Marketing

5th Edition

**by Jeanette McMurtry, MBA,
with Alexander Hiam**

for
dummies®
A Wiley Brand

Marketing For Dummies®, 5th Edition

Published by: **John Wiley & Sons, Inc.,** 111 River Street, Hoboken, NJ 07030-5774, www.wiley.com

Copyright © 2017 by John Wiley & Sons, Inc., Hoboken, New Jersey

Published simultaneously in Canada

For general information on our other products and services, please contact our Customer Care Department within the U.S. at 877-762-2974, outside the U.S. at 317-572-3993, or fax 317-572-4002. For technical support, please visit https://hub.wiley.com/community/support/dummies.

Wiley publishes in a variety of print and electronic formats and by print-on-demand. Some material included with standard print versions of this book may not be included in e-books or in print-on-demand. If this book refers to media such as a CD or DVD that is not included in the version you purchased, you may download this material at http://booksupport.wiley.com. For more information about Wiley products, visit www.wiley.com.

Library of Congress Control Number: 2017940029

ISBN 978-1-119-36557-0 (pbk); ISBN 978-1-119-36555-6 (ebk); ISBN 978-1-119-36558-7 (ebk)

Manufactured in the United States of America

C10004459_091318

Contents at a Glance

Introduction 1

Part 1: Marketing in a Consumer-Driven World 5
CHAPTER 1: Understanding Consumers Today and What Matters Most 7
CHAPTER 2: The Psychology of Choice and How to Trigger It for Lifetime Value 25
CHAPTER 3: Laying a Foundation for Growth 45

Part 2: Building a Strategy for LTV and ROI 63
CHAPTER 4: Researching Your Customers, Competitors, and Industry 65
CHAPTER 5: Creating a Winning Marketing Plan 89
CHAPTER 6: Content Marketing and Marketing Content 117

Part 3: Creating an Omni-Channel Plan 137
CHAPTER 7: Creative That Engages the Mind 139
CHAPTER 8: Digital Tools and Tactics That Work 165
CHAPTER 9: Using Print in a Digital World 195

Part 4: Powerful Ways to Engage for LTV and ROI 217
CHAPTER 10: Going Direct with Data, Personalization, and Sales 219
CHAPTER 11: Building a Website That Engages and Sells 247
CHAPTER 12: Leveraging Networks and Events 271

Part 5: Building a Brand That Sells Again and Again 289
CHAPTER 13: Making Your Brand Stand Out 291
CHAPTER 14: Finding the Right Pricing Approach 313
CHAPTER 15: Distribution and Merchandising in an Augmented World 329
CHAPTER 16: Succeeding in Sales and Service 345

Part 6: The Part of Tens 367
CHAPTER 17: Ten Common Marketing Mistakes (And How to Avoid Them) 369
CHAPTER 18: Ten Ways to Measure Results (Beyond ROI) 373

Index 377

Table of Contents

INTRODUCTION 1

  About This Book 2

  Foolish Assumptions 2

  Icons Used in This Book 3

  Beyond the Book 4

  Where to Go from Here 4

PART 1: MARKETING IN A CONSUMER-DRIVEN WORLD 5

CHAPTER 1: Understanding Consumers Today and What Matters Most 7

  Coming to Terms with the State of the Consumer Mind 9

  Addressing the Generation Gaps 9

  Creating Trust Equity among Today's Consumers 12

    Defining a common purpose 13

    Building relationships with customers 15

  Improving Customer Experiences for Sustainability 16

    Guiding the decision process with customer experience planning 17

    Creating powerful experiences beyond the sales process 18

  Pushing Boundaries with Guerilla Marketing 20

    The Fun Theory 21

    Other guerilla marketing examples 22

    Guerilla marketing and community building 23

CHAPTER 2: The Psychology of Choice and How to Trigger It for Lifetime Value 25

  The Unconscious Mind: The Real Driver of Consumer Choice 26

    The influence of schemas and the unconscious mind 26

    The conscious and unconscious minds often disagree 27

  Psychological Drivers That Drive Sales 29

    Neurotransmitters and how they affect choice 29

    Moving from USPs to ESPs 31

    Rewards versus loss 32

    Survival insticts 32

    Understanding the basics of human psychology 33

Aligning with Powerful Social Influencers 35
    Authority. 36
    Social proof. 36
    Reciprocity 37
    Scarcity 38
Appealing to Consumers' Happiness and Purpose 39
Putting It All Together 42

CHAPTER 3: Laying a Foundation for Growth 45
Measuring the Growth Rate of Your Market .46
Responding to a Flat or Shrinking Market 47
Finding Your Best Growth Strategies 48
    Go to market 49
    Grow what you have for higher profitability 50
Growing a Market Segmentation Strategy. 54
    Customer segments 55
    Niche marketing 56
Developing a Market Share Strategy 56
    Define your metrics. 56
    Establish a benchmark 56
    Do the math 58
Designing a Positioning Strategy. 58
    Envisioning your position: An exercise in observation
    and creativity 59
    Aligning your positioning strategy with growth initiatives 59
Growth Hacking to Build Leads and Market Share. 60
    Search 60
    Build links 61
    Fish for emails 61
    Try tripwires 61
    Hire a growth hacker. 62
Selling Innovative Products 62

PART 2: BUILDING A STRATEGY FOR LTV AND ROI 63

**CHAPTER 4: Researching Your Customers, Competitors,
and Industry** 65
Knowing When and Why to Do Research 66
    Monitoring social chatter to better understand
    your customers 66
    Following thought leaders to get current with reality 69
    Researching to discover what really drives your customers. 71
    Asking questions that get valid results. 73
Checking Out Net Promoter Scores and How to Find Yours. 75
Asking Really Good Questions on Surveys 76

Writing ESP Surveys. 78
Paying Wisely for Market Research. 80
Discovering Low-Cost and Even Free Ways to Find Out
What Matters Most 81
    Observe your customers 82
    Do competitive research 83
    Harness the power of one-question surveys 84
    Establish a trend report 85
    Probe your customer records 86
    Test your marketing materials. 86
    Interview defectors 87
    Create custom web analytics. 87
Riding a Rising Tide with Demographics 88

CHAPTER 5: **Creating a Winning Marketing Plan**. 89
The Marketing Plan Components You Need. 90
    First, the basics 90
    Now a bit more complex concepts. 91
    And now some even bigger questions. 92
Addressing the Four Ps. 92
Conducting a SWOT Analysis. 93
Focusing on Functional Alternatives. 95
Why Collaboration Matters So Much 96
    Teaming up on CSR. 97
    Building kinship, not just relationships 98
Expanding Your Target. 100
    Monitoring and reacting to trends 101
    Developing the customer experience. 101
Creating a Working Marketing Plan 102
Mapping Out Your Action Steps 104
    Step 1: Complete a situational analysis/summary 104
    Step 2: Establish your benchmark. 104
    Step 3: Define your goals 105
    Step 4: Take note of lessons learned 105
    Step 5: Outline your strategy. 105
    Step 6: Commit to action items. .106
    Step 7: Build learning plans 107
Keeping It Real: Do's and Don'ts of Planning. 108
    Don't ignore the details 108
    Don't get stuck in the past 108
    Don't try to break norms 108
    Don't engage in unnecessary spending. 109
    Do set reasonable boundaries 109
    Do break down your plan into simple subplans. 109

Preparing for Economic Influences..............................110
Budgeting Your Game...111
Managing Your Marketing Program 113
Projecting Expenses and Revenues 113
    Buildup forecasts...114
    Indicator forecasts.......................................115
    Multiple-scenario forecasts 115
    Time-period forecasts....................................116
Creating Your Controls...116

CHAPTER 6: **Content Marketing and Marketing Content**.......117
An Overview of Content Marketing............................118
    Creating content that delivers...........................120
    Channeling your content 121
Creating a Credible Content Marketing Plan..................122
Taking Advantage of User-Generated Content.................125
Flipping to Marketing Content.................................126
Content Marketing Writing Tips for Better Results............128
    Try the inverted pyramid 128
    Toss out some click bait 129
    Give ads greater stopping and sticking power 131
    Be consistent 132
    Be as persuasive as possible 133
    Be professional 134

PART 3: CREATING AN OMNI-CHANNEL PLAN 137

CHAPTER 7: **Creative That Engages the Mind** 139
Creating Compelling Creative 140
    Conducting a creativity audit............................140
    Changing (almost) everything 141
Applying Your Creativity.......................................142
    Building your creative strategy 143
    Color your creative psychologically.....................144
    Words, copy, and click bait..............................147
Writing a Creative Brief..149
    Goals 149
    Promise and offer 149
    Support statement 150
    Tone or persona statement..............................150
    Emotional drivers 150
    Wannabe profiles 151
    Color palette...151
    Golden triangle pattern 151

Constraints 151
Execution 152
Applying Creativity to Branding and Much More 153
Creativity and product development 153
Creativity and branding 154
Simple ways to spark new ideas 156
Making creativity a group activity 157
Managing the creative process 161
Elevating your creative thinking 163

CHAPTER 8: **Digital Tools and Tactics That Work** 165
Exploring Digital Channels You Can't Ignore 167
Using Facebook for Engagement That Builds Sales 167
Developing a successful Facebook plan. 169
Creating content that gets response, dialogue, and leads 172
Advertising on Facebook 173
Building Your Twitter Presence 174
Igniting Your Social Presence on Instagram 175
Expanding Your Network through LinkedIn 175
Groups. 176
Engagement 177
Promoting Your Brand with Pinterest 177
Discovering Digital Tools That Drive Brands 178
Podcasts 179
Webinars. 181
Videos 183
Online review sites 186
Fun and games work, too. 187
Advertising on the Web 189
Search-term marketing. 189
Google AdWords for ads as text, banners, and more 190
Getting the most out of each format 191
Using Automated Customization to Work Smarter and Faster 192

CHAPTER 9: **Using Print in a Digital World** 195
Creating Printed Marketing Materials 197
Exploring elements of successful print materials. 197
Designing print materials that capture attention and sales 198
Working with a professional designer 199
Using online sources for design services. 201
Doing the design on your own 201
Figuring out why fonts matter. 202
Using flow for engagement and clarity .206

Producing Effective and Efficient Print Collateral 207
Designing fliers for grounded results 207
Developing brochures and self-mailers with
specific marketing goals 208
Drafting an effective layout for your print brochure 209
Placing Print Ads That Generate Leads 210
Cheap but powerful publications 212
Ad size 214
Ad impact 215

PART 4: POWERFUL WAYS TO ENGAGE FOR LTV AND ROI

PART 4: POWERFUL WAYS TO ENGAGE
FOR LTV AND ROI 217

CHAPTER 10: **Going Direct with Data, Personalization,
and Sales** 219
Understanding the Metrics of Direct Marketing 220
The Basics of Direct Marketing 222
Getting direct about direct marketing 224
The more you do, the more you get 225
Digging Deeper into Data 225
Using a CRM system 226
Putting DMPs and DSPs together for ROI 228
Creating Direct Campaigns for Direct Profitability 231
Messaging matters 231
Outside matters 232
Actions that matter 233
Mailing tips 234
Purchasing lists 235
Going Direct with Email 237
Triggered email 239
Personalized email 240
Testing direct 241
Maximizing direct response online 243
Integrating Call and Chat Centers 244
Making use of phone time 245
Capturing useful information about each caller 245
Telemarketing: To call or not 245

CHAPTER 11: **Building a Website That Engages and Sells** 247
Creating and Managing a Web Identity 248
Understanding what consumers expect .249
Standardizing your web identity 250
Creating an Engaging Website 251
Watching your KPIs 252
Making content king on your website 255
Driving traffic with content 256

Integrating Key Design Elements 259
   Using the golden triangle 259
   Developing your web persona. 260
   Going from design concepts to an actual website 261
Driving Traffic via SEM and SEO 263
Creating Landing Pages, Blogs, and More 266
   Using landing pages effectively 266
   Using blogs to build brands, not bog them down 268
Monetizing Your Web Traffic 269
   Pay per impression 270
   Pay per click 270

CHAPTER 12: Leveraging Networks and Events 271
Harnessing the Power of Social Hives 271
   "Face" your customers: Events that inspire engagement,
   loyalty, and referrals 273
   Mix it up to create interest and ROI 276
Launching Your Own Public Event 276
   Hosting events with meaning 277
   Funding and monetizing your event. 277
   Getting help managing your event 278
Sponsoring a Special Event 279
   Hosting and supporting cause-related campaigns
   and events 279
   Sponsoring a cause-related event. 280
   Finding a good fit. 281
Maximizing Trade Show ROI 283
   Building the foundation for a good booth. 284
   Locating trade shows 285
   Selecting space on the expo floor 285
   Doing trade shows on a dime 286
   Getting people to your booth 286
   Offering premiums or "swag" that works. 287

**PART 5: BUILDING A BRAND THAT SELLS
AGAIN AND AGAIN** 289

CHAPTER 13: Making Your Brand Stand Out 291
Building Sustainable Brand Equity 292
   Brands defined by service 292
   Brands defined by experiences. 293
   Brands defined by product distinctions and innovation 294

Telling Your Brand's Story 295
    The characters 296
    The plot 297
    The climax 297
Branding Your Identity 298
    Unifying your brand identity 298
    Developing your brand's iconography 299
    Identifying your brand's personality traits 300
    Developing brands within brands 302
    Updating your brand 303
Designing a Product Line 304
    Eyeing depth and breadth 304
    Managing your product line effectively 305
    Protecting your product line and brand 306
Strengthening an Existing Product 307
Introducing New and Successful Products 308
    Partnering with experts to build new products 308
    Getting insights from customers 310
    Using the significant difference strategy 310
Upgrading or Expanding an Existing Product 311
    Passing the differentiation test 311
    Passing the champion test 312
    Branding across channels 312

CHAPTER 14: **Finding the Right Pricing Approach** 313
Pricing Opportunities and Obstacles 313
    Raising your price and selling more 314
    Avoiding the dangers of deep discounting .315
    Exploring the impact of pricing on customers' purchases 315
    Increasing profits without increasing prices 316
Setting or Changing Your List Price 317
    Step 1: Consider all the influencers 318
    Step 2: Examine your costs 318
    Step 3: Evaluate customers' price preferences 319
    Step 4: Consider secondary influences on price 320
    Step 5: Set your strategic objectives 320
    Step 6: Master the psychology of pricing 321
Designing Special Offers 323
    Creating coupons and other discounts 323
    Figuring out how much to offer 324
    Forecasting redemption rates 325
    Predicting the cost of special offers 326
    Keeping special offers special 327
Staying on Top of U.S. Regulations 328

CHAPTER 15: **Distribution and Merchandising in an Augmented World** 329

    Considering Distribution Strategies 330
        Shelf strategies to avoid getting benched 332
        E-commerce channels pros and cons. 333
    Tracking Down Ideal Distributors 335
    Understanding Channel Structure 336
    Reviewing Retail Strategies and Tactics 338
        Attracting traffic. 338
        Creating atmosphere 339
        Developing merchandising strategies 340

CHAPTER 16: **Succeeding in Sales and Service**. 345

    Selling for a Lifetime 346
        Calculating lifetime value 346
        Understanding the importance of customer loyalty 348
    Selling for Sustainability. 348
        Subscription and retainer–based selling 348
        Selling channels. 350
    Getting to Yes via ESP Selling. 354
        Generating sales leads 355
        Purchasing lists for B2B lead generation....................357
        Consultative selling 358
        Creating sales presentations with ESP power.................360
        Responding to problems 362
    Organizing Your Sales Force 363
        Determining how many salespeople you need................363
        Hiring your own or using reps. 363
        Compensating your sales force...........................365
    Retaining Customers with Great Service 365

PART 6: THE PART OF TENS. 367

CHAPTER 17: **Ten Common Marketing Mistakes (And How to Avoid Them)** 369

    Making Assumptions. 369
    Ignoring Customer Complaints 370
    Faking Popularity. 370
    Using Dirty Data. 370
    Competing on Price. 371
    Ignoring the Emotional Drivers of Choice 371
    Forgetting to Edit. 371

Offering What You Can't Deliver 371
Treating Customers Impersonally. 372
Blaming the Customer 372

CHAPTER 18: **Ten Ways to Measure Results (Beyond ROI)** 373
Establish Clear Objectives 373
Tie Your Metrics to Your Objectives 374
Set Learning Priorities. 374
Establish a Target ROI. 374
Know Your Customer Lifetime Value 375
Know Your Allowable Customer Acquisition Cost 375
Establish Benchmarks. 375
Turn the Funnel Upside Down. 376
Adjust Your Funnel Benchmark Assumptions When
You Have Real Data. 376
Avoid the Dashboard Trap. 376

INDEX 377

Introduction

Marketing is part science, part art and is truly one of the most fulfilling roles you can play in business.

Today, marketing embodies science through data and predictive analytics; psychology through consumer behavior studies and applications; emotions through events and engagement that spark inspiration and excitement; technology that breaks down boundaries; and art that invites imagination, innovation, and creativity beyond limits. And, as you read throughout this book, marketing involves fun and games, too.

But even with all the technologies available to create compelling programs to take products to market and capture a consumer's lifetime value, marketing is a challenging endeavor. Consumer expectations and demands change frequently, their attention becomes increasingly fragmented due to all the time spent on mobile and social channels, and they have more purchasing options than ever because e-commerce took down all the walls and barriers associated with location.

This edition of *Marketing For Dummies* helps you get a solid and working understanding of the marketing strategies, techniques, and technologies proven for today's markets and consumer-driven world that can help you build your business, no matter your size or whether you're in B2B or B2C.

To succeed in any field of business, you need to clearly communicate what you do in a way that's personally relevant, compelling, and exciting and taps into your customers' aspirations, values, and ideals. You also need a plan. You need to map out your journey to take a product to market, increase its real and perceived value, partner with distributors and retailers or B2B channel managers, and secure loyalty and evangelism from your customers — all while you're continuing to innovate new ideas for products and services that will keep your brand current and set you up for future success. Marketing isn't for the fainthearted, but it is for those who love fun, creative, and exciting challenges.

As you read this book, remember, *everything is possible!* The key is to craft a plan that enables you to work smart and efficiently with the resources you have. It's like mapping out a journey with a specific destination in mind and staying the course instead of veering off at tempting detours.

This book will serve as your guide whether you're a business owner, marketing executive, or small business manager and want to plan and execute your marketing yourself. It will also guide you to think more about big-picture ideas and identify smart ways for getting the job done instead of stretching yourself too thin. If you work for a business or marketing agency, this book will guide you on what you need to include in your marketing plan to achieve the goals given to you and advance your own career journey.

About This Book

This book caters to every marketing function and role — from small business owners and managers to staffers of larger organizations who work on plans, programs, product launches, ad campaigns, printed materials, websites, and other elements. It's also for those managing political campaigns, public health educators, directors and board members, museums, nonprofits, and the army of independent consultants who must not only be experts in their own field but also promote their personal brands to guarantee a steady flow of clients.

Ultimately, *every* marketer can benefit from the insights in this book about the consumer-driven world in which you operate, the media tools and channels you have at your fingertips, the technologies available to manage, deploy, and measure all that you do, down to the individual level. You'll also discover the key to executing successful customer journeys and experiences as well as direct, email, digital, and print campaigns that drive sales and profitability and, of course, how to do all of this while reducing costs and increasing efficiencies.

Foolish Assumptions

Even though we admonish you to avoid assumptions about your customers and markets throughout this book, we have clearly made some about you while writing this edition.

>> We assume that you're entrepreneurial and have the responsibility and desire to find out how to market a business or product successfully in your current business environment. But we don't assume that you have all the technical knowledge you need to do great marketing, so we explain each technique as clearly as we can. We also assume that you're willing to try new ideas, technologies, and processes to improve sales and grow your organization.

>> We assume that you realize when a task or skill is outside of your competency and when you need to call on others — such as agencies, data experts, and designers — to help. Marketers often use outside services, and it's important to build a long list of service providers you can trust to do good work on time and on budget.

>> Of course, we assume that you're willing and able to switch from being imaginative and creative one moment to being analytical and rigorous the next, because being successful at marketing requires both approaches. As you read this book, you'll find formulas so you can run the numbers and do projections for sales, ROI, and cost per customer. Other times, you'll be guided to use your imagination and think of fun and "guerilla" type of activities to help you communicate with emotional relevance and appeal. But most importantly, you'll be guided to think like consumers think today and to understand how to appeal to the psychology of choice — the unconscious mind that drives most people's thoughts and behavior.

>> We certainly do *not* assume that you have an unlimited budget. You'll find outlines and ideas for creating programs that you can execute on any budget and ways to engage customers that take price out of the equation for them as well as for you.

Icons Used in This Book

Look for these symbols to help you find valuable info throughout the text:

EXAMPLE

All marketing is real-world marketing. This icon means you can find an actual example of something that worked (or didn't work) in the real world for another marketer.

REMEMBER

When we want to get you up to speed on essential or critical information you need to know to succeed, we mark it with this icon.

TIP

This icon flags specific advice you can try out in your marketing program right away. And because sometimes you need the right perspective on a problem to reach success, this icon also points out suggestions on how to handle the task at hand in an easy manner.

WARNING

You can easily run into trouble in marketing because so many mines are just waiting for you to step on them. We've marked them all with this symbol.

Beyond the Book

In addition to the great content in the book or e-book you're reading right now, you can find more marketing tips and suggestions at www.dummies.com by using the search box to look for "Marketing For Dummies cheat sheet." These, plus the numerous narrow-topic books on marketing in the *For Dummies* line, give you lots of additional options for researching your marketing program.

Where to Go from Here

If you read only one chapter in one business book this year, make it Chapter 2 of this book, which explains the psychology of choice and how to trigger consumers' unconscious minds for unthinkable ROI. Unless you know what really drives people's emotions, joys, fears, anticipations, and aspirations, you can't be effective in building a sustainable business founded on lifelong relationships with valuable customers.

Perhaps you have a pressing need in one of the more specific areas covered in this book. If fixing your website is the top item on your to-do list, go to Chapter 11 first. If you need to increase the effectiveness of your sales strategies and approaches, try Chapter 16. Working on a direct mail campaign? You'll discover the role of data and direct channels, such as email and direct mail and how to execute both successfully, in Chapter 10. Chapter 5 will help you build a marketing plan, and Chapter 8 will guide you on using and managing digital tools and tactics that can help you execute campaigns that build sales and profitability.

Whatever you do and whatever your role, this book will provide you with new ways of thinking and doing, all of which are proven to work for businesses, both big and small and B2B and B2C, throughout all industries. So start reading, get going, and let your marketing light shine.

1

Marketing in a Consumer-Driven World

IN THIS PART . . .

Fight through consumer distraction, and discover how to market to different generations.

Discover what really drives consumers' choices, and make use of social influencers.

Determine your market's growth rate, and then implement market share and positioning strategies.

> » **Marketing to different generations**
>
> » **Building trust**
>
> » **Creating great customer experiences**
>
> » **Having fun with guerilla marketing**

Chapter **1**

Understanding Consumers Today and What Matters Most

There's never been a more exciting time to be in business, especially in marketing. With all the communications channels and technology available today, you can truly learn about and communicate with customers one to one while marketing to millions. You can know with certainty how customers spend their leisure time, what media channels they use and how often they use them, what their interests are, their brand attitudes, shopping patterns, preferences, likes and dislikes, and what their precise value is to you over their lifetime of purchasing. With all this knowledge, you can determine when and what they're likely to buy, how much and how often, and you can communicate specifically to their needs and relationship with you.

You can also monitor their attitudes, political preferences, and lifestyles on social media and insert your messages into their personal pages and sites when you see an opportunity to influence or inspire them. And you have the ability to analyze past behavior and scientifically predict their future behavior. It gets better all the time.

With the advent of artificial intelligence systems like IBM's Watson, you can program machines to have conversations with your customers, millions simultaneously and one to one, and learn even more so that you can deliver exactly what they need and want when they want it. And all these communications can happen in real time. Any day. Any time. Limitless possibilities await.

On the flip side: All this technology gives more knowledge and shopping power to customers as well and has changed the game significantly. They don't have to shop at the local pet store; they can order just about anything online and get it delivered within two days, often free. They want you to communicate and serve them like they're your only customer, and they'll abandon you on a whim if they don't like your values or if you don't support a cause that's important to them. People have so many options available today that loyalty is becoming obsolete. Consumers tend to choose brands based on their doing good in the world and the overall experience they offer rather than just the product and price.

As a result, marketers have to change their game. You have to change the way you distribute your products and services, how you reach and communicate with your customers and prospects, and how you engage them emotionally and physically. And you have to offer much more than a great product and value point; you have to offer consumers a fulfilling experience that adds value, happiness, or excitement to their lives.

This book is about doing all the above, effectively and affordably, for any business in either the B2C or B2B space, local or regional, national or global in scope. It's also for entrepreneurs starting a new business or marketing managers wanting to have a big impact on their job and their careers.

Beyond going through the essentials of building marketing plans, growth strategies, distribution channels, and pricing and merchandising strategies, this book guides you on developing emotionally relevant, creative experiences, websites, and online and offline promotions and marketing campaigns. You'll also discover the essentials of selling for a lifetime to capture lifetime value and loyalty in a world where both are hard to come by. And in Part 6, you find out how to measure your marketing in ways that can give you deep insights on how to grow your brand much more than just your traditional ROI and response analytics.

Before we get into the how-tos and guidelines for doing all the above, you need to focus on the mindset and behaviors of today's customers and this new era of consumerism. You need to understand what distractions you must overcome, generational influences that make or break brand relationships, consumers' level of trust in businesses like yours, and expectations for brand values and behavior. We cover these topics and more in this chapter.

Coming to Terms with the State of the Consumer Mind

Today's consumer mindset can be summed up in one word: *distracted.* And it just keeps getting worse as people spend more and more time looking at screens.

Reports by eMarketer and Nielsen show that people spend about ten hours a day on a screen — computer, TV, mobile phones, and other connected devices. About three of those hours are on mobile phones.

The vast majority of adults 18 years and older have smartphones and on average check them 46 times a day, or 8 billion times collectively, or so says a Deloitte report on smartphone usage. If you have 16 waking hours (and get 8 hours of sleep), that means you're checking your phone about every 3 minutes.

The bottom line for marketers is that pretty much all consumers are highly distracted and not paying attention to much around them.

Now add to that how much people multitask when it comes to media consumption. Accenture put out a report showing that 87 percent of consumers use more than one device at a time — for example, watching TV while chatting, posting, browsing, texting, or playing a game on their phone. That doesn't leave much attention span for marketers to capture and engage.

REMEMBER

The best armor you have when fighting the battle for attention is a good marketing plan that directs your actions, budgets, and customer experiences across all the channels that are getting all that attention.

In this book, we show you how to develop creative that's emotionally relevant so you can break through some of that clutter and engage consumers in inspirational common causes, open distribution channels that address their lifestyle, and execute direct marketing programs using email, print, mobile, and more that get noticed, acted upon, and generate sales.

Addressing the Generation Gaps

This is not your father's marketing book, nor is it the same book that was released in 1999 under this title. Times, technologies, channels, and needs have changed and so, too, has the way you connect, engage, and sell to your customers. With all this change, the gap or differences in the various generations is getting wider as people's attitudes, perspectives, and the way they live, shop, and engage with brands is redefined by technology, media channels, and social trends.

This section provides some insights about some of the different values and attitudes that drive behavior among the generations most businesses target today, in both a B2B and B2C setting.

The primary "shopping" generations are roughly broken down as follows:

>> Millennials: 18 to 34 years old

>> Generation X: 35 to 54 years old

>> Baby boomers: 55 to 70 years old

Although a ton of information about each generation is available — from books to white papers to videos and more — the main thing marketers need to understand is what each generation thinks of brands, what they expect about brands, and what they respond to in terms of values and stimuli.

Tables 1-1 through 1-3 list some of the characteristics of the various generations that impact their "marketing ability" and what you can do to address and engage them in meaningful ways. These attributes, mindsets, and potential actions should be front and center when you create your customer profiles and emotional selling propositions (ESPs), as outlined in Chapter 2, and your creative, as discussed in Chapter 6.

TABLE 1-1   **Marketing to Millennials**

Value	Suggested Response
Want self-expression.	Involve in user-generated content.
Respect is earned, not given.	Use statistics, industry knowledge, and experiences to position your marketing leadership and authority.
Trust equity is low because many don't trust brands to be truthful or operate in others' best interests.	Be transparent. If you don't have the best product, don't say you do. If your customer service is poor, fix it before making promises. Listen and admit to wrongdoing when you've made mistakes.
Crave change.	Keep your brand energetic and change things up to add interest and novelty.
Respond to bold colors, ideas, humor, and interaction.	Use digital channels that provide interaction, such as games (discussed in Chapter 8) and bright colors that fit their energy level, and engage them in disruptive events, like guerilla marketing tactics (described later in this chapter).

Value	Suggested Response
Seek relevance.	Your products, not just your marketing, need to fit their lifestyle and add value. Marketing should demonstrate how.
Open-minded, intelligent, responsible.	Always communicate with transparency, and never talk down or misrepresent the value of an offer or product. When trust is broken, you won't get a second chance.
Expectations for brands.	Involve them in user-generated content and product design and respond to them promptly.

TIP

Millennials don't trust brands or authority in the same way their parents did and do, and they have high standards for how brands should behave toward consumers, employees, and the greater good, which is a strong trend in consumerism.

REMEMBER

Each generation has a unique way of looking at the same brands and assigns different expectations for how it wants to be served.

TABLE 1-2 **Marketing to Generation Xers**

Value	Suggested Response
Want to feel they are contributing to something worthwhile.	Involve in volunteerism and corporate social responsibility (CSR) initiatives.
Like recognition for what they do.	Send thank-you emails, invite to VIP clubs, and reward with experiences, content, discounts, or products.
Thrive on autonomy, freedom.	Give them options for pricing, packages, service agreements, and product inventory. Enable communications options as well.
Seek a balanced life.	Align your brand's values with their values and personal life.
Accept authority but are skeptical.	Position your leadership and authority in an objective manner.
Skeptical about economy, fearful of job loss and financial setbacks, and skeptical of big business.	Communicate the security, comfort, and peace of mind that your product and brand deliver. Be transparent about pricing and product claims. Design brand offerings around their need to feel in control and have peace of mind.
Entrepreneurial.	Appeal to their desire to initiate new programs, ideas, and movements.

TABLE 1-3   **Marketing to Baby Boomers**

Value	Suggested Response
Want to feel they are in control of their choices and lives.	Provide information that informs, provides guidance, and assists in decision processes.
Like recognition for what they do.	Thank them for their business, invite to VIP loyalty programs, and reward frequently.
Thrive on prosperity.	Because they have worked hard for years and want to enjoy the perks of successful careers and financial planning, promote perks, pampering, and themes around "you deserve this."
Seek self-actualization.	Align your messaging and experiences with what matters most, such as leaving legacies, making an impact, achieving personal goals, and recognition.
Collaborative.	Invite to your causes centered on your common goals associated with charity, environment, and so on.
Optimistic.	They see good in communities and people and like to believe people can be trusted to be who they say they are.
Goal oriented.	Like to set goals and have a plan and a purpose.

Creating Trust Equity among Today's Consumers

Worldwide consumers are losing trust in business, media, and government. In just one year, the level of trust dropped three points and reached an all-time low in 2017, according to Edelman Trust Barometer for 2017, an annual report worth reading to help you get a better understanding of your customers' mindset and how it may have changed year over year. Visit Edelman.com for consumer studies on trust and other key topics.

The most trusted source for business information today is peers, or "people just like me," while CEOs and other business executives continue to lose ground. Note that the most trusted industry is technology and the least trusted industries are financial services, chemicals, and banking.

TIP

Research shows that about 30 percent of insurance customers believe that their providers will follow through on promises made regarding claim fulfillment. If you're in a low-trust industry, find ways to change this for your brand by communicating with transparency and providing objective information that serves your customers' decision processes over your own self-interest.

What does all of this mean? If customers don't trust business, and if you're in a business that consumers don't trust in general, you need to build content, customer experiences, and messaging around the things you do to be trustworthy. Your customer experiences need to show that you and your people are honest, care about customers' needs, not just your own, and that you do what you say you'll do.

REMEMBER

The best competitive advantage is the ability for consumers to trust you. This is far more important than price.

In Chapter 2, you read about the emotional and psychological influences of choice and how to appeal to these emotions in ways that build sustainable trust among your consumers.

Defining a common purpose

Traditionally, consumers demanded fair prices, good quality, and good service from brands in order to go back for more. Today, the demands are so much more. Consumers want to know what you've done for employees, communities, the earth, and the underprivileged and needy, not just what you've done for investors, stakeholders, and executive compensation. In fact, as we cover in Chapter 2, more than 80 percent of consumers (Cone Communications CSR study) state that their purchasing decisions and brand loyalty are based on what a brand has done and is doing to improve the world. A large majority, close to 90 percent, of global consumers are willing and likely to switch brands to one that's doing good in the world if price and quality are comparable.

More than 80 percent of consumers say that a brand's actions and positive impact on the world influence what they buy or where they shop and also which products they choose to recommend to others. As consumers continue to say, the most influential source for their purchasing decisions is actually other consumers, friends, and peers, and a brand's altruistic behavior becomes exponentially more critical.

TIP

Ninety percent of consumers say that they're more likely to trust a brand that supports social and environmental issues, making CSR efforts and positions even more critical for brands that want to thrive in this consumer-driven climate.

So what does this mean to you, the marketer? And for small businesses, regional, or large global enterprises?

>> You need to stand for something.

>> You need to commit some of your resources to doing good in the world just like you commit resources and budget to your advertising efforts and media spend.

>> Doing good is not just a good thing to do; it's a competitive advantage that makes your brand worth shopping, referring, and being loyal to.

This movement to align with good brands has become so powerful that it has actually sparked an era of anti-consumerism. A leading consumer activist group called Adbusters has grown consistently since the late 1980s and actively engages in what it calls "culture jamming," which describes its movement to interrupt consumer experiences and expose underlying and not-so-positive truths about large corporations while jamming their profits from sales. It has exposed advertising it believes communicates unrealistic and misleading promises from companies that engage in child labor or other unethical practices, and it organizes movements that send messages to big corporations. Its best-known movement is Occupy Wall Street, which successfully jammed New York's Wall Street district in 2011 and sparked similar protests against big banks worldwide.

REMEMBER

What marketers need to know most about Adbusters is its mantra: "Fight back against the hostile takeover of our psychological, physical and cultural environments by commercial forces."

Although this statement may be an extreme expression of an extreme consumerism group, it reflects the level of distrust and angst toward big brands that other research from Neilsen, Edelman, and Cone Communications has reported in reports on trust, consumer social media, and so on.

As you go about reading this book and developing your own positioning strategies, messaging, and marketing and engagement programs, keep in mind the power of transparency, truth in all communications, integrity of your deeds and alliances, and the values you stand by and spread. You don't want to be featured on Adbusters' website or in its widely circulated magazine.

We've seen a lot of consumer action toward brands because of their positions on social issues. Remember what happened to Target's stock value when it announced customers could self-identify their gender to decide which bathroom they wanted to use? And all the boycotts of Chick-fil-A when the CEO's comments opposed same-sex marriage?

You need to consider your company's positions and how you'll communicate them if the need ever arises, because in a market driven by consumer expectations and demands that transcend products and prices to social issues, you need to understand how your actions and words can trump even the best and most carefully crafted marketing plan. We're not suggesting that you change your values for financial gain but rather that you consider how you communicate about and respond to social issues. There is power in taking a stand for what you value and believe. As a brand, you need to plan for both positive and negative feedback.

REMEMBER

A marketing plan is not just a road map for how you'll develop products, build distribution channels, and earn profits; your marketing plan must also define the following:

>> What you stand for

>> How you'll act responsibly for society and the environment

>> What causes you'll support and how you'll engage your customers accordingly

>> How you'll build relationships with customers based on common values and causes

>> How you'll communicate with transparency to build trust equity for your brand

Building relationships with customers

Your biggest competitive advantage is not how clever or fun your social and traditional marketing campaigns are, and, as you'll read throughout this book, it's not your price. It's your ability to build relationships with customers on trust, value, and relevance.

TIP

Customers seek to align with brand personas that are "just like them." Your brand is first a reflection of what matters most to you and the customers you serve. It's also a community of like-minded people — your executive staff, frontline employees, customer service representatives, and customers.

Your marketing plan is thus not just about building a sustainable and profitable business through the right sales channels, distributors, social engagement, and advertising strategies; it's about building a community.

Brands that have done this well and which are referenced in detail in this book include TOMS, Wildfang, and Patagonia. Check them out online after reading their stories in later chapters and stay on top of what they're doing to build strong emotional bonds with customers who have like values and purpose.

Building a community around your brand is more than announcing your CSR program action items. It's about inviting people to engage with you, to volunteer together to impact local communities, and to donate time and money to a common charity, maybe the Salvation Army, Red Cross, or children's advocacy groups. Communities are also centered around sharing information to guide others on their journeys, whether it be to make a sound and wise investment or to join an association, support a cause or a political campaign, and so on.

Communities need to make sense for the products you sell. If you sell clothing, creating a community effort around helping people in underprivileged situations to get professional clothing for job interviews and jobs is likely to be meaningful to your base. Building a community around carbon emissions or climate change, not so much.

Ask yourself the following questions to help guide your actions that present your values as you build a community of like-minded people:

» How can we make our brand about consumers' needs, not our business's?

» What common goals and ideals do we share with our core customer groups?

» How can we align marketing, community relations programs, and brand values with those common goals?

» What programs can we execute that bring us together, online and offline, with our customers to further our common goals?

» What is the reputation for the retailers that distribute or sell our products and how could their reputation, positive and negative, potentially impact our reputation with customers and communities?

Improving Customer Experiences for Sustainability

As customer expectations and demands change from generation to generation, so, too, does the nature of marketing campaigns in general. Changes we've seen recently include refocusing the marketing department to become the customer experience department.

Some businesses have even renamed their chief marketing officer (CMO) to a chief experience officer (CXO) and are replacing advertising campaigns with customer experience initiatives for both their online and offline worlds.

How is customer experience defined today? Customer experience is the entirety of interactions between a brand and a customer beginning with her first purchase to the end of her purchasing life cycle. Interactions take place during each step of the decision process, which includes the following:

>> **Problem or need identification:** Consumers realize that they need to purchase a product to solve a problem or fill a need. For example, they need a good home computer.

>> **Discovery:** Consumers conduct research and explore options for products that fit their need and decide on the functions and features they need. For example, should they buy a laptop, notebook, desktop, or tablet?

>> **Evaluation:** After they've found options or product categories they want to purchase, consumers start to evaluate brands.

>> **Trial or purchase:** After research, and engaging with various brand representatives online or in stores, consumers make a purchase.

>> **Confirmation and reassurance:** Consumers gather information after the decision or purchase to reaffirm their choice was the right one. They read customer reviews, talk to others who chose the same product or brand they did, post decision on social media to get more validation, and so on.

>> **Assignment of loyalty:** A brand experience doesn't stop after the purchase. It continues as consumers use the product and access the resources available, such as customer service and technical support.

You must address all these decision steps in your marketing plan and customer experience strategy. The following sections walk you through how you can integrate each one into a concerted, mapped-out marketing plan.

Guiding the decision process with customer experience planning

Charles Graves, mentor of author Jeanette McMurtry, offered this great piece of marketing advice: "Consumers don't want to be sold; they want to be told." In other words, they want to be told what is in their best interests so that they can make informed decisions. When marketers educate rather than sell, they become trusted partners, not just suppliers and vendors, which often leads to lifetime value and loyalty (discussed in detail in Chapter 16).

Education-based marketing is not only a strong marketing communications strategy, but it is also a sound customer experience strategy. Providing guidance, decision support, and information for each step of a customer's experience with your product and brand can help set you apart from the competition. Here are some customer experience activities that can help you succeed at this important task.

>> **Problem or need identification:** If you're selling computers, your plan may include white papers and educational materials for a content marketing plan that you execute online via social and digital channels. You can read more about this in Chapters 7 and 8.

>> **Discovery:** If you've done your customer research as mapped out in Chapter 4, you know what matters most to consumers shopping for home computers today, and you likely know how involved the decision process is. You can tap into this stage of the decision process by creating how-to guides or checklists to help consumers make wise choices and posting links to those guides on social media ads (discussed in Chapter 8) and direct marketing initiatives (outlined in Chapter 10).

>> **Evaluation:** You can increase support for your brand and product line by engaging influencer marketing so that others are endorsing your products and validating your claims. We cover tips for content that you can share via influencers, such as bloggers and media writers, in Chapter 7. You can also engage in emotional selling practices to get prospective buyers to recognize the emotional or personal outcomes you offer, which are known to secure sales for both B2B and B2C. Tactics for emotional selling propositions (ESPs) are outlined in Chapter 16.

>> **Purchase:** After you've secured a purchase, your job isn't done. You need to continue to communicate your emotional and functional value and invite customers to engage with you on a great journey through the communities you build and causes you support. You've read about this already in this chapter and can get more information on how to do this in Chapter 5 on marketing plans and Chapter 12 on building brand communities and hives to which customers want to align.

>> **Confirmation, reassurance, and loyalty:** Again, building hives or communities is critical here as well. Sending customers thank-you notes, inviting them to join VIP programs for rewards, and sending them digital games to play that reward them as well are all key marketing tactics to create loyalty and capture lifetime value. We discuss these programs in Chapter 8.

Creating powerful experiences beyond the sales process

Customer experiences clearly start with the sales process, as outlined earlier in this chapter, but your marketing plan must address a bigger journey after you close the sale that builds loyalty, referrals, and of course captures lifetime value. As part of your customer experience strategy, you need to map out your customer's journey or the steps necessary from first sale to lifetime value that you need to address.

Again, a customer's journey encompasses the steps you must take and deliver upon at every touch point. For example:

>> How do you thank or recognize customers for their purchases?

>> How do you resolve conflict when you're right or wrong?

>> How do you validate customers' decisions to continue purchasing from you?

>> How do you reward them for loyalty and referrals?

>> How do you engage them in meaningful activities, causes, and so on?

The purpose of a customer journey is to build and maintain emotional bonds with your brand and get customers to refer others. To do this most effectively for your brand, it helps to look at the most powerful affiliations people have in their lives that aren't associated with purchase of products or services. Not to be politically incorrect or controversial, but these are your political and religious affiliations. In many cases, people don't know why they believe what they believe or take the stand they do on social issues other than somewhere, someone taught them to believe a certain way or embrace certain values. Right or wrong is not the issue.

The issue is that people hold powerful beliefs that guide them, and they make life-lasting choices and decisions based on these values and beliefs. People's commitment to their chosen organization is so strong that they commit their time and even money to organizations that don't give anything in return but intangibles, such as hope, faith, and anticipations of rewards if they stay the course and further the cause.

Experiences that keep people faithful to belief structures and value systems are present in all religious and political organizations despite how different they may be. For example, the same tenets are present in Christianity and all the various churches within this genre, Buddhism, Judaism, Islamism, and so on. These tenets exist in political organizations, too. These include symbolism, sensory appeal, promises, community, and rituals.

Successful brands integrate these same tenets. Think of your favorite brands. Note how they embrace these tenets. Apple is a great example of a brand using these cornerstones of religion to create a faithful following. Here's how:

>> **Symbolism:** The simple Apple icon recognizable by most consumers worldwide represents creativity, innovation, and personal power to communicate, self-express, create, and enjoy music and other forms of entertainment.

>> **Sensory appeal:** Apple's products appeal to people's senses by delivering music and videos with ease and giving them the chance to create their own creative and media events, which appeal to even more senses.

>> **Promises:** People believe and experience the promise of quality and innovation and novelty as Apple releases new applications and capabilities.

>> **Community:** Apple has many communities you can join online, such as iTunes, and has become a community itself through market penetration. Many people you know own Apple devices, and you can easily exchange ideas, tips, and enthusiasm.

>> **Ritual:** Shopping at an Apple Store is a fun ritual. You have a cool setting to explore products; you're assigned your own personal assistant when you walk in the door; your transactions are done causally via a hand scanner, not at a sterile divisive counter, so you feel more engaged with your assistant; and you can sign up for the Genius Bar and get one-to-one attention.

How can you create religious-like events and thus loyalty for your brand? This book is full of ideas for doing just that. Check out Chapter 8 for digital tactics, Chapter 16 for emotional selling, and Chapter 2 on how to trigger the unconscious mind for unthinkable ROI.

Pushing Boundaries with Guerilla Marketing

Beyond getting religious about your branding and marketing programs, you need to push the boundaries of traditional marketing. Guerilla marketing is one way you can do this.

Guerilla marketing, also known as ambush marketing, is all about ideas that are outside the boundaries and take competitors and customers by surprise — competitors, because you did something that took attention or market share away from them, and customers, because you did something fun and engaging that exceeded routine expectations or experiences with competing brands.

A short definition is

Actions, messaging, creative, experience, and events that transcend the bounds of traditional marketing that focus on product, service, price, and other common messages

In addition to commanding attention, one of the primary goals of guerilla marketing is to change behavior for the better, or at least how you want consumer behavior to be to drive more sales and loyalty.

The Fun Theory

One of our favorite examples of changing behavior by changing up routines comes from Volkswagen who created The Fun Theory. This program was built around the notion that fun can change behavior for the better, kind of like the discussion in Chapter 8 about the power of gamification in building customer engagements.

For The Fun Theory initiative, Volkswagen asked people to create ideas for changing routine behavior for the better. It then tested and executed winning ideas to see whether they would indeed work.

Here are a few attention-grabbing ideas that successfully changed routine behavior by doing something new and fun. As you review these ideas, ponder on how you can build on them to create "fun" customer experiences through every touch point of your customer journey — from need identification to purchase confirmation.

>> **Will fun reduce the amount of speeding in a city?** This project involved setting up signs throughout Stockholm that showed people just how fast they were going. It was really nothing new because speed meters are located in many places these days; however, this program made it more fun to stay at or below the limit. The speed camera would track your speed and light up according to whether you were under or over the speed limit. If you were over, you were sent a ticket. If you were at or under the speed limit, you were entered into a lottery in which you could win a cash reward from the money collected by the speeders. It worked beautifully. In three days, the cameras tracked the speed of nearly 25,000 cars and found that the average speed for traffic went down from 32 kilometers per hour to 25 kilometers per hour, which is a 22 percent reduction in speed.

>> **Will fun get people to use stairs over escalators?** Another "fun" experiment designed to get people to make healthier choices was to turn a staircase that sits adjacent to an escalator into a keyboard. If people could play music with their feet as they moved up or down the stairs, would they choose the stairs, the healthier option? The answer was yes as 66 percent more people than normal chose to take the stairs.

>> **Will fun get people to increase their use of recycle centers over trash cans?** The Fun Theory's bottle bank arcade experiment turned a bottle recycling depository into an arcade. Every time a bottle was placed inside, the

depository would light up and make noises like a machine at an arcade. It would even add up points for each bottle people deposited. People flocked to see how many points they could rack up with bottle deposits, even though there was no way to cash in their points for a tangible reward. In just one night, nearly 100 people used the arcade depository as compared to 2 people who used the conventional depository that was routine and void of fun.

You can watch videos of these experiments in action at www.thefuntheory.com.

Other guerilla marketing examples

So, yes, fun and games motivate behavior, and if used for building brand images and product sales, they can be a highly effective form of guerilla marketing. With enough fun involved, you create a movement or a society frenzy like Pokémon, the game that uses augmented reality to present Pokémon characters on your mobile screen in a depiction of a real setting so that you and your avatar can capture the Pokémon and train them to help you battle against other players doing the same thing on their phones.

Some other activities along the lines of surprise or guerilla marketing include

>> **Augmented reality (AR):** You can use augmented reality games or apps to make your products pop up spontaneously so you can suggest a need to go buy your product. It's a great app for food and drink brands. You can see how Valpak is using AR in a very clever way later in the book.

>> **Flash mobs:** Imagine if all the pedestrians at Times Square were suddenly surprised by an impromptu performance of people dancing and singing in your company's uniforms and handing out coupons for a free drink, cosmetic item, or such at your store around the corner?

>> **Captivating displays:** What if a tall building in your town was lit up all night long with images of your products and logo on it and a coupon code flashing that offered a not-to-miss discount to those savvy enough to see it?

Things like these get people's attention and break into their routine.

Other forms of guerilla marketing can be as simple as offering the best in industry:

>> **Return policies:** Be better than Nordstrom's if you can and take the fear out of committing to high-end purchases or subscription-based services.

>> **Free product trials:** Let people try a product for free with an easy return process if not happy. Once it's in home, a very high chance exists that they won't return it no matter what they think.

>> **"Freemiums":** Offer for free what others charge for and make your money through sponsorships, advertising on your sales websites, or upgrades to your basic service.

Blending guerilla marketing with CSR can have a really powerful impact as well.

Guerilla marketing and community building

The best guerilla marketing tactics are those that are fun both for you to execute and for your customers to experience.

Earlier in this chapter, we discuss building a community around a women's clothing store and helping distribute clothing to underprivileged women trying to enter the workforce. Here's how guerilla marketing can blend social giving and outside-the-boundaries thinking.

What if you asked your customers to adopt the cause of helping abused or homeless women get out of shelters and into jobs? You can tap into the emotions of their own personal journeys to success with a campaign on the theme of "Remember when . . . ," such as "Remember when you were just starting out and people said you couldn't, wouldn't, or shouldn't, but you proved them wrong by becoming the successful businesswoman you are today?"

Your campaign could go on to invite women to "adopt a woman" just starting her journey to success like you did at one point in your life. UNICEF encourages people to adopt a child through monthly donations for education, food, and shelter. You could ask your customers to donate a small amount every month for clothing items that you donate to the woman they have adopted (anonymously so privacy is maintained, of course) or to women in shelters in their community. Upon purchase of items they buy for themselves, you could send them an email or insert a statement with their receipts asking them to recycle the clothes they just purchased by donating to a local women's shelter when they no longer need them. You could even host donation days where you invite customers to come in and donate old items at your retail outlets and get 20 percent off any new items they buy. You'd be building a community among "people just like them" and helping others find joy by doing good in the world — a powerful way to bond with customers and communities.

A campaign like this shows guerilla marketing at its best because it not only involves customers and surprises them with a new idea, but it also takes them away from considering the competition as you've given them a strong emotional reason to stay loyal to you. People buy TOMS shoes knowing a kid in need will get a pair, too. The clothing guerrilla marketing idea has the same appeal. Buying a new blazer or winter coat from your store provides them with warmth and fashion and a good feeling because someone else is getting what she needs as well as a result of their choosing your brand.

REMEMBER

Your marketing plan is not just a guidebook for getting your product out to the world and making money; it's about creating an experience, event, and outcome that makes people's lives better or more enjoyable and brings people together for the better. When you deliver emotional fulfillment and build a community around the value you deliver, it's difficult to fail.

» Discovering what really drives consumers' choices

» Making use of social influencers

» Acknowledging people's need for happiness and purpose

» Creating ESP profiles

Chapter **2**

The Psychology of Choice and How to Trigger It for Lifetime Value

When asked what really drives consumer choice, common answers include quality, reputation, brand awareness, convenience, and of course price. However, although these are influencers at some level in most decision processes, they're not the most powerful driver as many consumers and marketers believe they are. Another more powerful influencer must be engaged in all decision processes, B2B and B2C, for both small and large purchases, before any of the others have a chance to influence people. That influencer is the unconscious mind, which drives 90 percent of people's thoughts and behavior, according to various neuromarketing studies, including those from Gerald Zaltman of Harvard University, widely known as the pioneer of neuromarketing.

So think about that for a minute: If 90 percent of all thoughts are unconscious, why do we market to the other 10 percent? If you're marketing to the conscious mind with "limited time offers," "act now," and "our quality is better than their quality" types of appeals for consumers to ponder and act on, you're targeting only 10 percent of the decision process. That is a lot of waste!

The Unconscious Mind: The Real Driver of Consumer Choice

Traditionally, advertising has been all about promoting prices, conveniences, brand reputations, price advantages, and other appeals that the conscious mind processes. Yet people don't always get far enough into advertisements to process the value of a given offer if the ad, content, posts, experience — whatever the medium is — doesn't first appeal to their unconscious mind. If the research is true, you're wasting 90 percent of your budget by appealing to just the 10 percent of the brain that drives the decisions people make. That doesn't make for good marketing returns.

The unconscious mind makes rapid judgments about marketing materials and messages and dictates immediately how it should "behave." These thoughts and actions are driven by our "schema," or set of preconceived thoughts and beliefs that drive what we believe to be "truth," real, and valuable.

The influence of schemas and the unconscious mind

We all have schemas associated with our political, religious, social, and brand beliefs and choices, and we typically pass off any outliers that don't fit the notions we believe as anomalies, even when evidence proves our schemas wrong, or at least makes us question what we believe.

Pew Research shows that scientists and the public are far apart when it comes to believing evidence of opinions about key social issues, such as vaccines, GMOs, and climate change. And no matter what people hear about their chosen politicians, religions, and other sources of ideology, they tend to believe what they've chosen to believe and ignore contradictory facts despite the sources of the scientific, validated data. For example, 88 percent of scientists say research shows that GMOs are safe. Only 37 percent of the public believes them.

TIP

Think about the things you've believed most of your life. How much would it take for you to change your attitudes and beliefs? Convincing customers to change brands, acknowledge your brand's distinctions and value, and try your product over another is not always that much different. You need to build a powerful case to get consideration and trial. And you're best able to do this by applying psychological principles related to choice rather than just sound marketing messages and personalized promotions triggered by automated CRM systems, data management platforms, and more, all of which we discuss later in this book.

Schemas reflect not only the attitudes and perceptions people have developed from their culture, community, and environments; they also reflect how the brain works in general. For example, schemas are unconscious expectations of patterns, rhythms, and such. When you listen to music, your brain has a set perception for how all the melody will harmonize, how the notes will scale, and how the rhythm will flow. People like music that fits this "schema," which was used by the masters and by modern-day songwriters and musicians.

Just like these mental schemas that guide expectations when listening to music, aligning with political and religious organizations, and more, people have "brand schema," or preset expectations for experience with brands they trust.

REMEMBER

These schemas associated with products and brands are largely built on prior experiences, memories, and people's conscious and unconscious values.

The conscious and unconscious minds often disagree

Young & Rubicam did a study in 2013 involving adults throughout the United States, South America, and Asia to see how close people's conscious values line up with their unconscious ones. What they found, and later published in a report called "Secrets and Lies," is surprising to most. It shows just how far apart the conscious and unconscious thought processes are. Take a look at Table 2-1. Just like psychologists have said for years, people are driven, unconsciously, for survival, to connect with outers in meaningful relationships, and by the traditions in which they were raised, although few want to admit that if you look at attitude reports for younger generations of consumers.

TABLE 2-1

Conscious Versus Unconscious Values

Top Conscious Values	Top Unconscious Values
Helpfulness	Maintaining security
Choosing own path	Sexual fulfillment
Meaning in life	Honoring tradition

Now for the secrets:

>> Most interesting is that the unconscious mind results showed "helpfulness" as dead last, 16 of 16 variables tested, while the conscious mind put it as the number-one value.

>> The conscious mind listed "sexual fulfillment" as number 14 of 16 variables, even though it shows up in the number-two spot for the unconscious mind. Perhaps people don't like to admit consciously that they need others in their lives to be happy? Most people probably like to think they're fine and independent on their own, but years of psychology studies show that people are all generally happier, more fulfilled, and reach their greater potential much more when they have fulfilling relationships with others.

REMEMBER

What you can take from this is that what people say and think is often *not* what they really do. This alone has huge implications for what marketers need to emphasize most in marketing content, which is not what they've typically been doing.

PSYCHOLOGICAL DRIVERS APPLY TO B2B EVEN MORE THAN B2C

Research shows that personal values influence people's choices for consumer goods and even more so for business purchases. In fact, Google/Motista research shows that

- B2B customers are more emotionally connected to their vendors and service providers than B2C consumers.

- When personal values are present in a business choice, purchasers are eight times more likely to pay a premium price.

- In contrast, only 14 percent of business purchasers see a real difference between suppliers and are willing to pay for that difference.

This research is very telling and can't be ignored in the highly competitive B2B marketing environment. If you're in B2B, identifying and addressing those personal values are key to helping you gain competitive advantage because most marketers in this space don't understand this or how to do it. This chapter sets forth what those values are and how the processes of the brain, and the conscious and unconscious minds, spark emotions and behavior associated with those values.

(To delve more into this research, check out www.thinkwithgoogle.com, "From Promotion to Emotion: Connecting B2B customers to Brands.")

Psychological Drivers That Drive Sales

Consciously and unconsciously, all human behavior is based on two emotional premises:

» The avoidance of pain

» The pursuit of pleasure

Everything we do is driven by these basic needs, socially, professionally, and personally. When marketers understand the pain their customers are consciously and unconsciously avoiding when purchasing their product category, they can much better align their messaging to be relevant far beneath the surface of the typical decision process.

Pain and pleasure in marketing terms are simply the fear and joy people experience as life events unfold or as they anticipate something bad or good happening in their lives. For example, when you choose to purchase auto insurance, you know that you'll be covered against losing your car or substantial amounts of money if you have an accident and gain a sense of joy as a result. You also know that you can avoid a lot of pain as a result of coverage, and both of these emotional outcomes drive your choices to purchase the category and the brand you chose.

TIP

When doing customer surveys, ask your customers what they fear about your product category. What do they enjoy about it? And what fears and joys are associated with doing business with your brand? Do they fear poor customer service, intimidating return policies, or paying too much for what they get? When you know the answers to these questions, you can create messaging, content, and experiences that are highly relevant to what drives your customers.

Neurotransmitters and how they affect choice

The most powerful forces that affect human actions related to finding joy or avoiding fear and pain are neurotransmitters, or the hormones that create strong emotional reactions to the stimuli people encounter daily in all areas of the world.

These neurotransmitters are

» **Dopamine:** Dopamine rushes occur when you anticipate a reward, such as a job promotion for doing good or a great deal on a new car, a great afterlife due to religious obedience, or reciprocal love. You feel euphoric, infallible, and ready to conquer your goals. This is the rush that makes people become addicted to drugs.

>> **Oxytocin:** This hormone is known as the love hormone. When you develop connections with others and you feel that powerful sense of validation and reciprocity for how you feel about them, and being with that person makes you feel valued and loved, your brain releases oxytocin. This feeling is often described as falling in love, and it feels good. As a result, people seek loving bonds with others via social and professional hives, and when they find it, they often become loyal supporters. Research shows that when people experience an oxytocin rush, the part of their brain that governs judgment and fear is shut off.

>> **Cortisol:** When you feel threatened physically, emotionally, socially, or financially, you experience a rush of confusion, insecurity, doubt, and fear. You respond by either fighting and taking on the challenge or by flying away as fast as you can to avoid the crisis and seek a safety zone, which often is just a state of denial. This is what triggers the fight-or-flight mentality that drives much of what people do.

>> **Serotonin:** This is the hormone that helps stave off depression. It makes you feel calm and upbeat and gives you the ability to face your daily challenges with hope, optimism, and confidence. Listening to music that has the right schematic patterns and tones often creates feelings of love, nostalgia, comfort, or confidence, all of which influence serotonin rushes and your mood.

When marketers trigger these rushes, knowingly or not, they create feelings that compel consumers to behavior — either toward or away from the behavior they're seeking to trigger. The challenge you have as a marketer is to create the rushes that create excitement for your brand, the experience and products you deliver, and not the ones that send people flying to the competition. Unwittingly, many marketers do both.

TIP

How does this relate to marketing? More simply than you may think. The first step is to know the emotions associated with the decision process for your category. For example: As mentioned earlier, most insurance customers don't trust their carriers to deliver on the promises contained in their policies. But they buy insurance anyway because they fear the consequences if they were liable in a car accident, if the house burned down, or if they got really sick and couldn't afford the care. Two emotions that insurance company marketers must address in their marketing, then, are distrust and fear. Three considerations may be to

>> Use testimonials validating your fulfillment of claims.

>> Cite industry awards from third parties showing that you meet or exceed the industry standards.

>> Identify and address fears related to your category and show consumers that you understand how they feel and why. Use empathy to let them know you're just like them, because people tend to buy from others they deem to be like themselves.

Moving from USPs to ESPs

One of the most important things marketers must do today is to move away from USPs — unique selling propositions — to ESPs — emotional selling propositions. ESPs are the messages that get through because they appeal to the emotions, such as those listed in the previous section.

A brand's ESP is a statement about how it fulfills a given emotion associated with its category. Understanding the emotional value you provide is key to your success in all forms of marketing — direct, social, personalized, mass, and experiences and events.

For example, if you're selling luxury apparel, what is the emotional fulfillment your customers seek by wearing something with your label or insignia and by paying much more than a functional alternative would cost? These emotions that drive the choice to buy your product at your most likely elevated price likely include

>> Feelings of glamor or beauty

>> Feelings of confidence and personal respect

>> Feelings of superiority to others who aren't wearing similarly unique or expensive clothing

The final emotion of superiority often stays in the unconscious as it relates to the most powerful of all related emotions: survival. When you know you have something most others don't, and that few can afford, you feel superior whether you realize it or not. And when you feel superior, you anticipate your ability to survive over others, and you experience a form of a dopamine rush that makes you feel joy about the products or experiences that set you above others. Much of this is unconscious but very real at the same time. That feeling of superiority and associated sense of survival drives some to purchase a $60,000 Gucci crocodile handbag.

TIP

If there's one emotion you must address in your brand's ESP, it is the survival ability that your product offers to your consumers and your superior ability to deliver survival over your competitors. No, this isn't a bunch of psychology babble. It's critical insight as to how you can craft emotionally and relevant messaging, offers, promotions and more to your customers and prospects and achieve what we call "unthinkable ROI."

Rewards versus loss

As you contemplate how to appeal to emotions in your marketing, keep in mind that humans are more risk adverse than they are reward seekers. People consciously and unconsciously want to hold on to what they have more than gain a reward, especially if they could lose something in return. It's part of the survival instinct.

Daniel Kahnemann, psychologist and author, has conducted a great deal of research about human psychology and how people process information and make choices. His research consistently shows that when people are faced with a choice to risk losing something in order to gain something, they most often choose to avoid the risk rather than take the chance of winning the award. In other words, he found that people will pay a high price to get a sure gain and to avoid a sure loss.

Ask yourself the following questions:

>> What potential losses can consumers experience by not buying your product?

>> How can your brand deliver on the promise of avoiding that loss in ways that competitors can't?

Being able to answer these questions and deliver on them is key to differentiating your product from others emotionally, and that is the most critical differentiation of all.

Brands can imitate and duplicate your product's features, functions, and price point. What they can't do so easily is replicate your emotional experience and fulfillment. This should be the top priority of your marketing program and everything you do based on the tactics and strategies discussed in this book.

Survival insticts

When viewing illusion art that shows either a woman looking in a mirror or a skull, most see the skull first. This is because the brain is wired to see threats to prevent harm before seeing the reward or joy.

Identify the fear that drives your customers and address it directly so you can put them at ease. After you diminish the fear or present a visible solution, you can then communicate better to the unconscious mind and more clearly to the conscious mind.

BORN TO SURVIVE OR CHASE THE THRILLS

Even with all the data and research over the years that show that people are molded by environments, psychology theories hold true that many people's attitudes and choices are part of their DNA. Psychologists maintain that humans are born with one of two affective systems that drives the emotional reactions to many of their life's experiences and the stimuli presented to them on a daily basis. One system is driven by the human need to survive and maintain security; the other by the thrill of the chase, or a desire to take risks and live off the adrenalin of excitement. The "born this way" theory explains why kids from the same family have such different approaches to risk taking and security, yet their environment and parenting is the same.

Knowing how each of these affective systems affects people's attraction to brands and their promotions is essential to succeed, as these drivers are some of the strongest influences over the choices we make.

Here's how common products tap people's survival instincts:

>> **Insurance:** Survive accidents or mishaps that could destroy critical possessions like homes and cars.

>> **Education:** Survive the economic woes of not being able to get good jobs, live a quality life, and provide for children.

>> **Luxury cars:** Survive the perils of not achieving a high social status, which could include exclusion from influential circles, interesting experiences, and respect in business.

Your ESP should encompass the fears and joys sought through your product category, consciously and unconsciously, and should be present in your marketing messages, content marketing, social dialogue, customer experiences, and sales propositions. Crafting your brand's ESP is as critical as writing a mission statement that guides your operations and values.

Understanding the basics of human psychology

To be an effective marketer in any industry, you need to understand some basics about human psychology and how the mind triggers behavior. Many agencies have popped up in recent years claiming to be experts in behavior marketing; however, most focus on projecting behavior based on past behavior. Although this is important for your database, CRM, DMP, and direct marketing efforts, it's not enough.

To be successful, you also need to focus on behavior that results from psychological triggers, such as the neurotransmitters mentioned earlier and other psychological processes. From psychologists and their proven theories, old and new, you can learn a great deal about how people think and act.

Following are some insights from two of the most well-known contributors to psychology theories, Sigmund Freud and Carl Jung.

Freud's personality theory

One of the key marketing lessons from Freud is his personality theory, which suggests that people each have three personalities, or voices, in their heads that compete with each other when making basic and complex decisions. These personalities are the id, ego, and superego:

>> The *id* acts like a compulsive toddler that has to have what it wants when it wants it and doesn't care about future consequences to self or others.

>> The *ego* wants to please the id but after thinking through a plan to get it in an appropriate manner.

>> The *superego* is the voice of reason, deciding appropriate actions to take based on social norms and life experiences to date, what is right, what is wrong, and so on.

Whichever voice wins out the most dictates people's individual personalities and, for marketers, predicts their behavior when it comes to shopping and assigning loyalty.

TIP

Think about which personality is most involved in making the decision to purchase your category and brand within it. Are you selling cookies or doughnuts and want to spark an impulsive drive to buy some, regardless of diet and health consequences? You need to appeal to the id in a way that overpowers the ego and the superego. Oreo does this well with its ads about dunking an Oreo in milk. Shops at malls that put out the inviting smell of fresh cinnamon roles, hot cookies, and such do a great job at sparking the impulsive id.

If, however, you're marketing fitness and nutrition products, apps, or the like, you may want to first appeal to the ego with information about responsible diet and exercise habits and then mention low-calorie cookies that satisfy the id without throwing out the plans made to stay on track for reaching healthy goals.

Jung's archetypal theories

Carl Jung, known for his archetypal theories, believed that the human psyche is nothing more than mass confusion because so much of all people do and think is unconscious. What marketers can learn from him is that people cycle through four main archetypes:

>> **Shelf:** The dark side of human nature or the unbridled carnal self

>> **Self:** The place where the conscious mind connects with the unconscious mind

>> **Animus:** The true person individuals are in terms of their values and personalities

>> **Persona:** The person people project to others to cover up their true self, their animus

And when you know where the core of your customers lies in terms of these stereotypes, you can again be more relevant. If you're marketing to young Generation X adults who are a few years into their career, you may be safe to assume that they're trying to project a sense of success, achievement, potential, and distinction in their business world to attract career opportunities. If your product can help them do this, reflect it in your messaging and creative.

Another perspective Jung gives in his book *Modern Man in Search of a Soul* provides great direction for a brand's positioning and messaging strategies:

> Faith, hope, love, and insight are the highest achievements of human effort. They are given by experience.

If this is truly what people seek in life, how does your product support the journey to attaining these emotional outcomes? For example:

>> If you're in education, does going back to school give people the insight to reach their highest achievements?

>> If you sell luxury goods, does buying your apparel, cars, or other items help individuals achieve the love they seek in life?

Ask yourself key questions about the psychological fulfillment your brand helps support. Doing so will help you see your product's value in a much different light — the light from the way your customers' unconscious minds see it.

Aligning with Powerful Social Influencers

Along with psychological triggers, social influencers that are rooted in some of the psychology described in the previous section drive people's thoughts, choices, and actions. The following sections explore some of these social influencers.

Authority

Yale psychologist Stanley Milgram did a study to see how the role of authority influences people to do things that go against their values and conscious. He set up an experiment with one volunteer playing the role of a student and another playing the role of a teacher. The student volunteer was fitted with electrodes that would deliver shocks each time the teacher pushed a button, which he/she was instructed to do each time the student got a question wrong. As the experiment went on, the student missed more questions, and the shock got stronger. The teacher volunteers started to get upset, even physically ill, hearing the pain and agony of the student who was sitting on the other side of a screen. But when the leader, someone in a white coat, told the teachers to increase the volume and push the button to deliver the shock, the majority kept doing it against their own conscious.

Remarkably, 65 percent of the volunteers kept following the instructions from the person in authority. According to the study's report, subjects were anxious and stressed about inflicting pain, and some so much so that they were "sweating, trembling, stuttering, biting their lips, groaning, digging their fingernails into their skin, and some were even having nervous laughing fits or seizures."

This shows how powerful authorities are in influencing behavior. From childhood, many are taught to respect authorities of various types — police officers, teachers, church leaders, parents, doctors, and so forth.

To tap into the power of authority in your marketing plan, you need to first do the following:

>> Determine which authorities have the most influence in your product category.

>> Find out what expertise they share that makes them an authority and how this expertise is related to your brand values, attributes, and so on.

>> Identify how you can align with authorities to validate your category and your brand. Some methods might include asking them to write a guest blog for your website, inviting them to speak at your events, or even paying them to be a spokesperson for your products.

Another way to tap into the influence of authority is to cite research reports, statistics, and testimonials from experts in your communications to validate your product claims and add strength to your messaging.

Social proof

No matter how sophisticated, intelligent, accomplished, or otherwise your customers are, they're still driven by social proof, whether they admit it or not. It aligns with the human need for survival as, unconsciously, people feel weak or disadvantaged when others have something they don't or are achieving something they haven't yet. In these cases, people often feel inferior, a contrast to the feelings that they unconsciously seek to feel fulfilled and secure.

Robert Cialdini, a psychologist and author, has done many experiments to see how this plays out in various settings. He found that by telling customers that their neighbors, friends, peers, and so forth were doing something worthwhile, like reusing towels at a hotel or participating in an environmental program, they were much more likely to do so as well than if he just told them it was a good thing to do to support a good program.

This is where testimonials play a strong role. Numbers like a 98 percent customer satisfaction rate, a high NPS, or Net Promoter Score, and like attributes show consumers that others are like you and substantially increase their willingness to try your product and/or brand.

When trying to influence behavior, let consumers know that others are engaged in the desired behavior, and watch your response take off. Note that on pages like Amazon.com, there's a list of like products that other "customers reviewed." Most people don't want to miss out on a good thing, so many will review them, too.

Reciprocity

No matter how much we accept the notion that life is not fair, we still hope it will be. At least when it comes to how people treat us. We thrive when one good deed creates another and embrace those who treat us reciprocally. This applies to our personal and professional relationships. Brands that understand that "giving back" is not just about their corporate social responsibility efforts but about giving back to the individuals who give their business loyalty to them are the ones with the most sustainability in good times and bad.

When people feel recognized and appreciated by businesses they patronize, their satisfaction is higher and so is their repeat business and referrals.

A favorite example of reciprocity for marketers is a campaign conducted by a regional bank called First Bank. It ran a billboard campaign with nothing more than the words *math tutor, dog walker, wedding singer,* and a name with a phone number below each title. Nothing more about the bank's offerings, advantages, and so on. It was truly running a campaign to help its customers. It really did have customers with those names and jobs, and when the phone rang, they really did refer people to that bank. This was a brilliant campaign because it showed customers that the bank truly cared about giving back to them, no matter how big or small, and instead of just using words to make that point, it used actions and a lot of its advertising budget. According to the VP of marketing at the time, it was highly successful in stopping attrition at a time when most banks were losing customers and also in gaining new customers.

TIP

Reciprocity is a simple and very affordable marketing program. It doesn't take a lot to give back to customers through better service, reward points, free gifts, mentions in your newsletters, content marketing, social posts, and so on. But the payback can be huge. When you develop your customer surveys, as discussed in Chapter 4, add a question asking customers to tell you how they would like to be rewarded.

Scarcity

A few years ago, Hostess Brands got in trouble and had to shut down, discontinuing some of America's favorite snack foods, including the Twinkie, almost overnight. Suddenly, people had to have what they hadn't even wanted in years. Adults who remembered the Twinkie from their youth stormed stores and bought boxes of Twinkies before they could no longer even buy one. Sales went up 31,000 percent (not a typo) in just days. This is a strong example of the huge power that scarcity has on consumers' thoughts and behavior. It's true. People often don't want or value something until they can't have it anymore. Then they can't get it fast enough or enough of it.

You see this all the time in marketing: "One seat left at this price," "One left in stock," and so on. Whether it's true or not and whether people believe it or not, they'll often buy it, just in case.

TIP

These psychological and social elements apply to all your customers generally and specifically. To be most effective, you need to identify your brand's "umbrella" position and then positions that are specific to the values, aspirations, and ESP profiles for each segment.

For example: If you're a retailer of organic, toxic-free household items, your ESP may read like this:

> We deliver *confidence* knowing that your home is free from toxins that affect your health and the *joy* of knowing your children are protected from issues that could affect their quality of life. Families that use our products can *relax* and focus on other life issues, knowing that they are protected at home.

Your ESP now involves creating messaging and positioning around confidence, joy, and relaxing as a result of using a product that delivers all three.

EXAMPLE

Here's a real-world example of how ESPs can work in the B2B world: I (Jeanette) once worked with a financial firm that was trying to get people to invest in their real estate fund by telling them how lucrative and smart real estate investing was. No one was buying it, especially since the big Madoff investment fraud scandal had just been exposed, and real estate had not performed well in recent years. So we changed the ESP of his sales presentation. Instead of walking in with a presentation about how solid real estate was and trustworthy my client was, we started off by talking about the potential clients' fears and their preconceived attitudes or schema about real estate. We actually said things like, "You know, real estate has had its challenges and has been risky. And we can see why investors have been leery." We just validated their feelings, confirmed their schema, and established trust. They listened, and they listened all the way to yes. My client closed four accounts with whom he had struggled to get a meaningful conversation.

Appealing to Consumers' Happiness and Purpose

Daily, we humans constantly strive to find and associate with happiness. Happiness is not only the greatest achievement we seek in life, but it's also a magnet for brands that truly understand its power. Coca-Cola has emerged as the beverage company in a league all its own and also one of the top brands globally for sales, loyalty, and brand respect. As of this writing, Coke has more than 100 million followers on its Facebook page. It became the leader of the happiness movement with its "Happiness" campaign that focused on delivering happiness to people in surprising ways around the world. Coke's content marketing and marketing content had no mentions of its product, just videos, ads, posts, and web and social content about how to find and share happiness. Subsequently, it has held a steady position as one of the top five brands for respect and revenue worldwide in listings by Interbrand and other top analyst groups.

Coke's marketing focuses on happy moments in its costumers' lives, putting Coke products at the center of their life's best memories. And it has created interactions between various communities that have traditions of not understanding one another and helping them find happiness by bridging their differences.

Jon Haidt in his book *The Happiness Hypothesis* points out the five fundamentals of human happiness are

>> Feeling connected to others

>> Making a difference

>> Associating with and experiencing "good"

>> Reciprocity

>> Fairness and justice

Whether we realize it or not, these are the things we all seek in our lives, personally and professionally, regardless of our culture, ethnicity, or nationality. And according to research on how people choose the brands they choose, these elements of happiness affect purchasing decisions.

According to various studies from Edelman and Cone Communications:

>> 71 percent claim, "I make a point to buy brands from companies whose values are similar to my own."

>> 80 percent are likely to switch brands when price and quality are about equal.

>> 90 percent will quit buying from irresponsible, deceptive brands.

>> 89 percent will buy from social/environmental-driven brands.

>> 80 percent will tell others about a company's CSR effort.

>> 76 percent will donate to a charity supported by a trusted brand.

>> 72 percent will volunteer for a cause supported by a trusted brand.

No matter our culture, ethnicity, age, and when we were born on this earth, we were all born with the innate desire for happiness and are also driven by our need to find a purpose and live a life that makes a positive impact on the world and others around us.

Doing good matters if you want your business to do good now and in the future.

As pointed out by Jonathan Haidt's list of five happiness factors, we find happiness most when we find a purpose and are engaged in fulfilling it. Consciously and unconsciously, people seek meaning in their lives and the need to actively make a difference and leave a personal legacy of good. Jung addresses this in his individuation process, and many studies on human behavior drivers validate that this instinctive need has not and is not likely to change.

Many people seek to find and fulfill a purpose, so much so that Rick Warren's book *The Purpose Driven Life: What on Earth Am I Here For?* became the second most translated book in the world, behind only the Bible. Many consumers today seek purpose outside of the traditional methods of religion and volunteerism and seek to further it by the choices they make at the grocery store, online shopping carts, and more.

TIP

This new state of consumerism doesn't just show that people still have a heart and soul; it's a big flag to brands in all industries to integrate CSR, or corporate social responsibility, into their brand fiber, customer experience, and marketing programs.

So just what is "purpose," and how can you integrate it into your marketing programs, experiences, and messages? *Purpose* is defined as a feeling of "determination to do or achieve something of importance." Identifying a purpose that drives your core customers, and each of your customer segments, should be a top goal of your market research programs. A simple question such as "What moves you most?" can provide some key insights as to how you can gain trust, support, engagement, sales, and more from your customers.

Toby Usnik, a philanthropic advisor and corporate social responsibility professional, with experience at Christie's and American Express, rigorously studies how purpose affects brands and suggests that CSR has moved far beyond writing a check to a cause and then moving on. It's about engaging with that cause in various ways to promote the good it does for the world and devoting your resources and intellectual talent rather than just a small percent of your revenue.

An article published in the March 21, 2015, edition of *The Economist* quoted Jack Welch, former CEO of GE, as saying "Pursuing shareholder value as a strategy was 'the dumbest idea ever.'"

Although that might be debatable to some of you reading this book, it's a big statement as to how critical it is that companies align their products and brands with what matters most to consumers today and find ways to engage with consumers, partners, and community leaders to further those issues and ideas. Statistics from many studies show that defining a brand's purpose and acting on it is anything but "dumb" and actually one of the smartest things you can do.

TIP

Defining your brand's purpose and corresponding CSR efforts is the first step to developing emotional and psychological bonds with internal and external customers. When you make your CSR actionable by engaging others in your cause, you can build passion and loyalty that defines not only your brand but also your profitability.

EXAMPLE

People are drawn to happiness that results from doing good in the world. TOMS, an example that is known to most as one of the pioneers in philanthropic branding, went from $9 million to $21 million in revenue in just three years by being a purpose-driven brand that enables people to give back to others simply by making a purchase. With a cost of goods sold of around $9 and sale price of more than $60, that is not hard to do.

The key to successful CSR programs and purpose-driven strategies is sincerity. Anything less simply backfires. Brands must be sincere about caring to support worthwhile causes related to their field, and they must be sincere when involving customers in charitable giving.

Sincerity is shown not just by the money you donate but by the way you use your marketing channels, budget, and resources to further causes beyond your own and how you encourage others to join your cause or movement.

Putting It All Together

As you build your business and marketing plans, ask yourself the following questions:

>> What emotions are associated with purchasing in my product category?

>> What roles do these emotions play in their purchasing process and final decisions? Outline specific manifestations for each. For example, "Customers purchase my product with the excitement that they may feel and look more glamorous and increase their social status and invitations."

>> How do I need to position my brand to appeal to those emotions?

>> What messaging is most critical to get attention?

>> What creative applications appeal to the feelings that drive choice?

>> What promises and offers will be the most credible for gaining attention and inspiring behavior?

>> What experiences can I create to appeal to and build on the emotions that get customers to trust, act, and remain loyal?

Answering just these questions will help you build out your ESP and action items for your marketing program. After you gather information about psychological, social, and emotional influences, your next step is to create ESP profiles, or grids, that enable you to map out and visualize the influencers that are most likely to result in the behavior and relationships you seek to achieve.

Because most brands market to more than one segment, you'll want to personalize elements to create and deliver content that's specific and highly relevant to each of your customer segments. Whether you segment according to generation, emotional needs, life cycle, history, attitudes toward category or others, you can and should adapt your ESP messaging to be more precise with what moves these personas.

Creating an ESP grid can help you see the differences in segment attitudes and the messages you need to deliver.

A grid for a company selling organic, toxic-free household cleaners per the ESP example earlier in this chapter might look like Table 2-2.

TABLE 2-2   **ESP Grid for Organic, Toxic-Free Household Cleaners**

	Millennials	Generation Xers	Baby Boomers
Trust in business	Low	Low to moderate	Moderate to high
Authorities	Low respect for authorities, don't believe many people, form own opinions, right or wrong Driven by peer support and reviews	Respect authorities but don't always follow them Listen to respected groups and peers	Respect authorities, and tend to believe their data and direction when it fits schema and logic Listen to news, groups, and peers
Values	Want health and clean environment for self; hate waste, chemicals; embrace natural products	Interested in environment and health; will try new products but not completely willing to give up old	Okay with products always used, believe health claims but not as driven to change habits
Messaging	Light on EPA evidence and strong on social proof Promises for clean air and health	EPA studies, other research to back it up, third-party testimonials Promises to protect family and environments	EPA studies, testimonials, promises Promises to protect self, family, and preserve environment
Creative	Bold messages, credible claims, social and mobile channels Bold colors around trust, interactive digital, video	News type messages, educational format, email and direct response Bold colors, mobile access, academic fonts	Educational format, email and direct response and banners Trust colors, traditional fonts, tones

These grids are simplistic for example purposes only. Your grids should include more defining subsets within each generational or demographic group you target. You may include ESPs for groups within each that reflect family-oriented, sunsetters, empty nesters, single young professionals, nervous nellies, and so on. Table 2-3 provides another example.

TABLE 2-3   ## ESP Value Grid for Female Luxury Apparel Purchasers

	Millennials	Generation Xers	Baby Boomers
Trust in business	Low	Low to moderate	Moderate to high
Emotional drivers	Confident, excited, driven, eager	Happy, optimistic, sure	Content, nostalgic
ESP for category	Luxury makes them feel powerful and rising toward goals	Luxury sends a symbol about achievements, status, and success	Luxury reflects life, traditions, and family, personal legacy
Brand choices	Brand reflects where they're going and their current values	Brand is a trusted partner to reflect who they are and provide what they need	Brand is part of who they are and is what they've always purchased
Brand expectations	Be honest, real, set trends, and have a cause that reflects their values	Transparency and innovation to help them stand out	Quality, tradition, service
Preferences	Self-expression, new, trendy, dare to be different, bold styles that reflect individuality	Classic fashion statements that reflect status, place in life, function, and individuality	Traditional styles, quiet statements, reflection of personal taste
Brand ESP	We design items that make a statement about you, your personality, your uniqueness, your values	Our styles reflect your journey, your achievements, your style	We are your partner in providing the styles you need for the times of your life

By doing market research, as described in Chapter 4, you can identify the emotions and values that influence your core consumers to purchase in your category. After you've outlined the psychological, emotional, and social values for your core customers and segments, following your ESP grids will enable you to create marketing materials and experiences based upon precise relevance.

IN THIS CHAPTER

» **Determining your market's growth rate**

» **Operating for growth**

» **Looking at market segmentation**

» **Implementing market share and positioning strategies**

» **Giving growth hacking a try**

» **Staying innovative**

Chapter **3**

Laying a Foundation for Growth

A mantra from the Native American belief says that elements of nature provide important guiding lessons for life. For one, we're taught that we should live our life like a river, always flowing and moving forward; otherwise, we stop progressing and become stagnant, like a pond that can be compromised by moss, fungus, and other elements that hinder growth.

As a marketer, you need to look at your business from this same perspective. Where are the white water rapids, or the growth waves, and can you ride them to capitalize your business?

The simplest and most reliable marketing strategy you can prepare for your business or product is to go where the growth is. One of your top priorities should be finding opportunities that exist today and riding those *growth waves* as long as you can. Doing so will better enable you to operate at a profit so you can capitalize your next round of product development, marketing campaigns, and expansion into new markets or new distributor relationships.

This chapter helps you determine what the growth rate of your market is and evaluate opportunities to find the best options for both short- and long-term growth.

Measuring the Growth Rate of Your Market

Typically, only a few markets are growing rapidly at any given time in a given economy. Some are actually shrinking. Knowing how quickly or slowly your market is growing is vital because it's a key driver of your sales growth and profits.

Continuously monitor and evaluate the current growth rate and future growth potential of your primary market and the opportunities or threats it presents to you. These factors should be part of your brand and competitive SWOT analyses, as discussed in Chapter 5, which will help you better determine your brand's *strengths, weaknesses, opportunities,* and *threats.*

Your core market should be experiencing a 5 to 10 percent overall annual growth. Anything slower than 5 percent makes it difficult for any business to thrive. If your primary market isn't growing fast enough to support your business goals, or is at risk of slowing down soon due to growth in other business sectors, you may need to find new markets you can serve, reinvent your business, or adapt your product line.

TIP

To assess your market's growth potential, you can use simple indicators of your market's current overall growth rate to guide you. These include

>> Year-over-year trends in industry-wide sales

>> Increase or decrease in the number of customers in market

>> Changes in the type and size of purchases per customer

Mapping out these growth indicators for the past one to three years can help you see what's happening and what to expect. Although these indicators will give you rudimentary guidelines that aren't based on statistical formulas or predictive analytics, they'll give you indications of growth nonetheless.

Here are a couple of examples of the kind of information you get on various markets from Statista.com, a statistics portal that provides data about numerous industries and markets from about 18,000 sources. Its reports share findings on industry growth year over year, projections for future years, and more.

>> If you're in the home furnishings space, you can review statistics on furniture sales for a given year. For example, in 2013 home furnishings industry reached over $101 billion. Statista's reports break down revenue per type of store and show the market share, revenue, and sales of top leading companies in the space. And much more.

>> If you're selling mineral water, you can see growth charts for the United States and other world markets, revenue per capita, and consumption per capita, in addition to growth projections and other insightful data.

Explore its reports and those of other market information providers to see whether you can get breakdowns for specific regions you're targeting. Analyst firms like Forrester and Gartner, chambers of commerce, and trade associations are also good sources of marketing growth trends.

Also pay attention to the business news in specific cities in which you sell your products. Follow the trends on home sales, new construction, real estate development, job growth or decline, and other economic indicators.

TIP

If you find that your primary market is shrinking or static, then it's time to look for growth opportunities and prepare for change.

Responding to a Flat or Shrinking Market

When faced with a flat or declining market, consider the following adjustments:

>> Reduce retail stores and other major investments to avoid losses.

>> Look for ways to move your sales online to expand your market reach beyond your current borders. This one step works quickly and powerfully if you're willing to invest in an e-commerce infrastructure. Be sure you find ways to efficiently fulfill and ship online orders before going this route to preserve your profit margins.

>> Eliminate low-margin products from your physical store sales and put those online only. This will help you cut waste from inventory not moving off your shelves while not disappointing customers with fewer options. You see Walmart and Target doing this quite effectively because it helps maximize revenue per foot and lowers overhead costs.

>> Look for other places to sell your product by exploring new distributors, intermediaries, online channels, and collaborators. You can also look to renegotiate your terms with existing partners to help increase your margins. The win for them is that they don't lose a client, end up with less to sell, or have to replace you with another account.

REMEMBER

By keeping an eye on market growth rates and your focus on growth markets, you set yourself up to grow your sales and profit potential at the same time. Slow-growth and no-growth markets are brutally competitive. To win sales in either case, you often have to slash prices, ruining your profit margins. That's why smart marketers make a strategic point of focusing on growth markets and pay close attention to growth rates in all their markets so they stay alert to slowdowns that may indicate a need to move on.

Learning to reinvent yourself before you have to is critical to staying profitable and alive. Never assume that you can glide on your successes. There is no rest for the successful business executive or enterprise that seeks sustainable growth.

TIP

Grow revenue by adding services to support your products. Look for services that appeal to all or specific segments. The goal is to add valuable new revenue streams in case your customer acquisition stagnates. Consider these examples:

>> Utility companies now offer ancillary services such as home delivery of air filters for furnaces and air conditioners, surge protection for appliances and electronics in case of lightning strikes, and more. These subscription-based services increase customer lifetime value and current revenue.

>> Software companies engage in licensing, or SaaS (software as a service) models, which ensures revenue flow every month instead of one-time big chunks of income by selling their systems for a high price one transaction at a time. In the long term, this typically adds up to much more than they could have charged outright.

Also, look at the geographic areas you target most to assess their economic health and strength. If your current market isn't growing, look for nearby markets with stronger population growth and economic projections. Look also at a market's workforce to ensure that it has the skills you need at affordable salaries. In recent years, Utah has become a hotbed for high-tech and software companies because the workforce is highly educated and the cost of living still relatively low. As a result, companies can operate at lower costs than Silicon Valley and make more profits without compromising quality of operations or human capital.

Finding Your Best Growth Strategies

Market growth and expansion are clearly the most common strategies in marketing and the foundations of sustainable brands. The ideas, respectively, are to get your product to customers as efficiently as possible and to start selling to new groups of prospective customers, in terms of demographics and geography, to grow and sustain profitability.

Clearly, your marketing strategies will differ if you're new to an established market, are an existing brand looking for growth, or are launching new products within an established brand to grow new revenue streams. The following sections cover some tactics for achieving success in these and other scenarios.

Go to market

Essentially, this entire book is about going to market. A go-to-market (GTM) strategy is your blueprint for getting your product to the end customer and achieving a high level of sales and awareness at the same time. Pricing, distribution, and publicity are key to GTM strategies. Following are some innovative ways to take a product to market that get you noticed and help you build your base.

Build a presence

Large companies with much to invest in new product launches may start out with their own retail stores to ensure that they reach their target customers and have total control over the product demo and buying experience. Apple carefully created the shopping experience and built a brand persona at its own retail stores before allowing its products to be sold elsewhere, like Amazon and Best Buy. If you have the money, this is a great way to build a strong platform on which a new brand can grow.

Crowdfunding

Even though campaigns on Kickstarter and other crowdfunding sites are designed to raise funds over selling products, they can help create a strong base of champions to help spread the word. If you create a strong campaign with product demos and great videos and gets lots of media talking about your kickstarter campaign, awareness will skyrocket without having to pay for most of it. Additionally, if your campaign can create enough emotional enthusiasm to succeed, you'll likely have a lot of excited backers who want you to succeed and thus are willing to tell your story and promote your products and brand to their networks. And if each of those people has a network of 500 people on just Facebook, Twitter, and LinkedIn, that's a lot of valuable publicity via the most credible channel ever — consumer-to-consumer communications.

Beta testing

Beta testing can work really well. For example, we helped get a new business off the ground recently, and one of the ways we did this was through a beta program. Instead of offering introductory or discounted pricing to get off the ground, because it's hard to raise it even after a launch price, we packaged it differently. We invited people to apply to be part of our beta test whereby they got reduced pricing if they let us tell their success stories in our marketing materials. It worked brilliantly.

People often want to be part of a test to find a new way to doing something better but shy away from "introductions" because they don't want to be the first to buy an unproven product. And deeply discounted products can send a signal that it's not worth much anyway, and you're just full of hype.

If you invite consumers to participate in a test, offer to share some information about your category or a how-to guide that is related to the product being tested so that the value of participation is more than price-oriented.

Once your pilot stage is completed, send participants a report and insights about next steps. Consider offering them a small discount on their next purchase or to renew a subscription to your services as a way to get them to remain an active customer.

Different experiences

Marketing today isn't about the price, special offer, or even the promise and function of a product as much as it is the experience. An experience is what creates the feelings that make people want to come back for more. The experience can come from using the product, trying the service, or from appreciating the service and kinship (see Chapter 4) that follows after the sale. To spark a new feeling of excitement for a new product, guerilla marketing can play a big role (check out Chapter 1).

Grow what you have for higher profitability

Two powerful ways to expand your market position and sales involve introducing more products into the market and using a bestseller to draw more customers to your brand and expanded product line. The sections that follow highlight how you can go about accomplishing both.

Offering more products

Introducing new products is a strong way to expand your share of a particular market — eventually. If you sold only 10 products last year and you offer 20 this year, you just may find that your sales double. Of course, there's a good chance your new products won't sell as well as your old ones at first, but if you persist, you should be able to ramp up their sales over the course of a few years.

When looking to offer more products, you have two options:

>> Add new products simply by reselling or distributing products that complement your current line and meet some need of your current customer base.

>> Innovate to create one or more new products that nobody else sells.

Either way, you have the twofold challenge of informing customers that you have something new to offer and convincing them to take a look — and then getting them to buy it before a bigger competitor gets wind of your idea and decides to offer its own version of a similar product, too. If this happens, the competitor is likely to undercut you on price and overwhelm you on distribution due to greater resources.

These reasons alone illustrate why being especially visible and persistent in the first few months of a new product launch or market expansion is so critical. A concentrated blast of marketing communications is the key to opening a new market successfully. With all the content management systems available today, doing this is getting more and more efficient.

TIP

Create visibility by showing people your brand or product often and in a consistent, professional manner. You can do this through publicity efforts to get visibility on blogs, news channels, and so on, advertising, direct mail, email blasts, search engine marketing, signage (such as billboards and transit ads), sales calls, or presence at conferences and trade shows.

EXAMPLE

Another great way to introduce a new product for both an existing brand or a new one is to sell it at kiosks, which are less expensive and often more visible than retail stores in shopping malls. Anson Calder, a luxury travel accessories brand, launched by opening a kiosk in a busy New York City building, which let people see its products firsthand. By doing this, it was able to introduce its style and quality and drive sales to the website, which is its primary commerce channel.

If your product is different, set up a demo station and offer coffee or snacks to keep people lingering longer and staying for the whole demo. Free food and drink have stopping power at malls or even stores like Costco. Collect email and other usable information before giving away that free coffee so you can build your database at the same time. (Find more on this in Chapter 10.)

WARNING

Risks and costs increase when you experiment with *new products* — anything you're not accustomed to making and marketing. Consequently, you should discount your first year's sales projections for a new market by some factor to reflect the degree of risk. A good general rule is to cut back the sales projections by 20 to 50 percent, depending on your judgment of how new and risky the product is to you and your team. It may also cost you double the time and money to make each sale when entering a new market, because your new prospects won't be familiar with your brand, and you likely won't have a well-defined marketing formula at the start. Budget accordingly.

Riding a bestseller to the top

If you have a *bestseller* — a product that substantially outsells your other products — it may make sense to put a lot of your resources toward maximizing sales for this product and using the profits to grow other areas of your business. Some marketing experts look for bestsellers to achieve sales that are at least ten times the norm; outstanding bestsellers can achieve a hundred or more times the normal level of sales for a product in their category. If you have just one bestseller in your line, growing your revenues and profits is fairly easy as long as it remains popular.

You can expand demand for a top-selling product by creating new experiences around it or partnering with others to help package or bundle your products with their products. Partnering or bundling works well with software and in retail. If you sell comfy throw blankets, for example, partner with a company that makes fuzzy slippers or single-serve coffee machines to help round out the cozy-at-home experience.

TIP

How do you create a bestselling product? First, look for one. Don't be content with products that sell moderately well. Keep looking for something that has more excitement and potential. Test many alternatives. When you find one that seems to have momentum (you'll know it has momentum when early sales figures surprise you by their rapid growth), quickly refocus your marketing efforts on that product. Make it the heart of sales calls and ads, feature it at the top of your website's home page, talk to the media about it, and offer specials for new customers who try it. Bestsellers are found and made by marketers who believe in them. Be a believer!

When you have a product with bestseller potential, your marketing strategy should be to ride it as hard and as far as you can. Write a marketing plan that puts the majority of your budget and efforts behind the bestseller and gives the rest of your product line as minimal a budget as you think you can get away with. The bestseller will tend to lift all sales by attracting customers to your brand, which will likely have a strong reputation for quality and service due to your bestseller, so you won't have to worry as much about the rest of your products.

After you have a bestseller, you should see your profits grow. Use some of these profits to look for the next bestseller because, like all good things, your current bestseller will eventually lose its momentum. Always be looking for your next top product so you can have it ready and waiting in the wings. Test ideas and options, and be patient. If you can't find another bestseller, switch to another marketing strategy. You don't have to have a bestseller to succeed, but it sure is nice if you can find a product that fits this strategy.

TIP

While your products are selling and your customer satisfaction is high, referral marketing and reward programs are critical to maximize your sales and profit potential. Reward your customers who continue to buy your products by giving them discounts for repeat purchases. Also consider giving referring customers a financial reward and see what that alone can do for profits. System Pavers pays

$500 for each customer referred that completes a qualifying project. It puts no limit on how much one customer can make in referrals. This act of reciprocity not only makes current customers happy but also keeps System Pavers's brand and new products on their minds. And it has helped grow profits very successfully as well. To date, System Pavers has paid out $1.3 million in rewards for referring customers.

So if, for example, a company paid out just $1 million in referral rewards, that is 2,000 projects. If a company's average sale is $10,000, that adds up to $20 million! With no advertising costs involved, that's a pretty amazing return.

Making a hot product even hotter

Another strategy is to influence the supply and demand for a product that's showing signs of being another one of your top sellers. You can influence sales and pricing by how you choose to distribute your product after it has established a stronghold in your market. One way to do this is to release a limited amount of product to specialty stores so that people have to seek out your product. If you distribute through the mass retailers, you lose the chance to build a competitive edge with exclusivity or scarcity — two elements we discuss in Chapter 2. You also have the freedom to change your price as demand increases, which you often give away when you contract with Walmart or another mass retailer that demands fixed prices.

EXAMPLE

Beanie Babies are a great example of this strategy. Creator Ty Warner released his Beanie Babies for short periods of time and then retired them, making them collector items that made people want them even more. And for some of his creations, he produced only a couple of hundred bears, making them instant and rare collector items. The value of some of his bears at the peak of the Beanie Baby frenzy reached upwards of $3,000.

Take a look at your distribution strategies for your top products. Can you produce less and make them more valuable? Can you change your access points to make them seem more exclusive? Or do you just want to keep selling a product until it doesn't sell anymore and pocket the profits while you can?

There are many considerations for how to maximize the profitability of your top-selling products. Just remember, what's hot now may not be hot in a matter of weeks. In the case of Beanie Babies, they were one of the biggest frenzies and crashes of the 1990s, as described by Zac Bissonnette, who wrote *The Great Beanie Baby Bubble: Mass Delusion and the Dark Side of Cute*. When the company announced that it would stop producing the toys that had become collectors' obsessions — leading to a murder and a custody battle in court over a divorcing couple splitting their "babies" — the frenzy almost dried up as quickly as it had heated up. Those big-priced little Beanie Babies on eBay lost value quickly, and the fad faded to where today many consumers don't really know what a Beanie Baby is or was.

TIP

Whatever your plan for maximizing the growth of your current top-selling products, have an exit strategy in mind, too. Be prepared to answer the following questions:

>> At what point will you cease production before you end up producing more than you can sell if trends and fads change?

>> At what point are you willing to let your product become a commodity, selling at a fixed price?

>> At what point will you replace this product with a new one that is likely to have the same appeal to the same consumers so that you have an opportunity to create another highly profitable product and cycle?

Growing a Market Segmentation Strategy

To succeed, a *market segmentation strategy* needs to be more than just sorting customers into like groups so you can build marketing around specific personas that appeal to each group with relevance. It involves messaging on psychological influences and producing relevant content for each segment, often simultaneously, to keep sales moving in large quantities rather than periodic spurts.

You can create segments along numerous lines. The key is to sort them in ways that make sense for how people process decisions to buy, past transactions, attitudes, and so on, and how you're set up to reach each segment efficiently. Digital asset management platforms that enable you to create new version and release content for all channels simultaneously are key to enabling you to communicate to all segments at the same time with high efficiencies.

REMEMBER

Step one in a segmentation strategy is to have a strong content marketing system that can automatically adapt your digital and print marketing material for each segment and enable you to put all versions in market at the same time instead of staggering sales promotions that can delay your sales and overall success.

The advantage of a segmentation strategy is that it allows you to tailor your product and your entire marketing effort to a clearly defined group with uniform, specific characteristics. If you find that one segment strongly outperforms all others consistently over time, you may want to consider a niche strategy whereby you drop your focus on all other segments and channel all your resources on the one segment. In a world that's looking for more customization and personalized service, niche marketing might just make the most sense. It helps you better compete with larger businesses because you can specialize and personalize in ways they can't.

Customer segments

One of the most proven and common segmentation strategies is based on RFM — recency, frequency, and monetary value of customers. When you sort customers accordingly, you identify those customers with the highest propensity for repeat sales and profitability for your business and establish groups with like values to which you can communicate with "mass personalization." RFM is one of the basic fundamentals of a strong data-driven marketing strategy (see Chapter 10).

You may build customer segments on the following:

>> RFM

>> Products purchased

>> Transaction value

>> Frequency of purchase

>> Generational attitudes

>> Trust equity in brand and/or category

>> ESP profiles (see Chapter 2)

>> Conversion channel (did they come in via social, web, retail, referral, or other?)

>> Purchasing and browsing patterns

>> Demographics (education, gender, income)

>> Geography

>> Relationship with brand (warm lead, cold call, or established customer)

With a strong database program and analytics tools, you can learn about your current customers and how you can build segments to capture growth trends or better nurture future leads. For example, if a subset of your customers is growing faster than the rest, consider specializing in those types of customers to gain more of their business or purchasing more lists that replicate that customer set. You can also adjust your product, pricing, promotion, or distribution plans for each segment. If you do this, you need to adapt your marketing content for each group.

TIP

If your customer base is shrinking or your current segments aren't responding as desired, consider adding a new segment. For example, a consulting firm specializing in coaching healthcare executives can decide to start offering a similar service to nonprofits, expanding its market base without having to change its core competencies or budget for expensive new product development.

Niche marketing

Specializing in a specific market segment can give you the momentum you need to power past your competition, but it may not always be the right approach for your operation. The niche strategy may work well for you if

>> You think your business can be more profitable by specializing in a more narrowly defined segment than you do now.

>> You face too many competitors in your broader market and can't seem to carve out a stable, profitable customer base of your own.

>> It takes better advantage of things you're good at.

>> You're too small to be one of the leaders in your overall market or industry. Maybe you can be the leader in a specific segment of your market.

Developing a Market Share Strategy

Scaling your business is obviously the best way to improve your ability to compete with larger, more established brands and increase your market share. *Market share* is, very simply, your sales as a percentage of total sales for your product category in your market (or in your market segment if you use a segmentation strategy). If you sell $2 million worth of widgets and the world market totals $20 million per year, then your share of market is 10 percent. It's that simple. Or is it?

Following are some insights on market share and how you can implement one effectively.

Define your metrics

Before you can completely determine your market share, determine the metrics that matter most to you. Is it better to determine market share by dollars earned, containers shipped, or units sold? Pick whatever seems to make sense for your product and the information you have access to.

Establish a benchmark

To effectively increase your market share, you must have an accurate picture of where you stand currently. Here's a simple method for estimating market size and share.

1. Estimate the number of customers in your market.

For instance, guess how many people in your country are likely to buy toothpaste or how many businesses in your city buy consulting services. With companies like Statista, a consumer statistics portal, and Hoover's, a commercial database of businesses and executives, you can get fairly precise insights on the size, sales, and market leaders for any industry.

2. Estimate how much each customer buys a year, on average.

Does each customer buy six tubes of toothpaste? Fifteen hours of consulting services? You can check your sales records for specific data for your brand or turn to industry research for specific information and year-over-year growth data.

3. Multiply the two figures together to get the total size of the annual market and then divide your unit sales into it to get your share.

You can also look at information compiled by the U.S. Census Data (www.census.gov) to get information about population and economic trends to help you with forecasting and growth plans.

Alternatively, you may estimate that three-quarters of the wholesalers handle low-cost, inexpensive teas and therefore don't compete directly with you. In that case, you can calculate your market share of the quarter of total sales that are similar specialty teas as $0.525 \div (0.25 \times 3.886)$, which gives you 54 percent. That's a much larger share based on a narrower definition of the market. Estimating your market share helps you determine which market share numbers are correct.

To create a market share strategy, you need to clearly identify and define your product and where it fits into your market. In other words, you need to know your *product category* — the general grouping of competitive products to which your product belongs (be it merchandise or a service). Knowing your product category is extremely important. If you don't know where your product fits into the market, you can't begin to develop a strategy to build on and increase your existing market share. For example, if you're a boutique business selling specialty teas from physical retail locations, you need to determine the following:

>> Are you competing with mass-market brands?

>> How do you compete with other specialty tea shops with physical locations that offer a gathering place rather than just a product?

>> Are you losing market share to online sellers?

>> Are there better opportunities for growth by selling as a wholesaler instead of a retailer?

You can learn about consumptions patterns and project consumer behavior by studying reports from trade associations, Statista data, and other sources that can guide you on what's happening and what to expect in your industry.

Do the math

If your goals are to increase market share by a certain percentage or dollar value, you need to do some calculations to determine what those figures really are. For example: If you own a tea store in Shanghai, you could have a goal of increasing share of tea sales by 1.5 percentage points. If each point of share is worth roughly $40,000 in annual sales (1 percent of the total sales in the market), then you'll likely need a plan that involves spending, say, an extra $25,000 to win that 1.5 percent share gain. If it works, you can gain an extra $60,000. But will it work? To be cautious, you, as the marketer, may want to discount this projection of $60,000 in additional sales by a risk factor of, say, 25 percent, which cuts your projected gain back to $45,000. If you exceed it, you can enjoy the reward. If not, you avoid setting your business up for missed sales projections, which can affect profitability and your own credibility.

Be realistic about the time it takes to reach market share goals. A sales projection starting at the current level of sales in the first month and ramping up to the projected increase by, say, the sixth month, may be reasonable. Dividing $45,000 by 12 to find the monthly value of the risk-discounted 1.5 share point increase gives you $3,750 in extra monthly sales for the sixth month and beyond. Lower increases apply to earlier months when the program is just starting to kick in. But the marketing expenses tend to be concentrated in the early months, reflecting the need to invest in advance to grow your market share.

REMEMBER

Market share gives you a simple way of comparing your progress to your competitors' from period to period. If your share drops, you're losing; if your share grows, you're winning. It's that simple. Base your goals on realistic, actionable items that you can measure. For example, if your goal is to increase share from 5 to 7 percent with a product upgrade and trial-stimulating special offers, be sure you can attribute market share growth to those actions so you know what's working and what isn't.

Designing a Positioning Strategy

A *positioning strategy* reflects the emotional fulfillment and psychological relevance of building ESPs (emotional selling propositions) over USPs (unique value propositions) because "unique" isn't a sustainable strategy (see Chapter 2). It's too easy for a competitor with more resources or a quicker time-to-market process to duplicate and take away a "unique" advantage. A successful positioning strategy focuses on getting customers or prospects to see your product by the emotional and functional values it offers, to trust your claims about quality and service, and to try your products before considering competitors' offerings.

REMEMBER

Your positioning strategy needs to reflect your ESP strategy. As you plan for growth, identify new markets where your ESP and positioning will stand out and be appealing to consumers. Do you need to adapt your ESP or how you position it and your other promises for various cultures or demographics that you're trying to penetrate or dominate? The more you know about each market you operate in, the more effective you'll be.

Envisioning your position: An exercise in observation and creativity

Good positioning means your product has mind share among consumers, which will in turn help you gain market share. Your positioning statement should be believable and actionable. It should reflect the core values of what you offer and make a statement about how you differ from competitors' or even functional alternatives.

As you do your competitive analysis, as discussed in Chapter 4, compare your positioning strategy against competitors to see whether you're saying the same thing in different words or whether your promise and emotional value really stand out. Just as important, do your product, sales, and service processes fulfill the promise you make in your positioning statements, sales promises, and other marketing materials?

Aligning your positioning strategy with growth initiatives

After you've defined the emotional value you offer in addition to the product value or competitive difference that sets you apart, you can start building growth plans accordingly. For example, if you produce and sell organic healthy snack foods for children that replace the abundance of junk food marketed to kids daily, your positioning could reflect the health benefits and emotional relief parents gain by knowing that they're not jeopardizing their child's growth by giving into demands for food that isn't healthy. As a result of having a healthier but tasty snack food for children, you can expand to niche and specialty markets that are showing big growth opportunity. Sometimes these may be geographical markets. Health food and fitness services are big in Boulder, Colorado, but may not be so big in some parts of the south where less healthy types of food are consumed regularly.

For a product such as this, you can target influencers who are directly related to parents who are highly concerned about the physical and mental impact of poor nutrition. Influencers whom you can target for resellers may include, for example, allergists, pediatricians, youth sports clubs, and associations and government bodies focused on nutritional research and education.

For any given industry, you can find a long list of organizations with whom you can build alliances for reselling your products, referring others, or introducing you to consumers who are right for what you offer, which leads to another critical strategy in today's world of many options and confusing alternatives: *growth hacking* (see the next section).

Growth Hacking to Build Leads and Market Share

Although the term *growth hacking* may be relatively new to this generation of marketing, the concept isn't. It's just a highly concentrated process for reaching out to your networks to build direct leads and increase your visibility and position in a marketplace by linking to others' social and digital assets and creating collaborative opportunities.

It's also about gaining mind share by taking advantage of the social and digital tools that enable people to find your brand ahead of others. The following sections offer some tips about growth-hacking strategies that cost little to execute but can pay off in a big way.

Search

Know what and who is getting the most attention in your market. Through tools as simple as Google's Search console, you can discover what websites are getting the most impressions and highest click-through rates and what keywords in your industry are getting the same. Pay attention to how the brands getting the most impressions are marketing themselves and what keywords are most popular for consumer searches in your industry. Make sure you include these in your positioning and marketing messages. And make sure you build your own search engine optimization (SEO) and search engine marketing (SEM) strategies around the keywords and products most searched by your core consumers. These will change and change frequently, so keeping current on these trends is critical.

Build links

There's a reason LinkedIn is growing in size and value to marketers in all industries and of businesses of all sizes. As of September 2016, it had upward of 106 million users, which presents a big networking opportunity for just about any business professional. Take stock of your own network (if you're not on LinkedIn, get on it now). How big is your network? Do you have 1,000 or more connections? How many of those can you name? And for how many of those do you have personal or work email addresses? Probably "not a lot" is your answer to both of those questions.

In today's world of digital networks, if you're not mining your network connections, you're likely walking away from a gold mine. You need to create templates for communicating with members in ways that get them to respond. Try emailing connections on LinkedIn and asking whether they'd be interested in a free white paper or participating in a brief survey. For either of these, they need to share their email address with you, which you can then add to your database for content marketing. You've just gained a critical email address and sparked a direct relationship that you or your sales team can nurture.

Fish for emails

Although *phishing* most often refers to unethical scams designed to get personal contact information to exploit consumers, *fishing* — the kind that uses bait to hook people on your brand — is still good and pays off. Fishing for emails is as simple as offering something of value to consumers in exchange for their email address. You don't need click bait (described more in Chapter 6) to get people to participate if you offer something real and of real value.

For example, if you're a marketing consultant and you design a banner ad or email that says, "Need help calculating your customer lifetime value?" you can require people to click on a form in your marketing template that sends their email address directly to you. Bam! You've got another email for your growth marketing campaigns and a lead with whom you've just started a new relationship.

Try tripwires

Tripwire is yet another new term, relatively speaking, for marketing tactics but not a new concept or strategy. Tripwire marketing is simply the act of offering something people can't refuse. It's one of those "big blowout sales" used car lots have been using for years. We see these all the time in infomercials on TV and now through digital channels all over the web. You sell someone on the benefit it offers and then offer it for a limited time as a free trial ("get now, pay later if you keep it" approach) or for such a low price that no one can say no. The trick according to Neil Patel, a growth marketing guru, is to keep your price pretty low (less than $50) and to offer a more expensive, better value product at checkout. According to Patel, at least 30 percent of your shoppers should end up buying the higher-end product or better value, which you can position as your "best value."

Hire a growth hacker

So how do you go about integrating these tactics into your growth strategy given that many are time-consuming? Simple. Hire a growth hacker who can dedicate her days to sending out templates for invitations to connects, offers for white papers, and other messages for you. If you have a well-connected sales or executive team, open their networks for your growth hacker. Your goal should be to establish a connection with about 20 percent of those to whom you reach out. Again, if you have a network of 3,000 people on your social sites, 20 percent is 600. Now multiply that number by five executives on your team and you'll have a new database of 3,000 highly qualified leads to nurture and grow.

To read more about growth hacking, follow Neil Patel's blog at `www.neilpatel.com`.

Selling Innovative Products

Every product category has a limited life. At least in theory — and usually in all-too-real reality — some new type of product comes along to displace the old one. The result is called *the product life cycle,* a never-ending cycle of birth, growth, and decline, fueled by the endless inventiveness of competing businesses. Product categories arise, spread through the marketplace, and ultimately decline as replacements arise and begin their own life cycles. If you're marketing an innovative product that's just beginning to catch on (in what marketers call the growth phase of the life cycle), you can expect rapid growth in sales and profits.

REMEMBER

Your growth strategy and actions will be only as good as your product. If you don't keep up with changing technology, consumer needs, and demands, no plan for growth will pay off. Imagine trying to sell a typewriter when personal computers were taking off and coming down in price. No amount of imagination, linking, connecting, and lead generation can overcome an out-of-date product that has no value in the current world. Your strategic imagination is the only limitation to your growth.

2

Building a Strategy for LTV and ROI

IN THIS PART . . .

Discover how to conduct valid and meaningful research about your customers, competitors, and industry.

Recognize key components of a successful marketing plan for any size business.

Check out content marketing strategies that work.

IN THIS CHAPTER

» **Conducting valid and meaningful research**

» **Identifying your Net Promoter Score and why it matters**

» **Using surveys to identify trends, needs, and emotional drivers**

» **Getting effective market research tools at the right price**

» **Keeping an eye on market demographics**

Chapter **4**

Researching Your Customers, Competitors, and Industry

One of the biggest mistakes any marketer can make is to assume. As a marketer, you need to be aware of assuming that you know what your customers think about your brand, products, overall category, and what inspires them to purchase or not. Just as dangerous is assuming that your customers are just like you. Chances are they're not. Making assumptions about the marketplace, trends, and your competition is also not a good idea.

The foundation of any successful marketing plan is a solid research program, and with all the technologies and sources available today, it's easier and more affordable than ever. Your research plan is your guide to how your customers decide what they like or don't like about your brand, expectations they have for products and customer service, their level of potential loyalty or attrition, and so on. It should also include insights about your category, local markets, and competitive landscape.

Regularly conducting surveys among your customers and prospects is essential to staying on top of what drives your customers to purchase from and stay loyal to you and how likely they are to refer others, which is critical to any company's success.

In addition, reviewing secondary research such as consumer trend reports, white papers on emerging technology, and market analyses and projections should all be part of your body of knowledge as you craft your product and marketing strategies.

This chapter outlines some tips and tactics for surveying customers to gain a better understanding of what really inspires your customers to act, how they process information, and what matters most to them. You also find suggestions for researching your competitors and determining how best to use your resources.

Knowing When and Why to Do Research

Research provides valuable insights about your customers, competition, and industry to help you make informed and thus better decisions about your brand positioning, messaging, offers, engagement activities, media purchases, and more. You can also use various methods to help you test your marketing campaign ideas and their likelihood to succeed before spending a lot of money on execution.

Following are some guidelines for gathering insights, information, and expectations about your market and consumers that will help you make wise decisions and communicate with spot-on relevance for your various consumer segments.

Monitoring social chatter to better understand your customers

In a world where trends change almost daily, or so it seems, so do the demands, expectations, and interests of consumers. The good news is that with all the social media outlets that capture consumers' thoughts, likes, shares, and other expressed interests, you can monitor the issues, attitudes, ideas, inspirations, and aspirations that are most on the minds of your consumers. This kind of information can stimulate your own imagination and new strategies while helping you see new business opportunities.

Don't fall into the trap of doing all your customer research online. Make a point of talking to people face to face, in groups and individually. Carry an idea notebook in your pocket or purse and try to collect a few insights from people every day. This habit gets you asking salespeople, employees, customers, and strangers on the street for their ideas and suggestions. You never know when a suggestion may prove valuable and lead to another.

Popular social media outlets

Get started by identifying the social channels your customers most use and follow in general as well as your subsegments. And follow them yourself. The most common among young and more mature adult audiences include

>> Facebook

>> Twitter

>> Pinterest

>> LinkedIn

>> Instagram

>> Flickr

Note what news, stories, photos, and videos are trending the most and what themes are getting the most likes and shares. Once you identify where you customers spend most of their time online, join those channels and then join the conversations. Monitoring and engaging in dialogue with customers and prospects provides the best information of all.

Take advantage of your own social media followers. Ask your virtual friends on LinkedIn, Facebook, and Twitter what's on their minds and for opinions, suggestions, and ideas about topics of interest related to your industry. You're not likely to get enough feedback to have statistical significance for any new idea or recommendation, but you'll gain insights on how some of your customers feel and identify trends you may want to research further.

Photo sites such as Pinterest, Flickr, and Instagram are highly visual, with members' selections of photos, graphics, and other visual art that provide insights into how people are thinking, feeling, and living and how trends, needs, and concerns are evolving. By studying such websites, you, too, can be an anthropologist of sorts, studying your own culture to seek business and marketing needs and opportunities, or even just to update the vocabulary, terms, or *shortcode* (abbreviated terms or acronyms for common phrases, such as LMK for "let me know") you use in your marketing communications.

Many social listening tools enable brands to monitor what customers are saying about them on social sites. You can monitor personas of customers and listen to their collective dialogue through various sites, and you can also track individuals, helping you identify which customers you're at risk of losing, those which may be interested in ancillary services, and most critically those that are spreading ill will about your brand. This ability gives you a unique opportunity to intervene with a solution in real time, something about which other generations of marketers could only dream. If your brand is big enough and you can afford a social listening platform, this can be critical to stopping customer attrition in a world where loyalty is diminishing among all age groups and customer personas.

Blogs

Other outlets you need to monitor are influencer blogs. No matter your industry, there are many voices out there, and you need to identify the ones your customers most listen to. For example, if you're positioning your products for those that value minimalist living, subscribe to the most popular blogs available. Today, one of those is The Minimalists, which is written by two leading subject matter experts with more than 4 million readers. Chances are they have a lot of influence on what products their followers view and purchase.

Bloggers are some of the most powerful influencers, so pay attention to what they say and recommend. After you identify the influencers in your market, be sure to not only subscribe to their blogs but also work to come up with blog or story ideas that support your products and encourage them to write about them. Just like journalists, they're always looking for new ideas, products, and insights to write about so that they can be relevant and gain more followers. These people should be on your lists for sending press releases, news bulletins, story ideas, and so on.

REMEMBER

When asking for input and information on websites and in virtual web communities, be honest about who you are and why you're asking for advice. If you tell people you're in charge of marketing your product and want to know what they think of your new ad, many people will offer their views freely. If, however, you pretend to be someone outside the company who's just trying to insert business questions into an innocent chat, people will see through you, and the loss of trust will outweigh any potential good you could have gained. Honesty and transparency are the keys to successful research in online communities.

Monitor blogs and social and news sites to read what people are saying about your category, competitors, and maybe even your brand. Take note about what makes them happy or not so happy, and identify appropriate actions to avoid making mistakes.

Following thought leaders to get current with reality

In addition to surveying your customers about their expectations from your category and brand, you can identify opportunities for your business, analyze choices, and determine product development plans by following thought leaders in your category and general business areas.

For example, if you want to see how other businesses spend their advertising budgets, you can find many associations and think tank organizations that provide insights on this every year. Knowing how similar or complementary brands are spending their advertising dollars can give you some insights on what is most likely to pay off and what channels are getting the most attention from consumers that you target as well. Large brands — business-to-business (B2B) and business-to-consumer (B2C) sectors — spend thousands on research to determine the best path to a strong ROI, or return on investment, so pay attention to what they're doing.

Some sources for learning how both B2B and B2C brands are spending their advertising and marketing resources include

>> Winterberry

>> HubSpot

>> The Data and Marketing Association (formerly the Direct Marketing Association)

>> Statista

>> eMarketer

Whatever decisions you're turning to research to help you make, it helps to plot out the variables so you can see clearly the pros and cons and the opportunities and risks.

Table 4-1 is a sample decision grid to help you get started. Plotting out the information you collect and insights you gain can help you visually see any situation more clearly and guide your decisions in the right direction. You can plot out questions for customer campaigns, media buys, product development, partnerships and alliances you seek, and so on.

TABLE 4-1   ## Analyzing the Information Needs of a Decision

Decision	Information Needs	Possible Sources	Findings
Choose between banner ads on influencer blogs or websites and email advertisements to purchased lists.	How many actual prospects do the blogs and websites under consideration actually reach?	Sales reps and media kits are initial contact points.	Three leading blogs covering our industry have a large following, but only half of these are among our top prospects. May not be worth it?
	What are the comparable costs per prospect reached through these different methods?	Analyze costs for each method and number of people reached. Divide cost by number of people and compare.	Email to purchased lists is one-third the price of banner ads on key blogs.
	Can we find out what the average click-through and response rates are for both approaches?	Contact other advertisers to learn about their ROI and quality of leads generated form sites listed. Ask for client references from email list brokers. Review industry averages for email results from sources such as HubSpot.	ROIs from other advertisers are below expectations for our current budget. Quality of leads from banner ads are not as strong as those we can purchase from target opt-in lists that have been identified as likely to buy within 30, 60, or 90 days. Extra cost may have higher ROI in long term.
	Which channel is most used by our larger competitors? And what is the average return? What email lists are available that replicate readers of sites with most industry presence?	Review media analysts' sites for ad spends and average return on web banners versus email.	Banner ads are producing lower results than in past years and reach many people we don't need to reach right now. We need outlets that produce leads more than brand awareness, which seems to be the biggest value for the sites we've monitored.

Decision	Information Needs	Possible Sources	Findings
Conclusions?	We need to find websites that cater to more specific, targeted audiences but cost less.	We can do this by identifying influencer blogs with small readership and small fees to maintain awareness among key audiences. We can find email lists that replicate these readers from various sources.	Our current plan should be to buy targeted lists while looking for smaller, less expensive sites to introduce our brands and identify future lists.

List the decisions you need to make and map out your questions. Creative information-gathering is key to determining the best answers. Figure 4-1 depicts a market research process that can be of value.

A good question is thought-provoking and affects your future actions and successes. If you come upon a really good question, research it carefully. You'll find that the first question breaks down into many more specific ones that, when answered, help you make a good decision.

Researching to discover what really drives your customers

As mentioned in Chapter 2, the success of any marketing plan for any business category depends on the ability to identify the ESP, or emotional selling proposition, that best applies to your core customers.

How consumers feel about your products or service, customer service policies, and their overall experience with your brand determines your success and your product's fate. Research can help you identify, understand, and eventually manage consumer reactions and feelings, which we've already determined influence 90 percent of people's thoughts and behavior. If you focus on identifying some of the more extreme views that customers express — both positive and negative — about your category and brand, you'll be able to connect with greater emotional relevance and stand out from competitors with the same old messaging.

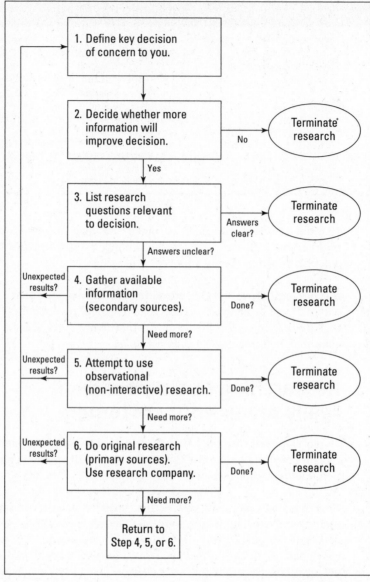

FIGURE 4-1:
Follow this market research process to avoid common errors.

Flowchart steps:

1. Define key decision of concern to you.

2. Decide whether more information will improve decision.
   - No → Terminate research
   - Yes ↓

3. List research questions relevant to decision.
   - Answers clear? → Terminate research
   - Answers unclear? ↓

4. Gather available information (secondary sources).
   - Done? → Terminate research
   - Unexpected results? ←
   - Need more? ↓

5. Attempt to use observational (non-interactive) research.
   - Done? → Terminate research
   - Unexpected results? ←
   - Need more? ↓

6. Do original research (primary sources). Use research company.
   - Done? → Terminate research
   - Unexpected results? ←
   - Need more? ↓

Return to Step 4, 5, or 6.

Instead of just asking routine questions related to customers' satisfaction, wait times, and so on, include some questions to help you identify how they feel.

Here are some ideas for questions to help you identify feelings that drive choice beyond just the feelings after a choice is made:

>> What was the emotional or functional fulfillment sought when making a purchase?

>> What is their main goal when purchasing your product category?

>> After doing business with you, how did they feel? You can leave it open for their input or guide them with feelings you want to assess. Maybe include words like *content, excited, creative, neutral, appreciated,* and *valued.*

>> Did you make them feel any differently from when they purchased from a competitor?

>> What was the main reason they chose to explore purchasing from your brand?

>> What was the primary element that influenced their decision to purchase from you versus a competitor?

>> What is their decision criteria for your product category?

>> What are the primary expectations they have for the brands they are considering?

>> What do they like most about your brand?

>> What do they like least about your brand?

>> How happy have they been with purchases and experiences from others in your category? What generated happiness or lack of?

These and other questions are key to helping you identify the feelings that drive consumers' research process and brand choices, which are critical to engaging in a manner that gets them to yes. When you add questions about feelings to customer satisfaction questions, you can get realistic and actionable insights on how to best communicate and engage emotionally with each of your customer segments.

TIP

As you gather information about feelings and satisfaction ratings, you can draw a graph of all the features of your product, rated from negative through neutral to positive. Most features cluster in the middle of the resulting bell curve, failing to differentiate you from the competition. A few features stick out on the left as notably negative — you must fix those features fast! Other features, ideally, stand out on the right as notably positive. You need to nurture and expand on these features, and don't forget to promote these in all your marketing communications.

Asking questions that get valid results

How you ask questions matters. If you are too vague, you'll get vague answers, which may or may not give you the right guidance. If you simply ask yes-or-no questions, you won't be able to identify the degree of positive or negative thoughts toward that issue and how to compare and prioritize answers.

We have found that the best scale on which to ask customers to evaluate their experience with you and your product is a scale of 1 to 5, with 1 being low and 5 being high. Anything more complicated makes it difficult for consumers to answer, which increases the drop-out rate and makes it more difficult to analyze and identify trends and feelings upon which you can act. For example:

1	2	3	4	5
Very poor	Poor	Average	Good	Very good

You can change the variables to Disagree Strongly, Disagree, Neutral, Agree, and Agree Strongly, and other attributes.

For example, a bank may want customers to rank checking accounts (average), savings accounts (average), speed of service (poor), and friendliness of tellers (very good), along with many other factors to describe the bank in detail.

Your high-ranking attributes from the survey represent the features you should be promoting to others and talking about in your social media posts and online sites. The low scores can help you identify your failings and set priorities for improving your customer experience. To clarify which ones are worthy of the most attention, you can ask customers to rate the importance of each listed item. Then you can focus your improvement efforts on the more important attributes.

Surveys are cost effective for getting a collective understanding of your strengths and weaknesses from your universe of customers and prospects and your specific customer segments. With all the affordable survey tools available today, such as SurveyMonkey and Constant Contact, you can afford to conduct surveys among your general customers and each of your core segments to better communicate to the specific emotional needs and current place in your product's life cycle.

For example, you may want to set up your surveys among demographic groups within your industry to identify different decision processes, emotional needs, price points, purchasing cycles, and so on. You should also sort out groups based on their relationship with you. These groups may include

>> Lapsed customers

>> Current customers

>> Potential customers with prior contact (often referred to as a warm list)

>> Prospects with no prior contact (often referred to as a cold list)

>> Male versus female shoppers

>> Baby boomers versus millennials

REMEMBER

When you create surveys for customers, you're not only asking them questions about themselves, but you're also sharing information about your brand. Use these tools to communicate key differences in an informative manner. For example, you may want to ask, "Did you know that ABC Brand maintains the highest customer satisfaction rates in the quick print industry?"

The leading question helps you identify how effectively your communication is getting across and lets you share something of value in a way that's more subtle than bragging on LinkedIn, which can get mixed results.

Checking Out Net Promoter Scores and How to Find Yours

Today, one of the most common benchmarks for how a brand is doing is its Net Promoter Score, or NPS. This is primarily a score on how highly you rate for customer referrals, yet it's something many consumers look for when choosing between brands. In short, the NPS is an index that ranges from –100 to 100, which shows the likelihood of customers to recommend a company's products or services to others. It helps marketers determine not just the possibility of referrals but also the satisfaction rates and thus potential loyalty of current customers.

Many tools can help you get a solid read on your NPS. If you use SurveyMonkey, these questions are already crafted and ready to be added to your survey in a way that will get you a valid response. You can also get real-time NPSs on a regular basis through tools such as those offered by Satmetrix. Do some research to find the tools that best fit your current digital and customer relationship management (CRM) platforms.

If you use your own survey platform and want to do your own calculations instead of using a tool from a software company, you can find calculators online to help you. One example of a free service you can use is www.npscalculator.com.

To give you some perspective, the average NPS for life insurance companies in 2016 was 31; it was 58 for department/specialty stores and 2 for Internet services (yes, 02). Companies with some of the top scores include Nordstrom at 80, USAA at 77, Ritz-Carlton at 72, and Apple iPhone/iPad at 60, according to Satmetrix, one of the leaders in NPS systems and findings (www.netpromoter.com).

A good benchmark for you is to look up the index for your industry and how your competitors score. Find your NPS and aim to execute marketing strategies that will help you get and stay ahead of your competitors. For consumers doing research on which brands to buy and which to avoid, these scores matter!

Beyond asking questions to determine consumers' likelihood to purchase from you and refer you, your surveys should also ask questions to guide you in developing your product line. For example, if you're in charge of a 2-year-old software product that small businesses use to do their planning and financials, you may want to ask questions that will help you determine the following issues:

>> Should we launch an upgrade or keep selling the current version?

>> Is our current marketing program sufficiently effective, or should we redesign it?

>> Is the product positioned properly, or do we need to change its image?

Asking Really Good Questions on Surveys

A survey is only as good as the insights it generates and your ability to get people to respond. How you write, present, and promote your survey all factor into the results you get. Before you can write a survey that provides insights that will enable you to stand out from the competition and increase customer loyalty, you have to define your goals. Ask yourself the following questions:

>> What do I need to know about my customers to really be able to serve them better?

>> What is missing in my body of knowledge about my customers in terms of who they are, what goals they seek to fulfill with my products, and how my products simplify or improve their lives?

>> What do I need to know about personality traits, emotional drivers, psychological states of mind, and feelings toward my category and brand that apply to my customers in order to prepare more relevant creative and promotional campaigns?

>> How do I plan to use the information I collect about customers and their needs?

>> What am I willing or able to provide customers in exchange for completing my survey?

You also need to ask yourself what level of statistical significance you're willing to accept and base your actions upon. Typically, you should strive for at least a 95 percent confidence level. The good online survey tools available for you to use for minimal costs include the ability to determine the number of responses needed for a given confidence level. A rule of thumb is that you need 385 responses among a national database of thousands reached to be able to append your results to the great population.

After you define your learning goals, it's time to start developing your survey. Your questions should be crafted in a way that is clear to understand and easy for respondents to answer quickly. Writing clear questions is essential to get statistically valid results that reflect not only your sample of respondents but also your greater population.

Here are some guidelines to asking questions that get answered and provide valid results:

>> **Ask only one question at a time.** Avoid questions like, "Do you think customer service and product variety are important?" If your response mechanism is yes or no, you really can't determine whether they are answering yes to customer service or product variety.

>> **Don't ask questions you don't need to know.** Do you really need to know what your customers' income or education level is in order to serve them?

>> **Don't get personal.** If you ask questions that go beyond their public activity or presence, customers will feel uncomfortable and could be concerned about how you will use information about them.

>> **Ask questions about things you can act on.** This way your customers can see clearly how answering this question can impact them in a positive way. For example, asking, "Do you agree that the wait time for us to serve you is too long?" clearly states that you are looking for ways to improve their experience with you.

>> **Mix up the format of your questions.** Instead of asking all multiple-choice or yes-or-no questions, intersperse all types throughout your survey to keep respondents' minds fresh and give you additional insights at the same time.

>> **Always include one open-ended or essay question so you can hear the voice of your customer.**

If you're not sure what to ask your customers or how to word your questions so that you get valid, statistically significant results, no worries. Tools like Survey-Monkey provide prewritten questions on themes most marketers need to explore that market research experts have vetted for unbiased results. You can also use their calculators to determine confidence intervals. One of the best reasons to use a platform like SurveyMonkey is the ability to easily collect responses and analyze them with the click of a button.

REAL-WORLD SURVEY TIPS

TIP

Here's a tip from small business expert Raewyn Sleeman, owner of Nimblwit in Vancouver, Canada: Don't assume that your preferences for staff, processes, and store environment match your customers'. Assuming preferences can slide you into failure.

Increase your chances of success by asking customers to complete an anonymous written survey in exchange for a small free gift. The survey could ask them the following:

- What would you change if this was your business?

- What would you change with the people?

- What would you change with the processes of getting service here?

- What would you change with the store (or online) environment?

After you get feedback, share it with someone that you trust to tell you the truth, who isn't in the business, to get his opinion of the overall changes to make.

Finally, know that if you ask customers and then don't make any changes, they will likely think less of your business than before you asked.

Writing ESP Surveys

Well, this is where it gets tricky. It goes without saying that asking the unconscious mind a question and getting a solid result is a difficult thing to do. But a big reason for doing surveys is to uncover the emotions that drive the decision process and ultimately choice and loyalty. Asking questions about how customers feel is a good start.

You may also want to ask a marketing expert with consumer psychology and behavior marketing expertise for some help asking questions. This person can guide you on how to ask the same question in two or three different ways so you can see how emotionally charged, or conflicted, or confused your customers may be about a topic. I (Jeanette) did this when surveying customers about climate change and learned a great deal. For one, what people said about their values did not match up with their intended or likely actions. And interestingly enough, those who highly valued environmental protection as a life goal scored very low on willingness to contribute even $5 a month to help out. I gained huge insight by that contrast. These are the kinds of questions you need to ask to see how customers truly feel versus how they say they will act.

Here's a sample question that can help you gain actionable insights based on feelings, not just past transactions:

> Of the following, which is most likely to cause you to donate $5 a month to reduce the amount of waste you contribute to landfills?
>
> - Knowing you are helping to preserve your local environment for future generations
>
> - Knowing you will be reducing your personal imprint on the local environment
>
> - Knowing the earth around you will be cleaner and safer for your family's immediate and long-term health

How consumers answer these questions reveal a great deal and helps you identify the values that are most likely to capture their attention and influence their behavior.

Today's consumers are less interested in receiving "personalized" information from you that just reiterates what they already know, such as what they just bought from you. Ask questions about what type of personalized information would be meaningful to them and add those variables to your customer profiles.

REMEMBER

Consumers are more willing to answer surveys if you make it about them and not just about you.

Preface your survey by indicating that you will use the information to better serve them. If you plan to keep all answers confidential, tell them that, too. Transparency regarding how you plan to use and share their information is critical to completion and building trust with your customers.

Be prepared for feedback about any controversial topics you may bring up. We did a survey for a client that was promoting a program to reduce carbon emissions, and by simply asking respondents whether they believed in climate change, we generated quite a bit of angry mail. However, we took those comments to heart and added them to our research findings as well.

TIP

Don't oversurvey. Use discretion as to how much and how often you ask. Keep surveys to 15 questions or fewer and do only one survey a quarter or less often if you want to get responses.

Paying Wisely for Market Research

With all the marketing technologies available today for monitoring the voice of the customer, you have many options to choose from for gathering information. You can do your own research, tap into existing systems to insert your questions, or hire a research firm to design and execute various tools for you.

Often, getting a list of prospects to survey is the greatest expense. To help lower this cost, look for opportunities to add questions to a survey being conducted by an industry publication or consulting firm. Some websites make customers answer questions to get access to a full news article. Check in to the costs of surveys like those that reach prospects to which you don't have easy access.

Some vendors that offer this option include Darwin's Data, PaidViewpoint, Bzz-Agent, Viewpoint Forum, tellwut, Opinion Outpost, MyView, KidzEyes, Opinion-Place, and Panelpolls. Browse the latest lists of survey panels through a Google search, or look at sites like www.surveypolice.com, which ranks polls based on feedback from users, and then collect price points and proposals from several before choosing one to run with.

In most cases, you can purchase survey accounts on a monthly basis or an annual basis. And in some cases, you can use these online tools for free — however, with limited access and data collection.

Online sources that enable you to design surveys and pay as you go or with a low-cost annual fee include tools like SurveyMonkey (www.surveymonkey.com), Polldaddy (www.polldaddy.com), Constant Contact's Listen Up option (www.constantcontact.com), and GutCheck (gutcheckit.com) for one-stop survey shopping. Working online, you can design survey questions, select a sample design, and (using your own database or, increasingly available, a sample arranged by the host site) send out your survey, collect data, and tabulate it. Does it make sense? Are you wiser as a result? Well, not every time. It takes practice and persistence to figure out how to extract useful findings from tables of survey responses, but at least it's less expensive to trial balloon some questions through these sites than through traditional full-service survey research firms.

If your website gets a good amount of visitors a day, put questions on your home page. A question with general appeal (something everyone's invested in or curious about) may actually boost visitors at the same time it generates useful data for your marketing decisions.

TIP

You can also add questions to the channels by which you communicate with your customers. For example:

>> If your customers order via a website, post questions for them there.

>> If they talk to a call center, script some questions for the call center staff.

>> If customers receive visits from salespeople or reps, brief the sales force about your questions and how to ask them without pressuring customers or prepare a simple email they can send with some questions to answer.

Discovering Low-Cost and Even Free Ways to Find Out What Matters Most

Knowledge is power. As trite as it may sound, knowledge is still the most powerful source you have to help you make smart decisions about your product and how to appeal to and build relationships with your customers.

As a marketer, you're never done learning. When you think you know all you need to know about your market and customers, you start to lose your competitive and profitable edge. You need to build and execute learning plans that cover all aspects of your market, your brand, your products, your customers, and the opportunities and threats you face. For example:

>> Who wants what?

>> Which markets are going to grow and be hot, and which aren't?

>> What really drives choice?

>> How do different generations react to different messages, themes, and promises?

>> What functional alternatives exist to our offers, and how do they impact our goals?

It's amazing how many businesses and other entities stagnate by working hard but not working smart to really know how to build their businesses sustainably.

The following sections provide a lot of ways — some cheap and others free — to boost your marketing intelligence.

Observe your customers

Consumers are everywhere — online and offline — shopping and observing all the messages and offers around them daily. As a marketer, you need to observe them, too, and with marketing technologies available today, it's getting easier. Offline, you can observe customers at your place of business and watch them browse your products, merchandising displays, pricing, and so on. Online, you can observe their attitudes and feelings and potential behavior through social listening tools.

Many different programs "observe" what customers are saying, pinning, and posting online and generate reports back as to what attitudes are prevalent among which groups, what people think about your brand, and most importantly what they are saying, and so on. You can find free tools that show the reach of your tweets, the likes and shares of your posts, and what topics trend the most on any channel on any given day.

Some of the technology available that helps you observe customers is social listening tools, which are available at many price points, including free.

One of the most recommended free listening tools per Brandwatch.com, a site that lists various marketing product reviews, is Social Mention, which reports back on the influence of social media posts on more than 100 social sites. With this tool, you can get regular reports about the strength, sentiment, passion, and reach of the posts associated with your brand and score how well you're doing with certain keywords, hashtags, and so on. You'll also find out how many minutes were spent observing your message, how many tweeted or commented on a given post, and whether the sentiment about a given message was positive, neutral, or negative.

If you really want to understand consumers and the themes, issues, beliefs, attitudes, and emotions that drive behavior in real time, it doesn't get much better than this. Other free listening tools include Hootsuite, TweetReach, and Addictomatic. Of course, you can purchase highly robust systems customized for your specific needs on a SaaS (Software as a Service) basis. Some recommended by *PC Magazine* in 2016 include Sprout Social, Synthesio, Crimson Hexagon, and Brand24. Before signing long-term contracts, look for services that offer free trials so you know what you're getting before you commit.

REMEMBER

Whether you're in B2B or B2C, you can learn a great deal about your customers by observing them online and offline. Integrating these efforts and technologies will pay off in the short term as you get new attitudes and intents in real time and the long term as you can cater your persona and messaging around the values that don't change with trends.

Observation is often underrated yet highly valuable. For example, when managers from the Boston Aquarium hired a researcher to develop a survey to determine the most popular attractions, the researcher told them not to bother. Instead, he suggested that they examine the floors for wear and for tracks on wet days. The evidence pointed clearly to which attractions were most popular. That was easy!

Observe customers at the point of sale and document what they spend the most time browsing, what questions they ask, what statements they make, and so on. Did they seem anxious, at ease, excited, or neutral about your offers if selling in B2B or while browsing your store? In B2B marketing, take time to observe what matters most to your clients' job security. Research by Google and Motista show that when you can tie a sales message and offer to personal value, you're eight times more likely to get a premium price for your product. Find ways to discover what matters most to your clients and link your product/service to those values.

You can find out about customer satisfaction every day by asking for feedback via email after a product ships or by leaving comment cards on sales counters. If you ask for a review directly, you can avoid unwanted and often unwarranted reviews on social channels like Yelp, which do influence attitude and choice, right or wrong.

When sending out surveys, always ask for email addresses and permission to contact customers with further information to better serve them, promotions, industry news, and so on. With their email address, you can monitor them with your social listening tools and add them to your survey databases.

Keeping up with customer opinion is a never-ending race, and continuously asking and analyzing questions is the only way to stay the course. The best way to succeed is by asking questions directly of your customers.

Do competitive research

Knowing your competitors' offerings and values is just as critical as finding out what your customers need and want. What emotional and tangible values do they promise and deliver, and how do you compare? Beyond knowing how your pricing and customer service differs, you need to know how they position themselves in the market so you can position yourself better. Create a grid like the one in Table 4-2 and refer to it often as you create your own messaging and time your own promotions.

TABLE 4-2   ## Competitive Research

	You	Competitor A	Competitor B
Slogan			
Promises			
Position			
Special offers			
Industry awards			
Social followers			
Pricing			
Customer ratings			
Product comparisons (strengths, weaknesses)			
Service comparisons			
Other			

Track their sales, promotions, and special offers and time yours accordingly. Keep track of what their customers like and don't like and position your brand as the better alternative.

Create and maintain a competitive grid to help you stay on top of your goals and the competitive environment in which you operate.

Also gather information on your competitors' marketing programs, especially how they're getting their marketing messages out. Are they advertising a fast-growing social network you hadn't considered? If you have even a modest budget, consider the options for online research by firms like WhatRunsWhere (www.whatrunswhere.com), AdClarity's media intelligence (www.adclarity.com), Competitrack (www.competitrack.com), Adbeat (www.adbeat.com), or AdGooroo (www.adgooroo.com), all of which can help you benchmark your ads (especially online advertising) against top competitors or role-model marketers (larger companies with the resources to spot new opportunities and trends quicker than you).

Harness the power of one-question surveys

One of the main reasons customers don't complete surveys is because they are too long and no one has more than a minute or two to give you, if even that. What works in a world where we communicate in sound bites for Twitter, LinkedIn, videos, and more is brevity. One of the most effective ways to get answers is thus asking one question at a time. Determine what you need to know most to develop better marketing programs and service, and ask just that question.

Delivery mechanisms for one-question surveys include emails, websites, and your social media assets. If you do one question at a time, you can get away with more surveys. Having a question or a poll on your web page makes your site more interactive and thus engages visitors longer. Just make the questions meaningful to both you and your customers. If they see answering the question as something that will benefit them, they're more likely to respond.

Ask questions that help you understand perceptions and value. For example, if your company focuses on environmental issues and you're trying to reduce plastics in the landfills, ask about the values that lead to purchasing products that are impeding your progress, such as the following:

> Do you think bottled water is healthier than tap water? Yes or No

You can pay news sites to ask your question before giving access to articles on their site.

REMEMBER

You can learn a great deal about markets, consumers, incomes, and so on by studying census data for your marketplaces. Every few years, to get useful data compiled and posted by various agencies of the U.S. government, go to www.census.gov, the main gateway into U.S. Census data on households and businesses. This site is your portal to U.S. data from the economic census (which goes out to 5 million businesses every five years) and the Survey of Business Owners. Another useful way to explore U.S. Census Bureau data is to go to factfinder2.census.gov.

Establish a trend report

Set up a *trend report,* a document that gives you a quick indication of a change in buying patterns, a new competitive move or threat, and any other changes that your marketing may need to respond to. You can compile one by emailing salespeople, distributors, customer service staff, repair staff, or friendly customers once a month, asking them for a quick list of any important trends they see in the market.

TIP

Your trend analysis should also include careful tracking of what bigger competitors in your space are doing because they may be setting marketing or product trends that affect the rest of their industry. Tracking media coverage is easy on Google or other search engines. Also read their press releases on PR Newswire (www.prnewswire.com) to see what they have to say about themselves. Track changes on major competitor websites, too, either manually or (if you want to follow several) by using a service such as LXR Marketplace (`www.lxrmarketplace.com`), Watch My Competitor (`www.watchmycompetitor.com`), Competitor Monitor (`www.competitormonitor.com`), Alexa (`www.alexa.com`), or Digimind (`www.digimind.com`). (You can also use these services to track competitor mentions in social media and compare them to mentions of your brand.) Benchmark your website against competitor stats on HubSpot's Marketing Grader (`website.grader.com`).

Note: Researchers wanting to do their own competitor monitoring at no cost may use Google Alerts to create customized search criteria for tracking competitor online activity (`www.google.com/alerts`).

Probe your customer records

Browsing your data files and models is also a good way to stay abreast of your market trends and your customers. Browse your data models and customer profiles to identify trends in demographics, interests, political affiliations, and lifestyle. Trends of interest around which you may build promotions or messaging include

>> Employment level

>> Personal hobbies and interests

>> Credit levels/debt levels

>> Family status

>> Political affiliations

Test your marketing materials

Before you launch anything to the public, you can easily get some feedback very affordably to help you identify any problems ahead of time. Send your email campaign or social media post to a handful of customers and get their feedback. Ask what made them want to read the ad or not read it. What intrigued them about the offer? How relevant was it to them? Fix any issues you identify and get ready to launch with more effectiveness.

Per emails, you can test the same body copy with different subject lines to see which generates the best open and click-through rates, enabling you to work more efficiently than ever. Testing is a great way to determine what emotions, offers, promotions, and so on really appeal to your mass consumers and your segments. See Chapter 10 on direct marketing strategies for more in-depth insight about testing your marketing programs.

Interview defectors

Losing customers is not always a bad thing because it gives you an opportunity to discover what you're doing wrong, which is critical if you want to keep getting it right. Following are some ways to find out where you're weak and need to improve:

>> Ask your customers why they're opting out of your emails instead of just providing an opt-out button. Ask whether it was the content, customer experience issue, frequency of emails, or lack of relevancy.

>> When customers abandon a shopping cart, program your CRM to send an email to find out why. Was it because they lost interest, found a better price, or simply forgot?

>> Stay in touch with lapsed customers and survey to find out whether they defected to a competing brand, had a bad experience, or just lost interest in your product.

When you find out why customers no longer want to engage with you or purchase your products and services, you often rekindle relationships that last for years. Customers like to know they're noticed and appreciated, and when you right a wrong, loyalty actually goes up.

Create custom web analytics

Make sure your web tracking/analytics program tells you more than traffic counts and sources. Attributes to follow include monitoring sales, repeat sales, lead collection, quality of leads (measured by rate of conversion), sign-ups, use of offers (such as you may post on a business site on Facebook, for example), and overall revenue and returns from web-based promotions. These numbers tell the story of your marketing successes and failures online and give you something to learn from as you go.

TIP

Many firms now offer quite sophisticated and powerful research tools for tracking your brand and competitors on the web, especially in social media. It may be worthwhile to look into the costs and benefits of options such as Brandwatch Analytics (www.brandwatch.com) or The Social Studies Group (www.social studiesgroup.com), a firm that studies conversations on social networking sites to gain ideas about attitudes and trends.

Riding a Rising Tide with Demographics

Monitoring demographics of your market, such as the ethnic makeup of your market, average age, spending power, and family structure, provide you with good clues as to how your marketing ought to evolve. If your business caters to women, for example, following are some of the sources and statistics you should know and monitor carefully.

>> The pay gap between men and women is closing, and women in their 20s are making 93 percent of the income of men of the same age. Still a gap but far smaller than in previous decades, which suggests growing purchasing power for women and an opportunity to reorient marketing toward them in financial services, realty, travel, continuing education, and many other markets. (Source: press release from PewResearch, dated December 11, 2013.)

>> More women than men are going to college, and the trend is growing over time. Add this to a slower trend toward pay parity, and the suggestion is that women will outpace men as the educated and leading gender at some point in the not-too-distant future. (Source: Forbes.com article on the trends in enrollment for men and women over several decades.)

>> Women outvote men, and they're also more likely to be socially liberal, which is producing (especially among younger voters) a big advantage for the Democratic Party, reinforced by the advantage it has with most minority voting blocks.

>> Women are having their first child (if they choose to have children) later than they used to, the mean age being 25.1 years. Record numbers are waiting to have children until their 30s or 40s. Also, births are declining slowly from year to year. These statistics are consistent with women going to college and pursuing professional careers at record rates. This tells you that you're better off introducing products for professional women than new mothers if you want to enjoy a growth market. (Source: "The Changing Demographic Profile of the United States," by Congressional Research Service.)

Whatever your business, pick a growing group you think you may be able to build long-term relationships with, and tailor your offerings and message accordingly. Back out of shrinking categories and regions, and go where the growth is.

REMEMBER

Knowledge is the foundation for success no matter what type of business you operate in. Continuously learning about your customers, market, and competition can often be the difference between success and failure.

size business

» Fleshing out the four Ps of your marketing plan

» Preparing a SWOT analysis for you and your competitors

» Putting your marketing plan and action steps on paper

» Checking out do's and don'ts for building a solid marketing program

» Forecasting and projecting for beat-the-odds survival and success

Chapter **5**

Creating a Winning Marketing Plan

Rome wasn't built in a day. Flight didn't happen overnight. Apple, IBM, Kraft Foods, and GE didn't become top of their game in just a matter of weeks, either. All had a carefully concerted plan with goals, action items, timelines, and more that would help them launch, scale to mass distribution, establish leadership, and grow as efficiently and profitably as possible.

In the past, it often happened that when people had an idea for a great new product, they built it in their basement and made their fortune by being in the right place at the right time. These stories are not so common now, unless you're a genius at building smartphone or software apps that a bigger company actually wants to buy. But again, those stories are few and far between.

To succeed, no matter what business you're in, you need that same kind of plan, a guiding blueprint that defines your brand, your market position, goals and vision, and customers. This same plan needs to map out how you plan to put a competitive stake in the ground and how you'll generate leads, close sales, and grow to reach your profitability, initial public offering (IPO), or exit plan goals.

In this chapter, we focus on building a plan or road map to get your business moving in the right direction in today's rapidly changing market climate. As you likely already have a product and customer in mind, we start with understanding how your product fits in to your current market and competitive landscape and suggest actions for giving your business the greatest possible chance to succeed.

The Marketing Plan Components You Need

The surest way to success today is to have a solid plan for building and growing business — one that covers product development, market identification, capitalization goals, growth initiatives, marketing and distribution programs, budgets, financial projections, and more, depending on your ultimate goals for growth or selling to investors or other firms.

The key elements or considerations in a marketing plan for today's technology-driven marketing world include but aren't limited to the ones we mention in the following sections. These just represent a start for any business, and we cover many of them in dedicated chapters throughout this book.

First, the basics

Just like a builder, you need to start your marketing plan by laying a strong foundation on which to build your branding, sales, customer engagement, and other programs. Your foundation needs to start with the basics such as defining your product, figuring out how it fills tangible and emotional needs, and determining how it fits in to the current marketplace. You also need to define what you want to accomplish with your business. Following are some basic questions to answer to get you started:

>> **Product:** What product are you selling, and what physical, emotional, and functional needs does it fulfill?

>> **Goals:** What are you goals? What do you hope to achieve in terms of revenue, profit, scalability, growth, and expansion? What are your short- and long-term goals for operating capital and profits?

>> **Customers:** Who are your customers? Who are your customers in your core and segment demographics? If your demographic is middle-aged women, how can you further segment this group to be able to reach those with the highest propensity to purchase your product? And who and what influences your customers?

>> **Market:** What other products can your target consumers buy instead of yours? How do you compare in terms of access, price, quality, reputation, distribution, features, warranties, and other elements that affect choice?

>> **Channels:** Where will you sell your product? Will you sell it online direct to consumers via your own e-commerce store? Will you sell to retailers via intermediaries and distributors? Will you have your own physical location/storefront? Will you sell direct to businesses via a sales team? You need to map out the pros/cons and costs of each so you can see a clear path to scaling distribution that's affordable and profitable, too.

Now a bit more complex concepts

After you have defined your goals and your product and how they fill valid consumer and market needs, it's time to start thinking about how you are going to sell your product to earn revenue and fund your business for growth. You need a plan for getting customers to purchase your product in the first place, raising funds from investors to help you scale quickly to capture current marketing opportunities, and deciding how you will build your brand through marketing initiatives that are sustainable and successful. Some of the questions you need to define follow:

>> **Promotion:** How will you launch your product to spark trial? How will you keep those that try it coming back? By referring others? What special offers and discounts can you execute without hurting profit margins? How often? How can you employ tactics such as guerilla marketing and growth hacking to get to mass distribution quickly?

>> **Financials:** What profit margin do you need to make to break even, expand, and engage in research and development for new editions, ancillary offerings, and expanded product lines? How much of your revenue will you allocate to marketing? Do you need investors? Can you secure enough capital through Kickstarter, or do you need some serious venture capital funding behind you to get you going? How much are you willing to give up? Check out *Venture Capital For Dummies,* by Nicole Gravagna and Peter K. Adams (Wiley), for a lot more critical insight on this topic.

>> **Marketing:** Clearly, this is the greatest focus of this chapter and this book, because this is, after all, *Marketing For Dummies,* 5th Edition. But to be reading this, you're clearly smarter than your peers because the biggest mistake

marketers can make is to assume that they know all the answers and that they can promote and sell their products with a few social posts, with articles by good bloggers, or by simply opening a cool e-commerce store. Anyone with that attitude toward marketing a product has dummied down the marketing process in a way that can seriously impact her success. And it's not good.

And now some even bigger questions

No plan is complete without an end goal in sight. There are many reasons for starting and building a business. These might include building a family business that can sustain generations, growing a business to sell so you can retire early, or building a business that enables you to change the world. Whatever your ambitions, dreams, or goals, map out a plan. Knowing your end goal will help you build a more efficient plan and help you avoid wasting resources and money, doing things that really don't matter "in the end." Here are some questions to think about:

>> **Growth:** What funds, resources, and plans do you have to grow your company, and how do you intend to reach your one-, three-, and five-year goals? If you don't have one-, three-, and five-year goals, this would be a good place to start.

>> **Year-over-year objectives:** Set objectives, or line-item goals, that you can measure to determine your business's true progress. For example, "Increase average annual customer value by 5 to 6 percent" and "Shift 25 percent or more of our catalog customers over to website ordering" or "Achieve 3 to 4 percent of market share in new territories" if you're opening any as part of an expansion strategy.

>> **Exit strategy:** Are you developing a product line or a brand that you hope to eventually sell to a larger company, maybe a competitor, so you can retire or start a new business? Are you hoping to build an enterprise that you can take public or just a successful business you can pass on to your firstborn should she prove interested and worthy?

Addressing the Four Ps

Every marketing plan needs to address the four Ps — *price, product, promotion,* and *place* — because, essentially, they represent the foundation of your business and the assets you have to sell and market your goods. You need to flesh out your product and pricing strategies, place of distribution strategies, and promotions so you can compare your strengths to your competitors', monitor your progress in each of these areas, and see how your efforts get you closer to or further from your goals. We discuss all these elements in other chapters throughout this book as well.

REMEMBER

The purpose of your marketing plan is really to outline the actionable items most likely to push your *product* forward in the market, building out your *places* of distribution as efficiently as possible, *pricing* your products for trial and loyalty, and *promoting* your product and brand using the channels and tactics that best reach and influence your customers and their influencers. These may include print and digital ads, content marketing, engagement, and events, online and offline, to create awareness and sales and to build customer acquisition and retention.

Conducting a SWOT Analysis

Even though the SWOT analysis has been around for years, it isn't and won't ever be old-fashioned or out-of-date. You can't define and improve your position in any market unless you know your

>> Strengths

>> Weaknesses

>> Opportunities

>> Threats

You need to continuously define these four elements. The world, consumers, and your markets are dynamic, not static, and if you don't continuously monitor your strengths, weaknesses, opportunities, and threats in real time (rather than the past), you'll fall behind, and once you're behind a competitor who adapts regularly to market and customer changes, good luck catching up and ever getting ahead.

One of the most efficient ways to do a SWOT analysis is to map out your answers and those of your top competitors' at the same time. This way you can more clearly see just how strong those "assumed" strengths compare to others. So open a spreadsheet on your computer, or get out the handy pen and paper, and start mapping out your SWOT. Do this frequently to ensure that you're on top of your own market position, focusing on the right opportunities and the right challenges to overcome, and are aware of what your competition is doing. You need to be only one step ahead of the others in your space to be in a position to dominate market and mind share — two important goals for any marketing plan.

Following are some starting points for what to include in your SWOT analysis:

» **Strengths:** Identify the strong points of your product(s), brand image, and marketing program so you know what to build on in your plan. Your strengths are the keys to your future success.

» **Weaknesses:** Pinpoint the areas in which your product(s), brand image, and marketing program are relatively weak. For example, perhaps you have several older products that are losing to new competitors or functional alternatives and your plan needs to address how to adapt or cut these products.

» **Opportunities:** Your situation analysis needs to look for opportunities, such as new growth markets, new communications, or distribution channels for reaching customers, potential partners for collaboration or bundling, and so on.

» **Threats:** A threat is any external trend or change that can reduce your sales or profits or make it difficult to achieve your growth goals. Common threats include new technologies that create new competitors, large competitors that can outspend you, and economic or demographic shifts that cut into the size or growth rate of your customer base.

Table 5-1 is a hypothetical example of how you can organize a competitive SWOT analysis. You should also take the time to outline each area for your business from a product, branding, market position, sales, capitalization, and growth perspective.

TABLE 5-1 **Sample SWOT Analysis**

	Your Product	Competitor 1	Competitor 2
Strengths	More features	Strong brand awareness	Lowest price
Weaknesses	Newcomer to market, not proven	Mediocre quality	Undercapitalized and may lack funds for product development
Opportunities	Take market share by communicating value of distinct features Bundle with complimentary brand with established channels in place	Completed IPO so could put more money into developing new features that could compete with ours	Opportunity to take market share due to pricing strategy
Threats	Higher price may prevent newcomers to category from trying Low marketing budget Economic slowdown, low consumer confidence levels	Lower quality can result in consumers switching to new brands like ours and so can the lack of features like we have	Competing mainly on price and that can be countered with ESP marketing tactics

Creating a SWOT analysis that compares you to your competition is a must if you want to keep ahead of the game or be aware at all times of what you need to do to get ahead if you're not there yet. Today's markets move fast, and you need to be prepared to act fast to jump over any hurdles you face and jump on opportunities before they disappear.

Before completing your SWOT grid, collect information about your competitors' promises, product claims, industry awards or rankings, pricing models, advertising messages, persona, and promotions. The more armed you are with information, the better prepared you are to identify your SWOT high points and low points and how they compare to competitors.

Some information worth gathering about your competitors include

>> **Company:** Describe how the market perceives it and its key product.

>> **Key personnel:** Who are the managers, and how many employees do they have in total?

>> **Financial:** How strong is its *cash position* (does it have spending power, or is it struggling to pay its bills)? What were its sales in the last two years?

>> **Sales, distribution, and pricing:** Describe its primary sales channel, discount/pricing structure, and market share estimate.

>> **Product/service analysis:** What are the strengths and weaknesses of its product or service?

>> **Promises and claims:** What promises and claims related to benefit, value, performance, and quality do they make, and how do you compare to these? Can you position yourself according to what they really deliver?

>> **Promotions and offers:** What promotions do they execute that can cut into your sales or tempt your customers to switch to their products? What is the timing and pricing differential of these promotions, and how can you schedule yours to offset any impact?

Armed with this information to add to your competitive SWOT analysis, you'll be ready to succeed more efficiently than you can imagine.

Focusing on Functional Alternatives

Another key analysis you need to do involves understanding how your product compares to functional alternatives — that is, products that aren't really the same as your product but perform some or many of the same functions and are designed for the same basic outcomes. Software platforms and applications compete with functional alternatives quite a bit. For example, in other chapters of this book, we discuss digital asset management platforms, content management systems, and marketing resource management systems. In reality, all are designed to do much of the same things and produce the same outcomes — higher efficiencies in creating new versions of content for cross-channel distribution that can be delivered to individuals with personal relevance. But each system is slightly different, which puts it in different software/technology categories and thus makes each system a functional alternative to another.

You need to decide how you support or compete with functional alternatives and then build action items into your marketing plan. Questions to ask yourself include

>> What business category best describes where you are now?

>> What business category best describes where you aspire to be to maximize long-term profitability?

>> Where do you currently fit in your primary category? If you made it on Gartner's Magic Quadrant, would you be considered a leader, challenger, niche player, or visionary?

>> Can you tether your brand in any similar categories to get visibility among those shopping for functional alternatives? So if your product is a content management system, should you also be promoting yourself as a viable option for those shopping for digital asset management systems? In the IT world, technology changes so quickly that there's a good chance your target consumers don't understand the difference themselves.

Why Collaboration Matters So Much

We are and will continue to live in a sharing society. Businesses that bring people together to share resources, collaborate on getting things done, and help each other with daily living are those that have thrived in recent years. Here are some fairly recent examples:

>> Uber, where drivers with cars helps travelers that need transportation

>> Airbnb, where homeowners share rooms with travelers who don't want the cost of a hotel

>> TaskRabbit, where people with time do errands for those who are stretching to get it all done

Many businesses collaborate with others, even competitors, to create a more robust product, service, or experience for customers whom they both target and service. Co-Society (www.co-society.com), a platform that brings international businesses and executives together to collaborate on new ideas and innovations, put out a report outlining several cases of successful business collaborations that create mutually beneficial outcomes. These include examples of innovations that improve the world, such as when Microsoft and Toyota teamed up to produce better information systems in cars, and marketing programs, such as when American Express funded a joint promotion with Foursquare to show how mobile technology can benefit consumers and restaurants accepting American Express.

TIP

Look around your marketplace. What common goals do consumers have? What challenges, goals, and aspirations do they share? What other businesses or organizations support your value proposition and align with your vision? And then ask yourself the big question: How can you bring brands and people together to solve a common problem or to achieve a common goal?

Try to build collaborative efforts around your brand's emotional selling proposition (ESP; see Chapter 2). When you do this, you end up with movement, not just a product and a brand. Companies that are perceived as moving toward a better world are those that are succeeding in this new era of consumerism.

Teaming up on CSR

Your corporate social responsibility (CSR) strategies for giving back, furthering environmental support, promoting charitable and community causes, and so on are a good foundation on which to build your collaborative efforts. Map out what you'll do on your own or with other groups as part of your marketing plan. Schedule your actions, measure them, and communicate them to your customers and stakeholders because knowing what you've done and are doing matters to consumers today. This likely won't change anytime soon.

Here's a good example of how collaborating for causes bigger than profits can pay off.

EXAMPLE

Ecologic Brands, Inc., is a young business dedicated to reducing the environmental harm of disposable bottles by making them out of recycled (and compostable) cardboard pressed into a thin, smooth bottle shape with a thin recycled (and recyclable) plastic liner. The innovative design needed to be tested in market to move from design stage to actual packaging for goods in market. So the company's founder, Julie Corbett, and her team looked for a marketing partner that strongly valued sustainability and had the visibility to introduce the packaging innovation. They were able to forge a partnership with Seventh Generation, Inc., a company that makes plant-based healthy household cleaning products, which featured the distinctive Ecologic packaging for natural laundry detergent. This partnership resulted in helpful sales revenue for Ecologic Brands and valuable visibility and publicity at a critical time in its development.

Building kinship, not just relationships

As we explain in the nearby "Legendary insights from J. Walker Smith" sidebar, marketers need to start building people-to-people not just brand-to-people connections. This supports what we cover in Chapter 2, and how we all have to be aligned with others and with good causes. Brands have typically focused on building relationships with customers based on their past purchases, product preferences, expressed interests, and so on. Yet, as J. Walker Smith pointed out, the new era of consumerism now requires building people-to-people connections, or kinship.

To include kinship strategies in your marketing plan, ask yourself the following questions and create action plans around your answers:

>> What elements does your company culture have in common with the core culture of your most valued customers?

>> What lifestyle values do your consumers embrace and live and that your corporate values support? Are these environmental, social, or charitable?

>> What opportunities exist within your markets and communities for bringing you customers and employees together in a common cause?

>> How can you build your CSR program around events and causes that you can do jointly with your customers?

>> What customer appreciation or thought leadership events can you host in your community that will bring people together with your customers in ways that provide value and benefits far beyond your products or services?

After you answer these questions, build action items around your answers and add these to your marketing action items and timeline.

REMEMBER

More than 70 percent of consumers say they'll sign up to volunteer alongside a brand's personnel for a cause they believe in. How can you organize events that bring your customers and staff together, not for transactions, but for moving the world in a better direction? When big companies organize their regional staff into teams that interact with their communities to further local causes, they suddenly become "local" businesses led by "friends or people we know" rather than another big corporation.

LEGENDARY INSIGHTS FROM J. WALKER SMITH

J. Walker Smith, executive chairman of Kantar Futures, a strategic insight and innovation consultancy service for global brands, and member of the North Carolina Advertising Hall of Fame, emphasizes the importance of building kinship among customers, not just relationships, which we've been conditioned to do for years. Here are some of his insights on what this means and why it matters.

Kinship is about the process of building social currency with others by how we treat them and by our familial connections. True kinship is built on utter transparency and the priority of fostering relationships that matter over building business and finally on purpose. Do you focus on maintaining close ties as you would within a family unit, and are you willing to make sacrifices to build those ties? Establishing kinship in business requires focusing on enhancing and supporting lifestyles, not just completing transactions.

Here are the fundamentals of a kinship economy:

- Culture, creed, commerce.

- Booming interest in relationships for which kinship is the gold standard.

- Social currency is the medium of exchange.

- The bottom line is how you treat people.

It's a world in which brand marketers must relearn the business they're in — no longer the business of brands but the business of kinship and social currency, or to put it in a word, *connections*.

Facilitating relationships is what brand marketers need to do as well. People will engage with a brand when it provides something they can share with kith and kin. Such social currency is what people want to spend these days, and only after that are people keen to spend dollars and cents. Brand marketers need to shift their focus to what people want most nowadays, which are stronger relationships with other people, not closer more revealing relationships with brands. People want people connections, and in a marketplace where relationships among people are the highest priority, the gold standard for brand marketers is the highest form of relationships, which of course, is family, which in turn means that kinship is the principle that must animate brands today to engage consumers in a compelling and effective way.

Expanding Your Target

Every marketing plan outlines who your target audience is, what they look like demographically, and the transaction and lifetime value they represent to your brand. It goes without saying that your primary goal is to reach and influence this group of potential consumers and purchasers to capture their lifetime value. In fact, if you're really as detailed as you should be, this marketing plan blueprint should include your calculated lifetime value as set forth in Chapter 16.

Yet you also have other critical targets you must communicate to and "sell" to if you want your core customers' business. These targets are the influencers over purchasing and brand choices within your category. Some are direct, others not so much. Some are obvious and others more subtle.

Influencers take on many different personas and attitudes and look very different if you're in B2B or B2C. Influencers are the most influential drivers of purchase choices because they're the most trusted sources to which people turn when making decisions. According to research from Nielsen's Global Trust in Advertising survey, 92 percent of consumers trust completely or somewhat trust recommendations from people they know, the number-one influential source. Second is consumer opinions posted online, which 70 percent completely or somewhat trust. Keep in mind that people don't know these consumers, but they still trust peers over paid advertising, which validates the wisdom of building strong communities to support your brand, online and offline.

Table 5-2 presents examples of influencers that can impact sales and loyalty in various industries.

TABLE 5-2   Examples of Influencers

B2B Influencers	B2C Influencers
Industry analysts (Forrester, Gartner, Hoover's)	Peers (family, friends, professional associations)
Media covering innovations, advancements, and business news in your industry	Reviews on sites like Yelp and Amazon
Peer networks such as associations or societies bringing together CMOs, CTOs, sales executives, product developers, graphic designers, architects, and so on	Social media sites such as Pinterest, Instagram, and Facebook
Product review sites such as bloggers that put out a Top 10 Widgets in 2015 report and so on	Bloggers on related topics (fashion, cooking blogs, and forums for consumer reviews, advice, and so on)
General print, radio, and TV news	Online news sites for category, general news outlets

B2B Influencers	B2C Influencers
End users who can influence department purchasing agents (radiology technicians influencing biomed purchasers)	End users who can influence selling channels via product, medical, and services requests
Peer reviews including testimonials on a brand's site and on review sites	Consumer reviews and posts on shopping sites

Monitoring and reacting to trends

Studying market trends to determine market influences on sales that are out of your control and how your sales and market share compare year to year and against your competition will help you better see your strengths, weakness, opportunities, and threats. When you do a trends analysis, you should include information about the following:

>> The size of your market — is the buying population growing or shrinking?

>> The transaction value of each sale and the annual value of each customer going up or going down.

>> Functional alternatives that have been gaining in prominence and sales.

>> Economic indicators that could impact sales in your category, such as housing starts, housing sales, unemployment, job growth, and wages.

Take note of all these and other market indicators so you can build your plans according to gains or losses. If the past period's program doubled your market share, seriously consider replicating it, if all the marketing and economic conditions remain constant. If you see a shrinking population that could impact sales out of your control, despite the best-made plans and product quality, adjust your output so you don't end up with inventory you can't sell and thus tie up your capital, which could be better spent elsewhere or put in reserve to protect your financial stability.

On the other hand, if your market share stayed the same or fell and no outside market factors influence this, perhaps you're ready for something new.

Developing the customer experience

Your marketing plan needs to encompass all the elements in the preceding section and how you plan to gain awareness to build sales — the overarching goal of any plan and business. In addition to the marketing campaigns you plan to execute and the sales goals and projections you need to identify, you need to plan out the customer experience.

Customer experience, or CX, campaigns are replacing marketing campaigns because, overall, customers care more about the feelings fulfillment and trust you create than the prices or benfits your offer. In fact, in the marketing department, we're seeing chief experience officers replacing chief marketing officers because the experience brings people back for more much more often than the price they paid.

Your customer experience needs to include plans for a meaningful journey on a path that evolves somewhat like the following:

>> Initial contact, sales support, and consultations (if applicable)

>> After-sale decision reaffirmation

>> Customer service protocols — how you respond to missed expectations, product issues, repairs, technical support, troubleshooting needs, and so on

>> Kinship opportunities — building intimacy beyond products through interaction at live events related to products and/or common causes

>> CSR — how you involve and engage your customers in your culture, values, and causes

>> Evangelism — how you enhance the emotional value of your brand relationship in ways that inspire your customers to introduce you to others

>> Communities — how you bring your customers and prospects together to form hives that support your brand and engage all in a joint cause and mission

>> How you adapt each step of the journey for your various segments, global markets, or cultures

Just like many software programs can help you execute a marketing plan, you can find many software applications for helping you manage and execute a successful customer experience and journey. Just do an Internet search for "customer experience software" and start reviewing the dozens of options that exist at various price points.

Creating a Working Marketing Plan

After you've worked through your goals and identified where you stand in terms of your SWOT analysis, functional alternatives, who your customers and influencers are, and opportunities for building kinships rather than just relationships, it's time to start putting your plan on paper and assigning actions, time tables, responsibilities, and metrics.

Taking the time to think through and write a marketing plan is essential to success for many reasons. It helps you and your entire team to clearly understand your goals, vision, current knowledge, actions you plan to execute, and the budget you have to spend on those actions. Essentially, it organizes your knowledge, defines your priorities, and sets your tasks and schedules and gets everyone on the same page.

A successful marketing plan encompasses all the elements discussed up to now throughout this chapter and assigns actions to associated goals. Here are some of the reasons that justify the time spent in organizing a workable plan:

» A plan helps you identify the best practices, eliminate the unprofitable ones, and keep everything on schedule and on budget. Many businesses don't have a plan spelled out and just react to opportunities that may or may not pay off. Having a plan helps you work smarter and more efficiently.

» The planning process helps you think through what needs to be changed to improve your results, and putting things in writing often adds clarity of focus to necessary tasks.

» Planning helps clarify and control key elements of your marketing plan, such as branding, pricing, content, selling strategies, and more.

Naturally, planning takes time and energy. But its payback is rapid and large. Unplanned marketing rarely, if ever, pays off. Without a plan, you risk making knee-jerk reactions to try to get ahead, and that can be very costly in the long run.

Another big benefit of planning is that it gets you thinking creatively about your marketing program. As you plan, you find yourself questioning old assumptions and practices and thinking about new and better ways to boost your brand and optimize sales and profits.

TIP

Software programs, like JIAN's Marketing Plan Builder (www.jian.com), can simplify and support marketing planning. Most planning tools include templates you can use individually or interactively with a team. Some options to choose from include

» LivePlan (www.liveplan.com) from PaloAlto Software makes it easy for a team to work remotely on the same plan at the same time.

» SecurePlan (www.secureplan.com), also from PaloAlto Software, offers sales and marketing plans as well as general business plans from the same source.

» Enloop's (www.enloop.com) online planning tools are slanted more toward financial plans but still of some use.

» Mplans offers free sample marketing plans and sells the quite sophisticated Sales and Marketing Pro software download (www.mplans.com).

>> Usually free, but less sophisticated, are the marketing forms and templates Entrepreneur offers (www.entrepreneur.com/formnet/marketingforms.html).

>> G Suite (Google's apps for businesses; https://gsuite.google.com) includes interactive tools that simplify sharing, editing, and creating documents and other resources collectively with multiple authors.

>> Smartsheet (www.smartsheet.com), a cloud-based planning platform that carries through to project management by the team. It also offers links for crowdsourcing.

>> SCORE (www.score.org; the nonprofit set up to help U.S. small businesses) offers a suite of free templates for marketing strategy and plans. You may also pursue mentoring and other forms of direct assistance by real live experts from SCORE or the nearest Small Business Administration District Office, Small Business Development Center, Veteran Business Outreach Center, or Women's Business Center, mapped on the U.S. SBA's website at www.sba.gov/tools/local-assistance.

Mapping Out Your Action Steps

The next step is to start mapping out your action items. Following is a solid way to organize your thoughts and outline your actions so your document becomes a true action plan, not just a good idea put in writing.

Step 1: Complete a situational analysis/summary

The first step is to outline the circumstances or situation that you are facing at the present moment. For example, where does your brand stand today in terms of marketplace and opportunities? What is your current position in your general market, and how are you poised to move ahead, or how are you at risk to fall behind? What are your constraints related to resources, funding, ability to scale, and so on? Explain the current situation as concisely as possible so all team members get an understanding of where you are and where you need to be.

Step 2: Establish your benchmark

When setting your goals, keep in mind what you have achieved, which actions have paid off, and set a starting point, or benchmark, from which you want to build and improve upon. Questions to ponder to help you do this include: What results did you achieve in the previous period in terms of sales, market share, profits, customer satisfaction, web visibility, or other measures of customer attitude and perception? What levels of customer retention, size and frequency of purchase, or other indicators of customer behavior did you end the period with? How capable are you today for delivering on current desires and expectations of customers? Your benchmark serves as a reality check for where you are and the foundation on which you should build your goals.

Step 3: Define your goals

While you are working on everyday goals for marketing and sales, don't lose sight of your long-term objectives. Learn from the moment to set goals for improvement and additional growth in the short and long term. What are your primary goals for the next period? Clearly, all objectives should lead to more sales, customers, and profits, yet you need actionable and measurable goals to help you get to the top of your game and stay there. What are your goals for market share? Quantify your goals by including sales projections and costs, market share projections, sales to your biggest customers or distributors, costs and returns from any special offers you plan to use, sales projections and commissions by territory, and so on.

Step 4: Take note of lessons learned

A postmortem on the previous period helps identify any mistakes to avoid, insights to take advantage of, or major changes that may present threats or opportunities. Also include lessons learned from competitors or even dissimilar businesses that have had good (or bad) luck with marketing initiatives you may want to try. Include any results from A/B testing of ESPs, campaigns, offers, promotions, channels, events, and so on. Review results of third-party testing organizations, such as BEHAVE.org, to help you learn from others' mistakes without having to pay the same price.

Step 5: Outline your strategy

This is the big focus of your plan and the way you'll grow your revenues and profits. Keep the strategy statement to a few sentences so that everyone who reads it gets it at once and can remember what the strategy is. Think like a sports coach: "Where is the opportunity to win, and what resources do we put in the game to score, dominate, and win?"

Your strategy outlines how you'll respond to the information you gathered in Steps 1 through 4 to help you find your strengths, weaknesses, opportunities, and threats to collaborate, influence influencers, and build kinship on top of relationships. For example, if you identify that you're strong at reaching middle-aged women, one point of your strategy may be to reach and convert young adult women to your products and brands so you can nurture the next generation of customers. Your action items (see next section) will then outline how you'll reach this goal.

Check out Figure 5-1 for an example of how a marketing strategy leads first to specific marketing objectives and then marketing tactics.

Sample Strategy
Create a hip new brand of dog treats and sell it to younger, active pet owners.

Sample objectives:
Brand the product to appeal to hip, younger consumers.
Build awareness and interest through the web, advertising, press coverage of events, and word of mouth.
Get at least 10,000 households to try samples of the product.
Build distribution through the web and retail grocery and pet stores.

Sample tactics:
Product: Design a product that makes dogs healthier and more energetic. Brand it to appeal to younger, hip pet owners.
Pricing: Price it slightly above competitors' products to signal that it is a specialty product and to fund an aggressive marketing campaign.
Placement: Make it available both on the web and through pet stores. Expand to grocery stores as soon as volume allows.
Promotion: Create a catchy, hip brand and logo. Use events, social networks, print advertising in magazines with the appropriate demographics, and in-store displays to communicate the product's special image and message.

FIGURE 5-1: How objectives and tactics flow from your marketing strategy.

Step 6: Commit to action items

You may want to outline the specific actions in your marketing plan and again in a spreadsheet so you can map out timing of execution, due dates for materials needed, roles and responsibilities, and the status of each action item. Here's an example of what this may look like:

Task	Description	Actions	Due Date	Owner	Status
Influencer outreach	Identify influencers over purchase and brand choice with voice among key constituents	Identify bloggers, analysts, columnists, speakers, and more	Deliver 5/17 Approve 5/19 Execute 5/24	Staff 1 Staff 2	Complete Approval pending

Step 7: Build learning plans

If you have a new business or product, or if you're experimenting with a new or risky marketing activity or trying new channels or offers, set up a plan (or pilot) for how to test the waters on a small scale first. You need to determine what positive results you want to see before committing to a higher level. After all, wisdom is knowing what you don't know — and planning how to figure it out.

To learn and ultimately succeed, everything you do must be measurable and testable. Set up tests for every action to determine how it worked against past efforts or to determine the best approach. (See Chapter 10 for more on testing plans.) Just be sure to identify the tests you need to do for the coming year to be as efficient and effective as possible.

You may want to include actions such as the following in a yearly learning plan:

>> Identify new research projects, such as Voice of the Customer programs, that help you identify what matters most, new attitudes, new customer demand expectations, satisfaction rates, and so on.

>> Try out direct marketing campaigns via A/B tests to identify a new champion or validate current champions that will still work in the new year's environment.

>> Test channels for promotions to identify best response and return.

>> Check new distribution channels to see whether you can identify more efficient and less expensive methods or partners.

>> Examine new market segments to identify secondary customer groups you can nurture for future gains.

>> Test lists to see which providers provide the best performing lists and the best overall returns.

>> Compare year-over-year (YOY) response for past and present campaign messaging and offers.

>> Experiment with engagement programs online and offline to see which best build relationships and kinship.

REMEMBER

Don't think of your plan as written in stone. In fact, your plan is just a starting point and is an evolving process. As you implement it throughout the coming year, you'll discover that some things work out the way you planned and others don't. Good marketers revisit their plans and adjust them as they go. The idea is to use a plan to help you be an intelligent, flexible marketer and guide your resources while being ready to change as quickly as markets and customers often do.

TIP

Always look for ways to maximize efficiencies in all you do. If buying advertising space is part of your plan, buy in bulk, or three insertions/placements rather than just one at a time. This way you save money and give a new channel a chance to pay off better, because one ad presented one time in one place likely won't get acted on as much as the same ad presented multiple times to the same people.

Keeping It Real: Do's and Don'ts of Planning

Marketing programs can easily get overwhelming, and when this happens, you set yourself up to fail. Keep your activities and goals reasonable, based on what you can do. If you try to do too much, you can waste a lot of resources and miss a lot of opportunities, both of which you want to avoid. The next sections illustrate common ways marketers lose money and some effective strategies for using your resources wisely.

Don't ignore the details

Good marketing plans are built from details such as customer-by-customer, item-by-item, or territory-by-territory sales projections. Generalizing about an entire market is difficult and dangerous. Your sales and cost projections are easier to get right if you break them down into their smallest natural units (such as individual territory sales or customer orders), do estimates for each of these small units, and then add up those estimates to get your totals.

Don't get stuck in the past

Don't rest on your laurels, and don't "do what you've always done" unless that is paying off and has every chance of continuing to do so. Build on your best-performing elements of past plans and omit those that didn't produce high returns. Be ruthless with any underperforming elements of last year's plan. Also, monitor your plan over the business cycle and adjust it as you go so you can catch problems early and avoid wasting too much time and money on underperforming activities.

Don't try to break norms

If you're trying to offer a product or service that interrupts life as usual for your customer groups, you'll likely be disappointed. Build a product or service and a marketing plan that your customer can realistically support. For example, businesses are seeing a decline in travel budgets for mid-level managers at large and small companies. If you're offering a workshop for this group of professionals that involves expensive travel to a resort town and a good share of play time, your audience likely won't be able to get it approved. *Junkets* (leisure trips disguised as business trips) don't usually get approved in any business culture anymore, even for higher-up executives. So instead of trying to change this reality, change your offering and your expectations to fit your customers' reality, not your own wishful thinking.

Don't engage in unnecessary spending

Always think through spending options, and run the numbers before committing to anything or any salesperson with the "perfect" solution. Just because something is new or you can buy it at a good price doesn't mean you should. Have a plan for what you need, what you can spend, and how you'll measure your ROI for each spend, and stick to it to avoid losing money on losing investments.

REMEMBER

Before committing to an expensive advertising agency with high overhead to cover, do some analysis to determine what outside resources you really need. With all the digital tools available today, can you do some of the ad and collateral design in-house? Also look for freelancers who can help with designing and deploying digital assets.

Do set reasonable boundaries

Don't make your ambitions greater than the resources you have available to pull them off. If you're currently the tenth-largest competitor, don't write a plan to become the number-one largest by the end of the year. You need to grow at your own pace, not a competitor's, in order not to overextend your financial and human capital resources. To build revenue, you may need to start out in a niche market and then expand as you have the capital to do so. Be careful how much debt you leverage, and always monitor your sales goals and actuals to ensure that you can stay ahead and not get in a deeper hole if you're in one to begin with.

Do break down your plan into simple subplans

If your marketing activities are consistent and clearly of one kind, you can go with a single plan. But if you sell ancillary services, like consulting or repair, to support your core products, you'll need to map out plans for integrating and selling these other services and products as well. They may fit into one sales proposal, or they may be secondary pitches to customers you close.

If you have multiple regions, locations, or e-commerce sites, how does your over-all marketing plan support these areas, and what specific plans do you need to add to address their specific needs and goals?

REMEMBER

If your plan seems too complicated, simply divide and conquer! Then total every-thing up to get the big picture for your overall projection and budget. For example, if you have 50 products in five different product categories, writing your plan becomes much easier if you come up with 50 sales projections for each product and five separate promotional plans for each category of product.

TIP

Every type of marketing activity in your plan has a natural and appropriate level of breakdown. Find the right level, and your planning will be simpler and easier to do. Following are some methods to help you break down your planning:

>> Analyze, plan, and budget sales activities by sales territory and region (or by major customer if you're a business-to-business marketer with a handful of dominant companies as your clients).

>> Project revenues and promotions by individual product and by industry (if you sell into more than one).

>> Plan your advertising and other promotions by product line or other broad product category because promotions often have a generalized effect on the products within the category. What is your budget for public relations/publicity, videos, collateral production, ad buys, social media site/page development, lists, promotions, printing/mailing, and so on?

>> If you have a single bestselling product that carries your company, consider a separate publicity and customer experience plan for it. You should also plan product-oriented activities on the web, such as blogs and fun videos that go viral, to keep a buzz going about your star product.

Preparing for Economic Influences

When preparing your marketing plan, you need to factor in economic trends and issues of which you have no control. Watch the leading published economic indi-cators and regularly monitor the numbers. If you notice a decline for more than two months in a row, look closely for any signs of sales slowdowns in your own industry and be prepared to take action.

Monitoring economic influences and cycles can help you avoid a false sense of security. In the 1990s, economic growth was fairly steady. When economic growth suddenly began to slow in December 2007, marketers faced major problems as their markets slowed down. To stay on top of economic trends by cities, and especially for those of the cities in which you do the most business, monitor the Milken Institute's Best Performing Cities annual list at www.best-cities.org.

The Conference Board (www.conference-board.org), a nonprofit in New York City, compiles an index of leading economic indicators that has successfully predicted the last half dozen recessions. However, it has also predicted five recessions that didn't occur, so if you slavishly cut back every time the economists publish negative forecasts, your marketing plans will be too gun-shy and conservative. You have to take some risk to grow, but if you watch the economic weather closely, you can scale back sooner than most marketers when it becomes obvious that economic growth is slowing.

TIP

When your own sales are weak *and* economic forecasts are poor, cut back aggressively on variable costs like printing, promotions, design of new materials, and so on. You need to ensure that you can always cover your fixed costs, which include your office lease, utilities, and so on.

Budgeting Your Game

A critical component of your marketing plan is clearly your budgeting. You need to come up with line-item expenses — costs for each line of activity you include and plan to execute — and manage your overall expenses accordingly. If you don't budget, you can easily overextend yourself by engaging in those "special opportunities" that arise unexpectedly. Add a few of those together, and you can really impact your bottom line, and not always for the better.

Your playbook should include your pricing estimates and allocations for each step of the way to your goals.

Figure 5-2 shows an overview of how to organize your marketing plan line items financially so you can better allocate your resources and see directly whether they align with your priorities and greatest competitive needs. If you evaluate your expenses against projected sales as shown in Figure 5-2, you can estimate your profit or loss from your marketing investments and activities.

Overview of Program to Target Retail Store Buyers	
Program Components	**Direct Marketing Costs ($)**
Primary influence points:	
– Sales calls	$450,700
– Telemarketing	276,000
– Ads in trade magazines	1,255,000
– New product line development	171,500
	Subtotal: **$2,153,200**
Secondary influence points:	
– Quantity discounts	$70,000
– Point-of-purchase displays	125,000
– New web page with online catalog	12,600
– Printed catalog	52,000
– Publicity	18,700
– Booth at annual trade show	22,250
– Redesign packaging	9,275
	Subtotal: **$309,825**
Projected Sales from This Program	$23,250,000
Minus Total Program Costs	– 2,463,025
Net Sales from This Marketing Program	**$20,786,975**

FIGURE 5-2:
A program budget, prepared on a spreadsheet.

© John Wiley & Sons, Inc.

Identify an initial cost figure for what you want to do with each component. Total these costs and see whether the end result seems realistic. Is the total cost too big a share of your projected sales? Typically, advertising and marketing spends are about 2 to 3 percent of projected sales. Are your estimates in line with your brand's historical marketing budgets?

Don't budget more than 10 percent of your revenue toward marketing unless you have good reason to believe (from past experience) that the return on marketing investment will be there. And don't commit to a full year of expensive marketing. A first-quarter plan is more cautious and commits you to only a fourth of a year's spending. Take it one step at a time.

TIP

If your marketing plan covers multiple customer groups, you need to include multiple spreadsheets (such as the one in Figure 5-2), because each group may need a different marketing program. For example, the company whose wholesale marketing program you see in Figure 5-2 sells to gift stores — that's the purpose of that program. But the company also does some business with stationery stores. And even though the same salespeople call on both customer groups, each group has different products and promotions. They buy from different catalogs. They don't use the same kinds of displays. They read different trade magazines. Consequently, the company has to develop separate marketing programs for them, allocating any overlapping expenses appropriately (meaning if two-thirds of sales calls are to gift stores, then the sales calls expense for the gift store program should be two-thirds of the total sales budget).

Managing Your Marketing Program

The main purpose of the management section of your marketing plan is simply to make sure you have enough human capital and bandwidth to get the work done. This section summarizes the main activities that you and your marketing team must perform to implement your marketing program. Use this section to assign these activities to individuals, justifying the assignments by considering issues such as an individual's capabilities, capacities, and how the company will supervise and manage that individual.

Sometimes the management section gets more sophisticated by addressing management issues, like how to make the sales force more productive or whether decentralizing the marketing function is worthwhile. If you have salespeople or distributors, develop plans for organizing, motivating, tracking, and controlling them. Also, develop a plan for them to use in generating, allocating, and tracking sales leads. Do you need a system like Salesforce (www.salesforce.com) to help them stay on track and optimize productivity?

Start these subsections by describing the current approach and do a strengths/weaknesses analysis of that approach, using input from the salespeople or distributors in question. End by describing any incremental changes or improvements you can think to make.

TIP

Make sure you've run your ideas by the people in question *first* and received their input. Don't surprise your salespeople or distributors with new systems or methods. If you do, they'll probably resist the changes, causing sales to slow down. People execute sales plans well only if they understand and believe in those plans. Getting them involved early with idea generation and strategy development also helps gain their buy-in and implementation.

Projecting Expenses and Revenues

Managing your marketing plan and the execution of such involves establishing processes, boundaries, timelines, and budgets, such as

>> Estimating future sales, in units and dollars, for each product in your plan

>> Justifying these estimates and, if they're hard to justify, creating worst-case versions

>> Drawing a timeline showing when your program incurs costs and performs program activities

>> Writing a monthly marketing budget that lists all the estimated costs of your programs for each month of the coming year and breaks down sales by product or territory and by month

TIP

If you're part of a start-up or small business, consider doing all your projections on a *cash basis.* In other words, put the payment for your year's supply of brochures in the month in which the printer wants the money instead of allocating that cost across 12 months.

Also, factor in the wait time for collecting your sales revenues. If collections take 30 days, show money coming in during December from November's sales, and don't count any December sales for this year's plan.

A cash basis may upset accountants, who like to do things on an accrual basis — see *Accounting For Dummies,* 5th Edition, by John A. Tracy (Wiley). Cash-based accounting keeps small businesses alive. You want to have a positive cash balance (or at least break even) on the bottom line during every month of your plan.

If your cash-based projection shows a loss some months, adjust your plan to eliminate that loss (or arrange to borrow money to cover the gap). Sometimes a careful cash-flow analysis of a plan leads to changes in underlying strategy. One approach may be to get more customers to pay with credit cards rather than invoices; this can shorten the average collection time and greatly improve your cash flow as well as spending power and profitability.

TIP

Several helpful techniques are available for projecting sales, such as buildup forecasts, indicator forecasts, multiple-scenario forecasts, and time-period forecasts. Choose the most appropriate technique for your business based on the reviews in the following sections.

You can use several of the following techniques and average their results. We've mentioned some of these earlier in this chapter. The following descriptions will help give you a better idea for how to execute on them.

Buildup forecasts

Buildup forecasts are predictions that go from the specific to the general, or from the bottom up. If you have sales reps, ask them to project the next period's sales for their territories and to justify their projections based on their anticipated changes in the situation. Then combine all the sales force's projections to get an overall figure.

If you have few enough customers that you can project per-customer purchases, build up your forecast this way. You may want to work from reasonable estimates of the amount of sales you can expect from each store carrying your products or from each thousand catalogs mailed. Whatever the basic building blocks of your program, start with an estimate for each element and then add up these estimates.

Indicator forecasts

Indicator forecasts link your projections to economic indicators that ought to vary with sales. For example, if you're in the construction business, you find that past sales for your industry correlate with *GDP* (gross domestic product, or national output) growth. So you can adjust your sales forecast up or down depending on whether experts expect the economy to grow rapidly or slowly in the next year.

Multiple-scenario forecasts

Multiple-scenario forecasts start with a straight-line forecast in which you assume that your sales will grow by the same percentage next year as they did last year. Then you make up what-if stories and project their impact on your plan to create a variety of alternative projections.

You may try the following scenarios if they're relevant to your situation:

>> What if a competitor introduces a technological breakthrough?

>> What if your company acquires a competitor?

>> What if Congress deregulates/regulates your industry?

>> What if a leading competitor fails?

>> What if your company experiences financial problems and has to lay off some of its sales and marketing people?

>> What if your company doubles its ad spending?

For each scenario, think about how customer demand may change. Also consider how your marketing program would need to change to best suit the situation. Then make an appropriate sales projection. For example, if a competitor introduced a technological breakthrough, you may guess that your sales would fall 25 percent short of your straight-line projection.

WARNING

You really can't be sure which scenario, if any, will come true. So another method involves taking all the options that seem even remotely possible, assigning each a probability of occurring in the next year, multiplying each by its probability, and then averaging them all to get a single number.

Time-period forecasts

To use the *time-period forecast* method, work by week or by month, estimating the size of sales in each time period, and then add these estimates together for the entire year. This approach helps you when your program (or the market) isn't constant across the entire year. Ski resorts use this method because they get certain types of revenues only at certain times of the year. Marketers who plan to introduce new products during the year or use heavy advertising in one or two *pulses* (concentrated time periods) also use this method because their sales go up significantly during those periods.

TIP

Entrepreneurs, small businesses, and any others on a tight cash-flow leash need to use this method because it provides a good idea of what cash will be flowing in by week or by month. An annual sales figure doesn't tell you enough about when the money comes in to know whether you'll be short of cash in specific periods during the year.

Creating Your Controls

The controls section is one of the most important elements of a marketing plan because it allows you and others to track performance. Identify some performance benchmarks and measurable values, often referred to as key performance indicators (KPIs), and state them clearly in your plan. You should set KPIs for your overall marketing program and actions and for each individual line item or business unit. For example, you can define KPIs for the following:

>> Sales activities

>> Marketing spends and action items

>> Web traffic from search activities

>> Customer service and support for resolving conflicts

>> Customer engagement sales from online and offline chats

>> Distribution channel performance

As you monitor the KPIs and results for various aspects of your business, you'll better be able to see where your resources are needed most, where you can cut back expenses, and where your strong points and weak points are when it comes to profitable operations and ROI.

Chapter **6**

Content Marketing and Marketing Content

Nothing points to the power of content marketing and publicity versus just advertising more than the 2016 presidential election. Per advertising and paid media expenditures, Donald Trump spent $239 million compared to Hillary Clinton's $451 million. You'd think that would make the difference because, in many cases, elections are popularity contests, and whoever has the most name recognition often wins. Well, that does hold true quite often. But the most credible name recognition comes from the "news" media or the many mentions, good and bad, that come from reporters, political commentators, community leaders, and other authorities we choose to believe. This is where Trump took over.

Throughout the campaign, Trump's mentions on the news were close to twice that of Clinton's. Any mention — good, bad, and ugly — helped. It got his name out and made him more popular than even he could imagine. For example, on October 9, 2016, when the news couldn't stop talking about his insults toward a beauty pageant contestant and just days after the release of the *Access Hollywood* tapes where he bragged he could get away with assaulting women because he was a celebrity, his media mentions totaled up to 4,079, whereas Clinton's were only 1,874 — almost one-third as many. Clinton thought that that scandal was the nail in his coffin, yet it actually turned out to be the nail in hers because it kept his name alive and consumed most media coverage for the remaining weeks of the campaign as indicated by an analysis by the GDELT Project, using data from the Internet Archive Television News Archive.

Publicity matters. And as Trump learned at an early age, long before he became a presidential candidate, the number of mentions matter more than the quality of the content. Like in middle school, the most popular kids often win elections, not because they are nice or good, but because people know who they are.

Getting mentioned on influencer blogs, media websites, printed media, television and radio shows, Twitter, Facebook — you name it — matters, and it matters a lot, especially as consumers today place less trust in advertising to guide their choices and an increasing amount on what they hear from peers and news sources.

Content marketing and marketing content are similar but not one and the same. Marketing content refers to your messaging, offers, and personalized communications in paid media outlets. Content marketing refers to the information you share with the world about your product, brand, industry, leadership, market trends, future predictions, and so on that position your brand as a thought and innovation leader, an authority, or just a popular player in your markets. The latter, because of its objective nature and often implied endorsement by others who share it, is most often more powerful for drawing consumers to a brand, engaging shoppers while in the process of buying, and securing loyalty and referrals, and of course, social media likes and shares.

This chapter sets forth some insights on content marketing and marketing content strategies and tactics and how to build successful plans no matter the size of your company. In terms of semantics, content marketing, marketing communications, public relations, and so on are pretty much the same, at least for the purposes of this chapter.

An Overview of Content Marketing

Just what is content marketing? According to the Content Marketing Institute (CMI; www.contentmarketinginstitute.com),

> Content marketing is a strategic marketing approach focused on creating and distributing valuable, relevant, and consistent content to attract and retain a clearly defined audience — and, ultimately, to drive profitable customer action.

In a sense, content marketing makes us all journalists as we pull together information, ideas, and insights and share objectively with consumers to positions ourselves as leaders and spark dialogue that, down deep in our marketing hearts, we hope will generate leads that our sales teams can convert to sales.

The goals of your content marketing should be to

>> Build awareness of your brand and offerings.

>> Get people and the media talking/posting/texting about you.

>> Position your brand as the authority in your field and/or market.

>> Get authorities and other influencers to talk, write, and tweet about you.

>> Inspire core consumers to engage with your brand online and offline.

>> Top the lists for mentions, shares, tweets, and so forth on social media.

If you achieve these goals, your ultimate goal of selling more and earning more will fall into place. That's how marketing works. We consumers hear about something and suddenly we buy it, or at least keep talking about it. Remember Super Bowl 2013 when the lights went out for 34 minutes and Oreo quickly tweeted, "You can still dunk in the dark"? Well, we may not know how many Oreos were purchased as a result of that tweet, but we do know that a lot of people are still talking about it several years later.

You can accomplish many of these goals in a world where everyone is a communicator and most people have a mechanism to voice their voice — via their smartphones and social channels — by giving your customers and consumers something worth talking about and the media more news to add to the news hole they have to fill daily. The first step is to increase the quality and quantity of your marketing communications.

This chapter helps you do just that by showing you how to put a plan in place for newsworthy, informative communications, prioritize your communications activities, improve your writing, spark dialogue, not just monologues, and more. Chapters 8 and 10 on digital and direct marketing techniques dig in to the technologies available to help you distribute your content in a way that is affordable and efficient.

Creating content that delivers

Content marketing doesn't just create visibility; it enhances many other aspects of your marketing efforts, such as the following:

>> Social media: Without a strategy for developing themes and messaging for your content that positions your brand as a leader or customer advocate/partner, your social media efforts become little more than a game of roulette, if they even get that much attention.

>> SEO engines tend to rank businesses that put out consistent content higher than those with spotty, infrequent content publishing.

>> Media outlets are always looking for content to add to their sites and printed publications, and with fewer people on payroll, this need for third-party content will continue to rise.

>> If you engage in pay-per-click (PPC) advertising models, your content will increase your chances of clicks and thus higher ROI.

>> Inbound marketing is built on content. If you want people to call you, give them a reason beyond an ad that most often sounds and reads like everyone else's.

Content that succeeds at drawing people to your brand and establishing you as the authority on the topic at hand and someone to be trusted is objective information. The goal is to deliver "objective" information that leads to your brand truths. Every marketer's content library should include "journalistic, objective" channels and tools, including

>> White papers

>> Webinars

>> News bullets

>> Industry trend updates and summaries

>> Media releases

>> Blogs

>> LinkedIn posts and articles

>> Columns in print and online magazines

Channeling your content

With all forms of marketing, the message, tone, and persona of your content need to seem personally relevant to the receiver. But so does the channel. Perry Kamel, an authority in content marketing and the corresponding technology that enables marketers to deliver it en masse efficiently and personably, suggests that most marketers work hard to deliver relevant content for all marketing channels — advertising and editorial — but often deliver it in a non-relevant envelope.

Channels, or envelopes if you will, for marketing content include the following, all of which can be narrowed down to specific channels that fit the information needs and patterns of your consumers and cater to their persona as well:

>> Third-party news sites (*Huffington Post* and online sites for your local newspaper)

>> Broadcast format (TV and radio news outlets)

>> News wire services (PR Newswire)

>> Blogs you own

>> Blogs written by influencers and followed by your audience

>> Twitter

>> Facebook

>> Informational, ideation sites, or those that people go to for ideas more than sales (Pinterest, Houzz.com)

TIP

Influencer marketing, or sending your content to influencers in a given industry, is not just a fad that sparked a new genre of marketing agencies; it's a concept that has worked for years just under different names. As social media continues to evolve, so, too, does the number of "experts" that arise in the self-proclaimed sector of authorities. Many of these people become experts simply due to getting a large blog or Twitter following quickly through shares, retweets, and so on. Find these people and send them ideas to write about. Keep looking for others that pop up because most of these "experts" turn over quickly as new bloggers with new ideas can rise quickly due to the low cost of entry for social media journalism.

For example, if you're selling men's high-end, contemporary fashion and travel accessories, you may want to pursue relationships with bloggers that cover the following topics:

>> **Men's fashion in general:** Styles, accessories, and total looks.

>> **Travel tips:** Target bloggers on tips for traveling light and fashionably.

>> **Minimalism:** Many bloggers cover fashion and minimalism, a really big topic for Generations X and Y.

Instead of blasting out your stories and news to every single blogger you find with Google searches, pinpoint those that have a lot of ads from respected brands on their sites and, of course, the highest number of followers. For example, the blog The Fashion Spot (www.thefashionspot.com) has so many big brand ads, like those from Volvo and Nordstrom, that you almost get lost. Although it has blogs that cover men's and women's fashion, its list of Top Men's Fashion blogs is pretty credible and one you'd want to be on.

Creating a Credible Content Marketing Plan

The best content is newsworthy, actionable, frequent, clear, consistent, attention-grabbing, persuasive, and accurate — no small undertaking. In fact, a lack of content is one of the biggest challenges facing CMOs today and is the thorn in their side when it comes to using their marketing technology efficiently.

Before embarking on a content marketing program by writing articles, blogs, news releases, white papers, and more and then pushing them out via social channels in hopes that some will get noticed, put together a plan that you can stick with every single week. A good first step to an effective plan is a *marketing communications audit.*

TIP

Perform your own marketing communications audit by first gathering examples of the ways in which you communicate with customers and the market in general. Include everything anyone sees, hears, or even smells and touches, including traditional advertising, mailings, web communications, packaging, signs, and so forth. Don't forget to add snapshots of public communications — or lack thereof — on your building and vehicles to the pile of samples.

After you have your samples of all the ways in which you communicate, create a spreadsheet or table with each type of communication down the left side as labels for rows (for example, blogs, trade magazine guest articles, news releases, and LinkedIn posts). Then create columns for the following items:

>> Your estimate of what you spend per year on that type of communication (for example, copywriters, PR Newswire feeds, and bloggers)

- » The *frequency* (quantity) of that communication, rated as very low, low, medium, high, or very high

- » The clarity of each communication (does it make its point sharply, quickly, clearly, well?), rated as very low, low, medium, high, or very high

- » The consistency of the communication's message (does it reinforce a clear theme that can be seen in the other communications, too?), rated as very low, low, medium, high, or very high

- » The *stopping power* of the communication (in other words, how attention-grabbing it is), rated as very low, low, medium, high, or very high

- » The persuasiveness of the communication, rated as very low, low, medium, high, or very high

- » The ability of the communication to reflect your ESP, rated as very low, low, medium, high, or very high

- » The reach among current customers

- » The reach among highly qualified consumers

- » The number of shares, likes, retweets, pins, and so on that you get from social friends and readers

- » The number of mentions or inclusion achieved for materials sent to news media to include in their news stories or feeds

Review periodically to see which topics, themes, stories, and ideas pay off the most, and then replicate often.

Quantity and quality are equally important in content marketing strategies. The goal of *quantity* or *frequency* is to get your marketing message out repeatedly to the majority of people in your potential market. On the flip side, *quality* is the effectiveness of the communication and its value to readers in terms of providing them something they're inspired to act on and potentially contact you to discuss further. The trick is to create high-quality communications for your own channels that others will want to include on their channels as well.

TIP

Here are some tips for increasing and managing the frequency of your content distribution:

- » **Create a monthly theme calendar for your content.** Your themes should cover objective topics, like how to select a CRM system, how to get the most out of your data analytics, or nutrition tips for your tween who won't eat veggies.

- » **Promote white papers on all your social channels.** Introduce your expertise and encourage prospects to opt in for future emails or research papers from you.

>> **Break out your monthly theme into four story angles and create weekly posts for all your channels accordingly.** Make every post point to a landing page with more information that readers can download in exchange for providing an email address and one other thing that may be important to you, such as work title or purchase cycle for your product.

>> **Seek out new media that offer prime exposure at a very low cost.** You can place ads on these new media sites that drive people to your blog or other site for your content. Weekly ads to promote your content elsewhere will help your readership levels and hopefully up your lead generation.

New media — whether new social networking sites or blogs or more traditional outlets that are just emerging on the scene — are a bargain until they mature, so take advantage of the low cost of advertising with them. Facebook ads are still quite reasonable, as are ads on newer channels such as Instagram and Snapchat.

>> **Promote your blog and website constantly.** URLs for your blog and website should be in all email signatures for all staff members, on all digital ads you purchase, and in all content you distribute to third-party publishers. Invest in search terms that will drive web browsers to your sites.

>> **Use QR codes to draw mobile customers to your website or attract leads and upsell with special offers.** Link QR codes to product demo videos, useful web content, brief surveys, or other links to your company news and resources that show your expertise on matters associated with your brand.

>> **Work the news media appropriately.** If you send a press release every week to news editors, you're likely going to lose their interest and respect. News media wants news, not promotional messages disguised as news, which they are very good at picking out. Sending a press release once a month, as long as it fits the topics they cover, is a good frequency to keep your name alive with the media for when they need a subject matter expert on your topic and for getting mentions about your brand in news sections.

Press release topics to consider as part of your content marketing mix include

- Business news, such as product expansion, new locations, sales growth

- Personnel news, such as new hires and promotions

- Partnership, merger, acquisition news

- Charitable or volunteer projects that impact communities

- Information about new studies, research results, consumer trends, and so on

Taking Advantage of User-Generated Content

Instead of coming up with new content each week for your social sites and talking mostly about your own accolades, let customers do the talking and posting. Campaigns that ask customers to share ideas for how to better use a product, how they'd design a new rendition if asked, or personal photos of stories about using a product produce some of the most powerful results ever. Studies show that the majority of millennials and baby boomers actually want options to generate content for brands they love, and other studies show that this content, created by users, not ad agencies, is the most trusted.

User-generated content campaigns can be entertaining and profitable, but not always both. Meaningful content that showcases happy customers and encourages others to view their posts pay off the most.

HubSpot identified a list of recent user content campaigns that actually built sales, not just entertainment value for people who spend a lot of time online. Here are some of the examples it shared:

>> **Burberry:** Needing to attract a younger audience and resurrect an old brand, Burberry launched a campaign called "Art of the Trench," whereby it invited customers to post photos of themselves in Burberry trench coats on its website. As a result of real photos of real people who invited other real people to see and like their photos, Burberry's Facebook fan base grew to 1 million, topping the luxury sector at the time, and its e-commerce sales grew 50 percent year over year.

>> **Coca-Cola:** You remember when Coke cans and bottles had names on them or labels like "Best Mom," "Beautiful," and so on? Coca-Cola asked customers to post photos of their bottles and cans that reflected themselves on Twitter and other social channels. Sales increased as a result, and it likely helped Coke get to more than 100,500,000 followers on Facebook as well.

>> **LEGO and Belkin:** As unlikely a duo as this one seems, they developed a successful user content strategy blending their two products. Belkin designed a case on which LEGO blocks would stick, and LEGO provided pieces to enable LEGO lovers to customize their phone cases continuously with new LEGO art whenever they felt so inspired. They then created a website where users could generate a lot of fun content showcasing their art and inspiring others to do the same.

LEGO'S BRILLIANT USER-GENERATED CAMPAIGN

One of the most successful user-generated campaigns of all time was launched by LEGO for product development, which also provided a great deal of strong marketing and social media content. The campaign, called "LEGO Ideas," invites LEGO enthusiasts to create play sets, which can be produced for sale and mass distribution. Each play set created for the competition needs to reach 10,000 supporters to be reviewed by LEGO's staff, which selects the winning play set to be produced for market. Brilliant. Customers are showing off fun ways to use a product on many social channels and promoting their designs using that product to masses of people to reach the 10,000 mark. Imagine the impact of 100 customers promoting your product to 10,000 others each for free? Multiple times a year? Just for fun, some of the winning play sets from 2015 were the Beatles Yellow Submarine and the Apollo V Rocket.

In addition, LEGO's user content includes a strong video strategy, which is getting millions of views per video featured on its YouTube channel. The channels and ideas are endless.

Flipping to Marketing Content

Marketing content refers to the content in your marketing materials, such as paid ads, brochures, web pages, Facebook profiles, and so on. Although the length for ads and sales-oriented materials is typically a lot shorter than industry reports, white papers, news releases, and other editorial-type content, the messaging and writing approach need to follow the same rules.

In terms of content, all marketing materials — informative and sales-oriented — need to include the following:

>> **Positioning strategy that appeals to your customers' minds:** Your positioning strategy needs to be clear. A *positioning strategy* is a reflection of your emotional selling proposition (ESP) and addresses how you want customers to think and feel about your brand, product, or service. It describes how you want to be positioned in their minds and hearts and the emotional fulfillment you deliver. If you can attach emotional values to your products, even those as non-emotional as a stone driveway or a new ultrasound probe for a healthcare clinic, your positioning strategy will directly appeal to what drives your customers and your ROI at the same time. See Chapter 2 on identifying and developing your ESP and positioning strategy.

» **Call to action:** Ads that just present a brand story are just that: a brand story that often gets a smile but not a sale. Ads with a call to action get action. You need to provide compelling content and then a reason to call you for more information or to close a sale. Calls to action include encouragement to

- Call for more information.

- Go to a website to download a coupon or get a discount code.

- Use a special code for a shopping discount.

- Like a Facebook or LinkedIn post to have a chance to win a prize.

- Refer new customers for discounts or cash in return.

Your informative or journalistic content should also have calls to action, just not positioned as calls to engage in a sales process. Calls to action in white papers, industry updates on social media, and so on can be as simple as to call your team for a more detailed report, for a free consultation on how the principles apply to your business, to participate in a survey to help with further research, or to simply call for further information.

» **Reasons to engage:** There are many reasons to engage with a brand beyond the products you buy and the price it offers. Research from Cone Communications shows that

- 89 percent of consumers will buy from a social/environmental-driven brand.

- 76 percent will donate to charity supported by a trusted brand.

- 72 percent will volunteer for a cause supported by a trusted brand.

If this is true, which it is per the actions of consumers today, engage your customers in a cause your company supports. If your passion is preventing animal cruelty or pet rescue, engage customers in activities that support pets — theirs and those that are waiting to be rescued. If someone close to your company has suffered from cancer and your team donates time or money to cancer prevention, invite your customers to do the same, and then recognize their collaboration somehow, even if it's just a thank-you email. If your team does local walks or events to raise money or awareness, include an invitation at the bottom of your ad for people to join you.

If 89 percent of customers are looking for do-good brands to patronize, give them a reason to choose you by mentioning your causes and your contribution and inviting them to join you. Pretty simple yet very powerful.

Content Marketing Writing Tips for Better Results

Writing for content marketing needs to follow the same rules as journalistic marketing. Following are some tips for making your writing more engaging, inspiring, and likely to interest readers in ways that generate leads. These principles apply to writing informative materials, ad copy, web pages, and email and print direct response letters.

Try the inverted pyramid

This is the basic rule of thumb for news writers, which applies to all marketing writing as well. You can never assume that your readers will read the entire news article, press release, white paper, ad, or social media post. So you have to start with the most important message first. This formula is really important for writing press releases you want others to publish or post for you because time is limited, and if people have to read more than a few sentences to get the point of your message, you're done as they check out and go read something else.

The inverted pyramid format goes like this:

>> Headline that states news and teases content

>> Statement of story lead in a compelling opening paragraph that clearly communicates the news but leaves people wanting to read more

>> Facts or statistics to back up news claim or story

>> Third-party endorsement about claim, anecdotes, and examples

>> Quote from authority of person of interest to the story

>> Summary of related news if applicable

>> Summary of news source — one-line statement about company releasing news, contact information, or URL for further news stories

If the main point you want to get across of the most important, actionable part of your story shows up halfway below the headline or after less substantial information is shared, you have buried your lead. In a world where people are used to getting news from Facebook headlines or photo captions, Tweets, Pinterest shares, and so on, you need to get to the point more quickly than ever.

Toss out some click bait

As we mention in Chapter 7, creative click bait, as tacky or unprofessional as it seems, works, in editorial content as well as social content.

Unfortunately, many marketers use this deceptively, posting bait that leads directly to ads, not the headline that turns out to be anything but true. You've likely taken the bait, too, from headlines like "Goodbye to Barbra Streisand," which implies that she has died, just to find out she hasn't and you are immediately directed to an ad instead of an article about her in the first place. Or the headlines that reads "20 Child Movie Stars 20 Years Later — You Won't Believe What #17 Looks Like." And of course you have to sift through pages of ads and other movie stars to find #17 only to discover that it's nothing interesting at all. But you sure saw a lot of ads in the process.

Although this isn't cool, the concept of curiosity is. We humans are curious no matter what stage of life, generation, income, or education we represent. Include curiosity in your marketing copy as often as appropriate if you want to increase your readership, open rates, and click-through rates.

Headlines that spark curiosity in an honest manner include ones like the following:

>> "What You Don't Know Could Be Destroying Your Business"

>> "10 Ways Your Website Could Actually Be Losing You Money"

>> "Warren Buffet's Best Kept Secret for Investing Revealed"

Here are a few things to keep in mind about click bait:

>> All the techniques in the following sections work for content marketing, such as articles, blogs, and white papers, and marketing content for ads, emails, and other sales-driven communications.

>> Clarity is more critical than creativity in both your advertising marketing content and your informative content marketing. If readers are not sure what your message is, can't relate to the value you're proposing, or lose interest in what you're saying, you pretty much just wasted your time, effort, and money.

>> Simply communicate the basic message in clear language.

>> State your call to action upfront so it's clear what value you're presenting and what they need.

You can be sure that your customer is bombarded with thousands of other marketing messages beside your own. This high level of noise in the marketing environment means that most efforts go unnoticed by most of the people they target. That's why adding a little stopping power with real and honest click bait to your marketing communications is helpful.

Leading questions

The best type of "click bait" that is actually responsible and ethical is to lead with timely and meaningful questions that not only get attention but also spark some of those emotional responses we talk about in Chapter 2. Asking the right questions, such as the following, can motivate consumers.

» Are you one of the business owners losing thousands every day?

» Is your CRM program working for or against you?

» Are you tapping your email program's potential?

If you create comprehensive ESP profiles, as we discuss in Chapter 2, you will better understand what types of questions or statements will get your customers' attention and inspire them to act. When working with a client that provides marketing services for small businesses, we followed the ESP guide for what is top of mind for small business owners. We crafted a subject line accordingly and got a 49 percent open rate, well above average for emails sent to purchase prospect lists.

Stats and facts

Going back to the influence of authority in capturing people's attention and motivating behavior, facts and statistics about issues of interest to consumers tend to pull strong results. Instead of making claims yourself about the growth of your product category or associated customer satisfaction trends, let the facts tell the truth for you. Subscribe to emails and newsletters from research firms and associations that produce reports on your industry and share findings that support your marketing messages and product claims. Some that we recommend for marketing insights include Nielsen, Edelman, Cone Communications, and Deloitte.

Testimonials

Most people use testimonials at the end of a brochure, email, or as a secondary message in a marketing campaign. Try leading with testimonials to create a sense of truth, transparency, and quality upfront. After you've created that foundation, you're more likely to get the rest of your story or marketing message read.

Give ads greater stopping and sticking power

Incorporating stopping power in your ads doesn't have to be difficult. You can give your ads for magazines, the web, TV, or radio (as well as catalogs and websites) stopping power by

>> **Being dramatic:** Tell an interesting story, create suspense, or draw the audience into an event in the life of an interesting character. The principles of good storytelling work well. And the best stories for marketing response are those that create a new, powerful reason to stop, read, and share.

>> **Creating an emotional response:** What emotions are most powerful for inspiring attention and action? Again, this is where your ESP profiles are critical. Do people buy your product out of fear of losing something or out of anticipation for a reward? Does your product make people feel more accomplished or actualized? Define the most compelling emotion for getting action and present it in a compelling manner.

>> **Surprising the audience:** A startling headline, an unexpected visual image, an unusual opening gambit in a sales presentation, or a weird display window in a store all have the power to stop people by surprising them. So, for example, a headline that says, "We go out of business every day," has more stopping power than a headline that says, "We have everyday low prices," even though both headlines communicate the same marketing message.

>> **Communicating expected information in a *detcepxenu* way:** (Here's a hint: Try reading that mystery word backward.) A creative twist or a fresh way of saying or looking at something makes the expected unexpected. Yes, you have to get the obvious information in: what the brand is, who it benefits, and how. But you don't have to do so in an obvious way. If you do, your communication won't reach out and grab attention, causing your audience to ignore it.

In addition to stopping power, you need sticking power so that people remember and act upon your ads sooner and later. Remember, facts fade, but stories stick. When you tell a compelling story about your brand, your product, your mission, your history, or your movement to change the world, people remember if it touched them emotionally. Tie your ads to your stories to present a company that is real, that is run by people whom they can relate to, and one your customers can and will want to associate with.

Figure 6-1 is an example of how a business-to-business brand presented a story about one of the company's leaders, vision, and values. By sharing what moves her to find new solutions for clients and better the industry, the ad communicates the company values and advantages in a way that is not pushy or salesy but inspiring.

Beth Morrison,
National Director of Service
Conquest Imaging

Being Bold Changes Everything.

Taking on the establishment takes courage. And many never do. But if you don't try, you will never know what lies within you, as a person and as a business.

This is the philosophy that inspired me to lead Conquest Imaging to take on the industry when it comes to First Time Fix performance. Others might have the same products to offer, but no one comes close to what matters most for optimizing uptime for ultrasound departments, First Time Fix.

Conquest Imaging stocks all critical parts so when you call us with a need, our experts show up with parts in hand. Even most OEM repair teams can't do this. With parts in hand, not just "in stock," we are able to diagnose and repair during the same visit, and get your ultrasound machine back up and running 9 out of 10 times the same day you call. This is how we established our 90% First Time Fix rate, while the rest of the industry averages 70%.

It's believing in what we can do, as a company and as an industry, that sets Conquest Imaging apart from all the others – regardless of size or years of establishment. And what sets us up to help you do your best work. Every day.

I am Beth Morrison, National Director of Service at Conquest Imaging, and this is what drives me:
Be Bold, Be Brave Enough to Be Your True Self.
– Queen Latifah

The Ultimate in Ultrasound

Call us today at **866.900.9404** to learn how we can help you reach your business and patient care goals. Visit **conquestimaging.com** for video demos of our process and products. And to schedule a free consultation about your ultrasound purchasing and maintenance needs.

CONQUEST IMAGING
Because Quality Matters
ISO 9001:2008 CERTIFIED

📞 866-900-9444
🔗 conquestimaging.com

Conquest Imaging is a proud and passionate supporter of the PANCAN – the Pancreatic Cancer Action Network. Cancer donating more than $10,000 annually to support research and victims, in honor of co-founder Jean Conrad who was taken by this disease in 2015.

FIGURE 6-1:
A business-to-business ad from Conquest Imaging.

Image courtesy of Conquest Imaging.

Be consistent

After you craft your marketing message and come up with one or more ways to communicate it clearly, be consistent! If you repeat a clear, well-focused message, people will eventually get it. Make sure you ask yourself how consistent your marketing communications are.

Even if an individual ad, web page, mailing, sign, or other communication is clear and well designed, it won't work well unless it's consistent with your other communications. Nobody remembers what you say in marketing unless you repeat yourself frequently, clearly, and consistently.

TIP

Don't fall for old-school tactics: Research that shows sex-based ads have stopping power also shows that these ads don't prove very effective by other measures. *Brand recall* — viewers' ability to remember what product the ad advertised — is usually lower for sex-oriented ads than for other ads. So although these ads *do* have stopping power, they *don't* seem to have any other benefits. They fail to turn that high initial attention into awareness or interest, and they don't change attitudes about the product. In short, they sacrifice clear communication for raw stopping power.

Celebrity endorsements can backfire and rarely pay off. If the celebrity does or says something that doesn't reflect your values, it filters down to your brand reputation. Imagine if a brand hired Miley Cyrus to represent it when she was Hannah Montana and then had to deal with her image when she changed her game dramatically to bad-girl Miley. Not a bridge you want to cross at any time. The expense of hiring a spokesperson for your brand is usually enormous and hard to achieve a ROI in short order if at all.

Be as persuasive as possible

Persuasive skills are key to writing content marketing and marketing content text and copy. You need to understand the power of persuasion, as we discuss in Chapter 2.

Here are some guidelines to remember for all your written materials:

>> **Avoid sales clichés.** Don't sound like everyone else out there. As obvious as that seems, it's amazing how hard it is to avoid. Before finalizing your ad copy, review your competitors' copy for ads, websites, and social media. If your message is the same, find another way to say it.

>> **Steer clear of so-called "power words" from the books and seminars on how to be a super salesperson.** *Power words* are terms the so-called experts tell marketers to use (they also date back to the 1950s — talk about being out of style). Some examples include *incredible, guaranteed, amazing, unlimited, immediately, proven, limited time,* and *exclusive.* Such power words are so incredibly overused that we positively guarantee you'll receive amazingly poor results and be incredibly disappointed by them immediately.

>> **Show the evidence through clear, simple language and illustrations.** The way to be persuasive is to *show* that your product is a success rather than tell people that it is. Share the statistics that show how good it is. Provide a sample of what it can do. Quote a happy customer's testimonial. Show and tell, with an emphasis on the "show" part, and your communications will be naturally persuasive. Just be sure to focus on the facts, not your opinions. YouTube videos demonstrating product use are a great way to show and tell. Embed them in your Facebook business page, your website, and a blog on the same topic to build awareness of the new video, and if they achieve popularity in social media, tweet about them to encourage more followers to find them.

>> **Present your brand's persona.** Show consumers that your brand reflects their personality, interests, and lifestyle through your copy, headlines, and stories. Use words and language that reflect a conversation among like-minded people versus a sales pitch to the masses. Keep your copy and message simple and don't try to be everything to everybody when presenting your persona. You'll just be confusing and end up appealing to no one.

REMEMBER

If you do everything right, your communications will be naturally persuasive. Clear, concise, well-written copy is naturally compelling. Accurate, informative messages are persuasive. Professional, clean graphics and designs are convincing. If you look, sound, and read like a top brand or a leading professional in your field, people will assume you are.

If someone has to tell you to trust him, you probably shouldn't. Present trust and transparency through examples, offers, and testimonials, not hyped-up claims. Let the professionalism of your presentation show how good you are. Your customer service policies, overall experiences, honesty, core values, community support and CSR, and your people say more than your words, so make sure that the expectations you create through your writing supports your brand's reality. If not, it's time to look at the core of your culture, which is a story for another book.

Be professional

Always have others proof your work. You can't really catch mistakes in copy you've written and edited many times over as much as someone who has never seen your copy. You can hire professional proofreaders for around $35 an hour, and it's well worth it. They'll find grammar issues, typos, spacing and layout problems, and other things that can make you look sloppy to customers, which in the end hurts their ability to trust you.

Another critical component is to always source your sources. Don't state research findings without including the source of the work. You can get in trouble if it appears that you're taking credit for others' work, and you can lose your customers if they don't see a third-party endorsement to believe a claim that is in your favor. When writing ads, white papers, and social media posts, this is an important component. When possible, include URLs that link to the actual studies you cite.

REMEMBER

All forms of marketing content need pull power. Pull power may be a limited time offer, a QR code for a mystery deal, a chance for an experience that may not come again, and so on. Pull power includes strong emotional appeals that address the "wannabe" persona of your customers, create a sense of self-actualization, or solve an immediate problem or need.

REMEMBER

You can only get to the essence of a communication by writing — and then rewriting and rewriting. Keep reworking, keep rethinking, keep boiling your words down until you have something that penetrates to your point with startling clarity in the fewest words possible. And then, stop writing!

Keep you copy and all content for all channels conversational, your message inspiring, your promises real, and your offers actionable, and then be patient. Most content marketing is like a personal relationship. It takes time before you build trust and are willing to commit time to engage.

Remember, too, that it takes at least five touch points on average before consumers buy from a brand communicating with them. Keep your content and communications flowing as long as it's relevant and meaningful. And whatever you do, don't stop at touch point four!

3

Creating an Omni-Channel Plan

» **Using color and words for creative that engages, inspires, and sells**

» **Crafting an actionable creative brief**

» **Exploring idea generation activities for product development and brand building**

Chapter **7**

Creative That Engages the Mind

O ften one of the elements of marketing most taken for granted is the creative presentation. After all, people act on words, not images, right? Wrong. As we mention in Chapter 2, people's unconscious mind makes a judgment about something, someone, or someplace based on the visual elements, and their hormonal triggers respond accordingly. Research put out by Xerox and other creative technology groups shows that people make a judgment about a brand by its visuals in about 60 seconds, and up to 90 percent of that judgment call is based on color.

Beyond color, the images, fonts, and even the layout of a marketing piece influences engagement. If those elements create anxiety, people get that cortisol rush and end up in flight mode most often. If the layout is too cramped, they move on before reading a word due to stress and concern over wasting precious time. If something is too busy, such as too many colors, designs, or competing call-out buttons and visuals, people just check out. They sense chaos and disconnect to restore calm. It's just human nature to do all the above, and all the above actions are most often unconscious.

Creative does not apply only to the layout and photos of your ads and brochures. It applies to all the design elements of your brand, or your iconology, which transcends ads, digital assets, packaging, in-store displays, sales materials, and more. Every brand needs to define its iconology — color palettes, fonts, and visuals that represent its values and persona — and then execute consistent creative applications across all channels for all segments.

In addition to the graphic design elements, creative applies to how you position your brand and engage customers. Your brand presence, events, experiences, and customer journeys will all be more successful if you can think differently to be different.

This chapter covers the elements of creative strategies that capture attention, engage, and inspire; tips for execution; and ideas for sparking imagination and creative thinking throughout your organization to create psychologically relevant creative that drives the psychology of choice.

Creating Compelling Creative

You don't have to be a creative genius to produce compelling creative. You just need to know what appeals to your customers' persona, aspirations, and ideals. Knowing your customers' ESP (emotional selling proposition) in general, and each subsegment, will enable you to develop compelling creative that engages, inspires, and sells. Following are ways to help you get started.

Conducting a creativity audit

A *creativity audit* can help you see whether you're taking the right creative approach for your audience and for the brand image you want to convey. Respond to each of the statements in Table 7-1 as honestly as you can with a yes or no answer. At the end, the more noes you have, the more you need to rethink and redo your approach to creative.

As this audit points out, don't leave anything alone in marketing. Every aspect of your product, brand, and marketing programs depends on creative applications and thinking. If you avoid addressing creativity for your products and brand and making appropriate changes to stay current, you could find yourself obsolete sooner than later. Just ask Smith Corona, Royal, and Brother how quickly their typewriters ended up in museums instead of shopping carts.

TABLE 7-1   ## Marketing Creativity Audit

Marketing Creativity Actions	Yes/No
We make improvements to the selection, design, packaging, or appearance of our product(s) based on what our research tells us about the personality and values of our customers.	Y / N
We integrate the fundamentals of color psychology to ensure that we are projecting the right attributes for our brand and mood among our consumers.	Y / N
We build iconology and experiences around present and wannabe personas of our customers to appeal to our current and future customer.	Y / N
We find new ways and explore new channels to bring our product(s) to customers, making buying or using the product(s) more convenient or easier for them.	Y / N
We update and improve our brand image and persona to appeal to the energy and interests of our core customers.	Y / N
We experiment with new ways to communicate with customers and prospects.	Y / N
We improve the look and feel of our sales or marketing materials to keep current with new attitudes, trends, and ideals of customers.	Y / N
We look for ways to be more creative with our customer experience and events, not just our marketing image and materials.	Y / N
We change our marketing message before customers get bored with it.	Y / N
We reach out to new types of customers to try to expand or improve our customer base.	Y / N
We share creative ideas and have brainstorming, inspirational discussions with all the people who are involved in marketing our product(s).	Y / N

Changing (almost) everything

Effort, time, and money are common reasons marketers give for not changing their marketing approach and product development. Again, unless you want to fall into the same graveyard as the 96 percent of companies that fail in ten years, make creative thinking and development a top priority.

TIP

Question everything. Start with the following:

>> Why did you choose your current logo and brand colors? Do they convey the right image and mood for today's consumers?

>> Do your customer events and experiences reflect your creativity and inspire people to further engage?

>> What characteristics and value are you presenting with your brand's creative assets? Are they in line with the characteristics of the customers you seek the most?

>> What elements of your marketing have gone unchanged for years?

Take stock of what your competitors are doing. What do other marketers ignore or fail to change and improve? Do they mail the same catalog to the same lists on the same schedule throughout the year? If so, send yours two weeks sooner. Or maybe the industry you're entering always uses the web to support its sales but not as its lead marketing medium (you can try reversing that formula).

List the patterns that exist in your industry. Question how you can be different in as many areas as possible. This will enable you to stand out and lead your industry.

Applying Your Creativity

Advertising and content marketing cross pretty much every channel available — the web, print, mobile devices, TV, radio, outdoors, point of sale, bathroom stalls, and warehouse floors — you name it. In most cases, your ads will be surrounded by others competing for attention. The most creative ones most often cut through the clutter, attract attention, and trigger behavior that can lead to sales, loyalty, and referrals.

Think of your creative as a vehicle for building relationships between your brand and your prospects. This vehicle forges common grounds on common values, interests, and personas and ultimately creates bonds that build sales. As a result, marketers need to consider creativity as a strategy — not just a tool to position their brands as unique — accentuate differences, and showcase commonalities with customer segments in terms of what matters.

TIP

To apply creativity to your business, identify your best sources of creative ideas. Assess each idea before spending too much time developing it. Can it be executed with your current budget and resources? Does it fit your positioning and messaging strategies? Is it unique? You get the idea. Make a table like the one in Figure 7-1 to help you identify your own list of sources and constraints.

Sources	Constraints
- Metaphors and analogies	- Your brand's personality
- Word play	- Good taste
- Humor	- Your budget
- New trends	- What competitors have already done
- New technologies	
- Unmet needs	- Other people's patents, trademarks, and copyrights

FIGURE 7-1: Identifying your creativity sources and constraints.

Building your creative strategy

In Chapter 4, we discuss customer profiles, and building your creative strategy is where having those handy comes into play. Your creative needs to reflect the values, personalities, attitudes, and interests of your core audience. Every element needs to speak to your customers' hearts and minds to capture attention and engage — two important yet difficult to achieve elements of marketing success.

Take a look at your customer profiles. What are some of the more powerful traits that affect attitudes and behavior? For example, if your top consumer segment is millennial males, you may find the following characteristics:

>> **Trust equity:** Low level of trust toward established authorities, government, and advertising

>> **Happiness drivers:** Freedom, self-expression, adventure, innovation, and justice

>> **Values:** Minimalism, friendships, technology, experiences, and excitement

>> **Entertainment:** Fast-paced action, dynamism, bold colors, and video blogs

>> **Shopping influencers:** Peers, online customer reviews, and corporate and social impact

If your profiles contain these valuable attributes of your customer group, you're more prepared to develop psychologically relevant and compelling creative. Otherwise, your creative may be interesting and clever but not as likely to drive your bottom line.

You also need to identify the colors, visuals, and iconology of the values and characteristics you defined for your customers' core characteristics.

Color your creative psychologically

The fact that color influences people's moods, productivity, and even appetite is nothing new. Researchers have been proving this over and over again for years. The fact that more marketers don't pay more attention to the findings is what's amazing. Here are just a few facts that can change engagement, response, and ROI:

>> Research conducted by the CCI Color Institute for Color Research and the University of Winnipeg shows that within 90 seconds most people make an unconscious judgment about something's value, trustworthiness, and so on and that between 60 to 90 percent of that judgment is based on color.

>> Studies from the Color Association of the United States as reported by Psych2go.net say that blue is a good color to calm people and make them stay longer and hopefully buy more when dining out.

>> Red is known to increase heart and respiratory rates and appetite. Some color theorists suggest that this is a bad thing for businesses that want customers to linger longer and eat more if they're a restaurant but a good thing for fast-food establishments who want to stimulate energy that triggers appetites in the order line.

The importance of color for brand identity and marketing materials goes far beyond the physiological effect on appetite and food consumptions. The big question is how does color impact attitudes toward brands and shopping behavior? And in the case of red and blue as dominant brand colors — logo, retail environment, and online shopping presence — does it really matter? According to some in-depth research conducted by professors at University of Virginia and Virginia Tech, yes, it does. And it matters a lot.

Associate Professor of Marketing Rajesh Bagchi (Pamplin College of Business at Virginia Tech) and Amar Cheema (University of Winnipeg) conducted a study to compare the sales influence of blue versus red. They studied sales in red online and offline settings compared to those in predominantly blue settings. Their research found that the likelihood of a purchase is lower with red backgrounds than with blue ones.

Could it be that too much red creates too much brain energy, making people more easily distracted or anxious to leave, while blue, as suggested by the restaurant studies, makes people relax and linger longer? Think of yourself when shopping at Target and Walmart with red and blue environments, respectively. Where do you spend the most time and money?

Colors and values

Colors also influence how people perceive a brand's attributes and values, which in turn determines their judgment about its value and alignment with their own goals and values. Every color triggers a different mood or value judgment, and most of this is unconscious. Do an Internet search for "color wheel meanings" and see for yourself the diverse range of moods created by colors. Here are just a few:

>> Blue is the color of trust, intelligence, respect, purification, honor, and faith.

>> Purple represents wisdom, maturity, dignity, virtue, and long life.

>> Red generates energy, courage, glory, inner strength, and passion.

>> Orange triggers energy, joy, creativity, excitement, and enthusiasm.

>> Yellow inspires enlightenment, awareness, consciousness, optimism, and warmth.

>> Green represents healing, awakening, learning, independence, and change.

If you're a bank, you can see that blue may be the best color for your logo because it speaks trust, intelligence, and honor to the unconscious mind and aligns your brand with the values customers seek in financial services.

TIP

Color meanings can change across countries and cultures. For example, in the United States, yellow is often a sign of caution. Yet in Malaysia, it's the sign of royalty, power, and wealth.

Instead of choosing trendy colors or your favorites just because, take some time to study what colors really mean to consumers' conscious and unconscious minds and choose those that reflect the personality you want to project to today's consumers.

Backing up the color wheel meanings derived by psychologists is some research by Faber Birren, a pioneer in color research and author of *Color Psychology and Color Therapy* (Citadel). He conducted a survey asking people to assign colors to a list of words. Here's a summary of what he got:

>> **Trust:** Blue

>> **Security:** Blue

>> **Speed:** Red

>> **Cheapness:** Orange, with yellow a close second

>> **High quality:** Black

>> **High tech:** Black followed by blue and gray

>> **Reliability:** Blue

>> **Courage:** Purple and red

>> **Fear/Terror:** Red

>> **Fun:** Orange, with yellow a close second

Although studying the impact and influence of colors on how people eat and sleep (supposedly, people sleep better in blue rooms) and their productivity levels can be fun, all that really matters for marketers are the attributes you associate with your brand. Are your colors projecting the values that attract customers to you, and do the values drive your mission and business processes?

REMEMBER

Work with your marketing team to identify values, attributes, and even personality traits that you want your brand to be associated with. Make sure the colors you choose reflect the emotional and non-emotional, tangible and intangible values you identified in your brand ESP. Choose traits that reflect the lifestyle, values, and interests of your core consumer.

Brand iconology

Dictionary.com defines *iconology* as "the historical analysis and interpretive study of symbols and images." As a marketer, you need to define it as the colors, hues, symbols, and persona that define your brand. Your choices need to reflect the images and colors that best fit the persona and attitudes of your core customers. Before building campaigns to sell products or increase awareness, set some graphic standards for your brand.

Choose the colors that reflect the energy, moods, and thoughts you want to evoke. Top brands spend a great deal of energy finding specific hues for the colors to represent their brand. Because colors have many shades, invest time to find the hues that best align with your customers. To see what top global brands use, visit www.brandcolors.net. You can view the specific color codes for the logos you know best, including Microsoft, Delta, and Coca-Cola.

Most brands have a primary color and secondary colors that complement it. Many also select the gray and black tones they want associated with their brands.

Beyond colors, your brand standards need to include the fonts you want to convey your brand. Fonts, like colors, need to be consistent across all signage, imagery, ads, promotions, and channels. They represent a tone and persona just like your colors do and need to be defined. As we cover in Chapter 9 on print ads, some fonts increase readership and message recall more than others when used for the body text. For your logo, you can be more creative. Just keep it simple, readable, and on strategy.

If you want to take a look at trendy fun fonts, many creative bloggers and experts share these online. Check out www.creativebloq.com for some of the top fonts from 2015. Just remember that your font needs to stay true to your identity for years, just like your logo. So pick something you can live with.

You can choose from many free fonts. Others that are more unique and artistic than fonts readily available with your word-processing or basic art software programs require a fee. Make sure you talk to your designer about font choices and pay for font rights if necessary (more details in Chapter 9).

Check out Figure 7-2 to see some free fonts from Microsoft Word that spark creativity for logos, iconology in ads, or digital assets.

Apple Chancery: If you want to be fancy but contemporary

American Typewriter: For a retro yet cool look

Avenir Heavy: If you want to be bold and simple

Comic Sans: For a lighter, more playful tone

Chalkboard: A fun choice for an informal mood

HERCULANUM: IF YOU WANT TO STAND OUT

FIGURE 7-2:
A small sample of
fun fonts.

Words, copy, and click bait

You used to be able to use a few proven words in your copy and you'd get lots of responses and sales leads. Well, it's not so easy anymore. You now need something that stirs up so much curiosity that readers are compelled to go deeper on your website or "click" from your banner ad to your web page, all the way to the shopping cart. We see ads all the time on our social media pages that appear to be links to other "stories."

Headlines that bait people to click and read, like "You won't believe what happens next," "These child actors died before 21," and "You'll never recognize her now," diminish the impact of those top words that used to always get attention, such as *free, discount, save, limited, guarantee, proven* — you get the gist. Click-bait tactics can be successful in the right context but can backfire if your leading question or statement is not authentic and does not lead to a real story about the topic suggested.

The best copy uses words to create the feelings that move people to behavior. If you want to ease someone's mind, you might say, "Relax. With our help, you've got this." These words are not likely to top a list of best advertising words, yet this phrase engages people's emotions and sets their mind at ease.

The most powerful words known for more than doubling response are "but you are free." Why? It's simple. They empower consumers to make their own informed choices and minimize the sales pressure, and when that happens, trust evolves, which opens the pathway to the unconscious mind and builds a foundation for success.

When people feel that they've made wise choices, they transfer those good feelings to the brands that supported and helped them. When this happens, a logo, color palette, and so on become symbols of trust and good energy. This should be the goal of all marketing campaigns: to tap into the psychology of choice in ways that make your logo and graphic images beacons of trust, reliability, and self-validation.

THE POWER OF "FREE"

In 2000, social psychology researchers Nicolas Gueguen and Alexandre Pascual conducted a study to see what words resulted in the greatest compliance for doing a simple task. They asked subjects on a city street to give money to a cause and were able to get only 10 percent of those asked to comply. When they added the phrase, "but you are free to accept or refuse," nearly 48 percent complied, and in many cases, the amount of the gift donated was greater than before. Subsequently, they found that by using these same words to get people to take a survey, the compliance rate was also substantially higher.

Although the implications of this "but you are free" approach may be more clear for selling techniques, creative can take some important insights from this as well. Think about how much research consumers do before buying just about anything. GE Capital Retail Bank's second annual Major Purchase Shopper Study conducted in 2013 shows that 81 percent of consumers research online before going to stores, up 20 percent from the previous year. On average, consumers spend 79 days gathering information before making their choices. This particular study focused on purchases of $500 or more covering many categories, including appliances, electronics, flooring, home furnishings and bedding, and jewelry. A single ad is not likely to replace 79 days of research and spark an imminent sale; however, a campaign that provides information and decision support and recognizes consumers' ability to make good decisions might.

Involving, informing, and inspiring people to make their own choices works because people have been oversold on hype for years. Most people no longer believe the fine print in red that states, "Only one left in stock" or "One seat left at this price," as they find that same price offered the next day and the next. And sales like Black Friday are no longer as strong a motivator as in the past because everyone knows that there'll be another sale in a matter of days or weeks.

REMEMBER

Bottom line: Your creative has to appeal to your aspirations, your wannabe personas, and your current self and needs. That is no small task, but if you follow the guidelines in this chapter and book, you can master the right message, emotional appeal, and ability to grow your business.

Writing a Creative Brief

Any and all marketing materials — ads, brochures, websites, trade show booths, and packages — benefit from the use of a *creative brief,* a document that lays out the goals, strategic elements, target audiences and associated characteristics, basic purpose of the marketing piece, and executional guidelines, and so on. Whoever designs your materials — someone on your team, a freelance designer, agency, or yourself — needs to follow this brief to make sure your end results support your strategy and ESP.

Successful creative briefs include the elements in the following sections.

Goals

Define what you want to accomplish. If you don't have a destination in mind, you can't map out the journey. List the goals you hope to accomplish, and make them measureable and real. One strong and spot-on objective is really all you need and is easier to accomplish than many.

Your goals will vary. Not all ads should be about driving imminent sales. You also need to build your brand's awareness, identity, and positioning so that you can be more successful in acquisition efforts.

Promise and offer

What promise are you making about your product or your brand? What is the offer for each specific campaign? Your offer may be "Buy One, Get One Free," and your promise may be personalized care, money-back guarantee, and extraordinary service. Your promise and offer are not the same, because offers change often and promises not so much, yet they need to support each other.

Support statement

Include the product's promise and the supporting evidence to back up that promise in your support statement. You use this point to build the underlying argument for the persuasive part of your marketing piece. The support statement can be based on logic and fact or on an intuitive, emotional appeal — either way, you need to include a basis of solid support.

Tone or persona statement

Every brand reflects a personality and a tone that others identify with, or don't. This is your brand persona. It needs to also reflect your values, interests, and attitudes and those of your core customer. For example, Apple appeals to a specific personality of innovation, self-expression, freedom, spunk, creativity, and individuality. These values largely appeal to consumers aged 15 to 50. Your tone is the mood you create in each piece.

For consistency, your brand should reflect the same persona in each ad or marketing piece you create. However, you can change up the tone. You may choose to change the tone with seasonal offers — from Christmas giving and charitable themes to spring sales promotions.

Emotional drivers

If you haven't already created your customer ESP profiles (in Chapter 2), we suggest you place a bookmark here and do that now. Or be sure to come back to this section after you do. Having them handy as you read this section will help you get the most out of it.

Review the top emotions for your core customers that influence choices in your category and include key insights in your brief, such as the following:

>> Which emotions overlap for the customers you're targeting in a specific add or content piece?

>> Do you need to address fear, anxiety, or expectations for joy or relief?

>> What promises can you make about the emotional fulfillment?

>> Do consumers easily trust your category? How can you get around industry trust issues?

>> What are some of the influencers of choice among your customers? Social proof? Authorities? List these as specifically as possible and include directives as to how to address in your copy and your visuals.

>> What disconnects exist around your product category or brand? Do you sell life insurance and need to make people face the reality that they will someday die and could leave their family compromised as a result? Do you sell weight-loss programs and need people to accept that they may need professional help? See the denial stages in Chapter 2, which are based on Freud's defense mechanisms. Outline messaging you need to include in your creative to help people accept reality and act on it.

Wannabe profiles

Appealing to the current identity of your customers isn't enough; you also have to appeal to their "wannabe" profile. All young adults have a vision of who they want to be in the near and long-term future. These visions usually are their future self doing something on their bucket list that's out of the norm or working in a successful position, owning their own business, and living their dreams. Tap into these visions in your marketing campaigns. Proctor & Gamble does a great job of marketing to wannabe profiles to expand its customer base beyond core users to future users, pulling them into its product lines at younger ages.

Color palette

When working with a graphic designer, you need to list the color codes and tones you've selected for your colors. Any additional colors you use throughout your marketing materials should complement and support these tones and hues.

Golden triangle pattern

People's eye-flow patterns on printed materials aren't that much different from digital screens. People tend to place their first glance in the upper left-hand corner, move to the upper-right corner, take a sharp diagonal to the left margin, and then glance downward. This pattern is called the golden triangle. Whatever format your marketing campaign takes — digital or print — direct your designer to place the key messages, offers, and calls to action in these key areas for higher visibility, recall, and response.

Constraints

Perhaps you face budgetary constraints or need to avoid certain terms, concepts, or images that your competitors have already used. Your brand image or product personality may also constrain you to approaches that are consistent with it. Be sure to give your constraints careful thought and list them as clearly as possible.

Ask important questions to ensure that you're aware of any potential constraints. Such questions include the following:

>> Are there actions a designer can't do with your logo, like change the color?

>> Are you trying to avoid looking like a particular competitor?

>> Do you have to have vector art so that all images can be scaled up for big posters and scaled down for a blog or web page?

>> Is it important to produce work that can be shown both in full color and in black and white, depending on the medium and variations in your budget, or that can be adapted easily from a still image to an animated one?

>> Do you have all the rights to use the images, fonts, and trademarks you've selected?

Execution

Your creative brief needs to cover execution as well. Given all the online and offline marketing formats brands use today that need to be adapted for each customer segment targeted, repurposing content quickly and affordably is key. And you must do this so your messages, images, and offers are consistent across all channels at all times.

Many tools enable automatic customization of marketing and promotional materials. These tools enable marketers to create a template for a given campaign and very quickly and easily adapt the content — message, visuals, languages, and so on — to be produced in various formats across all channels and with direct relevance to various customer segment groups and geographical locations. Look for tools that enable you to adapt quickly for all the channels you use, including digital, social, point of sale, and print (ads, posters, bus boards, and so on).

If you are marketing on a national or global basis, its important to include marketing asset management and content adaptation into your creative plan to allow you to get campaigns to market quickly and to save you a lot of money. If you have to manually adapt each format for each campaign, you will spend a lot of hours preparing each element of your campaign, and that adds days to getting a campaign ready to launch. And if you are paying an agency or freelance designer to adapt your promotional material for print, Facebook ads, banner ads, bus boards, and so on, the changes can add a lot of cost. According to Perry Kamel, CEO of Elateral, a cloud-based content adaptation hub, you can get campaigns to market up to 90 percent faster and you can reduce your unit cost per creative piece you distribute by 80 percent or more with automated content adaptation systems.

Being able to adapt content quickly for market distribution is critical, not just to save money, but to be competitive. If you are competing with brands that use these systems and can deploy campaigns in days, not weeks, to be relevant in a more timely manner, you could be left behind. These tools are discussed in greater detail in Chapter 8.

Don't assume that you can't afford automated creative technology. Many systems and many price points are available and in most cases you can access this type of technology on a subscription or per user per month basis, making it affordable to access the same kind of services your bigger competitors use to improve their efficiencies.

REMEMBER

Knowing in advance what channels you'll use for your marketing piece gives structure to your ideas and sets a framework for execution so you know what's realistic and what's not.

For example: If you're designing a promotion around a new service or a limited-time promotion, your creative brief will include the details, special discounts, and expiration date. If your customers are used to connecting with you via online and offline channels, you'll need to execute creative across all channels simultaneously. What goes out in print needs to be backed up by what they see on Pinterest, banner ads, Facebook feeds, and so on.

Applying Creativity to Branding and Much More

The creative brief gives you a clear focus for projecting your brand value and competitive advantages in a given campaign, but creative thinking should not stop here. Creative processes can and should also be used to guide your product development and branding. Answering the same questions as listed earlier in this chapter for product development can help you come up with new products or services and/or improvements to existing ones.

Creativity and product development

New products must be innovative to stand out. Managing a product development team so that it's optimally creative and effective means first putting together the right team. That generally means a *diverse* team, one that includes the full range of knowledge that may be relevant. You need to include different functions — from sales and marketing to manufacturing and engineering — in the creative process. Involving diverse team members and even outside partners, suppliers, or customers from the beginning helps secure ownership throughout the organization and can lead to faster and smoother approval processes.

When discussing new ideas for new products, it is important to keep in mind the needs of your target consumers. What problem are you trying to solve? What past products are you trying to improve? What is missing in your product category that can make lives easier?

If you let creativity overrule practicality, you might create a new product that is fun to think about but not something consumers think is worth spending money on. A favorite example of a creative idea that resulted in a product that likely didn't get vetted for practicality is the battery-operated marshmallow roasting stick. This idea defies logic on many levels. If you are willing to rough it by camping or cooking outdoors, you likely are prepared to turn your roasting stick manually instead of idly hold a stick that rotates without any effort on your part beyond keeping it close to the fire. This product is now marketed mostly as a toy, and you can see it on sites that sell overstocked items.

REMEMBER

Be creative and think of new ways to solve real problems. Producing products that contradict the overall experience for which they will be used — in the preceding case, camping in nature and getting away from the routine of modern conveniences — could result in your producing a lot of white elephant gifts for holiday parties, and that is not likely a good business investment.

Creativity and branding

Creating a strong, appealing, distinctive, and easily identifiable brand image is critical no matter what size your business or industry is. Everyone recognizes the logos for top brands, such as Google, Microsoft, eBay, and IBM. Apple's apple and Nike's swish are unmistakable and represent images of consistent quality, innovation, and service that people have come to expect. These images have become brand beacons largely due to using creativity appropriately and consistently.

As you sketch out ideas or review concepts with your designer about your brand's logo and iconology, keep in mind that your goal is to create an identity that represents the persona and value of your brand, not to win awards. You're not in a competition for the most clever logo or web design. Most often, graphic design that wins awards and graphic design that wins attention and sales are not one and the same.

REMEMBER

Your brand's visual identity needs to appeal to your customers' personas and reflect your brand experience and values. Your logo is the first impression most will have of your brand, so it needs to be relevant. But it also needs to be sustainable. It's not something you can change often without confusing your customers and jeopardizing sales if people don't recognize your products. Change is also expensive because you have to update your product packaging, signage, displays, printed materials, and digital assets.

Updating versus completely changing your logo is a safer strategy if the time comes that you need to be more relevant. In 2015, *Business Insider* listed some recent logo changes, including

>> Google's update, which simply changed the font from serif to sans serif (see Chapter 9 for input on fonts)

>> IHOP, which kept its font intact but turned its red arch into a red smile and softened the background

>> Verizon, which replaced its oversized red checkmark to a smaller one at the end instead of over the top of its name

Simple changes like these don't change your brand recognition but do make you more relevant for what appeals to your current customers.

TIP

Creativity is important to get noticed, but clarity, consistency, and positioning are even more important for sustainability and sales. Keep in the mind the following guidelines:

>> **Start with a clear, simple, strong logo.** Logos are supposed to symbolize the product and persona, so keep your logo clear and simple and use it consistently until it becomes highly recognizable.

>> **Your logo is the quality symbol of your brand.** You earn brand equity by doing a good job. Your product and service are valuable to customers, and your logo should be a symbol of what they can expect.

>> **Include a steady flow of good marketing communications to create a brand that everybody knows and respects.** Never let your marketing program fall silent. Your communication can include everything from packaging and ads to websites. Always keep communicating the value you offer, the expertise you provide, and the experience that defines your brand. What you say and what you do determine what your logo symbolizes over time.

REMEMBER

Although great brands usually stick to simple, clear fonts and conservative colors, you want to build identities through creative advertising, product designs, and distribution to make sure consumers are excited about them. Keep your creativity simple enough for others to understand and recognize, but have fun creating experiences around the identity you build.

Artists don't paint legacy murals the first time they stroke paint on a canvas. And chances are you won't come up with the right design the first time you experiment with your graphics software. Give yourself time to explore ideas and presentations.

To spark your own ideas, seek out inspiration. Collect stories of creative marketing, browse logos of companies around the world, create a bulletin board on Pinterest of your favorite designs, and share these with others in and out of your company and space altogether. What's the first word that comes to mind when viewing these elements?

When you have some concepts for your own brand's identity, share those with friends, associates, and customers in person or in an online survey. Ask them to view each concept quickly and note the first thought that comes to mind. Is that the attribute you want associated with your brand? Is that a characteristic or value statement that will attract your core customers?

Simple ways to spark new ideas

Creativity isn't a science. It's the product of imagination, individuality, and one's ability to look at a routine event or product differently and then communicate or portray a new idea in a meaningful manner. Many times new ideas come from soaking up information, researching what others are doing, questioning the problem, looking at issues from an emotional angle rather than a functional one, tossing ideas back and forth with an associate, and then experimenting until something relevant sticks.

TIP

Here are some ideas that can help you engage your imagination in new and unusual ways:

>> **Seek ways to simplify.** Can you come up with a simpler way to explain your product or your business and its mission? Can you cut your website's message down to ten words? Can you reduce the length of a headline in your print ad without losing meaning? Much marketing content is too complicated and makes the reader work to understand it. Simple is good because people often can get the point with a glance rather than a longer read, and simple can project your key values immediately.

>> **Think of a celebrity or current role model who reflects your brand persona and imagine that he or she is your spokesperson.** How would Malala, Taylor Swift, or Macklemore, for example, change your packaging, advertising, and website, and what words would they use to describe your brand value? Silly idea, yes, but silly ideas lead to some pretty successful ones.

>> **Have fun.** How would Stephen Colbert, Jimmy Kimmel, or Jimmy Fallon describe your product or brand experience in their opening monologues? What stories would they tell about your brand, and what jokes might they come up

with to describe its value to consumers? Maybe outline your own three-minute monologue, or come up with answers to what consumers might say if interviewed outside *The Late Show* studios in New York City about the three best uses for your product. You never know what you might come up with for a fun, attention-getting campaign or even just a headline.

>> **Browse faces.** Search for images of your core customers in various settings. For example, search for male millennials socializing, shopping, and working, or female baby boomers in a professional setting, working out, playing with children, and sitting in a classroom. Note the expressions on their faces. Do they look confident? Enthusiastic? Content? This should help you better "see" the many faces of your customers and how you can adapt your creative for the moods that move them. Browse Facebook pages to view real people and ads to see how various personas are most portrayed.

>> **Go small.** Try communicating your message in a really small format. This constraint forces you to clarify and codify your message in interesting ways. Try communicating your brand's value in three bullets or a sticky note. You'll be surprised at the powerful outcome this exercise often generates.

>> **Go big.** Think of statements to communicate to customers, using really big formats. Forcing yourself to change the scale of your thinking can free creative ideas. How would you present your ESP on a billboard, moving truck ad, scoreboard, or banner at a local sports arena?

>> **Find new places to advertise.** Can you think of ways to reach customers that nobody in your industry has used before? Maybe fliers for ice cream at a gym for those moments when fitness buffs feel they've earned a reward? Promote children's entertainment venues or products at a place that attracts seniors so grandparents get ideas for family outings, not just the parents.

>> **Be your own customer.** Are you marketing to young males? Spend time at a nightclub, an outdoor concert, a recreation center, or a restaurant that attracts your customer. Observe. Observe behavior, language, clothing, and attitudes. Start conversations. And take notes. Go home and look at your brand from this new perspective. Do your colors, words, language, and even layout and information flow of your materials fit the energy and attention span and project the key values you discovered?

Making creativity a group activity

When confined to a conference room, most groups do little more than rehash old ideas or sit silent in fear of looking stupid in front of their peers. When someone dares to speak up, others are often too ready to agree to avoid having to think themselves or to end the meeting sooner so they can return to their to-do lists. To avoid group think and wasted time, brainstorming needs to take on a new process.

The following sections highlight some of the best group creativity techniques. Note that these techniques generally produce a list of ideas, some useable and many not. But sometimes the strangest ideas lead to others that actually work, so don't hold back.

Brainstorming

The goal of brainstorming is to generate new ideas and inspire the team to think of the unusual. To be effective, you need to conduct a meeting in which people feel safe to allow their minds to wander from traditional and current ideas to extraordinary scenarios and feel free to speak up without ridicule or harm to their career path. Establish the "no rules" rule to your meeting and start the flow by sharing ideas of your own, some good and some not so good, to help others feel confident and free to do the same.

If you offer daring ideas, like turning your trade show booth into a circus funhouse, a giant cave, or a replicate of your product that visitors can go inside, you're likely to spark a lot more fun ideas among your team.

The rules that guide many successful meetings include

>> **Quantity, not quality:** Generate as many ideas as possible.

>> **No criticism of any ideas:** Nothing is too wild to not write down.

>> **No ownership of ideas:** Everyone builds off each other's ideas.

TIP

If you need to narrow down a long list of ideas, ask participants to vote for their top three choices, and then tally the votes. Try to build on each of these ideas to identify the most actionable and potentially profitable. If nothing seems to fit, throw out new ideas and start over.

Question brainstorming

Question brainstorming follows the same rules as brainstorming, but you instruct the group to think of questions rather than ideas.

So if you need to develop a new trade show booth that draws more prospects, then the group may think of the following kinds of questions:

>> Do bigger booths draw much better than smaller ones?

>> Which booths drew the most people at the last trade show?

>> Are all visitors equal, or do we want to draw only certain types of visitors?

>> Will the offer of a resting place and free coffee do the trick?

These questions stimulate good research and thinking, and their answers may help you create a new and successful trade show booth.

Wishful thinking

Wishful thinking is a technique suggested by Hanley Norins of ad agency Young & Rubicam and one that he has used to train employees in his Traveling Creative Workshop. The technique follows the basic rules of brainstorming but with the requirement that all statements start with the words "I wish."

The sorts of statements you get from this activity often prove useful for developing advertising or other marketing communications. If you need to bring some focus to the list to make it more relevant to your marketing, just state a topic for people to make wishes about.

Analogies and metaphors

Analogies and *metaphors* are great creativity-inspiring devices. Gerald Zaltman, a pioneer in neuromarketing, wrote an entire book about the power of metaphors, *Marketing Metaphoria: What Deep Metaphors Reveal about the Minds of Consumers* (Harvard Business Review Press). He explains how consumers think in metaphors about most of life's issues and how you can use these in your marketing copy. What metaphors are associated with your category?

Some that I (Jeanette) have come up with for brands I've served include "A Pass-Go-and-Skip-the-Walker Card" for the health supplement industry and "A tracking device for my teenager" for the smartphone industry.

Often illustrations based on metaphors or analogies hit home to your consumers' mindset. Create a picture in which they can see themselves. Are they the hero that saves the world? The teacher that turns around a failing student? The scientist that holds the key to curing cancer?

Ask the members of your group — from sales to customer service — to come up with their own metaphors for your brand.

While metaphors are simple expressions of speech that show similarities among different things, analogies are more complex and are more based upon arguments rather than elements of speech to draw similarities between two different things. An example of an analogy could be that we are all like caterpillars. We must learn to be patient, sit tight, and allow ourselves to transform into the beautiful person we have potential to become.

Metaphors can be fun, quick ways to get attention for your content or ad copy. Analogies can be used to help prospects and customers discover within themselves what your product's true value is for helping them achieve long-term goals.

For example, if you are selling software systems to help marketers work faster and better, you could communicate the analogy that all marketers are tasked with completing a big obstacle course. Whoever has the tools to overcome the hurdles and cross the deep chasms most efficiently will ultimately win the prize of competitive advantage.

WARNING

Analogies can also backfire, so be careful. For example, a classic ad from the 1950s introduced DuPont's then-new miracle plastic, cellophane, by showing a stork delivering a baby wrapped in a clear plastic bag. Apparently, nobody at the ad agency noticed that it looked like the baby was about to suffocate. And watch out especially for tasteless, biased, or offensive analogies, such as in a recent print ad for the Mercedes-Benz S-Class sedans that boasts about their high safety level by comparing their air bags (where more really is better) to a woman with eight breasts. Not as appealing an illustration as they hoped it would be, as you might imagine!

And Jaguar's "Good to Be Bad" campaign launched in a very expensive Super Bowl ad in 2014 positioned its F-TYPE Coupe as the car of villains. As most people don't see themselves as a cold-hearted villain, the ad actually lost substantially on purchase intent scores tallied that year. And it was banned by the Advertising Standards Authority in the United Kingdom for promoting irresponsible driving. Neither of these outcomes is what any marketers seek to achieve.

Pass-along

Pass-along is a simple game that helps a group break through its mental barriers to reach free association and collaborative thinking. You can read the instructions here, in case you've never heard of the game:

>> One person writes something about the topic in question on the top line of a sheet of paper and passes it to the next person, who writes a second line beneath the first.

>> Go around the table or group as many times as you think necessary.

If people get into the spirit of the game, a line of thought emerges and dances on the page. Each previous phrase suggests something new until you have a lot of good ideas and many ways of thinking about your problem. Players keep revealing new aspects of the subject as they build on or add new dimensions to the preceding lines.

If you're doing this for a bank, this game might develop as follows:

Subject: How can we make our customers' personal finances run better?

Pass-along ideas:

- Help them win the lottery.

- Help them save money by putting aside 1 percent each month.

- Help them save for their children's college tuition.

- Help them keep track of their finances.

- Give them a checkbook that balances itself.

- Notify them in advance of financial problems, like bouncing checks, so they can prevent those problems.

Here's another fun pass-along idea: Ask people to help you find 20 words that rhyme with your company or brand's name in the hope that this list may lead you to a clever idea for a new radio jingle, YouTube video, or banner ad. Sound silly? Research shows that prose or text that rhymes has a higher recall rate. So drop your guard and dare to be silly. It can pay off.

Managing the creative process

REMEMBER

If you think of creativity as generating wild and crazy ideas, you're right — partially. Yes, you have to do some open-minded thinking to come up with creative concepts, but you also need concepts you can develop into practical applications in your ads, products, sales presentations, customer journeys and experiences, or other marketing activities.

Following this four-step process can help you turn ideas into profits.

1. **Initiate.**

In this step, you recognize a need or opportunity and ask questions that launch a focused creative process. If you look at opportunities to fulfill an emotional need, not just a functional or pricing need, you'll achieve greater success in the long term. For example, you may take a look at your content marketing campaigns to identify ways to better build intrigue while tapping into the "but you are free" concept, discussed earlier in this chapter. You may want to look at the promises on your website's home page to see how much they relate to fears, concerns, or lack of trust among your consumers.

2. Imagine.

In this step of the creative process, you engage in the imaginative, wild-and-crazy thinking that taps into your artistic side. Brainstorm about your product's functional value, competitive positions, and, very important, emotional fulfillment. For example, if you're selling luxury apparel, you're not really selling clothes for warmth and function; you're selling a sense of self, the power of expression, and a sense of superiority and success among your customers. Brainstorm on those angles and see how different your ideas will be.

3. Invent.

Take a critical look at all the wild ideas you imagined and choose one or a few that seem to best represent your ESP and your product's function. Find ways to make them practical and feasible. Build creative concepts around these ideas in ways that support the persona, values, and promises of your brand and don't clash or conflict with other branding efforts. Keeping your brand's image consistent across all communications and campaigns is essential.

4. Implement.

Identify ways to execute your campaign and new ideas across all channels and throughout your content marketing strategies. When launching a new idea, offer, or value, identify one or two words or a short phrase that can transcend all channels, including the following:

- POS displays
- Email
- Mobile messages
- Social media and website content
- Games
- Trade shows
- Print ads

REMEMBER

Your marketing themes can change from campaign to campaign, or product to product, but your brand value and positioning statements remain the same. You don't change your slogan with each new campaign, but you need to make sure any new themes you introduce support and complement your slogan and overall value statements.

You may need different sets of talents to imagine wild ideas and to implement them in a practical way. In fact, each of the four steps in the creative process (initiating, imagining, inventing, and implementing) requires different types of behavior, so invite more than your marketing team to participate. Invite people who represent your distribution, call center, research and development, accounting, and customer service teams to get their insights as well.

Elevating your creative thinking

Need some help getting your creative energy flowing? Check out these tips and real-life examples:

>> **Cross-promoting with a dissimilar business:** A nursery created a spring cross-promotion with a local bookshop. It provided the bookstore with bookmarks that featured garden plant identifications and photos, along with coupons worth 10 percent off all plant purchases. In exchange, the bookstore provided the nursery with a reference library of gardening books; the nursery included a sign on the rack, thanking the bookstore for providing the books, along with coupons offering 10 percent off on purchases at the bookstore.

>> **Making a splash in public:** A chiropractor had one side of his car decorated with a gigantic picture of a comfortable-looking sleeping person. On the other side was a picture of the same person, shown as a skeleton to illustrate how well aligned her spine was. The car drew considerable attention and increased new patient inquiries by 200 percent in the month following its introduction.

>> **Creating a game:** Games that can be played on mobile devices and result in free product as a prize can be highly successful in generating new sales and loyalty.

>> **Hiring a creative professional to brainstorm ideas with you:** Consider artists, inventors, and/or consultants who understand your space.

REMEMBER

Creativity is key to standing out in a cluttered marketplace among numerous ads, messages, and content to which consumers are exposed daily. But creativity has to be managed in a way that maintains relevance for your consumers at all touch points of the brand experience — from products to promotions, content, advertising, and sales and service. Use creativity to capture attention and engage with customers in ways that are memorable, not just different.

» **Developing a Facebook marketing strategy**

» **Using Twitter, Instagram, LinkedIn, and Pinterest**

» **Getting the word out with podcasts, webinars, and videos**

» **Making the most of advertising campaigns on the web**

» **Being smart about the digital tools you use**

Chapter **8**

Digital Tools and Tactics That Work

Marketing with digital channels today is somewhat like trying to hit a moving target as the tools, tactics, and trends change more quickly than most can imagine. And because nearly all marketing today is connected to a digital channel, platform, analytics tool, or device, the term *digital marketing* is somewhat of an oxymoron.

No matter what business you're in, the role you play, or the size and scope of your market, you need to understand and stay on top of digital marketing tools to succeed on any level.

Although digital technology introduces exciting opportunities to open new markets and engage with customers like never before, it also comes with the following challenges:

» Digital tools are constantly changing. As soon as marketers master one, another comes up.

» Because of the ability that digital technology offers for highly personalized communications, customers have grown to expect it, making traditional marketing methods less effective and putting more pressure on marketers to keep up with rapidly changing technological developments that enhance customers' overall experience.

» Being able to manage the breadth and depth that digital channels offer marketers for communicating to customers any time and any place is another challenge. In the old days of marketing, brand managers just had to worry about developing a clever campaign with a good offer and getting a good media buyer to negotiate ad buys with magazines, newspapers, radio and television stations, and outdoor companies. Now, we have to identify the best opportunities within numerous channel categories for several customer segments and then customize versions of all elements of each campaign to be personalized for every customer segment or persona, adapt the format for every channel we plan to use, and then deploy quickly and frequently. Oh, and then we have to monitor social media dialogue and online review sites and respond quickly to avoid losing consumer interest, our reputation, or sales.

Mind-boggling! But thankfully, manageable. The trick is to map out a detailed plan based on how your customers use and respond to digital channels to guide how you spend your time and resources communicating, placing ads, and creating meaningful experiences online. Otherwise, you can keep yourself busy and not really go anywhere.

After you have a plan in place as to which channels you need to use and how you need to use them, you then need to have a plan for which technology investments make the most sense for your desired reach, outcomes, and budget.

This chapter provides some insights on several digital channels that drive customer engagement and sales and some tips for how you can integrate these into your marketing plan. We also include guidelines on how to efficiently manage and deploy content across multiple channels in addition to those covered in Chapters 7 and 10.

TIP

If you want more in-depth information on the channels discussed here, check out *Social Media Marketing All-in-One For Dummies*, 4th Edition, by Jan Zimmerman and Deborah Ng (Wiley).

Exploring Digital Channels You Can't Ignore

To start, Table 8-1 lists current digital channels and tools you need to embrace, manage, and at least begin to master as you build your marketing plan and allocate your time and money. If resources are slim, pick a few to start with and then expand as you're able. Regardless, you need at least a basic understanding of the channels and tools your customers (and competitors) use to execute a sustainable marketing program and competitive business.

TABLE 8-1 **Digital Channels**

Social Channels	Digital Tools
Facebook	Podcasts
Twitter	Videos
LinkedIn	Webinars
Pinterest	Games
Instagram	Content management systems

Because Facebook has more monthly active users (MAUs) than Twitter, Instagram, and others combined, we'll start there.

Using Facebook for Engagement That Builds Sales

Facebook is an incredibly important marketing tool. If for some reason you don't believe us, check out the nearby "Facebook facts" sidebar. To effectively use Facebook for customer conversations, promotions, and relationship building, you need to build a content marketing plan specific to this channel and an advertising plan. Don't post anything just because you can. Posting without a messaging plan may actually do more harm than good because if it's not meaningful, you'll lose likes, follows, and readership, and each of these is hard to build back.

FACEBOOK FACTS

Following is some information from a report recently compiled by Zephoria Digital Marketing that helps to answer the question, "Just how big is Facebook?" These statistics may or may not surprise you; regardless, they're very telling that you can't ignore Facebook for your business. It's not just a "brag book" for parents and pet owners.

- 1.87 billion monthly active users — 16 percent year-over-year (YOY) growth

- 1.18 billion daily active users

- 1.03 billion mobile users daily — 22 percent YOY growth

If these facts aren't boggling enough about social media's role in our lives today, here are some more.

Facebook has daily:

- 4.75 billion pieces of content shared — up 94 percent YOY

- 4.5 billion likes

- 300 million photo uploads

Every 60 seconds:

- 510,000 comments

- 293,000 statuses updated

- 136,000 photos posted

And another fact for marketers to note: The average time per visit is 20 minutes. With all this content, that's not a lot of time to get customers' attention, engage them in meaningful dialogue, and inspire them to act in a desired manner.

Following are some guidelines for putting together a content and advertising plan for Facebook; however, this planning guide applies to all other social media channels mentioned in this chapter. Instead of repeating these tips for each channel, use the following as your guide for building a presence and dialogues with your customers on Twitter, Instagram, LinkedIn, and other sites.

Developing a successful Facebook plan

Facebook is where many people document their life story and share their greatest moments. It's also a great place for brands to tell their stories and do so in ways that support the values of their core customers. As you build a plan to tell your story and engage in dialogue with core customers, keep in mind that Facebook is for stories, not sales pitches. Using this channel the way consumers use it will help you achieve greater success and return on the time you spend posting, sharing, liking, and more.

Here are some key elements you need to establish as you work on your Facebook marketing plan:

>> **Define your purpose.** Do you want your Facebook page to be a place where you have meaningful dialogues with your customers? Or a site that promotes your products, provides promotional codes and discount coupons, announces your sales, and the like? Or is your page a place to share stories about your people and business to better humanize your brand? When you answer and prioritize these questions and others like them, you're better poised to make your Facebook efforts pay off.

>> **Set your goals.** Facebook offers many different opportunities and outcomes for businesses in all areas. The trick is to set specific goals and have a plan to help you measure your progress toward achieving them while using your time wisely.

Some goals you can achieve through Facebook include

- Learning what trends, attitudes, and needs are important to your customers at a given time

- Interacting with customers to discover what they like about your products and brand and what else you can be doing

- Attracting more prospects by posting about relevant topics

- Driving customers and prospects to your website where you can better direct them toward a transaction

- Growing your email permission database through Facebook promotions

- Communicating with customers and prospects for whom you don't have an email address

- Building your social presence and prospect base through likes, comments, and shares of your current followers

- Creating a stronger brand image

- Putting together a community, or a hive, around your brand

These same steps apply to other social media pages and channels, so just repeat the steps that apply when building out your brand's digital presence.

The following subsections present some tips and examples that will enable you to succeed at reaching many of these goals. But first, remember that you can't achieve any of these goals unless you have followers and friends connected to your page. Use all your social channels to invite people to connect with you on Facebook (and others like LinkedIn) and post content that's worth sharing with their friends to build your base. Always include links for your page on your website, emails, content elements, and in marketing materials.

Consider doing an email campaign for the sole purpose of getting people to follow you on Facebook and other channels. Let consumers know what they'll gain in terms of insights and interaction if they choose to follow or connect with you.

Determine your metrics

Like any program, make sure you have a mechanism to measure the impact of your efforts toward your goals so you can see whether you need more resources to keep up with the opportunities created or need to make some changes to have a better impact.

Facebook Insights — a dashboard with metrics and analytics for your page — is available on business pages and provides valuable insights to help you see what your followers liked and didn't like, engagement level per post, which posts got the most likes, and whether you got likes from searches, shares from others, or Facebook advertisements, and more. It's important to pay attention to trends and comments on your page so you can discover what matters most and identify problems before they escalate.

Learn

Opportunities to learn valuable and actionable insights on Facebook are many. For example, you can find out what matters most to your followers and what drives behavior from the dialogue you create, the questions you post, the comments you get back, the posts your customers like or don't like, games your customers play, and by watching what your competitors are doing.

Ask questions. Most people like to comment on Facebook and have their voice heard. Just look at all the "talk" during a political season, surrounding a common cause, or a sports matchup. Posting questions for your followers can provide some great insights from their answers and comments.

For example, if you're a carpet cleaning company, here are some questions you may want to ask:

When it comes to cleaning your carpets, what motivates you most?

- Having your house look clean and fresh?

- Getting rid of germs that can affect your health?

- Getting that brand new look back again?

People often respond if they like you, want to voice their opinion, or if you offer an incentive. Facebook has a poll application (find it at www.facebook.com/simple.polls) you can use to create and post and monitor results, making it easy to analyze. Or you can just post a question and see what kind of dialogue it inspires. With Facebook's poll application, you can share your poll by email, which helps increase traffic to your page.

TIP

If you have a small following, be careful about using the polls app versus just posting questions to spark dialogue. If few people respond to your poll, it can send a signal that you aren't worth following on Facebook.

Make your question or poll open-ended and thought provoking rather than a yes-or-no question. Instead of, "Do you like watching soccer?" ask, "What do you like most about watching women's soccer matches?" Doing so will help you discover your customers' values and motivators.

REMEMBER

You need to monitor your page and control the content instead of letting others control it for you. You don't want customers to go to your Facebook page and see customer complaints to which no one responded. When this happens, newcomers to your site see a good reason not to do business with you and no explanation or resolution that could inspire them to still give you a chance.

Interact

Clearly, you can interact with customers in many ways on Facebook; you're really just limited by your time and imagination. Because Coca-Cola has one of the most liked and followed Facebook pages, with more than 102 million likes and followers, its page is a good one from which to gain ideas and inspiration.

Coke interacts with Facebook fans by frequently posting about things that matter to them. On January 9, 2017, it posted a congratulations to Clemson University for winning the college football championship. It got 36,000 views, 966 likes, and 104 shares. Never missing an opportunity, it also posted a reminder on January 19, 2017, about National Popcorn Day and encouraged fans to enjoy a movie with a friend. This got 22,000 views, 630 likes, and 60 shares.

And when someone posts about Coke, the brand responds. One fan commented on how he liked the little Coke cans but couldn't find them. Coke responded by asking for his zip code (in a personal message, of course) so it could help him find them. On another occasion, a fan asked whether Santa would give him a job. Regardless of whether this was sarcastic or serious, Coke responded with a link to its employment page.

The key to building relationships on Facebook is twofold:

>> Post content worth reading and commenting on.

>> Respond to the good, the bad, the funny, and the serious.

If consumers feel ignored or invisible on your page, you'll lose them.

If you want shares to help build your reach, the most effective way is to post things that are fun, engaging, humorous, or just really cool. Cool photos, funny videos, and inspirational stories seem to get the most shares.

Build

Keep in mind that the best content isn't always about driving a sale but more about engaging and creating rapport, trust, and communications with your followers. When you achieve these attributes, sales will follow. The best content strategy is to post fun, positive, inspiring, and relatable content that tells a story in which your customers can see themselves.

Creating content that gets response, dialogue, and leads

Creating a story in which readers can easily see themselves is the best way to spark interaction, dialogue, and new leads. But simply posting a well-written status update is not likely going to fill up your inbox with new prospects waiting to be sold something. However, if you post content that invites response and interaction that includes others' thoughts, feedback, and expertise, you will be more likely to start a conversation that could get you the right kinds of leads for your business.

Here are some tips for lead-generating content on Facebook:

>> **Be brief.** Remember, people typically have short attention spans, which seem to be getting shorter all the time with all the distractions and demands on their attention. To up engagement, keep your content short. If you want to

provide more information about a topic in a post, provide a link to a full article.

» **Direct to website.** Directing people to your website for more information on a post you shared is always a good idea, and then be sure to follow up by asking people for their email to get the full story. Offer white papers, links to columns, links to news coverage for your brand, and so on. You can also post about special sales and discounts available on your website.

» **Invite a response.** Don't just post a point, an opinion, or a fact. Spark dialogue by asking fans what they think. Do they agree? Share your stories and encourage followers to do the same. One comment often inspires another, which makes your page more interesting and gives fans more attention for their own voice, too.

» **Provide tips.** People like how-to tips and will often follow a site just to get more. If you have something of value that's actionable and helps others, post it. If you can, break up your list of how-to tips into a series to give you content that inspires people to come back for more.

» **Use hashtags.** Hashtags simply give your post more chances of getting seen, on Facebook and on other channels. Include at least one but not too many, and some research says that two work best.

TIP

Prepare a content plan and stick with it. It's easy to spend all day posting and reading comments on your page and others' pages and accomplish little, if anything, else. To avoid wasting your time and that of your followers and friends, make your content meaningful and actionable.

REMEMBER

Facebook is best used for interacting and building relationships. If you use it too much to promote sales and offers, you risk losing credibility and fans.

Advertising on Facebook

If you're not able to build your base through the tactics in the previous sections, or you want to get to mass quickly, consider advertising on Facebook. You can do this through boosting your post for a nominal fee or by purchasing Page Like or Offer ads. Here's the difference:

» **Boost post:** You pay a nominal free, maybe $5, to get your post pushed out to people in a demographic you choose. The more you pay, the more people see your post.

» **Page like ads:** These are ads with a Like button for your page that are sent to audiences of your choice. If they "like" the button, they become followers of your page.

>> **Offer ads:** You can use an Offer function provided by Facebook to post offers on your page. You can pay to have that offer boosted to people not following you to get more exposure for it. If you have a Facebook page, you likely see these in your News Feed quite a bit.

Building Your Twitter Presence

Although Twitter can be frustrating for the long-winded because you have to keep your posts to 140 characters or less, it does add value for building your brand's presence. For one, Twitter helps start conversations with followers and can be used to post links to your more in-depth content on LinkedIn, Facebook, and, of course, your website.

A key advantage of Twitter is that it helps you find people with similar interests by suggesting people you can follow. And if you post enough interesting content on a given topic, Twitter encourages others to follow you, too.

You can build your Twitter base by doing the following:

>> Searching a keyword related to your brand and then clicking on People associated with that term. For example, searching "consumer behavior" on Twitter results in dozens upon dozens of people to follow.

>> Including hashtags for your tweets so that people can find your posts.

>> Posting your Twitter handle in your email signature, on your web page, and on handouts for trade shows and live events. Encourage followers on your other social channels to follow you on Twitter as well.

>> Creating an interesting profile page and tweeting regularly about things that are of interest to consumers interested in your product and brand.

>> Tweeting about something more than just your latest offer or white paper. Start conversations on objective themes to attract like-minded people.

>> Linking your Twitter account to your Facebook account so that your tweets show up on Facebook, too.

REMEMBER

Twitter has more than 300 million users and is still growing. It keeps you connected in real time to your customers and maintains your presence in channels that consumers use daily in all industries.

Igniting Your Social Presence on Instagram

Instagram is a photo-centric social network that lets you tell your story through imagery — photos and videos. It's popular among younger audiences and omits a lot of the chatter, good and bad, from other social sites. In January 2017, Instagram had around 600 million users, making it another must-use site for reaching today's consumers.

Because a picture can be "worth a thousand words," Instagram is a great way to communicate quickly about brand events or happenings and to tell your story through the power of images. Most people access it via their smartphone, which limits your reach, but it helps boost your mobile strategy and share your brand stories.

The best way to be successful on Instagram is to use high-quality photos that are interesting, inspiring, and engaging. You can also upload your Instagram photos to other social sites, including Facebook, Twitter, Flickr, and Foursquare.

Expanding Your Network through LinkedIn

Although many people use LinkedIn to advance their careers and build far-reaching professional networks, LinkedIn also serves a valuable role for businesses. It's different from other social media channels and needs to be treated as such, or it can backfire on you. For one, LinkedIn is *not* for promoting products and attracting leads; it's for promoting your industry expertise, knowledge, insights, and business happenings and for posting your job openings. LinkedIn is widely used by B2B brands to identify decision makers at companies with whom they'd like a relationship and to strike up a meaningful conversation. Many companies in the B2C space use it to promote their workplace culture and attract new employees because it has a popular job center, which attracts job seekers and employers.

As of this writing, LinkedIn has 467 million members, making it another must channel for businesses, especially B2B. IBM's page is a great example of how businesses can use LinkedIn. It has more than 3.2 million followers and keeps the content on target and worth reading.

Here's a brief overview of the fundamental elements of a LinkedIn page for businesses:

>> **About Us:** Like personal profiles on LinkedIn, your page starts with a summary of your business. You can state whatever you want to about your company and change it as often as you want to.

- >> **Connections:** LinkedIn shows visitors to your page any common connections you both have so they can see who else values your page and who they can reach out to for an introduction or conversation. Having a big network makes you and your brand more valuable to others and sends a signal that you're successful at what you do because people want to follow your insights.

- >> **Showcase pages:** You can add showcase pages to your main page that provide details about your product lines. IBM has 11 showcase pages, which include IBM Watson Health, IBM Internet of Things, and IBM Mobile.

- >> **Updates:** Your updates are your posts, articles, links to articles, insights you want to share, and other information that helps define your brand. For a business, these may include inspirational quotes from your CEO, financial results, announcements about live events on other channels, such as Facebook, and insights about your product and development and of your corporate social responsibility.

The following sections explore some of the best features on LinkedIn for businesses and marketers alike.

Groups

A good use of LinkedIn is to create your own group. Find a topic of interest in which you're a thought leader and start a group to share insights and exchange ideas. If you start a group, your role is to set the rules, monitor posts, manage posts, initiate conversations, and keep it going. Every time a new post is made on your group page, all members get an email notification, which helps to keep your topic and expertise on members' minds. A group is tough to keep up with if you're stretched for time, so make sure you have a plan for keeping your group active and inspired.

Here are some tips for getting a group going:

- >> **Define the purpose.** Is this group for exchanging ideas about innovations, solutions, trends, breakthroughs, and case studies on a given topic?

- >> **Set the rules.** Put your purpose and rules on your site for all to see. If your rules are no job posts or promotions of any kind, follow through. As the manager, you can delete posts and eliminate violators.

- >> **Invite members of your network to join, and promote your group on your individual page as well as other social channels.** Keep inviting people to join regularly, because the bigger the group, the greater your network and reach.

>> **Monitor all activity.** If you set your group up to be an open group, you'll likely get a lot of fake accounts and spam posts. If you don't delete these, you may lose the members you value.

>> **Post often.** Post articles, insights, links to white papers, videos, research findings, event coverage, and personnel news. Keep your content business-oriented and leave the promotional, fun posts for other channels like Facebook and Twitter.

Engagement

The best way to get noticed on LinkedIn is to post meaningful articles or updates several times a week if possible. Topics that get engagement include articles you've written, news coverage of your brand, events, trade shows, personnel news, how-to guides, checklists, and links to your blog or new information on your website.

Here are some tips for driving engagement:

>> Include a link to a landing page in your posts; by doing so, you can double your engagement.

>> Post thoughtful questions and encourage others to share their insights.

>> Add an image. LinkedIn claims that images can result in a 98 percent higher comment rate.

>> Link to your videos on YouTube, which will play directly in your LinkedIn feed and could increase your share rate by 75 percent.

>> Respond to comments in a way that encourages more comments and gets more people commenting.

TIP

For every post, LinkedIn provides analytics, such as the number of impressions, clicks, interactions, and percentage of engagement to help you see which topics do best. Like other sites, you can pay to sponsor an update for more money and more exposure.

Promoting Your Brand with Pinterest

With an average monthly active user number of around 150 million, Pinterst can't be ignored, especially by B2C businesses that want their products and creative uses of their products to go viral. Pinterest is widely used as a bookmark of ideas for recipes, home decorating, crafts, holiday décor and goodies, fashion, and do-it-yourself projects.

Per a report from October 2016 posted on www.expandedramblings.com, a site that posts stats about various social channels, 85 percent of Pinterest users are female and roughly 13 percent are male. Nearly 70 percent of all users are millennials. Around 55 percent of online shoppers in the United States claim that Pinterest is their favorite social media platform.

So if you cater to women who like to make, bake, follow fashion trends, and the like, Pinterest just might be for you. If users like your post, they can really increase your exposure by sending it to their email and Facebook contacts or sharing it on other social channels.

REMEMBER

Pinterest is an idea board. You pin what you like, and your pins get communicated via other social channels, giving the creators of those ideas added exposure. The better the picture and the most clever the ideas, the greater the number of pins you'll receive.

You can create boards of images and ideas of interest to you and include images from others on these boards. If people click on these images, they can be directed away from your page so be careful about sending viewers to other pages or sites.

Pinterest can also be a good place to sell your products. You can promote your pin like on other sites and even set up a shopping cart so people can purchase from you without leaving Pinterest. The shopping cart works much like those on Amazon.com and eBay. You're buying from a seller using its platform. If you use Pinterest for business, make sure you set up a business account so you can get analytics about your most popular pins, shares, repins, likes, and demographic information about those visiting your Pinterest account.

For more details about setting up and managing Pinterest accounts, check out *Pinterest For Dummies* and *Pinterest Marketing For Dummies,* both by Kelby Carr and published by Wiley.

Discovering Digital Tools That Drive Brands

Beyond understanding the basics for using popular social media channels, you need to discover how to use popular digital tools for building your brand presence, network, customer base, and, of course, sales. When choosing digital tools and activities, you should focus on those that can best help you build your visibility, grow your social networks, and, most importantly, grow your in-house email list. Building your email list is truly one of the most important outcomes of all digital activities because email drives some of the best ROI you can get from any marketing activity today. Check out Chapter 10 for ROI comparisons for various marketing channels.

Some of the most visible and affordable digital tools appropriate for any business include podcasts, webinars, videos, and games, which we discuss in the following sections.

Podcasts

Started in 2003, podcasts are making a big comeback, and for good reason. For consumers, they play right to their mobile and digital lifestyle. You can listen in the car, at the gym, at the spa, while grocery shopping, while walking, while riding the metro — anywhere you can take your phone or tablet.

For marketers, podcasts are a great way to achieve many of the goals we discuss in this book, which include

» Educating your target consumer groups to provide objective decision assistance while positioning your team as trusted advisors and sources for key information

» Establishing you and your leadership team as authorities in your space

» Building your email list and social networks

» Increasing your SEO results

» Adding value to your website through more valuable content

Doing a podcast gives you access to key businesspeople who wouldn't otherwise take your call. Instead of calling to sell them something, you're calling to invite them to get exposure. This can help you establish relationships with influencers in your space and get them talking about you and your products. Whenever you interview a guest, encourage him to email his networks to listen to the podcast, introducing you, your content, your podcast, your leadership, and your brand to a network that you otherwise wouldn't have access to.

Before starting a podcast, you need to be sure you're fully committed. It doesn't do any brand any good to spend time and resources to launch a new program and then not stick with it. Podcasts take planning, time, and effort, but, when done right, they can deliver a strong return.

Here are some tips from various podcasters to help you get started:

>> **Target a niche group.** If you start a podcast on a broad topic trying to reach a broad audience, you'll likely be broadly disappointed. You'll be more effective if you specialize with a niche topic to build momentum and get you noticed.

>> **Decide on a format.** Most podcasts are between 20 and 30 minutes. Formats range from interview-type shows to how-to tips, tutorials, and such. Choose a format that you can keep up with and that keeps your listeners listening.

>> **Keep it brief.** Our society suffers from attention deficit due to all the information overload we experience daily, so treat your podcast accordingly. Get your main message across early on to avoid disconnects, and don't ramble on just to fill the time. Stay focused, meaningful, and on target.

>> **Commit to frequency.** Some successful podcasters claim that they podcast three times a week to get started; however, a good frequency to maintain is once a week.

>> **Build a library.** Before you promote and launch your podcast, record several sessions so you can air content consistently and build your base.

>> **Invest in quality.** Make sure you have a good microphone and deliver good quality without noise clutter that can be distracting and cause people to stop listening.

>> **Link to your digital assets.** Post your podcast archives on your website and link them to your Twitter account and your blog. Make them easily available for people to find and of course share with others.

>> **Promote it everywhere.** Invite people to listen to your podcasts through email campaigns, LinkedIn announcements, Facebook posts, and so on. Post links to your podcasts on bookmark sites, like Reddit and Quibb, and YouTube channels.

You can use your podcast to grow your email base as well by offering free material to your listeners. Encourage listeners to go to one of your social sites to download a paper, a coupon, and so on in exchange for registering with their email.

TIP

If you get enough downloads and listeners, you can even monetize your blog through sponsorships. Some of the top podcasts, like *Entrepreneur on Fire*, get thousands of dollars a month in sponsorships.

The most popular platform for podcasts is Apple iTunes. Other platforms include Stitcher, TuneIn, and BlogTalkRadio. And given that 55 podcasts are being recorded at any given moment and that 24 million podcast minutes are recorded a month, it's time to get thinking about how you can join the fray but be better and more interesting.

TIP

Just for fun, the top podcast, which has broken all records with more than 59 million downloads, is hosted by comedian Adam Carolla, who rants on social topics in ways that make people giggle out loud. So take note: Make your podcast fun, a bit disruptive, and borderline irreverent, and dare to be daring. People like listening to things that have a little surprise element, not just what they expect to hear.

Webinars

Although podcasts work well for B2C and B2B brands, the webinar is a powerful tool mainly for B2B brands that can help with lead generation, relationship building, and cementing a position of authority in any given industry. In many ways, webinars are easier to pull off than podcasts because you don't have to commit to a weekly schedule or produce a series to have ready to go before you launch your program.

The benefits of webinars are many. Here are just a few:

>> **Affordability:** You can use free apps such as Google Hangouts, or you can subscribe to a service like GoToWebinar, WebEx, or ReadyTalk. Google Hangouts has limitations, like no ability to charge attendees and can handle up to only ten people in a single video/audio call, which can seriously limit your success. Skype also provides a free service for group voice and video calls and screen sharing, but you're limited to 25 people.

You can subscribe to services that can handle up to 100 callers for around $50 to $100 a month. Your fees will depend on what features you want and your attendee number limits. Check out some of the webinar platforms to find what works for your budget. Some of the features you may want beyond audio and voice calls and screen sharing include

- Archiving

- Mobile-friendly features

- Multiple rooms

- Ability to edit your recordings

- Integration with social media and Outlook

- Ability to change presenters

- Ability to monitor attendees' focus (get signals when they open other screens on their computer during your presentation)

>> **Authority:** When you share knowledge that enhances a customer's life, you become a valued advisor and authority, and quite often, that positioning can

take price out of the equation for purchase decisions. Also, when people learn from someone, they tend to trust that person and give him their business.

>> **Awareness:** Even if you get only 20 people to attend your webinar, you'll likely get a lot more visibility than that. If you promote your webinar on your social networks and to your email list, news channels for your industry, and more, you can get literally thousands of impressions for your expertise and position as an authority on the topic on which you're presenting. This is worth it alone because most of this visibility is free.

As you consider systems to subscribe to, look for a system that will grow with your needs. If you want to do small-group events or weekly webinars with client teams, you can keep your numbers small and use a free system.

Following are some tips for organizing and pulling off a successful webinar, or two:

>> **Be free.** Consumers are used to getting good content for free these days and are more and more reluctant to pay for it. So even though you may charge for strategic advice or in-depth training courses, you should still create a webinar that has substance. Just don't give away so much that you cannibalize sales of your other programs. This mainly applies to consulting services or agencies that provide strategic advice and sales or marketing training as part of their revenue streams.

>> **Be smart.** A webinar should help to tease your bigger offering — be it consulting, training, software services, and so forth. You need to position your webinar as valuable on its own while subtly getting people more interested in your programs that aren't free. You have to give away a little bit of your expertise to whet the appetite for more. Just pay attention to how much you give away that attendees can execute on their own so that you don't end up cutting yourself out of future sales.

>> **Be relevant.** Pick a topic that's meaningful, current, and provides realistic actionables for attendees. Purchasers will invest their time if they believe they'll gain something they can put to use toward achieving their business goals.

>> **Be professional.** If you use an app and decide to use a webcam and your screen for the webinar, keep it professional. Nothing is quite as distracting as seeing a speaker talking in his bedroom with a messy bed in the background. True story.

>> **Be giving.** Provide takeaways that are actually useful. Many presenters offer their slides as a bonus for attending the webinar. Others offer discounts on products, services, or further training programs that aren't free. And others

offer white papers or free audits of attendees' marketing material or other items. Many times those free audits turn into great long-term clients, and they can signal a vote of confidence in what you do and your willingness to invest in the process.

>> **Be present.** Market your webinar everywhere. Post invitations on all your social media channels. Send notices to trade associations, chambers of commerce, and business alliances. Email invitations to prospects, customers, and channel partners. Post on LinkedIn groups as well as your own page. Get it out there that you're an authority and are sharing secrets to success. After you're done, record your session, create a PDF, and send links to anyone who didn't attend. Archive it on your website, too.

REMEMBER

A big reason to do webinars is to build your base. You're giving people knowledge for free so make sure you get their email address in return. Require contact information to register for the event and access any archived files.

No-shows to webinars are quite common. We've had around 1,000 people register for a webinar and only 600 actually show up. That's okay and expected. The attrition rate is fairy high for free events because things come up, and if you haven't paid for it, you're not losing anything. Be sure you get emails for all registrants so you can offer the archive link both to those who attended and those who didn't.

Videos

You've likely noticed videos have been taking over photos in your Facebook and LinkedIn feeds and are popping up more frequently in your email boxes, and slide shows on websites are moving over for videos. HubSpot shares some powerful statistics to validate why this happening and why you need to jump on this bandwagon, too. Here are just a few:

>> Videos in email lead to a jump in click-through rates of between 200 and 300 percent.

>> Videos on a landing page can help your conversions increase by 80 percent.

>> Videos combined with a full-page ad can boost engagement by 22 percent.

>> Videos can increase likelihood of purchase by 64 percent among online shoppers.

>> Videos included in a real estate listing can increase inquiries by 403 percent.

>> Videos inspire 50 percent of executives to seek more information about a product.

>> Videos inspire 65 percent of executives to visit a marketer's website and 39 percent to call a vendor.

>> Most importantly, 90 percent of video watchers say that videos help them make purchase decisions, and 92 percent of those viewing them on mobile devices share videos with others.

We could go on, but the point is clear: *You need to create videos if you want to engage customers and sell more products.* And because YouTube is the second-largest search engine, next to Google — well, enough said.

Another reason you must include video is because most of your competitors are doing it, and that can leave you out in the cold if you're not.

The following sections explore ways to create effective videos for any business as well as specifics for B2C and B2B.

Creating effective videos

The one challenge of using videos is that a lot of videos are competing with each other. In fact, on average, users are exposed to 32.3 videos a month, or roughly 1 a day. So how do you create videos that build your business and use them effectively in your marketing mix? Check out these tips:

>> **Create an emotional reaction that drives people to contact you for further information.** This is where it gets fun. Like all things you do in any medium — print, digital, or mobile — your content needs to have actionable value, and that value can be improving people's circumstances, inspiring them to live a better life, or guiding them to do their job better so they achieve their goals and advance their career.

>> **Regardless of your business genre, keep your video short and to the point.** This isn't your chance to produce a Hollywood blockbuster. It's simply a way to tell your story with a medium that appeals to the senses and makes your brand come to life. Keep your videos around two to three minutes long.

>> **Before you debut your videos publicly, test them.** Ask non-employees and even non-customers to sit through your videos and give you feedback. Good questions to ask include

- Did it keep your interest?

- What was the main message you took away from this video?

- Did it inspire you to inquire more about our product or service? If yes, why? If no, why not?

- Was the length appropriate?

- Did you think the production quality of this video was in line with other brand videos you've watched?

>> **Like any marketing communications, always include a call to action and a response mechanism.** Stay away from promotions because they'll expire before you're ready to stop using the video. Make it clear how to contact you for more information through email, website, phone numbers, and social channels.

>> **Use professional footage and images.** Your video can be text based, like a slide show, or it can be a true video with all the moving parts. Regardless of the format you choose, use the highest resolution and quality possible. Your reputation is on the line per the quality you project. If you're a high-tech company and you use low-tech video, that transfers to the perceived quality of the products you develop and sell.

>> **Create a YouTube channel to house all your videos.** You can archive videos on YouTube and on your website. For either option, include a transcript of your video to help you achieve higher SEO results.

Looking at B2C and B2B considerations

For B2C, you can add a little more fun and focus on life messages, not just brand messages. Coca-Cola does a great job of this. Its YouTube channel has more than 1.2 million subscribers and its views have topped more than 22 million for a single video that's about spending more time offline and enjoying the journey of life in the real world. Coke's "Happiness Truck" video, which shows a Coke truck dispensing gifts to people on the streets in Rio, has more than 1.6 million views — another inspirational mission and message that helped build the emotional equity of the Coke brand.

Here are some tips for using videos in the B2B world:

>> Create product demo videos to showcase the features that set your products apart.

>> Show how your products compare to competitors' when applicable and how your products fulfill your viewers' needs.

>> Include statements from your company leaders to show their vision and help tell your brand story.

>> Include customers talking about their experience with your product and your team. Video testimonials are powerful because viewers can see the body language, the smiles, and the looks of relief and also hear the excitement in voices that written testimonials don't provide.

Again, consumers like to see brand stories in which they can see themselves. They want to be the proud father or the mom being thanked by her Olympian child as shown in Proctor & Gamble's "Thank You Mom" ad series that makes many moms cry no matter how many times they watch it. They want to be the vacationer on the beach, the newly engaged couple, the happy family, or the thriving executive.

Find ways to associate your brand with what matters most to your consumers and then get creative and start writing video scripts that tell your story in conjunction with the goals they have for their lives.

Online review sites

Another digital tool you can't ignore are online review sites, like Yelp and Google. Although you don't populate content directly on these sites, you can influence it.

When you have a happy customer, ask him to write a review on Yelp, Google, and other sites you know your customers use. Research by Nielsen shows that more than 70 percent of consumers trust online reviews, even though they don't know the reviewers. If people read a bad review about your business, you could lose their interest right away.

TIP

You need to continuously monitor all review sites to look for comments about your brand. Respond immediately to negative comments and offer a solution. You can turn an angry customer into a happy one if you resolve his concern quickly and appropriately. And you're showing prospects that you're willing to do what it takes to keep customers happy.

Many of the complaints on these sites are petty, but the one-star review from a customer that had to wait five minutes more than expected can take your average down and make you look bad in comparison with competitors.

Monitoring reviews will also help you determine whether you're being sabotaged by competitors posting fake reviews to ruin your reputation. If this is the case, you can report it to the review site and try to get this resolved.

REMEMBER

You can't repair your reputation if you don't know it's damaged. Monitor review sites regularly and always respond. Thank good reviewers for their time and words and offer to work with those who weren't so happy with you. Research shows that when you resolve customer issues, you increase their loyalty to you.

Posting testimonials on your website isn't as credible as a review posted on a third-party site, which you didn't review and approve ahead of time. Take the time to ask customers to do this. If you treat them well, they'll usually find time for you.

Fun and games work, too

Marketing is really all about fun and games — literally and figuratively as gamification is rapidly increasing as a profitable way to engage customers and build relationships. Everyone likes the thrill of trying something different, playing a game to test his chances for success, and getting unexpected surprises.

REMEMBER

Games tap into people's most powerful drivers of choice — the neurotransmitters that trigger hormonal rushes that make people feel happy, excited, energized, or fearful and threatened. Those feelings dictate behavior, and when people get feelings that make them feel confident and powerful, they go back for more. Games do this! And when games are associated with brands, people assign those good feelings accordingly and often go back for more.

In a world that seems to thrive on instant gratification, games can be very rewarding. Games reward behavior, and that behavior can be as simple as making a purchase, sharing a post on social media, referring a friend, and so on. Brands win, too, by getting results pretty quickly when they deliver a game that has a reward attached to it. For example, if a consumer completes a behavior, such as registering for your newsletter, you can send him a game that has a reward attached to it as a token of appreciation. He plays the game and gets a reward, and that makes him happy and willing to engage with you again.

Todd McGee, CEO of CataBoom, an automated game company, points out that giving customers a game to play that enables them to win a reward has a more powerful reaction than just giving them a reward because "winning" releases that dopamine rush (as discussed in Chapter 2). When that happens, it increases positive feelings about the experience and brand exponentially.

You can create games in various formats, such as digital scratch cards, slot machines, trivia, puzzles, and polls. You can even create skill-based games that present a little more challenge but can also increase engagement as consumers keep trying to win.

While the nature and creativity of games played may change over time, human nature never will. People like the thrill of the chase and the chance to win something. And the more you can tap into that for your brand and provide a "winning" experience, the greater your loyalty will be.

TIP

Game platforms come in a variety of options and include SaaS models like that offered by CataBoom. To see examples of how you can create games and use them to engage your customers, visit www.cataboom.com/games.

To do games right and within regulations for social media and others venues, you need to work with a game expert.

Getting customers to come back

Brands using gamification find that customers do indeed come back for more. Games that offer a prize, such as a free product, for winning are becoming regular points of engagement between brands and consumers. If it takes just a few seconds of time to engage and the payoff is to win something worthwhile, people keep going back.

McGee has seen 80 percent of customers who were sent a game from a brand return to that game to keep playing for prizes. This kind of return participation is making games a new type of loyalty program, especially if games pay off in product prizes or points that can be redeemed for products of choice.

REMEMBER

Rewards aren't always tangible. A good reward can be just knowing you beat your own score or reached a level of play you didn't think you could. It's not always about the end reward but more about how you felt during the experience. Brands that spark dopamine experiences are more likely to spark greater customer satisfaction and loyalty.

Consumers like to win experiences, not just "stuff." Think about offering unique content, special access to VIP services or offers, or a chance to do something people wouldn't normally get a chance to do.

Engaging customers

When customers play your games, they're engaged with your brand even when they're not actively shopping. This kind of increased engagement often leads to more sales and enhanced loyalty. CataBoom has seen 50 percent of targeted consumers engage with brands when games are delivered along with a reward.

Higher engagement pays off in many ways, such as the following:

>> Positive experiences that drive positive feelings make people want to engage with the brand in various settings, online and offline.

>> Customers tend to tell others about their positive brand experiences by posting online or verbally referring others to a brand.

>> When people engage with a brand on multiple levels, they tend to trust it more, and when they trust that brand, they purchase more.

TIP

Games can be used to accrue points to cash in for big prizes or to reward instantly with $1 or $5 off your next purchase. Instead of sending coupons like others do, you can give your customers a more engaging experience through games.

Advertising on the Web

Given the huge amount of time consumers spend online, we can't dismiss the importance of online advertising in addition to social media activity. Here's some perspective: Nielson reported in June 2016 that American adults spend about 10 hours and 39 minutes consuming media each day across various screens and channels, including tablets, smartphones, computers, multimedia devices, video games, radio, DVDs, DVRs, and of course TV. Of a 24-hour day, that is substantial. Think about it. If you add 8 hours for sleep, you're now up to 18 hours a day of time committed, leaving about 6 hours for all else, like eating, dressing, finding your keys, commuting to work, and then, of course, your work activities that don't involve a screen.

Although that number may seem staggering, it's also very telling of the importance of your brand being "seen" on screens. Following are some insights and guidelines for how to do this through advertising.

Search-term marketing

People conduct millions of online searches a day on search engines like Google, Yahoo!, and Bing. Advertising on these sites in any format can clearly get your brand name exposed to a lot of potential prospects.

The challenge is to get your site to show up on the first page of a search listing that likely produces millions of results. To do this, you can bid to purchase the top search terms, but that is usually very expensive. If you're in a general category, like pet supplies, bidding on and getting the best search terms to boost your ranking may be out of reach per your resources, and there's a good chance that others in your space have locked up those best words that currently fall on the first page of results.

For example, if you're in the pet supply business, consumers searching the term "pet supplies" will likely get millions of results. Good luck getting on top of that list and buying those terms.

An alternative is to purchase *long-tail keywords* — that is, long descriptive terms, not just the main universal term. A long-tail keyword search may be "pet supplies Denver, CO," which generates a lot fewer results because it's a narrower search. If you go a bit deeper and search "pet supplies self-grooming Denver, CO," you'll get even fewer results.

Various groups researching search trends have discovered that 60 to 70 percent of page views result from long-tail keywords. If consumers are using long-tail searches so should businesses when it comes to buying search terms, not just because you can capture a lot of views for your URL but also because they're much cheaper.

TIP

For marketers, this signals a big opportunity. Find out what customers like best about your products and determine what you want to be known or found by — your inventory, special services, experiences, or location. Buy those long-tail terms on Google AdWords and see how much more exposure you get.

Google AdWords for ads as text, banners, and more

With Google AdWords, you create a campaign, such as an offer, and then decide whether you want to have it show up as text in search listings, a display ad, such as a banner on the top of the page, a video ad on YouTube, or an app ad, which runs across the entire Google network. You then choose the following:

>> Geographical area, or target searchers in a given area.

>> Radius, or target searchers within a certain radius of your place of business.

>> Which search terms you want to bid on so your ad gets top visibility.

>> Your budget. You may pay $30 a day to have your ad get top billing for browsers in your area searching the terms you bid on. You pay only for actual clicks so AdWords sends you only as many as your budget allows.

You get continuous access to your results — how many people see your ads, how many clicked through to your website, or how many called you for more information. AdWords also manages ads on YouTube because Google owns it.

TIP

WordStream, an online advertising agency, offers a free AdWords performance grader to help you see whether you're getting good results or wasting your money on your current words. Although it wants you to buy its services as a result of your score, it may be worth checking out at www.wordstream.com.

Here's a brief outline for starting an AdWords campaign:

1. **Set up a free AdWords account.**

   Just go to www.adwords.google.com.

2. **Decide on the format you want — search-term ad or text among the listings, display/banner ad, video ad, and so on.**

   AdWords has templates you can use for pretty much any format.

3. **Link your ad to key terms you think people will use in searches.**

   Do this by following a specific search engine's instructions for advertisers and entering your bids for specific search terms in the relevant form. Again, long-tail keywords are less expensive, more available, and work.

4. **Tell the Internet search engine how much you'll pay for a click on your ad.**

   This is your *bid*. For example, we may commit to a bid of 50 cents for a click on the search term "marketing advice." So if someone follows our link from his search to our website, we owe Google 50 cents. If our bid is higher than anyone else's bid, our listing appears before any other commercial listings at the top of the searcher's screen, which increases the probability of that person clicking on our listing.

5. **You track the results.**

   Based on what you learn, you can keep tweaking your ad, the formats you use, your terms, your reach, and so on until you get the results you want and need.

TIP

Take a look at monthly and year-to-year trends in searches on Google by using Google Trends (www.google.com/trends). This site can alert you to slow periods (searches for many business-oriented terms fall off sharply in December), allowing you to time your pay-per-click advertising to peak search periods.

Getting the most out of each format

With a text search ad, you pay to have your URL and brief description at the top of the search listing. This consists of a headline, your URL, phone number, a one-line description, your address, and some links to key pages on your website. You may want to have a page go straight to your top seller, or your About Us page. You need to use your words wisely and stick to terms that create emotionally relevant reactions, intrigue, and interest for these to work.

Banner ads (those brightly colored rectangles at the top of popular web pages) are the web's answer to display advertising in a print medium or outdoor advertising on a billboard. They're good for building awareness of your brand, but not much more than that. Whether you place them through an online agency or AdWords, you need to have a good, compelling headline that gives people a reason to click and learn more. It can be a strong call to action or a statement or visual that creates curiosity and intrigue. Have your ad direct people to a landing page about the offer you promoted so you can keep the momentum going toward a conversion. For ideas on banner ad designs, offers, headlines, and creative that work, just search for "good banner ads" and you'll get plenty of sites with fun examples.

TIP

Like with outdoor billboards, a lot of copy won't get noticed or read. Keep it simple and to the point. It helps to have your URL on your ads in case people don't click through right away so you have at least gained exposure for your web page.

You can place your ad on sites beyond the AdWords platform. Explore online ad agencies and brokers for good rates on good placements, and then monitor your results.

In addition, web ad agencies offer lots of creative options, including interactive ads such as *widgets*, which are banners with an overlay of a pop-up interactive box that usually asks for an email address in exchange for a chance to win some contest or prize. You can also animate a pop-up or regular display ad or include video in it. Or you can use one of the skyscraper formats to create something that looks like an old-fashioned printed coupon, with the addition of a live form for entering an email address and linking to a landing page where the offer's details are provided and the deal is sealed.

Then there's the *interactive*, a web display ad that invites the viewer to try his hand at something entertaining or useful. For example, a kitchen design company may run an interactive display ad with content aimed at homeowners and remodelers with a call to action, such as "Click here to use our kitchen design software for free." The trick with interactive web ads is to quickly send people to a landing page where they fill in a short registration form, allowing you to capture their information before you give them access to the free tool or toy.

TIP

Like anything with marketing, it's easy to get carried away and not realize how much you're spending on a given initiative. Set a budget before you start purchasing space online and AdWords. If online marketing seems to be working well, maybe spend 10 to 25 percent of your ad budget accordingly, or 1 to 2 percent of your revenues.

If your web marketing efforts lose money by not delivering enough leads to pay off, move on. Don't spend good money on bad results. Remember, too, that if an ad doesn't work on a small scale, it's not going to work on a big scale. Keep experimenting with formats, messages, and offers until you find a combination that produces results you need.

Using Automated Customization to Work Smarter and Faster

With the advent of all the digital channels and data-driven insights we have today, we face a new set of challenges. One of the biggest challenges is how to manage, produce, and effectively deploy all the content needed to reach target audiences with relevant messages across an expanding array of digital and even traditional channels.

As mentioned earlier and throughout this book, you need to customize content to individuals and personas to gain attention, influence behavior, and capture sales. But if you market to thousands of customers, sorted into various customer segments, with different needs, different cultures, different locations, and different generational attitudes, you have a lot of repurposing to do for each campaign you execute. Being able to do this quickly and efficiently is often the difference between a brand's success or failure. No small task or amount of pressure here.

Consider this scenario: You want to promote a new product that supplements an existing one. You want to communicate this to each of your target segments and your current customers in all the markets in which you operate. And you want to use email, Facebook, mobile, web banner ads, and printed point of sale (POS) displays at all the retail outlets that sell your products. You need to customize each element for each persona targeted, maybe even each geographic location targeted. Oh, and you want to target Spanish-speaking and English-speaking customers at the same time. On top of all of this, you're offering an introductory price for a limited time only so it's critical that all pieces are in market at the same time for all markets you serve. And you have to get it out in a matter of weeks to take advantage of seasonable buying cycles.

So think about that for a moment. If you're targeting even just four consumer segments in just a handful of different locations, you need a lot of versions for each element you use in your campaign. In many cases, your content customization costs can increase by 300 percent or more according to Perry Kamel, a leader in the content management technology field and CEO of Elateral, a cloud-based content hub designed to manage and deploy content in all formats across all channels. If you're paying an agency $50 to $250 or more per piece (varies by type of content) to build out those versions, that adds a lot of time and money to the cost of your campaign and makes your ROI goals all that more elusive. And if you don't meet the ROI goals set by your CEO or board, your job could be on the line. The pressure builds.

Thankfully, marketing technology has evolved to include robust systems that enable mass multi-channel customization, which provides an affordable and quick solution to this scenario. With the right technology and relevant messaging, you can increase your outcomes by 30 to 40 percent, Kamel points out, who has achieved this level of results consistently for clients in various industries. Add that to the savings in production, and now your ROI can be mind-boggling in a good way.

Table 8-2 presents a more detailed comparison to see how time and cost savings can add up.

TABLE 8-2   **The Time and Cost Savings of Automating Content Versions**

Task	Conventional	Automated
Design and assemble templates for segments	12.25 hours @ $110 per hour	0.25 hours
Brief agency, await concepts, review concepts, check art, await edits, and review edits	7 days	1 day with no agency involved
Approve artwork and deliver production-ready art to producers	$1,348	$28

REMEMBER

The point here is simple: A successful marketing plan can and should embrace all channels without worrying about the cost and time to produce and deploy, no matter how big or small your business is. Technology exists to make it actionable and affordable to execute omni-channel campaigns and communications to thousands, even millions, of customers and prospects efficiently.

TIP

Here are some tips for choosing the right platform for your budget and marketing plan:

>> **Look to the clouds.** Cloud-based systems are the most efficient way to store, access, share, and use your digital assets. Your team players, employees in remote offices, agencies, resellers, distributors, channel managers, and so on can then access all assets any time and get items to market quickly. Just be sure to choose proven systems that will meet your security requirements. Cloud systems are most often priced as SaaS models, allowing you to buy monthly subscriptions to use the platform based on your needs and budget.

>> **Use templates.** Creating a new design and/or shape for every content element you need can be cumbersome. Look for a system that has templates that support all content types, online and offline, that you can customize for your channel and production needs that are then automatically resized and reshaped for various channels and screen and production requirements.

>> **Consider multi-format options.** Many campaigns integrate printed and electronic POS material with mobile, social, and digital channels. You'll need these materials to be produced in sync with each other, especially if you're sending display materials to distributors or retail outlets that you want in place while social channels are engaged to drive customers to those locations.

>> **Check content analytics.** Look for a system that can help you track content usage across your enterprise for specific assets and determine outcomes for various elements. This capability can help you eliminate wasteful elements and focus on executing those that drive the most revenue and profitability.

Chapter **9**

Using Print in a Digital World

Print is not dead. And it never will be because consumers still react more emotionally to tactile communications. It's just human nature. As the world increasingly turns digital, you may think it's okay to bypass printed direct mail, newspaper ads, and collateral. It isn't.

The 2015 Response Rate put out by the Data & Marketing Association shows

» Printed direct-mail response rates outperform digital channels by nearly three times with an average of 3.7 percent response rate versus a 0.62 percent rate for digital channels targeting current customers.

» For ROI, printed mail generates the same return as social media, which is between 15 and 17 percent.

And other studies confirm that print still matters:

» Brand recall for print ads is 75 percent compared to 44 percent for digital. (Canada Post)

» Baby boomers, which make up a large population of the buying public, still read newspapers — 38 percent daily and 44 percent on Sundays. (Nielsen Scarborough data, State of the News Media 2016)

>> Print actually generates greater comprehension than digital. Many studies show that people read printed articles longer and are more engaged because they're tangible and create a greater sensory experience. They also have fewer distractions, such as moving objects and links on web pages.

A Canada Post/True Impact study alone shows that print takes 21 percent less cognitive effort to process and that recall for a print piece was 70 percent higher than a digital ad.

Although print media options are shrinking due to the advantages of web-based advertising and promotions, it should still be a major part of your marketing program. When done in conjunction with your digital programs, it can be very cost effective. Print is a powerful tool as a first introduction to your brand and a mechanism to drive people to digital assets to learn more and engage directly.

Understanding the basics of a print campaign is essential, whether you're a do-it-yourself marketer for your own small business or a marketing manager for a mid-sized or larger organization. This chapter helps you create and design print materials that can build your brand awareness, generate leads, and help drive customers to your advertising with digital programs, such as email, websites, and social channels, and use them together to create better brand engagement with your customers. Print, even in a world where many are addicted to screens, can have a powerful impact on sales and ROI.

REMEMBER

When designing anything in print, your purpose is to spark engagement and drive consumers to your point of sale, be it a physical location or online store, and ultimately stimulate a sale. Think ahead to that goal:

>> If your product sells in stores, create signs, packaging, displays, or coupons that echo your print brochures and ads and remind the buyer of that theme.

>> If the sale occurs on a website, make sure the ad sends prospects to a landing page where the offer from the ad is highlighted and it's obvious what to do next.

>> If you make the sale in person, use handouts like catalogs, white papers, fliers, order forms, or brochures that are consistent with the promises and brand positioning in your print ads and online presence, including Facebook, Twitter, and LinkedIn.

REMEMBER

Always maintain the same brand persona and value propositions in your print material that you do in your online and point-of-sale materials. Even if you're writing something that's informative or instructional (like a product manual), the professionalism and utility of the communication will make a strong impression about the character of your brand. If you're in healthcare and your material is sloppy and full of mistakes, bad grammar, or confusion, consumers likely won't trust you with their health. Every detail matters.

Creating Printed Marketing Materials

In general terms, print materials need to follow the same rules as digital to capture attention and secure engagement. Brochures, *tear sheets* (one-page, catalog-style descriptions of products), posters for outdoor advertising, direct-mail letters, catalogs, and even blogs and web pages all share the basic elements of good print advertising: good copy and visuals mixed with eye-catching headlines. They also all require a common look and feel that unites the separate pieces and furthers your brand position and persona. Understanding print and how to use, design, and integrate it into your omni-channel marketing plan is critical to building your brand's visibility, value, customer engagement, sales, and ROI. The following sections cover the essentials of print materials.

Exploring elements of successful print materials

Just like newspapers tell a news story, your print material — collateral, brochures, fliers, and ads — tell your brand story. Print materials you should integrate into your marketing mix include display ads for local and regional publications and fliers and brochures to hand out at networking events, trade shows, and so on.

Following are some of the necessary parts to help you tell your story at a glance and with detail after you get readers' attention.

>> **Headline:** Your headline, the large print at the top or most visible in your design, must present your emotional selling proposition (ESP; see Chapter 2). This is one chance to attract customers to your story.

>> **Subhead:** The optional addition to the headline provides more detail, also in large (but not quite as large) print. Copy here usually backs up the headline but in a way that creates more curiosity or clarification.

>> **Copy or body copy:** The main text section tells your brand story and is laid out in a readable manner, much like what printers use in the main text of a book or magazine.

>> **Offer:** If you're placing an ad or building a flier around a sale, make sure your offer is one of the most dominant aspects of your piece, followed by a strong call to action, or CTA. Your offer is the specific product or promotion you're promoting, and your CTA is the mechanism by which you want customers to respond. For example, your offer may be 15 percent off regular prices for a limited time, and your call to action may be to go to your website, email, or call you. Regardless, these elements must stand out and be easy to find.

>> **Visual:** Because 90 percent of people's reaction to marketing materials is driven by their unconscious mind, colors and images you use are critical to your success because they set the tone for your message and brand story before consumers read a single word.

>> **Caption:** Copy attached to the visual explains or discusses that visual. You usually place a caption beneath the visual, but you can put it on any side or even within or on the visual.

>> **Trademark:** A trademark is a unique design that represents the brand or company (like Nike's swoosh). You should always register trademarks and copyright all your materials so no one can infringe on the unique way you tell your brand story.

>> **Logo:** A company's logo often serves as a trademarked version of its name. Often logo designs feature the brand name and include the company's slogan.

>> **Slogan:** A slogan is an optional element consisting of a short phrase evoking the spirit, personality, and ESP of the brand. One of our favorites is Michelin's "Because so much is riding on your tires." This statement coupled with a visual of a baby on a tire makes you think hard on what matters much more than price. It works. Despite a higher price, Michelin continues to be on the top-sellers' list for tires worldwide.

>> **Digital links:** One of print's most valuable roles is to drive people to your website where they discover how your product can improve their lives and can interact directly with members of your team. Also directing them to your social sites like Twitter, Pinterest, and Facebook is important because it helps consumers do the research they most often do before making brand choices. If you give them only a phone number and they don't want to call anyone for risk of being pressured to buy, there's a good chance you just lost a prospect.

Designing print materials that capture attention and sales

Design embodies the holistic feel and layout of your brochure, ad, or other printed marketing materials and is vitally important: It's the first impression people have with your brand's story and values and helps them determine consciously and unconsciously whether your persona reflects their own and whether to engage. Your colors, fonts, layout, images, and other visuals have less than three seconds to signal relevance and intrigue to your reader. Photos reflecting the way your readers see themselves, or want to see themselves, often successfully spark engagement and so does your color palette.

The following tips and insights apply to all print formats — ads, fliers, and brochures. These same design elements apply to much of your digital assets as well.

>> Great advertising has to rise off the page, reach out, and grab readers by appealing to the values and aspirations that drive them. In the cluttered world of modern print-based marketing, this design goal is the only one that really works! If you're designing an ad for a local magazine or newspaper, spend some time looking at the current ads for various businesses and your competitors to see which ones stand out. Avoid designs like those that don't, and gain inspiration from those that do.

>> Many software programs offer design templates for brochures, fliers, and other print materials that can guide you. Many are inexpensive and easy to use, such as Microsoft Publisher.

>> Regardless of your role — sole proprietor, business owner, or marketing manager — you should always design your ads with the intent to repurpose your design for other channels. You should be able to scale your design to be printed as a flier that you can hand out at trade shows and networking events or as a poster that you can display at community events that you may sponsor, and then you should be able to easily transfer your design to a digital format for a web banner, social media post on LinkedIn or Twitter, pin on Pinterest, and so on. Be sure you use high enough resolutions of all images in your design to be able to scale up, which is critical for print quality.

Working with a professional designer

If you don't have the time, talent, or desire to design ads and other printed materials, you can find many affordable options for hiring freelancers. Just search the Internet for "freelance graphic designers," and you'll get lots of options. Another great resource is your local college. You can hire design students at a lot less per hour or project, and they'll often work together with fellow students to offer you even more creative perspectives.

This section walks you through the process of working with a designer. When selecting a designer, review each candidate's portfolio thoroughly. Only hire someone whose body of work matches your sense of style and quality and get recommendations from past or current clients to make sure the person has a reputation of getting the work done on time, on budget, and on goal.

Before hiring any designer, write up a creative brief. This is the blueprint from which the designer will work to build your brand's image and lay out your offer and message. This creative brief should contain elements from your marketing strategy, such as colors and fonts. You should direct your designer to include the following items:

>> **Colors:** Which colors and color combinations reflect the emotions and attributes you want associated with your brand and specific message?

>> **Fonts:** Do you want sans serif or a customer design, size, and so forth? Which fonts best appeal most to the generation you're targeting?

>> **Imagery:** What icons and logos should your designer use?

>> **Visuals:** Do you want photos, cutout boxes, charts, and so on? Provide stock photos you've purchased or original photos you own that you want to use.

>> **Layout:** Do you want columns to make your ad look like a news article or body copy that flows like a letter? Which best reflects the mood you want to create and the credibility you need?

Your designer should provide you at least three options for designed pieces, based on your creative brief. After you choose a design, you then need to make sure the design fits the right specifications for how it will be printed.

You also need to ensure the following:

>> All photos are at a high enough resolution to ensure good print quality. Typically photos that are 300 dpi (dots per inch) or higher will work well.

>> Your design needs to be able to scale up or down to easily go from a flier to an ad without losing clarity and quality. Scalability is important because many publications today have print and digital versions, and often purchasing a print ad gets you a place in the online version as well.

>> You have purchased rights to use any photos or images you've included.

>> Your ad or brochure wasn't created in a template from a software program that contains images and other design elements for which you haven't purchased the rights to use.

Always get a project fee, not an hourly rate. Low hourly rates can cost more than projects done at higher rates if the designer isn't as good or efficient. It's about the end cost to get the end product — concept, design options, edits, and final execution.

Using online sources for design services

If you're just starting out and need a good graphic identity for your brand, you can check out some fun and cost-effective ways to tap some of the best talent available. Sites that can connect you to designers who in turn bid on your project include Freelancer (www.freelancer.com), Crowdsite (www.crowdsite.com), LogoArena (www.logoarena.com), DesignContest (www.designcontest.com), Hatchwise (www.hatchwise.com), Logo Design Guru (www.logodesignguru.com), DesignCrowd (www.designcrowd.com), and 99designs (99designs.com).

You can get great prices and work from these freelancers that are heavily vetted and proven to participate in the bidding process. Another route is to set your project up as a contest and purchase the one that wins. For example, 99designs hosted a logo contest for Alchemist Distilleries, a local beer brewer from Waterbury, Vermont. The cost of the contest was less than $300, drastically less than most traditional logo designs.

Doing the design on your own

Anyone with a basic computer and printer can now set up shop and create her own fliers, brochures, business cards, and ad layouts. In fact, Microsoft Word and Pages both include a number of excellent templates that simplify layout and allow you to bang out a new brochure or other printed marketing piece quickly. Any graphic designer you hire will eschew Word and Pages and use the Adobe professional design programs (currently available at a fee of about $50 a month from Adobe Cloud at www.adobe.com/products/creativecloud.html).

If you have experience using these programs, then you may want to design your own print materials (as well as websites and so much more), but if you've never used them, we don't recommend them. It takes a while to figure out how to use the programs, make edits efficiently, and create a design worthy of your brand. In the end, your time may be better spent managing your marketing and sales rather than learning how to master a software application and design processes. Do, however, take a look at Adobe Marketing Cloud, which many marketing departments now use to help them manage programs.

If you're a consultant or own and operate a small business regionally, you can use design software for just about anything, including your logo, business cards, signs, website, and so on. Take a look at the do-it-yourself logo options on sites like www.flamingtext.com, www.logogarden.com, and www.logomaker.com.

Designers often experiment with numerous layouts for their print ads or other printed materials before selecting one for formal development. Whatever approach you take to becoming a do-it-yourself designer, we strongly recommend that you experiment with layouts the way pro designers do. The more layouts you look at, the more likely you are to get an out-of-the-box idea that has eye-grabbing power.

Figuring out why fonts matter

Just about every element of advertising, print, email, website, and other marketing material design has been tested, and testing which font best is no exception. Studies show that which font you choose not only increases comprehension, but it affects response to your call to action, making your font one of the most important choices you make regarding your printed marketing materials.

The right font for any job is the one that makes your text easily readable and that harmonizes with the overall design most effectively. For a headline, the font also needs to grab the readers' attention. The body copy doesn't have to grab attention in the same way — in fact, if it does, the copy often loses readability. The following sections help you find the font that will make sure your printed marketing materials improve readability, comprehension, and action.

Choosing a font style

You have an amazing number of choices, because designers have been developing typefaces for as long as printing presses have existed. Your word-processing software will have many of the basic options, including classics like Helvetica, Times New Roman, and Arial. Check out Adobe Typekit (www.typekit.com) for nice displays of many more options, where you can call up most popular fonts or create lists by style and type.

A clean, sparse design, with a lot of white space on the page and stark contrasts in the artwork, deserves the clean lines of a *sans serif typeface* — meaning one that doesn't have any decorative *serifs* (those little bars or flourishes at the ends of the main lines in a character). The most popular body-copy fonts without serifs are Helvetica, Univers, Optima, Arial, and Avant Garde. Figure 9-1 shows some fonts with and without serifs.

Traditional fonts used for books, newspapers, and similar materials are serif fonts like Century or Times New Roman. The most popular body-copy fonts with serifs include Garamond, Melior, Century, Times New Roman, and Caledonia. Figure 9-2 shows an assortment of typeface choices, in which you can compare the clean lines of the sans serif typefaces with the more decorative designs of the serif typefaces.

FIGURE 9-1:
Fonts with and
without serifs.

© John Wiley & Sons, Inc.

Fonts without serifs that are easy to use include Arial, Avenir, Calibri, and Gil Sans. These have a more contemporary clean look and are good for readability and comprehension as well. However, studies show that serif fonts test higher in comprehension and recall tests.

Sans Serif	Serif
Helvetica	Century
Univers	Garamond
Optima	Melior
Avant Garde	Times New Roman

FIGURE 9-2:
Popular typefaces
for ads.

© John Wiley & Sons, Inc.

REMEMBER

In tests, Helvetica, Times New Roman, and Century generally top the lists as most readable, so start with one of these typefaces for your body copy. Research also shows that people read lowercase letters about 13 percent faster than uppercase letters, so avoid long stretches of copy set in all caps. People also read most easily when letters are dark and contrast strongly with their background. Reverse font, or font that is lighter than the background, such as white font on black, has been shown to lower comprehension by more than 80 percent, so if you use it, use it sparingly to make key points stand out in a design but not for your body copy or main story. Black 12-point Helvetica and Times New Roman on white are among the most readable fonts for a printed marketing piece, even if it seems dull to a sophisticated designer.

As a general rule, use complementary fonts for the headline and body copy. For example, you can use Helvetica for the headline when you use Century for the body, and vice versa. Or you can just use a bolder, larger version of the body copy font for your headline. Work to make the headline grab readers' attention, stand out from the body copy, and ultimately lead vision and curiosity into the body copy's text.

Making size and style choices

All fonts are available in many sizes, most readily from 8 to 72. The main thing to consider is how the size looks in the format you have to work within. Make sure your ad doesn't look too crowded by using larger font, and don't make it so small that it's hard to read. If people's first impression is that your ad or brochure will take energy or time to read, they'll typically opt out. Studies show that size 14 has the greatest readability, but 11 and 12 are common.

WARNING

Consumers don't like to have to work to read a message, they tend to read type quite conservatively, and they find traditional designs instinctively appealing. The spacing of characters and lines, the balance and flow of individual characters (with some white space around them or an appropriate illustration to break up the text) — all these familiar design elements please the eye and make reading easy and pleasurable. So when you need to provide emphasis, try to do so in a conservative manner. For example, try simply bolding your body copy before resorting to a new style of type. Too many type styles may reduce your design's readability.

REMEMBER

A good design uses two type families and varies the size of them, mixing in appropriate italics, bold, or reverse type if the overall design benefits from it. Figure 9-3 shows a black-and-white print ad laid out using Garamond and Helvetica, which are traditional, easy-to-read fonts. Some graphic designers avoid them because they like to be less traditional and more creative, but as the figure shows, these two type families lend themselves to clean, attractive, appealing, and (most important) *readable* designs.

Don't just use a new or different type of font because you can. Stick with popular fonts, in popular sizes, except where you have to solve a problem or you want to make a special point.

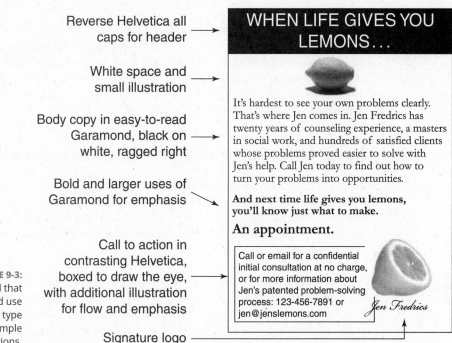

Reverse Helvetica all caps for header →

White space and small illustration →

Body copy in easy-to-read Garamond, black on white, ragged right →

Bold and larger uses of Garamond for emphasis →

Call to action in contrasting Helvetica, boxed to draw the eye, with additional illustration for flow and emphasis →

Signature logo —

WHEN LIFE GIVES YOU LEMONS...

It's hardest to see your own problems clearly. That's where Jen comes in. Jen Fredrics has twenty years of counseling experience, a masters in social work, and hundreds of satisfied clients whose problems proved easier to solve with Jen's help. Call Jen today to find out how to turn your problems into opportunities.

And next time life gives you lemons, you'll know just what to make.

An appointment.

Call or email for a confidential initial consultation at no charge, or for more information about Jen's patented problem-solving process: 123-456-7891 or jen@jenslemons.com

Jen Fredrics

FIGURE 9-3:
A print ad that makes good use of traditional type styles and simple illustrations.

FONTS, TYPEFACES, COPYRIGHTS, AND OTHER MINUTIAE

If you decide to be your own designer, you should familiarize yourself with some of the minutiae you don't know you don't know. These include

- **Font versus typeface:** A typeface refers to the overall style, and the font, the specific variation of that style. For example, you can use Arial, Arial Narrow, Arial Black, Arial Rounded and then add bold, italics, and so on.

- **Copyright:** In most cases, a typeface such as Arial is not copyrighted and can be used in your ads and marketing materials. Customized fonts, such as the font created for the classic Coca-Cola logo, are usually copyrighted and require purchasing rights to use.

If you want a wide variety of unique fonts you can use for your materials, you can use sources such as Google Fonts and Red Hat, which provides a line of fonts called Liberation.

Your eye can't distinguish easily between fonts that are only one or two sizes apart, so specify a larger jump than that to distinguish between body copy and subhead or subhead and headline. For example, if your body copy is set in 10-point Times New Roman, you need to set subheads at least two steps up (steps being defined by standard point sizes: 9, 12, 14, 16, 18, 24, 36, and 48, although in-between sizes can also be used).

Using flow for engagement and clarity

How pieces flow and look to readers is critical for securing engagement, without which you have no response. *Flow* is the smooth movement of attention from an entry point, around the page, and to an end point. In marketing, the entry point is almost always the headline, and the end point is either the brand name and logo or a call to action.

Whether in a brochure or a print ad, white space matters. Psychologist Ken Larson did a study at MIT on how font and layout affect people's emotions, which in turn affect their interest and engagement with an ad. He found that how copy flows on a page and the amount of white space affects interest in reading, clarity, and cognitive focus. In a lab setting, readers were given an ad designed for *The New York Times,* one with a poor, busy design and one with a good design where copy flowed more easily around the visuals and left more white space. Results showed that readers of the good design felt more positive emotions while reading the same copy as those with the bad design, and they experienced higher cognitive focus, mental processing, and clarity. Another key finding was that the readers felt that it would take less time to read the good copy, and, in today's world, that is critical because consumers don't have a lot of time to give, nor are they willing to do so, to read your sales message.

As you create your ad, you need to create visual interest while creating the right flow and copy/visual balance.

In a really well-designed print ad, brochure, website, or blog page, the writing and the selection of font styles are just a part of the bigger-picture design, which ought to draw the viewer through a well-planned flow of reading and viewing experiences. If the flow is inviting, the design appears simple and the copy easy to read, and the likelihood of your ad getting noticed and read significantly increases.

Producing Effective and Efficient Print Collateral

Word-processing or graphics software, a good inkjet or laser printer, and the help of your local photocopy or print shop allow you to design and produce brochures, fliers, and more quite easily and affordably. Print collateral that still provides that tactile connection with a brand and its message includes fliers, brochures, and sales kits where fliers designed in a cohesive order are organized in a printed folder. The following sections provide some tips for making each of these formats effective in today's highly digitized world.

Designing fliers for grounded results

Fliers serve a big purpose for just about every brand. Gone are the days when prospects pour over long brochures to determine interest in your product and brand. People have been trained to think and read in sound bites and short statements that fit the word count limits of social media. Your print material needs to cater to that new way of processing information. This is the value of producing what we call at-a-glance sheets, which are one-page fliers that present your brand's value when customers have time to only glance at your material.

At-a-glance fliers that work consist of the following elements:

» **Imagery:** A powerful visual that represents the end result of what you sell. Peace of mind about your financial investments? A happy, healthy pet? A software platform that increases efficiency, making staff happier as they perform better? This visual can be a photo around which you wrap text, or it can be a soft undertone creating the desired emotional connection and impression over which you put text with your key messages.

» **Bullet points:** Instead of trying to fit your brand's dissertation onto one page with 10-point font, identify the top three key values you offer, the top solutions to problems you provide, and your competitive distinctions and craft brief but powerful bullet points about each.

» **Brand anchor:** Following the bullet points that show what you offer and how your brand fulfills real and emotional needs, include a summary statement about your brand that anchors your overall value and advantages of functional alternatives and competitors. This may include information about your Net Promotor Score (NPS), industry awards, company growth, and other details that communicate your strength and back up your product promises.

>> **Contact information:** Your bullet points and anchor serve as teasers to encourage readers to go online to your website and social pages to learn more and, ultimately, inquire about a product or service. Make sure all your contact points are clear and easy to find. List your LinkedIn, Facebook, and Twitter contact info, not just your email and phone number.

Developing brochures and self-mailers with specific marketing goals

Brochures, especially those that can double as a self-mailer, are still worth the investment because they're still appropriate in some forums, such as trade shows, networking meetings, and customer events.

REMEMBER

Many brochure designs foolishly waste money because they don't accomplish any specific marketing goals. Like any marketing efforts — print, digital, or live — you need to ask some key questions about how you'll use a brochure before your put the time, energy, and money into producing one. For example:

>> Who will read the brochure?

>> How will they get the brochure?

>> What should they do after reading the brochure?

WARNING

Without a specific focus and purpose, your brochure is likely to miss the mark and risk being just another boring marketing piece that could represent any of your competitors and fail to engage prospects in your message and encourage them to reach out for more information. The most common and appropriate purposes for a brochure are to

>> Act as a reference on the product, or technical details of the product, for prospects

>> Support a personal selling effort by lending credibility and helping overcome objections

>> Help prospects identify how you differ from the competition

>> Determine how your product and brand fill a real or emotional need or solve a current problem

>> Generate leads through a direct-mail campaign

When planning your copy, review your ESP (as discussed in Chapter 2). The headline on your front cover needs to address your ESP, and the key copy points that you focus on need to show how you do just that. Revisit the copy points you chose in your at-a-glance flier (see the earlier section "Designing fliers for grounded results") and add more substance, evidence, examples, and such to each of those points.

You want your copy to be consistent and story the same across all touch points. The difference is how much space you have to back up your claims (use references and authoritative stories to add credence) and how much detail you can go into about your products and services.

Instead of using three bullet points to tell your story, turn those three bullet points into sections and use headlines that describe what's in those paragraphs.

If space allows, consider including some of the following elements:

>> Key competitive distinctions, differences, and advantages

>> Customer satisfaction scores, NPS, and testimonials

>> Customer testimonials or case histories

>> Quotes from staff members illustrating their passion for quality and commitment to serve customers

Drafting an effective layout for your print brochure

An effective print brochure follows this standard layout:

>> The appeal, with its enticing headline and compelling copy and visual, goes on the front of the brochure — or the outside when you fold it for mailing, or the central panel out of three if you fold a sheet twice.

>> The sections covering the main three points of focus go on the inside pages.

>> The fact base, needed for reference use, goes in the copy and illustrations beneath your subheads.

>> When folded, the back page should leave ample space for mailing insignia and postage information. Be sure to check out current guidelines for mailing requirements at www.usps.com before you print your mailer because regulations and requirements change.

You can produce your brochure in small or large format and be effective either way. For larger brochures, plan your copy and design elements to cover the span of 11-x-17 paper, which when folded in half makes for a four-panel 8.5-x-11 brochure. Smaller formats span an 8.5-x-11 paper size, which folds into three narrow panels about the width of a single newspaper column.

Designing a brochure is relatively easy to do. Just pick your favorite publishing software and get started. Whether you use a Mac or PC, you have many options for designing both small and large format brochures

WARNING

If you don't know what each part of your brochure does, then you need to redesign it. Otherwise, that brochure becomes a waste of time and money.

Although you can lay out a brochure in many ways, you should choose the format that is most cost effective for you to produce and which format you're most likely to mail. If you don't include a section for mailing insignia on the back, then produce it for the least-expensive mailing costs, which would be a #10 envelope which fits an 8.5-x-11 piece of paper folded in thirds. Larger format brochures that unfold as full 8.5-x-11 pages are a good format as well and can be folded in half for a larger mailer, which does get better response than the smaller mailing pieces; however, the larger the foldout size, the heavier the brochure and the higher the price to mail.

Most copy stores accept emailed copies of files and can produce short runs of your brochures (as well as pamphlets, catalog sheets, and other printed materials) right from your files. However, if you need thousands of copies, you should look into offset printing, which is a more cost-effective option at that quantity. *Offset printing* is how most books, magazines, and newspapers are printed. The printer makes a plate of each page, and the printing press automatically inks the plate, transfers or "offsets" the ink to a rubber blanket, and then transfers that to the page.

You can also do smaller runs (100 or less) right from your own color printer. Buy matte or glossy brochure paper designed for your brand of printer (HPs work well for this) and simply select the appropriate paper type in the print dialog box. Today's printers can produce absolutely stunning brochures, but you have to fold these brochures yourself, and the ink cartridges or toners aren't cheap, so print as needed rather than inventory a large number of brochures.

Placing Print Ads That Generate Leads

Print ads are still productive and cost effective, especially for niche or small businesses. The key to successful media purchases for ads of all sizes is twofold:

>> Purchase space in publications that directly reach your prospects with a high propensity to engage or purchase.

>> Have a goal in mind. If you're not Pepsi, Apple, Honda, or another brand with household recognition around the world, advertising to promote your brand's name isn't likely to pay off quickly, if at all. Advertising with a specific call to action is much more likely to generate leads. Successful print ads have a value-add offer, such as a seasonal sale, limited time free gift with purchase, and so on.

You don't have to be a big brand with a big budget to purchase advertising space. You just need to be smart about it. If you live in a big city, you're going to pay big prices to get in your daily newspaper. However, many other affordable options can help you get the awareness and attention you need. The following sections provide just a few ideas to pursue. Before you commit to any publication, though, keep the following in mind:

>> What are the rack rates? Advertising tends to be priced on a *cost per thousand of readers* reached basis. Rates are calculated by the cost of buying that ad, divided by the number of readers who read the publication, and then multiplied by 1,000, so you generally get as much exposure as you're willing to pay for. Buying ads in small-circulation publications allows you to reach specific niche audiences more effectively and increase your ROI while avoiding the risks associated with larger, more general publications.

>> Who does it reach? Does this publication reach decision makers or influencers? Ask sales reps to give you a breakout of the readership demographics so you can determine whether they represent your customer base or not.

>> How many highly valued prospects does it reach, and what percentage of the total readership do they represent? If a publication has 10,000 readers and you care about only one-tenth of the readers, you're paying to reach 10 percent and wasting money on the other 90 percent.

>> What are the costs? Just like with digital media, you need to determine your cost per reach. Sales reps for each publication other than your local, nonprofit newsletters should be able to give you an idea of the average response current advertisers get so you can determine the potential cost effectiveness.

>> How much can you negotiate? Just because a rate is printed in a media kit doesn't mean that is what you have to pay. If you're a first-time customer, ask for an introductory rate so you can test the publication. If you want to place your ad more than once, look at the 3x, 6x, and 12x rates. Also check for rates that include your ad in both the print and digital version of the newspapers.

>> What are your values? Beyond the monetary value of each publication you choose, you need to keep in mind the values and causes with which you're associating. As we mention in earlier chapters, aligning with like values and demonstrating support for worthy causes and ideals is critical for building your brand's value and sales. Just because a rate is low doesn't mean it's a good value because associating with the wrong values can do more long-term damage than you can add up.

REMEMBER

Also keep in mind that frequency in print matters. Placing an ad once will likely disappoint because consumers need to see something on average three times before it really sinks into their psyche, and even more than that in most cases to act on it. Choose a publication you can afford to keep purchasing to create continuity and brand awareness. If you can afford a rate only one time, move on to something you can keep up with because in most cases, one ad isn't going to do much for your bottom line.

TIP

In addition to finding a publication you can afford to advertise in regularly, use economical print media, such as brochures, blogs, mailings, and emails. (We help you figure out how to design a brochure earlier in this chapter.) If you operate on too small a scale or budget to afford print advertising, try turning your ad design into a good flier and mailing it. You can send it to 500 names and see what happens. That's a lot less risky and expensive than buying space in a magazine that goes to 200,000 names — some of whom may not care at all about what you're offering. Or you can search for smaller-circulation publications with a more local or specialized readership where the rates may be much cheaper.

Cheap but powerful publications

Following are some ideas for local organizations that produce publications that are not only affordable but also powerful channels for reaching the right customers for your brand and elevating your brand position at the same time. To be most effective, include a line of support for the cause at hand rather than just your sales message.

REMEMBER

Keep the scale of your print advertising (or any advertising for that matter) at such a level that you can afford to run an ad that may produce zero sales. Although zero sales certainly isn't your goal, it's always a possibility, and you want to base your buying decision on that possibility while you're experimenting to find an effective venue for your ads.

Nonprofit clubs and charities

No matter where you live — city, suburb, rural America, or resort town — many local organizations communicate regularly to members of your community, and they're often looking for brands such as yours to help underwrite the cost of publishing their newsletters. As a result, they offer inexpensive opportunities to advertise in print and digital newsletters. These are powerful outlets to reach people united in a worthy cause, and when you support their passion, they'll often support you over competitors that choose not to support them via advertisements. Some groups to look into include

» Rotary, elk, and lions clubs.

» Library districts.

» Charities such as the American Cancer Association, Muscular Dystrophy Association, and the Red Cross. These often have publications they use for fundraising and member communications.

» Sports clubs, such as youth soccer, ski racing, volleyball, and lacrosse.

» Homeowners associations. Many homeowners associations produce magazines to keep residents informed and connected. These offer a specific reach and are ideal for local businesses, like carpet cleaners, veterinary practices, restaurants, and spas.

Local theaters

Community theaters are another great resource for inexpensive advertising. Placing your ad in a play bill shows your commitment to the arts.

Professional associations and networking groups

Small and large cities all have local chapters of larger professional organizations and often produce print newsletters or even magazines to communicate regularly to members. Often many options exist within one organization.

» Chambers of commerce.

» Business partnership organizations.

» Local chapters for professional organizations. Every industry typically has a few options in a given community, so do your research to find them. Here are some examples of the kinds of local chapters you can find for the marketing industry in just about every medium to large city:

  • Business Marketing Association

  • Data & Marketing Association

- American Marketing Association
- International Association of Business Communicators
- Advertising Federation
- American Association of Advertising Agencies

Local and small-town newspapers

You can find hundreds of newspapers and weeklies with circulations in the tens of thousands and rates one-fifth to one-tenth the price of big-city newspapers (and even less expensive when compared to major national magazines). Even though you don't reach as many people, you can reach high-quality prospects nonetheless. When browsing which newspapers to buy, ask about circulation trends. Some are losing print readers to their website, so be sure to know what you're really getting from your investment. The challenge is that readership is declining for local papers, and many of them are folding or going to online-only formats.

Ad size

What size ad should you buy? The answer depends in part on the design of your ad. Does the ad have a strong, simple visual or headline that catches the eye, even if it's only a third of a page in size? Or does the ad need to be displayed in a larger format to work well?

You should also consider goals associated with your ad. If you're promoting an end-of-season sale and want to move inventory fast, you may want a bigger ad to make sure you get a lot of attention to drive big amounts of traffic. If your goal is more to introduce your brand to a new audience and establish a presence or awareness, you can probably achieve this with a series of smaller ads with compelling copy that tells your brand story over time.

Table 9-1 provides some general statistics on what percentage of readers *notice* an ad based on its size, according to a study by Cahners Publishing Co.

TABLE 9-1 ## Selecting the Right Size Ad

Size of Ad	Percent of Readers Noticing Ad
Fractional (part-of-page) ad	24%
One-page ad	40%
Two-page spread	55%

No surprise here that the bigger the ad, the bigger the impact. But also consider the fact that the percentage of readers noticing your ad doesn't go up in proportion to the increase in size. Doubling the size of your ad gives you something like a quarter more viewers, not twice as many. That's partly why the cost of a full-page ad isn't twice the cost of a half-page ad. For example, a full-page, four-color ad in *Health* magazine costs 59 percent more than a half-page, four-color ad. The same ad run at full versus half size probably attracts, at most, about a third more reader notices, meaning your cost per reader exposed to the ad is higher for that full-page ad than for the half-page ad (although your impact on each of those readers may be greater with a larger ad, which is why the cost per reader can be set at a higher level for a larger ad).

Ad impact

After placing your ads, it's time to sit back and wait for the phone to ring. Or not. If only it were that easy. Measuring print isn't as easy as measuring direct response where you can link a sale to individuals in your database and to specific promotions. And asking new leads how they heard about you isn't reliable because many will tell you they heard your ad on the radio. Now what?

In truth, measuring the impact of your ad needs to start long before you place it. Here are some ideas for simple, affordable ways to determine whether your design, message, offer, and publication choices worked:

>> **Ask for feedback.** Although focus groups were a common way to generate feedback in the past, they're not as popular now due to the high cost to facilitate and the lack of reliable feedback due to group think and other issues. You can get some of the same insights for free by simply asking people you know for candid feedback. Ask friends in your industry and outside of it for their first reaction to your ad and how likely they are to act on the offer. Even if they're not in your customer segments, their feedback on readability, emotional value of the headline, and interest in and believability of the body copy is valuable.

>> **Test outlets, messages, offers, and designs.** You can code your ads by the size, day of week, and offers to determine which works best and produces the greatest ROI.

>> **Post on LinkedIn or Facebook.** Before spending a lot of money to go to print, post your ad in its creative form on your social media pages. Gauge likes, shares, and comments to determine how people reacted to the offer and message. No comments or likes? Post again and incentivize people to give you feedback by offering a small token, such as a Starbucks gift card.

>> **Email your ad.** This is a cheap and great way to test your offer but also, most important, your headline. Use the headline as your subject line to see how many opens you get for each headline tested. Use the top-performing subject line as your headline for best results in print. You can email your ad to friends, associations, and people that follow you on social media. Doing this also ensures that they see your ad in case they missed it in their daily newsfeed and enables you to get the feedback you want from high-propensity prospects.

>> **Code each ad you place.** Every ad you place in print should have a specific code to help you identify specific leads generated. Set up your codes to help you determine which publication, ad, call to action, and offer worked best. Consider the following when coding your ads:

- Use a different phone number or email address for each publication purchased.

- Direct readers to a separate landing page for each publication and/or each offer you promote. Give the landing page a URL that will help you identify which outlet and which ad generated the best traffic.

- Use discount codes for each outlet. If you advertised in a local weekly and a local entertainment guide, you may want to code your ads as such to determine which offer and which outlet worked best. For example, in a weekly newspaper ad with a 20 percent offer, ask customers to reference 20OFFWeek when ordering in person or online (maybe differentiate between print and online by adding "print" and "web"). Or in an Entertainment Guide, use an offer code like 20OFFFUN.

Always use different codes and response mechanisms for different outlets and digital versus print formats to help you identify the best use of your media budget in the future.

REMEMBER

Any experiments you can run as you do your marketing give you useful feedback about what's working and what isn't. Always think of ways to compare different options and see how those options perform when you advertise, giving you useful insight into ad effectiveness.

4 Powerful Ways to Engage for LTV and ROI

IN THIS PART . . .

Discover why direct marketing is critical for any business and understand why data matters and how to use it.

Create a strong website for engaging customers, building relationships, and driving sales.

Build your network and gain support through events and trade shows.

Chapter **10**

Going Direct with Data, Personalization, and Sales

F irst and foremost, direct marketing isn't simply direct mail, or what most customers call "junk" mail; direct marketing is the process and methodology of marketing directly to your customer via many channels, of which just one is the kind of mail that the USPS delivers.

The goal of direct marketing is to establish a one-to-one relationship directly with your customers to achieve lifetime value (discussed in Chapter 16).

Although the terms used for direct marketing strategies and tactics change often with the advent of new technologies and apps, the principles remain constant as, again, human nature doesn't change with semantics. To this point, other terms for direct marketing efforts include *relationship marketing, one-to-one marketing, personalization,* and *direct response.* Whatever term you use or channels you employ, the goals remain the same:

> Connect directly with your consumers to facilitate direct sales, create emotional bonds and relationships that drive purchase, secure loyalty and lifetime value, and spark evangelism for your products and brand.

Direct marketing is the most powerful form of marketing for achieving these goals. Direct communications that are all about the customer is the best way to initiate relationships, nurture them, and achieve lifetime value among your highest value customers. Invest in the data, the processes, and the technology to help you achieve highly personalized direct communications across all channels. Doing this ups your game not only for winning profits but also for beating your competition, both of which are critical for sustainability.

Understanding the Metrics of Direct Marketing

Here are a few statistics from the Data & Marketing Association's (DMA) and Demand Metric Response Rate Report 2016 to validate how important it is that you engage in data-driven, direct marketing activities (see www.thedma.org for more information).

Response Rate for Selected Media

Mobile	0.2%
Paid search	0.5%
Online display	0.9%
Social media	0.6%
Email house list	0.6%
Email prospect list	0.3%
Direct-mail print for prospect, purchased list	2.9%
Direct-mail print for house/total list	5.3%

Note: Response for all digital channels — mobile to email — was calculated by multiplying click-through rate (CTR) by conversion rate.

One of the most important metrics for any medium or advertising spend is cost per acquisition (CPA), which tells you just how much money you're spending to acquire each new customer. For optimum ROI and profitability, your goal should be to keep this as low as possible. Per the DMA report, B2C email campaigns using house lists generated the lowest CPA of all digital media with an average cost of $6 and $7. The highest digital media CPA was for paid search using generic words, coming in at $36 to $37. This number alone shows the importance of growing and managing your customer contact lists and communicating directly with them for direct sales.

Here are some more response comparisons that may reshape your reality about the impact of direct marketing:

>> A full-page magazine ad typically pulls a response between 0.05 and 0.2 percent of circulation, giving you only two responses per thousand from a decent ad.

>> An individually addressed direct-mail letter typically pulls between 3 and 5 percent of the names you mailed to. So you can expect 50 responses per thousand from a strong letter.

>> A direct-mail piece showing your product among other products, as in a catalog or coupon deck, pulls far less. Divide the 50-per-thousand by the number of competing products for a rough idea of the average response rate. For example, if your product is 1 of 50 shown, the maximum response may be 1 per thousand. That's nothing to write home about.

>> A call center calling a qualified list may get a response of about 10 percent for B2B brands, but the CPA is often much higher than direct mail because of the labor costs. Because unsolicited calls are often not welcome, you could lose more than you realize from this method.

>> Email may have an open rate of 10 to 20 percent, but what matters most is the click-through rate, which is typically in the 1.5 to 3 percent range for consumer marketing and as high as 4.5 percent for business-to-business.

If you take anything away from the response rate findings in this section, it should be that relationships matter if you want to achieve a high ROI for your business and that direct mail, the printed kind, isn't dead. Some studies show that roughly 80 percent of consumers still go through their mail daily and actually open and read it, especially if it comes from a brand with whom they have a trusting relationship.

The DMA's Response Rate 2016 report shows the following median ROI for direct marketing channels:

Social media	28%
Online display	18%
Paid search	25%
Direct mail	27%
Email	122%

You also should note that most businesses in both B2B and B2C plan to use direct mail and email among their top channels. For example:

Direct Mail	Email
56% of businesses that target both B2B and B2C	80% of businesses that target both B2B and B2C
38% of businesses in solely B2B	91% of businesses in solely B2B
59% of businesses in solely B2C	71% of businesses in solely B2C

So there's a good chance your competitors are engaging in direct marketing to build emotionally fulfilling relationships with the same customers you're targeting. If you're not doing the same, your challenge just got that much bigger.

The Basics of Direct Marketing

This section covers some basics about the tools and techniques to get you started on a successful direct marketing program to help you achieve optimum ROI and customer lifetime value.

First, the foundation of direct marketing is creating and managing customer data centered on individual needs, life cycle, value, and more, which you can use to develop and deliver highly relevant, personalized information. With a solid and detailed database for customers and prospects, and a customer relationship management (CRM) platform, you can automate emails around customer preferences, browsing patterns, shopping cycles, past purchases, offers used, and so on. You can also affordably test combinations of messages, channels, and offers to find the perfect mix for generating the response you need. Your database will help you identify high-quality prospects and find lists for purchase that have a greater chance of paying off.

Additionally, a good database program sets you up to retarget customers, which means you can identify the social sites they visit frequently and place ads in sidebars when your customers visit those sites, thus reinforcing the offers and messages in your emails and other campaigns.

REMEMBER

Direct marketing, no matter what channels you use, is only as good as the emotional appeal of your content, message, and offer. Before you can succeed, you need to develop your emotional selling proposition (ESP) messaging and psychological profiles so you know the messages, emotions, and triggers that will capture attention, trigger the right reaction, and inspire engagement and trial. (See Chapter 2 for more on ESP profiles.)

Initially, in the days of Lester Wunderman, who is heralded as the father of direct marketing, the approach was about getting a sale directly from a customer, often with strong calls to action that created a sense of urgency, and then nurturing that relationship for additional sales over time. He introduced subscription-based selling and loyalty programs.

Today, direct marketing focuses on delivering highly personalized, relevant communications designed around creating a sale, loyalty, referrals, and brand equity. The technology and processes today allow you to monitor your customers' needs, group them in like segments or personas, and communicate to them about specific past behavior, interests, even sentiments expressed in real time. As a result, messaging has evolved into personalized offers and correspondence that is all about the customer. This is why direct marketing works so well.

Direct marketing is quickly taking over other forms of marketing because it substantially outperforms mass media in results and accountability. Display ads, outdoor, radio, and other mass media formats are now more about keeping a brand's name visible so that when you deliver personalized communications, customers are more likely to open and act on it.

This chapter shares some insights on the top channels for direct marketing in terms of affordability to execute and likelihood to pay off. These are print and email. We cover other forms of direct communication in Chapter 8, which discusses digital channels. Telemarketing has traditionally been a good method of direct contact with customers, but because of the expense compared to email and print, it's becoming less efficient. It's also getting more difficult to execute due to the Do Not Call List options and privacy concerns consumers have today.

Getting direct about direct marketing

The primary tool you need to achieve strong results from any and all direct marketing efforts is data. You need data that tells you the following information:

>> Who your customers are

>> Where your customers shop and how often they shop for your category

>> What their preferences are within your category

>> Your customers' relationship with your brand

>> Their lifestyle, social, and attitudinal attributes

>> Their sentiments about your category, products, and brand

>> What channels they engage with the most

>> What types of offers most inspire their behavior and purchases

>> Their expectations for brands they choose

>> Basic demographics about age, gender, household income, geographic location, education, profession, and so on

Without good data, you can't develop relevant messaging and offers, and you'll produce a lot of waste by targeting the wrong customers or the right customers with the wrong message. The benefits of good data and direct marketing channels are huge. Just a few capabilities include

>> Personalizing every aspect of your communications piece, including

- The customer's transaction history

- Needs — for example, "It's time for an oil change."

- Lifestyle (parent of a teenager or toddler, single, LGBT, and so on)

- Age and income

- Gender

- Life cycle phase for your product category

>> Tracking responses to each individual you send a marketing piece or offer to — no other medium allows you do this.

>> Affordably testing your messages, creative, and offers across various channels and within various markets to help you discover which message worked best in which market for which age or demographic and by which channel — email, letter package, mobile, and more.

The more you do, the more you get

It's simple. The more you send and the more you test, the better your results and the more you'll understand what works and what doesn't. If you test and track your campaigns closely, you can tell when a change, even as slight as the envelope teaser or color or one word in the subject line, improves response rates. Even if you have little or no experience in direct marketing, know that a small effort can generate enough information to help you execute better the next time and on a larger scale.

TIP

As the statistics from the DMA show (in the earlier section "Understanding the Metrics of Direct Marketing"), building a strong in-house mailing and email list is critical to your success. You can improve and grow your lists in many ways, which we cover in detail throughout this chapter. In short, you can do the following:

>> Include a warranty registration card with shipments of product and add a registration option to your website to begin building your in-house list.

>> Buy a list of prospects from an established list broker and test it with a mailing or emailing. You may add positive responses to this test mailing to your in-house list. Then keep mailing and emailing your in-house list regularly so as to keep it fresh and up-to-date.

>> Reach out to your LinkedIn connections and ask permission to send them information or surveys or just exchange email addresses.

>> Offer incentives for your Facebook, Pinterest, and Twitter followers to send you their email addresses and give you permission to contact them directly.

>> Engage in growth hacking activities, which involves using digital channels to build databases with connections on social media such as prospects, peers, thought leaders, and others of influence.

REMEMBER

The risk associated with direct marketing is lower than other channels, especially if you use email to test your messages and offers before using print because the production costs are low and so is the execution and measurement.

Digging Deeper into Data

Your data investment is one of the most important you can make — not only the mailing and email lists you may buy that replicate your current customers but also the data systems that allow you to quickly sort your customers and create groups based on persona, ESP, recency, frequency, monetary variables, and other triggers of purchase so you can easily and quickly deploy campaigns with high relevance to groups of like individuals. You need a CRM system that can store multiple attributes about each customer, enable you to personalize messages to individuals in real time, automate communications deployment, manage leads and monitor their overall value to you, and of course track the ROI for each customer group and even individual. Using a data management platform (DMP) and a demand side platform (DSP) can enable you to communicate with the same kind of relevance to prospects. The DMP follows the online behavior of people who fit your customer profile, and a DSP places your ads on the sites most likely to reach them as a result of the behavior monitored. If you have a social media account, you've likely experienced these ads quite frequently yourself.

Using a CRM system

A wide variety of CRM software platforms are available. You'll need to do some research to find a system that fits your budget, anticipated scalability, and functions that are most critical to your growth goals. Many CRM systems are now cloud-based so you don't have to set up or manage your own infrastructure. You just need to log in to access your data, analytics, and tools.

CRM systems also provide critical insights through analytical functions so you can work smarter and more efficiently than ever. These may include

>> A comprehensive view of the customer across channels, campaigns, and online communities; behavior such as store visits, online/offline purchases, blog comments, partner site visits, ESP triggers, and purchasing trends so you can sort by behavior, price sensitivity, campaign response, and more.

>> Engagement levels that tell you which campaigns, blogs, social media posts, offers, and campaigns were of the most interest to which individuals and customer groups.

>> Lifetime value, which, as we discuss in Chapter 16, is critical to sustainable growth. CRM systems let you analyze the net value of each customer so you can identify the customers who cost you a lot to serve and thus deliver a lower profit margin and those who are lower maintenance and generate a higher return per transaction.

CRM systems offer similar functionalities with a few distinctions. Some of the more popular systems today include

>> **Oracle CRM on Demand Marketing:** This is a simple, integrated solution that helps small to large enterprises automate the full marketing process, from designing and deploying campaigns, lead management and nurturing, to measuring ROI. It has built-in email and web marketing automation and

analytic tools. It also has a robust response management system, which can enable users to build qualified databases easily.

>> **Salesforce Marketing Cloud:** Some of the features this CRM system offers includes an audience builder, which allows you to create a single view of each customer, automate customer journeys across channels, and pair customer profiles with machine-learning algorithms so you can automatically deliver highly relevant content. It also has a content builder and performs predictive analytics to give you new insights about customers.

>> **Microsoft Dynamics 365:** Microsoft has partnered with Adobe Marketing Cloud to offer a robust CRM system that can easily and affordably scale with a business's growth. This system enables one-to-one personalized communications, delivers content and offers based on a customer's behavior, and provides real-time insights into results and attribution.

For a lot more detail on CRM systems and how to use them, check out *Microsoft Dynamics For Dummies CRM 4*, by Joel Scott, David Lee, and Scott Weiss; *Salesforce. com For Dummies,* 5th Edition, by Tom Wong, Liz Kao, and Matt Kaufman; and the more comprehensive book, *Social CRM For Dummies*, by Kyle Lacy, Stephanie Diamond, and Jon Ferrara (all published by Wiley).

TIP

Managing your in-house data effectively with a CRM system can save you a great deal of money in the long run. The DMA response rate report mentioned earlier shows that your CPA is substantially lower with a house list versus a purchased prospect list. Compare the following:

Direct Mail	Email (B2B and B2C)
House list CPA: $27.35	House list: $10.23
Prospect list CPA: $42.20	Prospect list: $25.61

TIP

If you're in retail, you can amass valuable data about customers every day through transaction records, loyalty programs, social media interactions, and credit card applications if you offer your own private label cards. This first-person data is yours to use freely and hopefully successfully as you work toward securing lifetime value from your core customers.

Sven Tarantik, VP of Retail Marketing Strategies for Oracle Data Cloud, provides some insights on how small to large retailers can enhance their CRM and personalization efforts through data management. Here are some actionable tips:

>> Build a digital strategy for your business that's focused around two main priorities:

- Understand, assemble, and organize your own first-person data and ensure that the right tools are in place to effectively utilize it.

- Find a reputable third-party data provider that can help you scale your marketing efforts with quality data and applications. You want a data provider that can build a model that reflects the analytics of your in-house data lists (for example, similar attributes, characteristics, and purchasing propensities).

>> Align your data strategy and your marketing team around clear key performance indicators (KPIs) so you achieve sustainable business goals from your efforts, not just cool, cutting-edge communications. This will enable you to directly evaluate how your efforts are driving performance, aligning with goals, or not.

Tarantik suggests that no matter what business you're in, your first step is to look at your in-house database and find ways to effectively organize it so you can deploy direct marketing campaigns in real shopping time. Knowing what you have will also help you know how much CRM system to invest in. Having your data in one location will enable you to see what you have, what is useful, and what you need to improve your insights and personalized communications.

TIP

As you build your lists and execute campaigns, you need to factor in multiple touch points to get to yes. To close a customer, you may need to email, call, send a letter, and call again to get the sale or meeting you seek.

Always include a way to opt-out of your emails, even for existing customers, or risk being seen as a spammer, which won't help your relationship-building efforts.

REMEMBER

CRM systems are designed to help you grow sales and customer communications. As your business grows, your needs for data management will, too. Purchase a system that will enable you to scale your programs effectively for tracking more transactions, performing more analytics, and adding more names to your lists.

Putting DMPs and DSPs together for ROI

Ways to scale your data-driven marketing programs include DMPs. This is a system that looks at online behavior of consumers that reflect the consumers in your own database and provides you with more in-depth, specific information about their demographic and psychographic and behavioral trends and aggregates this information with your own data so you can identify spot-on customer segments. With all this information provided, you can pinpoint social sites, Facebook groups, and so on that your target customers frequent and place ads precisely where they'll actually be viewing.

As Tarantik sums it up, DMPs create highly targeted look-alike segments and highlight online sites in which to display ads, giving marketers in B2B and B2C spaces a very inexpensive and productive way to acquire new customers at a relatively low cost of acquisition. DMPs can retarget ads from a website to a Facebook page for specific customers in your database and are essential to helping your social media efforts pay off.

DMPs, like CRMs, are available from multiple sources. Some to consider include Adobe Audience Manager, Oracle BlueKai, and Neustar PlatformOne.

DMPs work in sync with DSPs, which are websites that give advertisers the ability to buy, track, and manage digital advertising across multiple platforms and websites. Sophisticated DSPs play an important role in online advertising, enabling marketers to target audiences in real time buying on multiple sites — from Google and Facebook to more obscure ones. This way, you can buy ads based on a site's performance for driving click-throughs and sales. Imagine having the command of Google AdWords but for many different advertising venues.

For example, using a DSP, you may test your ad on Facebook's News Feed against other online news platforms and compare to see which pulls best. You can get these results in a single day and then allocate your resources accordingly. For current options, search for the top 20 DSPs and you'll find many great options and reports from analysts such as Forrester.

TIP

Moving to a DSP model can help ensure that your campaign is optimized by real-time tracking, comparing, and buying/placement. DSPs also stay current when rules and algorithms of social sites that present advertising opportunities change. Having a system that stays up-to-date on its own can save you a lot of time reviewing, monitoring, and managing your ad placements.

For prospecting, data-driven advertising via DMPs and DSPs allows you to pinpoint products and channels of immediate relevance and retarget customers who have shown interest in both. This can produce substantial ROI in short order as you can deliver an ad to consumers while they're thinking about your product and shopping for alternatives. We call this communicating in real shopping time.

LEGENDARY INSIGHTS FROM ERNAN ROMAN

Ernan Roman, president of ERDM Corp. and 2011 inductee into the DMA Marketing Hall of Fame, is a pioneer in current-day direct marketing. Here are some of his insights on the role of data in marketing today. You can get more of his insights from his blog Ernan's Insights on Marketing Best Practices, which appears in *Huffington Post*, CMO.com, *Forbes*, and other sites.

What is human data and why is it critical for customer experience (CX) and data strategies?

Marketers must make a profound shift to human data, which is based on *explicit, self-profiled opt-in preference data*. This data enables customers to *identify their individual* issues, needs, and expectations regarding messaging, media, and frequency, among other things.

Findings from over 15,000 hours of Voice of Customer research we conducted for clients such as IBM, MassMutual, Microsoft, QVC, and Gilt, show customers today *expect* high levels of personalization in all communications and across all channels. And they want personalized experiences and interactions based on their *individual preferences*. Our study also shows *traditional implicit* data from web-browsing behavior, shopping cart and wait-listed items, previous items purchased, and data mined from social media are just not providing the necessary depth of information to drive relevant communications and offers. As a result, today's personalization attempts are falling far short of expectations.

Human data is unique in that it lends itself to segmentation based on *self-described* personality types, attitudes, and life stages. This powerful data should complement your traditional database information, such as previous purchases, demographic, behavioral information, and so on.

What are the seven critical points where customers want explicit data-driven personalized engagement?

1. Purchase
2. Onboarding
3. Anticipatory responses to decreasing engagement (visits, responses, purchases)
4. Immediate responses to negative experiences
5. Surprise-and-delight thank-yous
6. Value-added cross-selling and upselling
7. Repeat sales/renewals

How should I get started with the right data, metrics, and segments to begin an effective personalization and CX program?

First, obtaining customer insights with a goal of deep understanding is a key element of CX transformation because it enables brands to look at touch points and interactions from a value-driven and customer point of view. Conducting research to understand in detail how your customers want to experience high levels of relevance and personalization with your brand, based on their individual preferences, is key to enabling you to build a high-value database that delivers meaningful and relevant personalization and an improved CX based on earning the right to opt-in self-profiled information and preferences from your customers.

Next, define the criteria for success for your CX, database, and loyalty strategies. Set benchmarks and determine what factors and data you'll monitor regularly to evaluate progress, success, and improvements. Doing so will also help you gain a true understanding of how consumers interact with your brand and enable you to further shape strategy.

Creating Direct Campaigns for Direct Profitability

To optimize the power of direct marketing, organize your customer data in segments of like customers, which you can identify through your CRM analytics. Your data analytics can help you sort customers by recency, frequency, and monetary value, browsing and shopping habits, social media activity, life cycle and LTV, and more. By creating ESP profiles for top customer segments, you can build personas and communicate with even greater relevance.

The direct marketing strategies and campaigns you create for your segments should cross over multiple channels to provide a comprehensive view of customers and communicate in real time on the real channels that matter most to them.

Messaging matters

With the right technology in place and the right messaging, you'll be set up to build campaigns that can increase your marketing ROI, sales, and customer lifetime value. Your messaging is key to your campaign's success and needs to include the following key fundamentals, whether you use digital or print channels:

>> **Relevance:** Content, visuals, and offers that directly relate to the consumers' needs, lifestyle, and expressed interests.

>> **Personalization:** References specific to each customer's name, relationship with your brand, past purchases, and so on throughout the copy, visual, and graphics.

>> **Solution:** Evidence that builds a case that your product provides a real solution to a real problem. Building your case emotionally and with a sense of urgency is often the difference between success and failure.

>> **Call to action (CTA):** The action you want recipients to perform, which is often linked to timely offers or benefit. Your call to action — to call, email, or order online, register, or donate, and so on — is the ultimate goal of your letter or email, and all elements need to lead to this outcome. Without a strong CTA, your letter or email could be "set aside" for later and forgotten altogether.

>> **Bait:** For email, its your subject line. For print, it's leading headlines before the letter copy. Whatever format you're using, this is your first opportunity to catch the readers' eye and attention and pull them in deeper to your message in hopes of getting them to complete your CTA.

Outside matters

When using print, the copy on the outside of the envelope or mailer cover is what entices readers to open your mailer for more information. The same is true for subject lines in email, which we discuss later in the section "Going Direct with Email." Following are some techniques to make your envelope enticing enough to open:

>> **The stealth approach envelope:** Use an envelope that looks like a bill or personal letter. Customers will open the envelope just to find out what's inside, especially if it looks like a utility or credit card bill.

>> **The teaser envelope:** Craft a statement that sparks curiosity about the offer or message inside. A teaser about the offer, such as "You can save thousands with this offer" or "See what our free gift can do for you," helps get your envelope opened by people who are actually interested in an offer from you.

>> **The special offer envelope:** Promote your call to action on the envelope, whether it be to enter a sweepstakes to win a million dollars, get free samples or a first month of service free, or find valuable coupons. Like the teaser, this envelope inspires the customer to open and learn more.

>> **The creative envelope:** If your teaser and creative are strong and unusual, you'll get people opening it out of curiosity. Tests from various groups show that dimensional mail, such as small boxes, and oversized formats, like big postcards or brochures, perform better than traditional formats, like a #10 envelope letter package.

In general, a letter combined with an insert, like a one-page flier or a small brochure, pulls better than a letter alone. This is another element worth testing because adding inserts adds to the cost of production and mailing. (See the section "Testing direct," later in this chapter.)

Actions that matter

Every letter you send must have a CTA for response or you're not likely to get much action from readers. Look at your CTA as the climax to your letter campaign's story. The action is what leads to the engagement you need to close a sale and the metric that will help you determine responses and ROI. Here are some examples:

>> Call a toll-free number to process an order/sale.

>> Register for our subscription program via an online form.

>> Email for more information on a product or to schedule a free consultation.

>> Sign up for coupons/discounts.

>> Take an online survey (which enables you to get feedback and capture emails).

>> Return a form in a postage-paid enclosed envelope to process a sale, subscription, or donation if you're in fundraising.

REMEMBER

You must be able to track the source for your CTA. If you have multiple campaigns in play at the same time, be sure to code each campaign separately so if you use the same CTA, say, a call to a toll-free number, you can track calls back to each specific campaign, mailing list, or customer segment. A simple method is to use a different phone number for every creative you send, a different landing page for every campaign directing consumers to your web page, and so on. If you're testing different lists with the same creative, be sure to send each list to a different response mechanism so you can determine which pulls best.

TIP

A coupon offer often improves response rates and can help you track sales easily. Give each coupon a unique code number so you can track the sale to a specific campaign, mailing, and individual customer.

Directing consumers to web landing pages will help you capture data and permission for further communications, so never leave these out of your contact options or sources for more information listed in your print material.

When it comes to mailing your letter package, you have options to consider: standard bulk mail, first class mail, and overnight packages. Traditionally, overnight packages get opened the most, but the open rate may not justify the cost unless each sale is substantial and can easily pay for the cost of the campaign.

Mailing tips

If your mailing is bigger than you can print, stuff, and mail out yourself, consider hiring a print services company to do it for you. You can hire a full-scale printer that does all formats and sizes on off-set or digital presses or a quick print shop like an AlphaGraphics or Allegra franchise. Either way, they'll be able to get your mailing out quickly and pretty affordably.

If you do your own printing and mailing, talk to your local post office to find out how to handle metered or permit mail and processes and prices for bulk mailings.

EXAMPLE

System Pavers (www.systempavers.com), a leading designer and installer of interlocking paving stone outdoor living systems, was using a traditional direct marketing piece that had worked well but was reaching a point of diminishing return. It wanted to create a direct marketing campaign around the psychological values discussed in Chapter 2 to test against its control. By using all the principles discussed in this book and executing them through a direct marketing channel, we were able to achieve a 3,100 percent ROI and generate at least 200 percent more revenue than the control. Here's a summary of the processes we took to achieve those results:

>> **Messaging:** We needed to find an emotional value that would resonate with potential customers. System Pavers creates beautiful paving stone driveways, walkways, BBQ stations, outdoor kitchens, water features, and so much more. None are necessary for daily functions, and the cost for outdoor living upgrades can be expensive, so we had to assign an emotional value to this non-emotional product.

>> **Survey and research:** To find the right emotional value that would spur a high-end home improvement project, we surveyed existing customers to find out how they "felt" about their new outdoor living systems. We then reviewed those results with testimonials gathered over the years to identify and build ESP. We discovered that many felt their home was like part of their family, so we built our ESP messaging around family values and rekindling love sparks, like when you first moved in to your house and when Mom and Dad first fell in love.

>> **Format:** Because the decision to upgrade and remodel your home's outdoor living spaces is a complex decision, we decided it needed more than a self-mailer with product photos and limited-time offer copy. So we created a newsletter — a four-page large format mailer that included a lot of content around our ESP and the customer decision process. Our copy centered around the theme of "Love Your Home Again," as, like with our family members, we see no flaws at the beginning of a relationship or living in a house, but over time we notice a lot of little things we want to change. We also included statements about our leaders and customer satisfaction results to build trust and confidence in our brand.

>> **Testing:** We then tested our new "Love Your Home Again" theme and format against the control, another large format self-mailer in select markets. We chose test cells in two regions where System Pavers serves and compared like cells in each region against each other to weed out any geographical influences. We assigned the test and control pieces to like homes in each cell so we could test messaging and not economic or social variances. We sent three mailings to our test cells to ensure that no anomalies existed in our process.

We also tested results among past customers or prospects we'd already mailed to and cold prospects with no prior contact with our brand. And we tested email against print direct mail.

Our results were very telling. Our ESP approach achieved a 3,100 percent ROI and outperformed the control for revenue generated. Interestingly, the print version outperformed email, reflecting that we still like to hold onto things that matter, and when you're making big changes to an emotional part of your life, tactile marketing material matters.

Figure 10-1 shows a visual of the first edition of "Love Your Home Again."

Purchasing lists

As evidenced by the DMA data and campaign examples shared earlier in this chapter, direct marketing tends to generate higher results from in-house lists. Yet purchasing prospect lists is critical to customer acquisition and to building your own lists of qualified leads.

List purchasing options are many, including

>> **One-time rental of prospect lists based on attributes you designate:** If a consumer replies, you own that name and can add it to your in-house list.

>> **Census-based lists that provide information about households in demographic areas:** These are less expensive than modeled data lists that come from in-depth analytics of customer groups, past transactions and behavior, and other attributes.

>> **Modeled lists from data companies that create, manage, and sell lists they compile from tens of millions of households:** These lists may be built upon household data they compile from various sources or from surveys they conduct to sort consumers in multiple segments according to preferences and needs, life events, and so on.

>> **New movers who help you find newcomers to your marketplace:** There are a few options for purchasing these so look around to find the best partner.

FIGURE 10-1:
Direct marketing from System Pavers.

Image courtesy of System Pavers

You can also participate in a co-op database, which is a compilation of your mailing lists combined with those of other companies targeting the same customers. Each contributor to the database has access to the full database, which is duplicated and often enhanced to make the database more valuable. These lists are often highly effective because they consist of customers who have been vetted in a sense by other brands and know their purchasing behavior. However, you have to be willing to share your lists to participate.

Create your ESP customer profiles, run analytics to find the common emotional, demographic, and functional trends, and then purchase lists that support those trends.

TIP

Take time to browse analytics you receive from your list supplier instead of just reading the report it generates. You may find insights about your prospects that didn't show up in the summary reports.

For example, I (Jeanette) was working with a client in the utility space and looking to buy lists to expand our lead generation for an ancillary service. We hired a data firm to run analytics on our households and show us purchasing, lifestyle, demographic, and even political trends. One thing we noticed that didn't show up on the data firm's report of strong attributes was that most customers paid off their credit cards regularly and carried little credit debt. This showed a trend toward responsible spending that we added to our messaging and our profiling for future data models.

Test various data models against each other as well. As you get results and reports from your data provider, you can even test the top percentile from one segment against the top or middle percentile from another to help you more precisely identify who you need to be targeting for optimum returns.

List suppliers usually have minimums. Start by purchasing the minimum amount of names and test them. This will help you more efficiently identify the types of lists with the highest return for you.

REMEMBER

If you intend to make direct marketing a core component of your marketing plan — and to succeed today, you must — it's important that you find a list supplier you trust. Take your time to ask questions about its sources and how its lists are managed to stay current and valid, analytical processes, and so on. Ask for referrals to see how lists performed and how much waste, if any, was experienced due to returned mail and other issues.

Remember the basic principle of list buying: The best indicator of future purchase is past purchase. Try to find lists of people who've purchased something similar to what you're selling rather than just a demographics-based list.

Going Direct with Email

Email is one of the most cost-efficient and highest-producing methods for direct marketing, especially among your current customers. As noted earlier from the DMA data for 2016, the return on ad spend (ROAS), or your media investment ROI, is 122 percent on average for email. You'll be hard-pressed to find a better return on any other advertising or communications channel. And the results for email-open, click-through, and conversion rates just keep getting better year over year.

This section explains how to develop direct email campaigns that get response, build customer relationships, and teach you about your customers and what they respond to most, all at the same time.

One of email's many advantages is that you can measure it in ways you can't measure anything else. With print direct mail, you never really know how recipients opened your letter or saw your offer before choosing not to respond. With email, you can know how many actually

>> Opened your email

>> Clicked through to read more information about your offer or message

>> Engaged with your sales team via phone or email, or other response

>> Purchased or performed another desired behavior

You can also discover with precision which message, offer, subject line, day of send, time of send, frequency of send, list, and so much more drove sales, down to the individual level.

TIP

Knowing how email performs in general will give you a benchmark against which you can compare your own results to see whether your campaign is really all that good. According to all the data out there on email click-and-open rates, both of which are critical to sales growth, the rates you need to achieve are . . . well, it depends. Both your open and click-through rates go up as the frequency of your sends go up until you cross the threshold of too many, and then both start to decline.

DMA data shows email rates for house lists as follows for 2016:

>> Open rate: 21 percent

>> Click-through rate: 10 percent, up around 4 points from 2015

>> Conversion rate: 5.5 percent, up from 1.5 in 2012 and 2.9 in 2015

Research from HubSpot, a software company for CRM, marketing, and sales systems, shows that the more you send, the more you gain. The "sweet spot" it identified is to send between 16 and 30 email campaigns a month to your various segments, not all to the same customer segments. Companies that operate at this range end up with more than two times the click rate of those that send only one to two campaigns a month, according to its research.

So create enough meaningful content that you can execute campaigns at that frequency. Another lesson is that you need a content management process or digital asset management system to help you adapt your content quickly per segment so you can maintain a strong pattern of frequency. If you stick with the 16 to 30 campaigns a month range, per HubSpot, you can expect median open and click-through rates, such as

>> Open rate: 32.4 percent

>> Click-through rate: 6.5 percent

More data shows that the average open rate for B2B companies is 30 percent and those companies sending 16 to 30 campaigns a month had the highest median click rate of 6 percent.

The most effective emails for short- and long-term sales are personalized and triggered emails, both of which are based on customers' known interests, past transactions or browsing history, and data profiles.

Triggered email

Triggered emails are those that your CRM system sends automatically in direct response to customers' browsing or shopping behavior, an event, action, missed opportunity, or change in behavior or status. According to Epsilon's research, triggered emails achieved an average open rate of 57.5 percent. Compare that with the numbers in the previous section from DMA and HubSpot, and it's easy to see how important triggered emails are for any business.

One of the most effective uses of triggered emails is to get people to go back to abandoned online shopping carts, a critical part of an email and overall marketing strategy if you're in the e-commerce space.

Industry vendor SurePayroll estimates that businesses are walking away from more than $18 billion in sales each year by not capturing sales in shopping carts before they're abandoned. That alarming figure comes from about 70 percent of shopping carts being abandoned, per a study industry vendors Bronto and Magento performed. If you have a bricks-and-mortar shop and 70 percent of the shoppers who walked through your door put something on hold just to never come back and buy, you'd be hard-pressed to stay in business.

TIP

Here are some amazing insights from Jeanne Jennings, a consultant and recognized expert in email marketing strategy (www.JeanneJennings.com) on creating powerful email campaigns:

>> According to research from Bronto/Magento and SaleCycle, at least 85 percent of shoppers say that cart reminders are helpful, and more than 35 percent of the clicks resulting from those reminders lead to purchase.

>> More than 60 percent of shoppers said a reminder would get them back to a site.

>> Less than 21 percent of retailers, which likely includes your competitors, are sending reminders (Return Path study).

Executing a triggered email campaign not only can help you stand out from those that don't, but it will likely help you capture wallet share that others are leaving behind. If you're in e-commerce and you're not monitoring cart abandonment and sending reminders, you're starting to get an idea of just how much money you're walking away from.

Jennings has some tips that work for retailers for making cart reminders work:

>> **Offer free shipping.** Most consumers expect free shipping these days, and it makes your customers feel rewarded for coming back.

>> **Include a product image, but not too many.** A few good images inspire click-through, but too many results in inertia.

>> **Add urgency.** Going back to basic direct marketing practices and your survival DNA, make the offer limited in time or availability. Statements like "Offer ends on XX date" or "Only one left" seem to get people to act sooner than later.

>> **Offer a discount.** Reward shoppers for coming back to their cart and give them a discount to close it out this time.

>> **Offer assistance.** Make it clear how to email or call, or better yet, offer live chat from the cart screen to help them get to yes without further delay.

>> **Send more than one reminder.** If they don't respond with the first reminder, send them another.

Personalized email

Like printed direct mail, email works best when personalized. HubSpot's research shows that when the recipient's first name is in the subject line, the click-through rate goes up. Other research from Statista shows that the open rate for a personalized email is upwards of 17 percent and closer to 11 percent when not personalized.

Personalization is key to success today and is not likely to change anytime soon. It's dependent on having strong CRM and content management systems (see Chapter 6 on content marketing) that enables you to customize your content for various personas, cultures, languages, segments, and even channels.

TIP

Direct-mail print or email needs to be seen like a series of communications. Although the first piece is designed to get a sale, it typically takes three or more touch points to achieve the desired behavior. Creating a series of touch points helps to increase the return and conversion. You can mix up your channels, too. Maybe send a first touch point by letter, reinforce it with a corresponding email, and then try to close the deal with another letter that's highly personalized and has a stronger call to action or offer.

REMEMBER

Your envelope and subject lines are the first strategic messages your customers see, so you have to master these to get action. Never underestimate the value of a good copywriter.

Testing direct

To work most effectively, test various messages and channels to see which work best for your industry, your customer database, and your offers. You can test messages and offers over email before utilizing more expensive channels to save money and time. Your tests should cover multiple variables to find the perfect combination of channels, messages, and offers for your brand and customer base.

One of the prime advantages of direct marketing is the ease and affordability it provides for testing. Truthfully, there's no reason you shouldn't be testing your campaigns, and if you're not, you're likely wasting a lot of money and walking away from huge opportunities to learn about what works and what doesn't, your customers' preferences and how to optimize efficiencies.

The list of testing variables is extensive, as shown in Table 10-1. What matters is not just that you test, but how you set up your test so you know precisely what you're finding out and can glean actual truths rather than assumptions.

Following are some guidelines for conducting a test that delivers clean and confident results:

>> **Variables:** Test only a few variables at one time. If you have too many variables in play for a single test, sorting out the actual influence of each is difficult. For example, if you're testing two creative options, keep the offer the same so you truly know what pulled response: the creative design or the offer.

>> **Metrics:** Have in place clear metrics so you can document actual response and sales from each direct campaign you execute. Code your response cards for the offer, incentive, and time of your campaign. For example, if you're sending a letter package to customers and prospects and offering a 10 percent discount, and you sent the letter out in May 2017, your code for new customers may look like:

> DM0517NC10 – Direct Mail May 2017 New Customer 10% off

>> **A/B Tests:** Straight A/B tests are the simplest ones to execute. You send out two versions of the same campaign at the same time to the same test cells and see which one, A or B, pulls the most. After you identify a winner or a champion, keep testing that piece against new ideas and offers. This is a simple yet powerful way to find out how little elements change results. You learn quickly and thus can adapt quickly.

> You can use marketing automation software to execute A/B tests to speed up the execution and analysis, enabling you to continuously test and learn. An A/B test can be as simple as testing the colors you use in your creative, the size and placement of your CTA graphics, and which incentive, headline, or subject line work best.

> If you don't have time or money to do a lot of testing, check out www.behave.org to see test results for just about everything.

>> **Document:** As you test offers, formats, creative, and such among your customer lists, keep track of which customers responded to which offers at which time. This will help you know how to segment customers according to when they're most likely to purchase and for what they're most likely to purchase.

>> **Goals:** Before executing your tests, have a learning plan or goal in mind. Outline what you want to learn, when you need this new knowledge, and when and how you'll execute the test. In addition to seeing what creative and offer combination sells the most product or generates the most leads, establish learning goals about your customers. What information can you gain from each test to better segment customers according to purchase cycles, lifestyle, preferences, and so on to increase your level of personalization and effectiveness in the future.

Table 10-1 lists some variables to consider testing in print and in email.

TABLE 10-1   Variables to Test in Print and Email

Print	Email
Database lists and segments	Email lists and segments
Responses based on CTA	Open rates and click-through rates
Inserts versus no inserts	Google sponsored ads (email ads at top of inbox)
Offers	Offers
Reply cards versus phone calls	PURLs and landing page views
Free gifts versus no free gift	Free gifts versus no free gift
Coupon for free lunch versus discount	Coupon for free lunch versus discount
Response mechanism	Response mechanism
Creative and layout	Creative design or text-only format
Envelope teaser	Subject line
Call to action	Call to action
Envelope color and return address	From line
Arrival time to HH — time of week	Send time — day of week, time of day

Maximizing direct response online

As pointed out earlier, creating an omni-channel direct response program is one of the most effective ways to build, nurture, and convert leads and maximize lifetime value. For example, if a consumer opens an email and clicks through to your website but doesn't purchase, you can use your DMP and DSP to post ads on social sites remarketing the product of prior interest.

Also invest in search engine marketing options that allow you to be above the scroll for keyword searches related to your category. With the right systems in place, your ad can pop up in a sidebar of a site that's frequently visited by someone who's actively searching for information related to purchases in your category.

Pop-up ads should integrate the elements of successful direct marketing by having an incentive and a timely call to action. Consider offering a discount, free shipping, or other incentive that has a limited time frame for response.

Purchasing space on websites relevant to your customer base is also a good channel for direct-response ads. Algorithms on various sites can tell you how often prospects are exposed, if you're at risk of overexposure, and whether prospects will be pulled from the pool after they make a purchase (if not, continued advertising may annoy them). You don't need to be an expert on how algorithms work to serve ads to site visitors, but you do need to ensure that your exposure is being managed sensibly. If not, do it manually by limiting the exposures and not allowing the same ad to run endlessly.

TIP

Monitor the results of your online ads so you can pull back on low-performing ad sites and shift to high-performing ones. The web offers very rapid feedback about performance, so request and review the stats often. An interesting statistic that sometimes can be tracked (for example, with the newest Facebook advertising support) is *viewthrough*, which is the percent of people who view your direct-response ad and then, say, within the hour, visit your website. They don't have to click on the ad itself for you to get a sale, so that's why it's interesting to track viewthrough along with ad response.

Integrating Call and Chat Centers

Whether you staff or outsource online chat or call centers, you need to integrate the messaging and tone of your direct-response campaigns with the experience and service that happens when a customer actually calls you. And even today, many still use the phone. So you need to include phone numbers in your direct-response mechanisms.

Here are some tips to making sure this part of the sales process moves smoothly and closes the sale you started with your direct mail campaign:

>> Keep in mind that every person is a call center or online chat representative, but most don't realize it. You need to manage these points of customer contact very carefully by outlining how you want your phones and emails to be answered, the tone you want for your brand correspondence, the process for getting answers to questions, and how you end the call so that you can encourage further action and follow-up. Having scripts and reviewing protocols in staff meetings is an important way to manage your live brand communications.

>> However consumers choose to engage with you via online chat, phone, email, or some type of online response mechanism, don't underestimate the importance of responding quickly. Consumers don't have patience to wait online or on hold to buy something. They'll disconnect and go somewhere else.

>> Even though most people use cellphones and don't use toll-free numbers much, still offer one. Giving customers many options for contacting you helps make sure they do, and toll-free numbers still carry a sense of added credibility.

Making use of phone time

Being accessible to your customers in part means having staff by the phones during the hours customers are most likely to call and making sure they don't sit on hold long. Research shows that the shorter the wait to get what they want, the greater the chance of getting the sale.

Make your on-hold messages matter. Don't just use them to keep promoting the products you mentioned in your direct-response campaigns; use them to keep customers happy. Tell them how to reach you via email or web if they don't want to wait, and be sure to tell them how long to expect to wait.

TIP

Keep your wait times relevant to what you perceive to be an acceptable amount of time. Depending on the nature of your product and customer, that time limit is probably less than two perceived minutes. A *perceived minute* is the time period a customer on hold thinks he has waited for a minute — and that time typically comes out to be more like 40 seconds when you measure it on the clock.

If you want to hire a call center, look for some that also do online chat so you can integrate all your messages across channels.

Capturing useful information about each caller

One of the most important functions for your call center is to field inquiries or orders from new customers as they respond to your various direct-response campaigns. These callers are hot leads that you need to gather information from. Ask how they heard of your company, and document the conversation to help with future issues that may occur and to add to the profile of the customers you talk to.

Telemarketing: To call or not

Direct-response phone efforts in the past worked well and generated a good response because live callers tend to say yes more than they do to other channels. However, with all the regulations, privacy concerns, and Do Not Call Lists in play today, this is an increasingly difficult channel. Add the popularity of online chat versus customer service calls, and you have even more reasons not to make direct calls.

Here are some tips if you choose to include phone calls in your direct-response mix:

>> **Call only those consumers with whom you have a relationship.** Cold lists produce cold results and waste a lot of time and can be a big turnoff to consumers who feel you've invaded their privacy. Many businesses today call people who have engaged with them through social media or who initiated a relationship by requesting information about their business or the industry in general. If your content marketing plan offers customers a free white paper, research report, checklist, or how-to guide, it's acceptable to many if you call them shortly after they've downloaded it to see whether they have any questions or would like a product demo. If you make such calls, be sure to tell them why you're calling and make the call about their questions first and your desired next steps, such as product demo or free consultation, second.

>> **Staff your call center with trained, competent salespeople.** You want people who can represent your company in a professional and engaging manner. Don't just let them wing difficult calls. Anticipate customer issues, comments, complaints. Prepare a response script and train each employee how to deliver the messages that script so your team responds professionally and consistently.

>> **Prepare a good call script and adapt for various scenarios.** Craft messaging for when customers call you, when you call customers, and how to respond to various concerns, complaints, and issues. If you have defined your ESP, your call scripts should address this as much as possible.

>> **Call to follow up.** No matter what business you're in, assigning a team member to call each customer after a service visit or product purchase is a great way to build rapport and loyalty.

>> **Consider closing each call with a survey-type question.** You can change this weekly or monthly or however often you want to. Doing so lets you learn about customers so you can better define your ESP and messaging.

own site

» Creating a strong website for
engaging customers and building
relationships

» Using design elements that enhance
the stickiness of your website

» Developing a web marketing strategy

» Driving sales with landing pages,
PURLs, blogs, and more

» Making money off web traffic

Chapter **11**

Building a Website That Engages and Sells

N ot all that long ago, websites were little more than digital brochures that simply served as informational pages about a business, its products, and how to contact it for more information. Now, websites have become dynamic communities where ideas are shared, advice is given, and live engagement takes place. More importantly, consumers have come to expect websites to be a place where they can get comprehensive information about a product and the brand and engage directly with brand representatives to learn more as they research their options and make carefully concerted choices.

In addition to having a website that sets forth your brand story in an engaging way that inspires others to stay tuned and want to be part of your story, you need to ensure that all your digital assets support the tone and persona of your site. This is critical because your website is like the mother ship, or the hub, of all your brand identity. Your digital assets, such as ads on Facebook, Twitter, and other sites you've chosen to appear on, point your customers back to the hub where they can engage with real people, learn about your brand story and products, and choose whether to engage on a journey with your brand or another one.

This chapter outlines some tactics and techniques for building a strong identity on your own site and supporting it with consistency across all your digital assets.

Creating and Managing a Web Identity

Your *web identity* is the sum of your messaging and persona on your own site and other digital sites, such as blogs, social media sites, search engine listings, and product review sites. Managing and controlling this identity should be a top priority for your marketing team. You shouldn't take it lightly because the values, persona, credibility, and trustworthiness you project affects consumers' interest in doing business with you.

Part of managing this identity involves managing the company you keep. Just like people often judge you by the friends you associate with in the real world, they will also judge your brand by the sites on which your logo, messaging, and promotions appear. If you don't want to be seen as a brand that supports unhealthy living, don't advertise on a site that promotes eating unhealthy diets. Just the appearance on a site implies indirectly that your values are the same. Again, don't take this lightly unless you want to take on the daunting task of reputation management.

When building a website, you need to start with the realization that a website is no longer a nicely designed information center but rather a portal for all your web activity and a tool that establishes your brand identity and image. For example: Your main home page creates the first impression many will have of your brand. Your site will also have many other entry points, or landing pages, for visitors coming through specific activities, such as social media pages, search engines, online contests you set up, specific offers, links directly to a form to register for an event or download a paper, and many more.

Each of these landing pages is critical and must maintain the same persona, projected values, and identity as your home page. They must also easily direct visitors back to your main site and overall menu.

The next sections take a closer look at what you can do to establish and manage your web identity.

Understanding what consumers expect

Just like perception is everything, "expectations" are everything when it comes to marketing. When shopping, most of us have expectations about a product price, quality, features, benefits and so on while looking at options for purchase. Consumers expect to find certain elements that meet those expectations when browsing on a brand's website during the purchasing process. Expectations are not just limited to product features and prices but also for information about the brand, its leadership, and values. The latter is especially true for B2B purchases. Some examples of the information we seek to fulfill or deny our expectations include

>> **Product detail:** Product detail is anything from features and functions to specifications and pricing. This information is important because shoppers are likely comparing the details of your product to others they are considering so sometimes the more detail you provide, the greater the chance of closing the deal.

>> **Leadership:** Many purchasers, especially in B2B, want to know about the leadership of a business. If they're buying an IT application that they'll need to live with for a few years, they want to know how stable and experienced your leaders are to determine your staying power. They may even want to know who some of your backers and investors are for added assurance that you have the ability to fund your growth and their account.

>> **Testimonials:** Consumers want to know what others are saying about their experience with your products and your overall persona. Even though most people don't put bad reviews on their website and those present are always positive, it still helps to see what others say so you can form your own expectations.

>> **Corporate social responsibility (CSR):** As mentioned many times throughout this book, consumers care what brands are doing to give back to communities and move the world toward a better place. They want to support movements such as those offered by TOMS and Patagonia, not just shareholder goals. Many turn to websites to see what a brand is doing, and what they find about CSR values, initiatives, and results often determines the brands they choose.

>> **Engagement:** Gone are the days when customers were willing to sit on hold to ask a question about a product or a return policy. Consumers now go to websites and expect to be invited to chat with a knowledgeable customer service representative in real time and really quickly. Online engagement and chat are becoming more and more critical for websites, especially e-commerce sites.

>> **Policies, FAQs, and terms:** Consumers want easy access to your return policy, shipping methods, shipping costs, customer service processes, sizing

guides, and so on. Being able to find these easily simplifies their research process. If they can't find this information on your site, they'll go to another site and likely find it there.

>> **Communities:** People want to engage with others with like values and compare ideas, products, insights, and more. Look at all the chat communities for car owners, computer experts, programmers, and home chefs. Making your site engaging beyond live information about your products is another key strategy for keeping people on your site and getting them to come back — two fundamental goals of web marketing for any business.

>> **Efficiency:** For e-commerce sites, people expect to be able to find what they want quickly and check out as simply as possible. Again, the longer it takes to check out, the more likely they are to leave.

Having all the information consumers seek on your website in an easy-to-find format is critical to making your web investment pay off and to capturing sales. The quicker people find what they want, the longer they'll stay on your site and the greater chance you have of closing the sale. "Stickiness," or how long a person "sticks" on your site before bouncing off to another, is a key metric for the success of your website and something you can easily measure with web analytics.

Standardizing your web identity

When building your web identity, you need to be clear and consistent, and all you do needs to reinforce the emotional selling proposition (ESP) and value proposition that define your brand and core values. A top goal should be to have your brand recognized and reinforced *everywhere* that you're present, on and off the web.

As simple as it seems, the URLs you use are important. Besides your company name, which is a given, find URLs that define what you do and purchase them for your website as well. For example, if your business is a pet boarding facility called Five Star Lodging for Pets, not only get the URL for that name but also consider purchasing a URL that will come up on the search engines, such as www.petlodging.com, www.luxuryhotelfordogs.com, and www.safeboardingforpets.com — kind of like hashtags come up for tweets or pages with common terms.

TIP

Your URLs should be consistent with your other social site names and tags, such as your blog, Facebook page, Twitter page, Instagram account, and LinkedIn account. Using your brand name as often as possible helps reinforce your presence, but in some cases it doesn't work for a handle or is too close to another account's name. In this case, you can add a simple defining word, such as *best*, *leading*, *info*, or *blog*, to help connect the account or page to your brand. Per the earlier example, a good name for a blog or Facebook page may be FiveStarLodgingBlogforPets.com.

Take the time to register all possible URLs that relate to your brand before someone else does and then tries to sell them to you for thousands. If you're a consultant, register your personal name and your brand name. If part of your name reflects your region, such as Intermountain, register the short versions and the long version.

For example, Intermountain Healthcare, which owns hospitals and clinics in a tri-state area in the mountain states, owns the domains of `www.intermountain healthcare.org` and `www.ihc.org`. It also owns the `.com`, `.org`, and even `.biz` versions of that name. Purchasing all potential URLs drives more people to your site as they search for you and helps them find you faster and easier, while also protecting your identity. If you own the `.com` version and someone else owns the `.biz` version of your URL, you can easily get caught up in a case of mistaken identity, and you just don't know what kind of business you may get mistaken for. Paying that minimal price for a domain name is worth all the hassles of repairing issues associated with confused identities or losing customers to another site or to the frustration of not being able to find your brand quickly.

REMEMBER

Also, make sure your domain name doesn't violate someone's trademark. Check web addresses against a database of trademarks (in the United States, you can do this search for free by going to `www.uspto.gov`, clicking on the Trademarks link at the top of the page, and clicking on Trademark Search), or ask a lawyer to do a more detailed analysis if you think you may run into an issue. The trademarked domain name you want may be available, meaning you can register it at a site like `www.register.com` because nobody else has yet, but if you begin using it, the owner of the trademark may sue you.

After you register your website, take steps to protect your new domain name. Purchase options such as multi-year registration and protection against lapsing due to late payment. Again, people are out there just waiting for a site to expire so they can quickly purchase it and sell it back to you for thousands. Consider purchasing private domain registration, in which your host doesn't give out your personal details as the owner of the site.

If an obvious misspelling for your site exists, register that, too. The alternate names can be set up as simple redirects, and they'll keep a competitor from owning a domain that may receive some of the traffic you generate.

Creating an Engaging Website

This is where it gets fun . . . and complicated. Fun because you have a blank story board in front of you and many tools at your fingertips for painting and telling your brand story in ways that make your customers want to be a part of it.

Complicated because at the time of this writing, more than 1.1 billion websites are active on the Internet. This means that there's a lot of competition to get people to go to your website and stay on it!

For perspective, if consumers search for "furniture stores in Colorado," today they'd get more than 3 million sites to browse. If you're one of those sites and you're lucky enough to get them to open your page, you have the added challenge of keeping them there. This is where the design and messaging of your home page needs to be more than just a pretty picture.

The first impression you create for visitors coming to your site is influenced by the color, fonts, and layout of your page. If you want people to feel excited and energized by your brands and products, you need energetic colors that stimulate happy, fun moods to dominate your color palette. You also need to have fonts that reflect their persona or sense of self. You can choose fun fonts like Chalkboard that create a playful, whimsical feeling, or traditional fonts like Times New Roman that reflect a tone of academics, knowledge, or news. Both have an impact on the browser's immediate snap judgment about the relevance of a given site. (For more on the psychology of color and imagery, see Chapters 2 and 7.)

After you've assured the unconscious mind that your site reflects their persona with your initial colors and style, you need to immediately engage your visitors and enable them to find what they're looking for quickly so they stay on your site. You can do this effectively in many ways. But before we get into design elements, you need to have a few goals in mind when designing your site, which we explore in the following sections.

Watching your KPIs

Clearly, your first goal to creating a web page is to drive traffic. The majority of this book is on how to do that through different marketing activities. But there's more to measure than traffic. You need to know what people are doing once they get to your site and how long they stay there. Without this information, you really don't know how your investment is paying off, and you can't monitor the activity and interests of your customers when it comes specifically to their experience with your messaging, branding, and sales experience on your own page.

The following sections present a few key performance indicator (KPI) goals from the experts on web analytics and marketing.

Bounce rate

This is the percentage of visitors that are directed to a page on your site and don't go past the first page they land on. Your goal is to get them to dig deeper to engage them with your message and move them toward a sale. Or two.

On average, according to various reports from many different analysts, bounce rates range from 20 to 90 percent of visitors, meaning that this percentage of people leave after viewing just one page. And with this huge range, it covers just about everyone.

The lowest rates tend to be for e-commerce and retail sites and the highest for websites that share news and information. A good bounce rate goal is pretty much any number under 50 percent.

Google Analytics shows the following bounce rates for a few specific types of sites. Use these benchmarks as a starting point for your own website and check your own Google Analytics reports to see whether you're above or below average. Google Analytics provides information on all the following for your website to help you monitor daily how well your site is working for you. It's easy to sign up at www.google.com/analytics.

Type of Website	Average Bounce Rate
Content websites	40–60%
Lead generation	30–50%
Blogs	70–98%
Retail	20–40%
Service sites	10–30%
Landing pages	70–90%

Here are some ways to keep your bounce rates low:

» Give visitors a reason to stay, such as a promotional offer they don't want to miss.

» Present something inspirational and relevant, such as a video on a topic that can help them solve a problem or feel better about the world.

» Don't offer links to go elsewhere. Don't tell them to check out a partner's page, an industry report, or link to a coupon somewhere else because they're not likely to come back to your site.

» Implement better design, content flow, and access to desirable information.

Average session duration

It goes without saying that the longer people stay on your website, the stronger your chance is of converting them to customers. Average session durations vary across the board, but what matters most is monitoring your own session duration. This is defined by the duration of each visitor, which you can track with Google Analytics, which divides the average length of each user's session by the number of sessions. It's not the same as *time on page*, which gives you the amount of time each user spent and an average for all users on each page of your site.

Your goal is to, again, give people a reason to come back to your site and stay longer. If your average session duration and time on page numbers decrease, it's time to think about changing your site so users get a new experience when they come back and doing some things differently to make it more engaging.

Following are some ways to do this:

>> Include a brief and emotionally relevant video on your home page to create a mood for your visitors and introduce them to the value you offer.

Referring to the earlier Intermountain Healthcare example, its home page does a nice job of this because it greets users with a video of people doing active things that keep people healthy and happy. The video has its mission statement scripted over it, which helps to depict how your life could unfold if you partner with it for health. The rest of the site's navigation could use some improving, but the home page does a good job of engaging you with emotional relevance and interest.

Samsung has a great video, or file as it calls it, inspiring viewers to get fit by using their smartphone and GearFit 2 application. It's fun and engages you while you contemplate your own fitness goals. Unlike the video on ihc.org, you have to click to watch this one. Samsung changes the videos frequently to promote more products and inspire more engagement and creates a different experience for return visitors to the site.

>> Try a slide show to showcase who you are or products you represent. Despite the advent of home page videos, slide shows are still widely used and can be just as effective if the images and messages are powerful and relevant. Apple uses a full-screen slide show to showcase its latest products.

>> Plant a live webcam in your office so visitors can see your place of work live and "feel" like they just walked into your real-world office. Customedialabs. com does this. You can get a view of its lobby or main work station. If you have something more interesting, like people installing a new kitchen, landscaping a public playground, or rescuing a puppy from a river, you're likely to really achieve more time on page and a great average session duration.

Pages per session

If you have a good site that's meaningful to your audience and provides them with the information or products they seek, they'll view more pages on your site. It's that simple. To see how you're doing, you can review your page view counts and unique page views. Page view counts tally in more than one view of the same page by an individual, and unique views count only one view per individual so you don't get skewed data if one person continues to go back to the same page during a given session, giving you the impression that that information or product is more popular than it actually is.

Again, averages bounce all over the place, but if you can achieve two pages per session and around two minutes per session, you're doing well.

Making content king on your website

So if you're not an e-commerce site with lots of product pages for people to view as they shop, how do you get people to view more pages when they come to visit so you can engage them longer and increase your chance of converting them to a sale or other desired transaction? You've heard it before: *Improve your content.*

Chapter 6 discusses content marketing across channels. Here, we're keeping the focus on websites and web pages. To achieve your web "stickiness" goals of more time onsite and more time per session, you need to keep your content focused on what matters most to consumers at the time they choose to go to your web page. Here's a little exercise to help you:

1. **List the top reasons people come to your website directly, not organically.**

For example:

- To get information about your product
- To check out your prices
- To read about your return policies
- To look for sales
- To assess your leadership
- To find your product or systems, results, and capabilities to see whether they meet needs
- To compare your products or systems, results, capabilities, features, and so on to competitors'

2. **List the top content themes or topics they most often seek.**

Some of these might include the following:

- **Product comparisons:** Be brave. Show how your product's features and prices compare to others. This level of transparency builds trust and most often takes price out of the equation.

- **Purchasing guides:** These are popular with both B2B and B2C customers because no one wants to experience decision regret. Purchasing guides can include how not to overbuy technology, insurance, or too much house for your income.

- **How-to guides:** Even if you offer a service, customers tend to bond better with brands that show them how to do it themselves. They often realize that they're not an expert or don't have the time, so they call you to come do it for them.

- **White papers on marketing, selling, and technology topics:** These don't have to be long, just meaningful and actionable.

- **Research findings:** Everyone loves research and learning what other people are thinking. Nielson makes many reports available to its website, as does HubSpot, which also creates infographics you can use in your own presentations. This is a great strategy because all who use its infographics help it strengthen its position as a leading marketing analytics CRM authority.

If you don't know the answers to complete this exercise, you just found a new question or two to ask in your customer surveys (check out Chapter 4) and on your web surveys (continue on to the next section for more).

Driving traffic with content

To use content to increase your website's time on page and engagement value and level, you need to think like a publisher, not an advertiser. No one reads the same news over and over again, and the same rule applies to reading website content.

TIP

Keep content newsworthy to attract and engage visitors and keep it in line with your sales goals to make sure you're not providing a free news site but one that will pay off for you as well. Craft stories, reports, insights, and guides that are meaningful and subtly drive people back to you to help them achieve related goals.

Today's most exciting web content is often published in social media first and then linked into the main website from Twitter, YouTube, and so forth.

The useful or interesting content you add to your site to boost visits isn't the same as that call to action that drives sales. Keep the call to action and the compelling sales copy top level and nest supportive content below it in the navigation hierarchy so as not to set up obstacles to quick sales or opt-ins.

What if you do everything you can to build traffic but your website continues to be ignored? Then you may want to hire a search engine optimization (SEO) consultant or agency. Most of these firms (such as Wpromote, which has a service called QuickList; see `www.wpromote.com/quicklist` for details) work for a fairly reasonable fee.

Web surveys

A great way to engage customers when they land on your website is to ask them to take a one-question survey to help you better understand what matters most to them. A lot of people like to take the survey so they can see how their peers voted or answered as well. Ask questions that spark curiosity and help visitors validate their own challenges and needs. If you're a B2B site selling marketing services, you may want to ask something like the following:

>> What is your number-one marketing challenge?

>> Does your CEO trust you and your marketing team?

>> What do you believe is your most powerful marketing tool for the coming year?

Many marketers are curious to see how their peers answer those questions. If you do this to increase your engagement and stickiness, here are a few suggestions:

>> Make respondents give you their email address to see other's responses and vote/answer the question.

>> Upon answering, automatically offer to direct visitors to your archived questions so they can see answers to other questions, again increasing engagement and time on site.

>> As applicable, have the answers to your questions direct visitors to more content on the topic on your site. If you asked the question about marketing tools, direct viewers to a free download for a white paper on the marketing tools/services you provide.

Critical components of content

In addition to populating your website with pages about your products, promotions, customer testimonials, leaders, and competitive advantages, some basic content has become important for consumers as they research and choose brands from whom they want to purchase. These include

>> **Compatible or complementary products:** This is especially important if you're a technology company. Purchasers may want to know what companies you've aligned with so they can assess compatibility and application program interface (API) with other programs they may have purchased.

>> **Your news:** Create a page to house all your business news. Include press releases and articles for which your leaders were interviewed or in which your people or brand were mentioned.

>> **Your blog:** People want to experience your thought leadership, and that is really what a blog is. Make it easy for people to read what your experts are saying by making your blog easy to find. Update it often to keep your messages current and your voice strong in your industry.

>> **Your videos:** If you have product demo or customer testimonial video, or videos of your leaders communicating about your brand, host them in one library on your site as well as throughout your site. Make them easy to find and share with others.

>> **Resources:** Do you have white papers you've used to get people to come to your website in the first place, research studies, customer survey results, NPS reports, and other information that would be of value to consumers' decision process? Even though you may have links to these materials throughout your site, house them in a library or separate page for easy access. Before enabling downloads, always ask for email addresses so you can build your permission-based email lists.

>> **Your jobs:** Be sure to build a page about your jobs that reflects your persona and enables you to attract people who are a good fit for your culture. Make this a mini-page that communicates about your values, experience, passion, and team. This is a critical component of your site because it influences your company's growth and competencies. Treat it accordingly.

REMEMBER

Your content is either static or dynamic. Static content is content that you don't change much, like your leadership profiles, contract information, mission statement/values, and so on. Dynamic content refers to the content you change often to change the experience prospects and customers have when visiting your site. This can include your promotions, web contests, new white papers offered, limited time information, news stories, product features and highlights, customer and partnership highlights, and so on. These can change weekly or bi-monthly or whatever works best for the frequency at which customers come back to your site or what your resources dictate you can do.

Now on to designing an engaging and effective website.

Integrating Key Design Elements

Unless you live under a rock, you've likely noticed that the design trends for websites change as often as, if not more than, politicians change their positions — which is a lot.

A few years ago, the trend was to make your page look like a digital version of *USA Today* — headlines with teaser statements everywhere in hopes of driving you deeper. Then, they went to a more boxy design with a large masthead for promotions, sales buttons, and other teasers or value statements, followed by a navigation bar, and then maybe a video and more boxes with links to product pages and so on.

And now the trend is to have a very simplistic visual presentation. Often, a single image, a slide show, or a video starts upon opening and takes up most of your screen, leaving you to have to search or keep rolling your mouse for navigation or click to enter buttons to appear. Maybe next year, they'll be back to the *USA Today* approach. Regardless, some key design strategies will never change with the trends because they follow how the human unconscious mind processes information. And remember, human nature never changes. For web browsing, that process is referred to as the *golden triangle.* We discuss this as well as how to develop your web persona and go from concept to actual website in the next sections.

Using the golden triangle

Google researched how people view search results and found that most people start on the left side of the masthead or top of the page, browse right, and then read the top three items and choose one. That kind of validates search engine optimization (SEO) and search engine marketing (SEM) expenditures. Other studies from other groups like Marketing Sherpa show that people do the same on web pages. They start at the left, shoot over to the upper-right corner, and then browse down the left side of the page. So what, you say? It's actually a big what.

You need your core messages, calls to action, and most valuable leads to get people to dig deeper on your page in this triangle. If your call to action buttons, free offers, and such are in that big vast space outside of the triangle, you likely won't fulfill visitors' needs to find something relevant immediately before they switch to another site. That's where you can lose a lot of gold in terms of engagement that leads to sales.

TIP

Skip the design trend changes for how a website should look and design it around how consumers look at sites.

Per the golden triangle, that top inch of your page, or masthead, is really critical because that is where the eyes stop and browse first. This is where you get to hammer home a consistent, memorable, clear brand identity on the web, tease a current promotion, broadcast new news, and so on. You'll note that sites like CNN.com and FoxNews.com often use the top inch (after highly paid advertisements these days) for breaking news and that their content then follows the flow of the golden triangle.

Web designers and users generally accept that the top inch or two of every web page is branding space for whoever controls that page. You want to use that top inch or two to present your brand name plus a short tag line, logo, and special promotional links and messages. Be careful, though, because this space can easily get cluttered with multiple logos, messages, and promotions.

TIP

To ensure that you're taking full advantage of this top inch or so, select type, colors, and a visual logo that tie into your overall branding. Change out your icons, news, or teasers/promotions so that they're fresh and capture attention of repeat visitors. You can do a quick audit of your web brand identity right now by looking at the top inch of every page you control. Is it as consistent and as strong as it can be?

Developing your web persona

Designing your website is as personal as how you dress every day. It's a reflection of who you are, your persona, your energy, your values, and your way of positioning yourself to be part of a hive of like people and attract them to your space, personally or professionally. So instead of letting someone tell you what your site should look like, start profiling the persona or type of people you want to attract. Following is an exercise to get you started. (Refer to your emotional selling proposition from Chapter 2 to guide this exercise.)

>> What's your brand's personality? Spunky, traditional, reserved, outgoing, daring, rebellious, or trendsetter?

>> Describe or list characters, celebrities, or people you know who embody that personality.

>> What do these people wear every day? To a formal event? Would they show up at a black-tie event in a tux with red high-top sneakers? Would they get married in a black dress?

>> What are the aspirations, goals, and status levels your characters or persona seek?

>> What books do they read? What television shows do they watch? Or what Instagram and Twitter pages do they follow?

» How can you include actual customers in your web strategy to help appeal to new customers?

» Can you create a movement around your persona? What values and causes move them? Can you engage them with design and with a joint cause?

Now take a step back and start thinking of creative elements that reflect this persona. How can you use some of these to appeal to your customers? How can you do this quickly with graphics, words, headlines, and invitations to join a common cause so that your customers immediately know, consciously and unconsciously, that they've found a website that's like them, part of their tribe, their hive, and a place where they belong?

Repeat this exercise to help you direct your logo design and print presence as well.

EXAMPLE

Wildfang is a good example of this very strategy. Its mantra is to be a wild feminist, and its clothing reflects the feminist style. It includes customers and causes and pretty much invites you to be part of its tribe the minute you visit. Check it out at www.wildfang.com.

Going from design concepts to an actual website

After you have some ideas, sketch out a story board for the images and elements you want to project in your home page and how you can adapt those into themes that transcend all pages. Then start designing, either by yourself or with a designer who can do it quickly for you. If you prefer the DIY route, tons of options provide templates you can use outright or modify to fit your style and needs. Check out tools available from GoDaddy, WordPress, eHost, Wix.com, Squarespace, and many more.

Before signing up for a "freemium" account, which always seems to get you paying for something somehow, ask around to see what platforms and tools others like and have had an easy time using, deploying, and updating. You can waste numerous hours on programs that don't work as easily or seamlessly as promised.

When you find a good template to use, you need to start adding your own photos and content. If you use your own photos, make sure the resolution is good as well as the artistry so you look professional, not haphazard. You can buy images fairly inexpensively from many sources, especially if you need them only for your website because you can purchase low resolutions at lower costs. Check out stock photography sources such as Corbis (www.corbisimages.com), Getty (www.gettyimages.com), iStock (www.istockphoto.com), or Shutterstock (www.shutterstock.com). Also look for useful images on Flickr, where photographers set up pages to share their work. If you like an image, contact the photographer directly. You may be able to use it for a modest price or even for free. The body of work there is growing rapidly.

TIP

Here are some ideas for improving your overall web experiences:

>> **Use streaming video and animation to engage.** You can use these for showing a speaker in action, demonstrating a new product or providing services, and supporting the consumer online.

>> **Keep the navigation clear and simple.** Make sure your site is easy to navigate and that your menu is easy to find and follow. Drop-down menus make it clear and easy to find what you're looking for.

>> **Take time choosing an Internet service provider (ISP).** As you're using your website to help build your business, look for a system that meets your current needs and can grow as you grow. It's not always so simple to switch down the road. If you used a template from an ISP to build a site, you'll lose that template and need to build your site again if you change to another one. Be sure to pay attention to what features are standard and which are extra, and whether shopping carts are included. Many basic website templates do *not* include a shopping cart, so make sure you choose one that offers this if you need one or think you may down the road.

>> **Check out *Building Websites All-in-One For Dummies,* 3rd Edition (Wiley).** This book by David Karlins and Doug Sahlin gives you the essentials of website construction as well as information on mobile site planning and social media integration.

REMEMBER

Because consumers browse websites on many different devices — smartphones, tablets, and desktop and laptop screens — you need to make sure your website automatically adjusts to each. Today, most website builders have responsive website design (RWD) capabilities, which serves all devices with the same code that adjusts for screen size so you don't really need to worry about this. It's a good idea to check your site on all your devices once in a while to make sure no glitches occur.

>> **Change up your content.** Because websites are relationship-building and informational tools, you need to change the experience and the content to keep them interesting. For e-commerce sites, you wouldn't have the very same promotion or product highlight on your home page every single day, either. If customers come to the very same site all the time, they'll lose interest as they've "been there, done that."

>> **Offer a clear and simple method for getting through your site and completing your call to action.** The fewer clicks it takes your customers to

find what they're looking for, the better chance you have of selling. Instead of just listing "ladies sweaters," make your site searchable by size, color, and occasion. This helps people find what they want faster and without having to sift through dozens of photos, which can lead to boredom, frustration, and a bounce off your page.

>> **Ask visitors to opt in right away.** One of your top goals should be to encourage visitors to complete a form with their contact information so you can add them to your database and nurture relationships based on their interest that drove them to your site in the first place. It can be an offer to qualify for a consumer discount, an upgrade, an informative B2B newsletter, registration for your frequent buyer program, and so on.

>> **Get personal.** Every time you go to Amazon, the home page is filled with suggested products that reflect your past purchases and browsing sessions. Thankfully, technology for all things on the Internet is developing so quickly that the ability to do this is getting more affordable to the point that small businesses can do it, too. Personalization platforms enable you to track the source of all visitors, monitor their behavior and intent, and create personalized web experiences for them based on past behavior. You can also personalize your web page for segments and fill these pages with product recommendations based on what a specific group of customers tend to browse and buy.

>> **Test.** Many web content management systems have A/B testing capabilities so you can continuously test what messages, offers, layouts, templates, and so on get people to go deeper into your site or complete your call to action. Never stop learning if you want to get ahead and stay ahead.

TIP

There are many personalization platforms and web content management systems to consider for delivering highly relevant content, conducting personalization, creating landing pages, integrating blogs, monitoring visitor behavior and intent, and more. Search for personalized webmail platforms and web content management systems, and compare prices so you can find a system you can afford. Personalization platforms are typically subscription-based or SaaS-based models and can vary from $59 to $250 or more a month, depending on the number of websites you manage and other variables.

Driving Traffic via SEM and SEO

SEM is *search engine marketing* and encompasses all things that you do to make your page more visible on organic search lists. SEO is *search engine optimization*, a subset of SEM, and is what you do to maximize the number of visitors to your site by making sure it's one of the top listed sites on all searches. HubSpot defines the different tactics as follows:

>> SEM involves tactics like paid search or pay-per-click advertising.

>> SEO includes tactics on and off your web page. On-page tactics include keyword placement throughout your site, blog posts, social sharing options within your content to get more shares, and so on. Things you do off your page may include forging links with other websites that support and complement your own site — for example, linking your site with a partner's site so you get more hits from search engines. Social bookmarking, such as sites like Reddit and StumbleUpon, are great ways to get higher search rankings as your page comes up in many different places.

Here are some guidelines or suggestions to consider for SEO and SEM. If you question the value of doing SEM, just remember, there are more than 1 billion websites out there, some say even closer to 1 trillion. So good luck getting found randomly.

>> **Make sure you have a strong presence on the web and then manage that presence.** Your web presence encompasses your sites or accounts that bear your name and drive people to your URL. Channels that help build your presence include YouTube, Facebook, LinkedIn, Flickr, your blog, and other accounts that help your name come up more often and higher in the search rankings.

>> **Provide a site map.** The fewer links a search engine has to navigate to find content relevant to a specific search, the higher it'll rate your site. A well-designed site map cuts the search engine's journey down to just two links. A large website needs a separate page for its site map, whereas simpler pages can place the map on a navigation bar that's visible from every page. On your map page or navigation bar, list all pages by title or topic and provide a direct link to each one.

>> **Communicate directly with your customers to build traffic.** Search engines look at traffic when ranking pages, so anything you do through direct communication with your customers to build traffic can help. Offer free informational or entertaining content people will want to visit and download. Consider making your website a resource for customers and noncustomers alike so as to maximize the amount of interaction with visitors. Free webinars and white papers can help boost your presence.

>> **Build links to related sites to improve your ranking.** Put a tab or button on your home page that's labeled Links, or if you want to pump up its appeal, label it The Best Links, Recommended Links, Our Pick of Links, or something like that. To find sites to link to, do your own searches and see what sites appear in the top ten listings. Then visit each of them and see whether you can find appropriate places and ways to link to them from your site (and vice versa,

if possible). A company that distributes products for you or a professional association in your industry is a natural to link to your site. Build such links and the higher-ranked sites tend to draw yours up toward them. But make sure you have useful content to justify those links! Very brief reviews of the linked-to sites may increase the value of your links page and thus build usage and traffic.

» **Build a family of sites and social networking site pages around your hub website.** Doing so may capture traffic out on the rim of your web presence and direct it toward your hub. Include single-purpose, single-topic satellite pages and optimize the META tags for these pages so they rank higher than your main site in searches specific to their topics.

» **Advertise steadily enough to amplify search engine traffic.** Traffic increases rank on most search engines, so a promotion that drives traffic to your website gets amplified by follow-on traffic that comes from search engine visibility, which in turn creates more visibility.

ADJUSTING FOR SOLE PROPRIETORS OR NICHE MARKETERS

If you're a sole proprietor, such as a business consultant, accountant, computer expert, or other professional, you don't really need to invest in web technology for sites designed to attract masses of consumers. Although you still want to build traffic, your greater need is to focus on a smaller audience of people who likely need your services due to their proximity of location or direct needs for your service. In many cases, these people know you from another setting. In this case, keep giving them reasons to go to your site. Email them links to information, reports, coupons, news about your business, your speaking schedule if you do public speaking, and so on.

To drive more people to your site so you can build your prospect base, use keywords effectively and bid on Google search terms that are highly specific to your area of business or niche.

As a niche marketer on the web, you may also find it more effective to emphasize your own expertise as the spokesperson for your brand. Blog in your own name and post a short video seminar or how-to demonstration on YouTube. In addition, look for ways to build visibility in professional online venues, perhaps by offering content to newsletters and signing up to be listed with professional associations and then linking those sites to your hub website. The more you build your voice in the industry as a thought leader or expert in a specific skill area, the more you can build your site's traffic and the more attractive you become to others whom you may want to link your site to for mutual credibility and traffic building.

Creating Landing Pages, Blogs, and More

As mentioned earlier, websites have many entry points besides the home page. Creating secondary entry points, also known as landing pages, is a common and wise tactic to get people to your site at the highest point of relevance and to enable you to track the effectiveness of an email, mobile, social, or print campaign. Google Analytics easily identifies the entry page for your visitors, so this is a solid and inexpensive way to test your campaigns. Landing pages are secondary pages to your main site and include direct links to and the same navigation as your other pages, just as all secondary pages do.

Some reasons you may want to do a landing page include

>> Testing a new campaign to see how many people respond to a new message or offer

>> Driving people to a page to register for a free gift, white paper, or a discount code to use when purchasing products on your main page

>> Getting people to take a survey as an objective way of initiating communications with you

>> Launching a new product or service and wanting this to be the focal point of your communications for a given time period

>> Creating a specialized website that will attract a different demographic or customer group

>> Supporting a specific campaign and maintaining the momentum of that specific message or offer while it's in play

Following are some guidelines for how to use landing pages effectively as part of your overall marketing program and web strategy and how to build your position of authority with a blog.

Using landing pages effectively

If you advertise on the web, you should consider a separate landing page for each ad campaign — and not just ad, but a full campaign. If you have a series of three to five ads in a campaign promoting the same product or service, call to action, or messaging, all those ads should include a link to one *landing page* that supports the corresponding strategy and goals. This will help keep the momentum of your campaign message and call to action and help you measure results better.

Following are some traditional ways to use landing pages:

» A *transactional* landing page (also called a *lead capture page*) finishes the job the ad started by persuading visitors to complete some kind of transaction, such as making a purchase or signing up for a membership or special offer. Special trial offers are often effective on transactional landing pages. Write a transactional landing page like you would any good ad or catalog copy by keeping the copy short and to the point to keep people on site. Because many people landing on this page won't complete the call to action you offer, include another way to engage so you can at least capture their information for your database and future communications, such as a free report or a coupon for their first purchase, which they can use then or later.

» A *reference* landing page is designed to fill the visitor's informational needs by providing useful content, such as links, reviews, and professional listings. Marketers for associations and nonprofits tend to use reference landing pages more than for-profit marketers do, but this type of page can be helpful in a wide range of ad campaigns. If you build a reference landing page that has rich enough content to attract a steady flow of thousands of visitors a month, you can sell advertising on it and turn it into a revenue stream.

» *PURLs* are personalized URLs that include the name of the recipient in the URL name. For example, www.johndoe.ABCInsurancerate.com, or www.bestinsurancerates/johndoe.com. This tactic plays a role in creating a personalized experience for customers and prospects and can help to increase the impact of a personalized website. You can use PURLs as links in digital campaigns utilizing email or mobile and print. In fact, PURLs initially were highly used in print direct mail and, when tested against non-PURL landing pages, have shown a substantial impact on results. Most realistically, PURLs aren't likely to increase your response rate because they're not as unique or unusual as when they first were introduced. However, they do create a direct sense of recognition and personalization, both of which can help you get a new relationship with a customer off to a good start.

If you have a complex business and product offering, you may want to create landing pages for each specific category you offer. IBM is a good example. It has landing pages that are actually complex websites on its different product categories and within its categories. It offers cognitive products, such as Watson, which is a supercomputer that combines artificial intelligence and deep analytics that can then guide digital conversations with consumers.

TIP

Regardless of the type of landing page you employ, be sure to track visitor traffic and conversion rate. Getting a lot of people to your website who don't do anything but browse isn't going to build your business and generate sustainable sales and profitability. Track your *conversion rate*, which is simply the percentage of visitors who fulfill your call to action or other desired goal, like signing up for your email list, accepting your special offer, registering for your newsletter or discount code, or making a purchase. Ultimately, you want to optimize this ratio. Experiment with ads that attract people who are easy to convert; also experiment with the copy, layout, and offer on your landing page. The more you experiment, the more you discover about how to convert visitors at a good rate.

Using blogs to build brands, not bog them down

Blogs serve many purposes for businesses of all types. Some use them as landing pages to get you to the main website in hopes of getting you to go deeper and engage in a sales transaction. Others use them to build their voice and credibility in their space. And others use them as sources of income by getting a lot of followers whom advertisers want to reach.

Blogs can build your position of authority in your space, attract partners and customers, and have a lot of other positive results. But if you don't commit resources to blogging frequently and effectively, it can really bog you down. It's like newsletters used to be. A lot of people could get the first one out but couldn't seem to execute a second. Don't let that be the case with your blogs.

Regardless of your purpose, blogs are an important element in your web strategy and overall marketing program. According to research reported by HubSpot, businesses that use blogs as part of their web strategy receive 67 percent more leads than those that don't.

Simply put, a *blog* is really just a column that you host that gives you a voice in your industry and social and personal circles. In business, blogs can help you secure a position of authority as the leader or visionary in your field. They can also instill a sense of trust as people tend to believe others who are top experts in a field in which they seek products, services, information, or help.

TIP

The trick to making blogs successful is to write simple, relevant, and actionable articles and post them frequently enough that you stay top of mind as a leading resource for your business category.

Your blogs can be hubs for written articles, visual storytelling, or photo essays and stories. Blogs that use images and even videos tend to do better than those that don't. In fact, video blogging — that is, using videos instead of written content — is gaining in popularity to the point that a new term has been coined, *vlogging.* One vlogger, Casey Neistat, has nearly 30 million views for his vlog, with many posts getting well over a million views. And they're simply vignettes of the interesting and adventurous life he lives. Creating a YouTube channel for your vlogs is a great way to increase views, which in turn enables you to better monetize it.

TIP

Most website building platforms include a blog as part of their website template and hosting plan. You can also use other services to host your blog. Just make sure you can measure the traffic, time on page, and other elements and how the blog leads to your main website.

REMEMBER

Your website is often the first impression people have with your brand and needs to be everything they expect to get them to engage. Do some research to find out what consumers in your space want when browsing brand and product websites, and follow through. Make your website about their needs first, and engage them through personal relevance to guide them deeper into your site toward conversion to a sale or other desired behavior.

If you were going to a job interview for your dream job, you wouldn't skimp on the details. You'd be prepared to talk about the business, how you can contribute, and your qualifications for contributing, and you'd make sure your appearance was spot on for the details and professional for the purpose. Do the same with your website. In a sense, it's a one-way interview with your prospects and customers. When you add online engagement or chat to your website, as described in Chapter 16, it becomes a dialogue. Be prepared to be relevant and interesting in either case.

Monetizing Your Web Traffic

If you can successfully execute strategies outlined in this chapter to drive traffic, and lots of it, you can start to monetize your website through paid advertising. The best way to get advertisers for your site is, of course, to build a site worth advertising on because of the interesting content, experience, or community that you've built. The next best way is to align with an affiliate network, which is an intermediary for ads just like you may have intermediaries for your product distribution.

REMEMBER

The trick to getting any of the following monetization methods to pay off is simple: Have good content that's worth visiting your site to get. The best content is not only emotionally relevant, as discussed in Chapter 2, but it's also actionable. Most people don't have time to read websites just because they're there; people read articles and content when it provides a direct value that they need at the time. Quite often, that great content answers a how-to question for personal or professional goals.

You can expect some various payment plans from affiliate networks. The most common include pay per impression and pay per click, which we explore further in the following sections. (We cover how to use these for your own advertising needs in Chapter 8.)

Pay per impression

This payment method accrues income by the number of times the ad is displayed on your site. Every time a unique visitor views your ad, that is considered an *impression.* According to www.monitizepros.com, at the time of this writing, the average payments are about $2.80 per 1,000 displays for display ads on your site, $5.00 per 1,000 displays for ads within emails, and about $3.00 per 1,000 displays for ads aligned with videos.

You can place your own ads on sites you think are relevant to your business or see what ads are going for on popular sites at www.buysellads.com. At the time of this writing, the cost per thousand impressions ranged from $0.25 to $8.00.

Pay per click

With this method, you get paid every time someone clicks on the ad on your site. Amounts actually paid out can be higher than paying for each 1,000 displays as described in the preceding section. The range varies greatly, so do some homework before deciding which method works best for you.

As companies in the web marketing space come and go quickly due to the increasing presence of groups like Google, it's best to do you own search and explore worthy options that come up.

The best affiliate network is one that focuses on the same genre of business, product, category, or customer needs that you do. If you're offering a nutritional product and want to attract ads about nutritional products that supplement yours, look for affiliates that have a presence in this same space.

Google AdSense is another option worth looking into for getting ads on your website. Essentially, Google AdSense places sponsored ads on websites it determines to be relevant to the advertiser through a series of algorithms. You apply for inclusion in the AdSense program and get a code you can very easily add to the HTML code of your site.

» Leveraging local events — your own and others'

» Gaining support through cause-related events

» Getting the most ROI from trade shows

Chapter **12**

Leveraging Networks and Events

The old adage of "Who you know is more important than what you know" still holds true and likely will for a long time.

In marketing, your network is one of your most valuable assets. Your ability to leverage your networks and those of your customers is one of the most critical skills to develop. This chapter shares insights on how you can leverage your network to spark dialogue and interest in your brand, build networks among your customer groups that inspire passion and referrals, and host events that encourage loyalty and sales.

Harnessing the Power of Social Hives

We humans seek and form hives in all areas of our lives. We find comfort, validation, and security in numbers and tend to seek out people who reflect how we see ourselves. Our social hives are usually made up of people who dress like we do, like the same entertainment, humor, and activities, and have the same religious and political viewpoints and affiliations. Professionally, our hives are made up of people who do the same line of work, have similar achievements, and so on.

Given that each of your customers belongs to many hives, you then have potential access to individuals in those hives that are just like them. Gaining access to customers' hives is critical for marketing success and to acquiring customers with some of the lowest costs of acquisition.

Most people belong to several formal and casual organizations compromised of people just like them. These groups provide support systems, structure, and opportunities to collaborate with others on common causes, or to just have fun. Most importantly, they provide emotional bonds and loyalty to causes and others that are hard to break.

For example, Rick Warren wanted to be a minister at a time when church attendance was declining. So he went door to door to learn what people wanted in a church and discovered that many wanted to be a part of something inspirational without the formality of traditional churches. He then started Saddleback Church and invited people to come as they were — no formal dress or rituals — just come and find inspiration to live their purpose and carry on while surrounding themselves with like-minded people. Rick wrote a book about purpose that summarized the theology he taught at church. His purpose took off and fast. His sermons moved from small assembly halls to bigger venues. When he couldn't keep up, he let followers form congregations that met in their homes and provided curriculum from his bestselling book *The Purpose Driven Life* (Zondervan). In a sense, he enabled his followers to form hives, inviting people of like values to get together once a week, discuss what mattered to them, share stories, and leave inspired to stay the course and invite others to join them and find the same joy that they had found. His church quickly became one of the fastest growing in American history (the sixth largest megachurch as of 2015), and his book is second only to the Bible in publication.

Brands can do this, too. And they must because the most powerful form of marketing is consumer to consumer, or C2C, which applies to both live and digital worlds. Despite all the time people spend socializing on "social media," they still thrive being around people, meeting with them face to face rather than just screen to screen. Events that bring customers together are powerful for not just delivering messages, performing product demos, or introducing new products; they're most powerful for building validation and passion for a brand and its products and escalating loyalty because to leave a brand means to leave your support systems, friends, and social network and risk being embarrassed among those you recruited to the group.

Our networks are powerful, too, for calling on others to help with important causes. In his book *The Power of Habit* (Random House), Charles Duhigg explains how Rosa Parks became the face of the Civil Rights movement. She was not the first black person to refuse to give up her seat, but she was a person with many circles of friends and associates in church and sewing, charity, and social groups. By tapping these networks and asking members in each group to tap their networks, a small group of civil rights leaders were able to organize the Montgomery Bus Boycott around Rosa's arrest and thus spark the Civil Rights movement in a matter of days.

TIP

Imagine the kind of movements you can spark for your category and brand by tapping your customers' social and real-world networks. Find out which groups and causes your customers tend to align with. Ask them in surveys or at the point of sale. Find out what matters most to them and find affiliated organizations that also make sense for your brand to support. These organizations often provide opportunities for live interaction, content marketing, sponsorship, and advertising options.

Following are some ideas for events and experiences that can help you build your relationships with customers and qualified prospects, strengthen your place in their lives, and inspire them to introduce you to their networks of like people and, of course, like customers.

"Face" your customers: Events that inspire engagement, loyalty, and referrals

Although you can use many tools to automatically communicate with large networks online, you can never underestimate the power of engaging face to face. Even in a digital world, there is still a need for human touch. People still like to shop at retail stores, see others giving them product advice, and touch the products. This is human nature, which will never change.

The possibilities for face-to-face marketing are many, but no matter what you do, all interactions in the real world, and the digital world for that matter, should provide a meaningful experience that is relevant to your consumers and the role you play in simplifying or enhancing their lives. The goal of your live interaction with customers and prospects should be to make every customer feel like your most valued, no matter how small or big his revenue stream is for you.

Here are some ideas for live marketing events designed to strengthen your bonds with customers and inspire them to introduce you to their hive:

>> **Customer events:** Events are important to building relationships with customers that create loyalty beyond just customer satisfaction. Today, events take place both online and offline. Online events can include instant messaging and voice discussions in chat rooms, such as those on Twitter or Skype, and webinars. Offline, clearly, are those that take place in the real world

where people mingle in person versus behind a screen. The key to success is to keep them meaningful and interactive and not just lecture about your brand or products. Think of events for your customers in general and for your segments for highly relevant engagement.

Consider the H.O.G. (H.O.G. being the acronym for one of the most successful customer groups ever — Harley Owners Group.) H.O.G. was formed in 1983 and, as of 2016, totaled more than 1 million members. H.O.G. members get together for organized scenic rides, charitable rides that raise money for the Muscular Dystrophy Association, and to have an amazing adventure with others "just like them." These events take place all over the country and bring together a wide spectrum of Harley customers, from the Fortune 100 CEO to the rebel leader of a biker club. Economically and professionally, many have little in common, but when they ride together, they bond over their Harley stories and passion for what Harleys do for them. The H.O.G. program is largely attributed to turning fledgling sales around and making Harleys the most popular bike, even at a time when owners joked that you had to buy two at a time — one to ride and one for parts.

>> **Trade shows:** Trade shows are great for building visibility and presence among customer and partner prospects within your industry. You can get a lot of value from exhibiting and getting in front of prospects or just attending for some informal networking. In some cases, after you register, you'll have access to a communications platform specific to the show, and you can see what sessions people are signed up to attend and then actually invite other registrants to connect with you via the online platform and in person at the event.

Setting up meetings at trade shows with key prospects or influencers is often more valuable than exhibiting because you can select who you want to meet instead of waiting for attendees to come to you. If you do exhibit, it's worth buying the attendee list in advance so you can mail an incentive to them to stop by your booth. Read more about trade show tactics in the section "Maximizing Trade Show ROI," later in this chapter.

>> **A client-appreciation event:** A party for entertaining and recognizing your customers can be a great way to strengthen relationships. At one point, automaker Saturn attracted more than 30,000 people to customer events to honor the car and its people whom they had to pay to attend. If you make it entertaining and about the passion your customers feel, an event like Saturn's Homecoming Weekend, which drew 38,000 from 47 states and some from abroad, is a great way to mingle with customers and reignite their excitement for your brand in ways that keep them talking for years — even after you've gone out of business, in this case!

Big-brand events for B2B customers pull in big numbers as well, such as Microsoft's Ignite event in 2015 that sold out (even though it was free) when it reached 20,000 attendees.

>> **A fundraising dinner for an important charity:** As we mention in Chapter 2, supporting worthwhile causes is critical to gaining trust, support, and loyalty among your customers. In May 2015, Cone Communications conducted studies that showed that more than 70 percent will donate to and volunteer for a group supported by a trusted brand. Hosting an event that brings customers and your employees together for a common cause is a powerful way to create emotional bonds and friendships that take price out of the equation.

>> **A community event for families:** Not everything has to be business-oriented. If you have the resources, consider organizing a fun, social event that enables you to mingle with your customers and build friendships. Try a pumpkin festival or educational event for families — something relevant that is worth attending. A community talent show is a fun idea that can attract publicity and crowds, raising your visibility and building your network.

>> **A client advisory board:** Invite a select group of good customers to join your advisory board. Organizing and funding meetings in interesting venues can make it worth their while to provide new ideas and open their networks to you.

>> **Local supply chains where you wholesale to your neighbors and local stores that sell to their own communities:** If this sounds like an old-fashioned trunk show, that's the point! It's face to face and person to person without any sales pressure. Trunk show businesses are popping up again and doing quite well, especially clothing lines like cabi and W by Worth.

>> **A workshop in which you share your expertise or solve problems for participants:** Live workshops are engaging, social, and a great platform for building trust with customers and prospects. For example, if you own a pet store, you can bring in an expert on dog nutrition or how to blend cats and dogs in one family and invite the public to attend for free. Collecting RSVPs in advance and names at the door will help you build your database as well.

REMEMBER

Live events are a great way to build better bonds with your network and your customers and prospects, and they're a great way to meet people in their collective networks. Send invites to customers and encourage them to bring their friends. Make them feel recognized and special when they come.

Find a way to mingle customers with prospects so that your customers become ambassadors at your events, spreading your message directly. Always make sure you collect names and contact information for attendees so you can add them to your database and follow up accordingly.

Whatever the business-oriented opportunity, keep in mind that you're still trying to attract and hold the attention of people, not businesses. You're interested in the people in any business who make the purchase decisions. Make sure your business-oriented events are relevant to people, not just an industry.

Mix it up to create interest and ROI

If you're planning your own event, keep in mind that it needs to be entertaining as well as professional and informative to draw attendance. To get someone to sit through two days of lectures on the impact of new technologies in the industry, or product demos of any nature, your chances are higher if you make it fun and social at the same time. Add cocktail receptions, outings such as golf, sunset hikes, dinner concerts, and other activities relevant to your invitee list. Attendance is often high at conferences and other corporate events at places like Las Vegas that attract tourists and offer a lot of interesting after-hours things to do. But be careful, especially when planning events targeting B2B purchasers. With corporate travel budgets declining, if you have too much fun planned and not enough functional take-away sessions, your event could seem like a junket, and your customers could fail to get approval to attend.

TIP

Some events become staples that gain visibility and impact with each repetition. Customer events, such as those hosted by Salesforce, Adobe, and Microsoft, attract thousands each year and are challenging attendance at long-running events hosted by trade associations.

If your event seems to be a success, find ways to do it again, and make it big enough to attract sponsors who add credibility, value, and of course funding.

Launching Your Own Public Event

In a world that is more about creating great customer experiences than clever advertising campaigns, hosting your own event is key to building relationships on your terms and for elevating the value of your brand beyond the products or services you sell.

First rule of success: Make the event about your attendees, not you. If you disguise a sales pitch as a customer-appreciation, thought leadership, or charitable event, you'll destroy the trust you have among your customers and harm your chances of sparking new relationships with others.

Second rule of success: Don't do an event just because you can. Only do an event because it's meaningful and offers something of value to your network.

The whole reason for doing events is to build relationships, people to people, and leverage your network to introduce you to others. People don't build relationships with brands; they build them with people within the brand, and when they feel fulfilled, they bring others to you.

TIP

A great example of leveraging networks is the classic MCI Friends and Family campaign. When you brought friends and families to MCI, you all got to talk for free. Give your network a reason to come, and reward them if they bring friends who become customers, too.

In the following sections, we explore different ideas for hosting events with meaning, for funding and monetizing your event, and for getting help managing your event.

Hosting events with meaning

Relevance, just like anything you do in marketing, is important to the success of events. If the theme, purpose, activity, or benefit gained from participating does not provide a direct value to your customer base, you will likely be disappointed in the turnout and thus your ability to build relationships with prospects and customers. Successful events are those that have direct meaning or impact to customers' quality of life, community, or a cause about which they feel strongly. Some examples follow:

>> Host a volunteer day for highway cleanup. Invite customers to an after party and hand out "road trip" swag as a gift.

>> Host a dinner event at your business or a nearby park, pack it with kickball tournament and other summer games, and make admission donated food items.

>> If you own a retail clothing store, set up an after-hours party to collect business clothes that customers no longer need. Offer appetizers, cocktails, and light entertainment. Donate the clothes to a local shelter for women and men in need or a program that helps place needy adults in jobs so that they can show up dressed for success.

Funding and monetizing your event

Events aren't cheap, and footing the entire bill with the hope of generating sales and acquiring new customers can sometimes be more than you can afford. Here are some ideas for how to get others to cover some of your expenses.

>> Partner with local restaurants or catering companies. Ask them to donate refreshments in exchange for signage and mentions in publicity material.

>> Is there a new venue in town that could use some publicity? Ask the owners to let you host your event for free in exchange for sponsorship mentions.

>> If you live near a college or community arts center, see whether you can find musicians and artists who need exposure and will perform or design promotional materials for free.

TIP

If you're in B2B and choose to host a conference or thought leadership workshop involving speakers and workshops beyond just your team, you can better justify charging an admission fee. The trick here is that your content needs to be different and more actionable than the many other events competing for attendees. It can be done. The value of hosting your own conference or professional summit is that it positions you as the authority, and authorities are naturally perceived as pioneers, leaders, and experts with a higher likelihood of success.

Some ways to help you monetize a conference follow:

>> List a price for your event to give it value. Then invite customers to attend for free and give a substantial discount to any friends they choose to bring.

>> Invite partners or companies that provide complementary services to yours and seek the same customer base to underwrite any speakers for whom you need to pay royalties.

>> Seek sponsors for special workshops, receptions, or as underwriters for entertainment.

>> Video record sessions and sell online access for a nominal fee.

Getting help managing your event

If you're like most small to medium-sized businesses or marketing departments, you likely don't have time to do your day job and pull off a full-scale event. Luckily, you can hire event planning consultants and firms to do this for you if your budget allows. Event managers can help you design and manage all aspects of the event, such as shows, speeches or activities, meals, conference and hotel room reservations, security, transportation, and all those sorts of details that you have to do right when staging a major event. A good place to look for a proven planner is The Event Planners Association (EPA) website at www.eventplannersassociation. com, which includes a list of members you can contact.

Other sources for help include the Event Planning blog by Cvent at blog.cvent. com (Cvent sells software for event marketing and management) and Event Manager Blog (www.eventmanagerblog.com) for examples, ideas, and promotion strategies.

Sponsoring a Special Event

A great way to create face-to-face marketing opportunities without all the liability is to sponsor a special event. Doing so is kind of like piggybacking on others' investments and efforts because you get visibility without the responsibility and all the costs. Choose events that not only cater to your customer groups but are also well publicized.

Sports events get the biggest share of sponsorship spending (about 70 percent), but lots of other options exist, too, including entertainment, tours, attractions, festivals, fairs, and the arts. To help guide you in choosing the right events to sponsor, ask your customers. Maybe put a one-question poll on your website, at your cash register, and so on. If you run a local business, ask customers whether they plan to attend any specific events you're considering.

The following sections break down the four actions you should take if you're considering sponsoring a special event. If you follow them, odds are your experience will be worthwhile.

REMEMBER

Whatever special event you decide to sponsor, make sure you get a clear, detailed agreement in writing about where, how, and how often the event identifies your brand name. That identification is the return on your sponsorship investment. Too often, sponsors complain that they didn't get as much exposure as expected, so make sure you and the event directors understand the exposure level upfront.

Hosting and supporting cause-related campaigns and events

You've heard the saying, "If you don't stand for something, you'll fall for anything." Today, standing for something takes on a new meaning because a large majority of consumers seek to align with brands that engage in responsible social and environmental causes. According to Cone Communications research from 2015:

>> 91 percent of global consumers expect companies to address social and environmental issues.

>> 84 percent seek out responsible brands whenever possible.

>> 90 percent would boycott a company for irresponsible or deceptive business practices.

Hosting or sponsoring cause-related events will help position you accordingly.

One of the first cause-related campaigns was American Express's "Charge Against Hunger," which started in the early 1990s. The campaign raised more than $21 million in four years and benefited more than 600 anti-hunger groups throughout the United States. It helped raised awareness about hunger throughout America and generated community support to ease the suffering of those affected. Not only did this campaign help launch the genre of cause-related marketing, but it also helped American Express improve relationships with its restaurant customers and add value to aligning with their brand.

To launch a cause-related marketing campaign and associated event, first decide what you stand for. Which societal needs matter most to you and your team and align with your product category and brand? Which causes are your customers also likely to support? Do you operate in an area with a higher than average population of at-risk youth? Or neglected seniors? Is hunger an issue? Do you have a personal connection to autism, cancer, or another cause you and your team can rally behind?

Ideally, you want to align with programs that are meaningful to your customers and your brand. Common causes bring customers and brands together in ways that are more powerful for relationships, loyalty, the greater good, and profitability than most other things you can do.

Regardless of your size, you can sponsor or launch your own cause-related marketing campaign and event easily and affordably. Consider launching a campaign that donates proceeds to charity for a sales period and then host an event to invite customers, donors, and others involved to celebrate the success. Imagine the emotional bonds of an event celebrating a successful mission you and your customers accomplished together.

REMEMBER

Aligning with causes is a great way to build your network and strengthen relationships with partners, customers, and communities. If you tap your existing network to support a cause or come to an event you sponsor or host, invite them to tap their networks. This way you have more impact on your cause and add new like-minded people to your network. Encourage them to sign up in advance so you can collect contact information for future communications.

Sponsoring a cause-related event

You can attract a lot of positive attention from the media and the community by sponsoring an existing fundraising event for a charity rather than hosting your own. You can generate extremely valuable goodwill through cause sponsorship, especially if the cause and event are appropriate to your target market, and relieve yourself of the planning and execution details.

Also, make sure to carefully examine a charity's books and tax-exempt status before sponsoring it or running an event to benefit it. Make sure that it has full charitable status — defined as a 501(c)(3) corporation in the United States, for example — and that its audited financial statements show that it has relatively low overhead and moderate executive salaries. You don't want to support a charity that turns out to be poorly or dishonestly run. A charity's records and financials should be available for public inspection, so all you have to do is ask. If an organization hesitates to share this information, move on.

Beyond sponsoring events, consider joining a local charity's board or advisory committee. This shows your ongoing commitment to the cause, not just business exposure, and sends a signal of sincerity to your customers. Transparency and sincerity matter a great deal to all customer groups, so don't try to disguise your marketing as charitable acts. This will always backfire.

Finding a good fit

Finding a good event or cause that fits your organization's purpose and business is important to your overall branding efforts and your ability to truly make a difference. The following sources can help you discover what type of events are available in your market area:

>> **IEG:** IEG is the International Events Group, which publishes a listing of many special event options, including just about every large-scale event. Check out www.sponsorship.com for more info.

>> **Local chambers of commerce:** Chambers offer lists of local events and can often shed insights about what to expect from each.

>> **Organizations that align with your category and cause:** These groups may know about or put on special events that are appropriate for your sponsorship. For example, if you market sports equipment, educational games, or other products for kids, you may want to call the National Basketball Association to see whether you can participate in one of its many events geared toward children (perhaps a stay-in-school event featuring popular musicians and basketball stars).

>> **Schools and colleges:** These institutions usually have a strong base of support in their communities, and some add a broader reach through their alumni, sports teams, prominent faculty, and the like. Call their public relations offices to get a list of events they have that may be worth sponsoring.

>> **The web:** A number of companies can help you locate good sponsorship matches. For example, check out www.eventcrazy.com for hundreds of possibilities in everything from sports and the arts to reenactments and museum shows. At this site, you can enter your zip code and limit the distance away from your location if you want to find smaller, local events to sponsor.

>> **Local television stations:** Call the local television stations and ask them what local events they expect to cover in the coming year. These events are naturals for your sponsorship because television coverage makes the potential audience bigger.

TIP

Like any marketing program, an event sponsorship needs to deliver reach at a reasonable cost. So ask yourself how many people will come to the event or hear of your sponsorship of it. Then ask yourself what percentage of this total is likely to be in your target market. That's your *reach*. Divide your cost by this figure, multiply it by 1,000, and you have the cost of your reach per thousand. You can compare this cost with cost figures for other kinds of reach, such as a print or radio ad or a direct mailing.

REMEMBER

Seek out events that are relevant to your product and the values you want your brand to be known for. Align with events that tie into your product or service in some obvious way. For example, a healthcare organization may sponsor a blood drive, and a bank may sponsor a first-time homebuyers' clinic. These events clearly reinforce the sponsor's brand image in its industry.

Sometimes going beyond direct relevance is okay, especially in community-based business, but always consider the pros and cons first. For example, an area savings and loan institution may sponsor a local youth soccer team, contribute to a campaign for the local homeless shelter, and help fund the preservation of conservation land, purely because these are good local causes and the managers of the savings and loan institution care about them.

Whatever charities you support, make sure they're working on issues that matter to you. Sponsorship is a great way to align your personal values with your business interests. For example, sponsoring events and charities aimed at making business greener may excite you — and also attract like-minded customers.

Of course, you don't always have to have a business reason to sponsor an event. Doing good for the sake of doing good is enough. And when you invest in charities, the return usually comes back in ways that you can't always measure on a spreadsheet.

Maximizing Trade Show ROI

Trade shows are one of the most traditional yet effective ways to mingle face to face with prospects and nurture your existing network. But you can't just show up and expect people to come to your booth. You must have a message and a plan, just like you do with a given marketing campaign. Components of your plan should include

>> **Messaging that is relevant to the attendees of the show:** If the show attracts millennials, incorporate messages that are meaningful to this group, such as transparency, your social impact, and promises that relate to their goals.

>> **Visuals that reflect the persona of the consumers attending to create an immediate common ground:** Upon entering the exhibit hall, attendees have lots of stimuli trying to capture their attention. Yours will stand out if you reflect the colors, fonts, images, and energy that appeal most to their "wannabe" goals and current self.

>> **A relevant experience:** Like your overall marketing plan, you need to provide a relevant experience for your attendees. Just talking to sales reps who want to scan a name tag is not the kind of experience that inspires intrigue or sales. Offer something of interest or fun to draw people out of the aisles and to your booth. Some things that work well include magicians, comedians, bistros, free personalized T-shirts printed at the booth, massage therapists, games with prizes, and so on.

Following are some tips to get the most out of your trade show investment:

>> **If you belong to associations, get a list of all events they host throughout the year.** Get information on attendance, expo hall activities, and what the organizers are doing to drive traffic to exhibitors.

>> **Get a list of last year's exhibitors and find out how satisfied they were with traffic and the quality of leads generated.** Just because a lot of people walk by your booth doesn't mean they're qualified leads you should spend your time trying to close.

>> **Ask for a preview of other companies signed up to exhibit to assess competitor presence.** If your competitors are there, you may not want to be missing.

>> **Look for potential partners on the exhibitor list.** Reach out for potential alliances and joint presentations to add interest and value to each other's booths.

Building the foundation for a good booth

Marketers traditionally focus on the booth when they think about how to handle a trade show. But you should consider the booth just a part of your overall marketing strategy for the show. Develop a full-blown show strategy by answering each of these questions:

>> How do we attract the right people to the show and to our booth?

>> What do we want visitors to our booth to do at the show and in our booth?

>> How can we communicate with and motivate visitors when they get to the booth?

>> How can we capture information about them, their interests, and their needs?

>> What can we send visitors away with that will maximize the chances of them getting in touch with us after the show?

>> How can we follow up to build or maintain our relationship with our booth visitors?

Booths can take on many different formats, which enable you to interact with visitors in various ways. Consider the following:

>> A small panel display on a table top and maybe a couple of chairs to chat with visitors in a 10-x-10 booth may be enough to have meaningful engagement that generates quality leads.

>> A table with information or product samples people can browse from the aisle.

>> A much bigger space with multiple interactive digital displays, sitting areas for groups to listen to mini-presentations, and sitting areas for one-to-one meetings.

REMEMBER

Your strategy should be built around your budget and the type of interaction with prospects that is most likely to spark a long-term relationship. You need to see high numbers of your target customers; otherwise, the show wastes your marketing time and money.

TIP

Don't overlook the drawing power of simple things, like fresh flowers or food. Offering a free fresh-baked cookie can be a big draw as can a massage chair or bottles of cold spring water.

Locating trade shows

Your most reliable source for trade show info is your customers. The whole point of exhibiting at a trade show is to reach customers, so why not just ask them where you should exhibit. Email your best customers and ask them for advice on where and when to exhibit. They know what's hot right now and what's not.

TIP

Here's where else to look for the scoop on trade shows:

>> **Virtual Press Office:** For recent listings and press announcements of trade shows and other industry events, visit www.virtualpressoffice.com.

>> **Exhibit & Event Marketers Association (E2MA):** This association can provide you with information about shows in your industry. The association also offers a great source of information and training for trade show booth designers and exhibitors. Find out more at www.e2ma.org.

>> **Trade Show News Network (TSNN):** This organization's website (www.tsnn.com) is a useful clearinghouse of listings for vendors and companies involved in the trade show industry. Check out the list of top 250 U.S. trade shows for venues that may be good for your marketing program.

Selecting space on the expo floor

Where your booth is located is often more important than the size of your booth. If you're on the outside aisles, you likely won't get much traffic. You need to have a booth that is on a heavily trafficked aisle, such as one near the entrance, leading to the back lunch or sitting areas, or near or adjacent to a large company that tends to get a lot of traffic.

If you can afford only a small booth space, consider using a tabletop display that you can use at other venues, such as conference rooms and chamber meetings. These smaller-scale displays can be effective in the right spot and often cost less than a trade show booth.

Experts can help you design and build your booth or other display, manage your trade show program, and handle the sales leads that result from it. Many firms design and make trade show booths, kiosks, and tabletop displays. Decide which format fits your marketing program and budget best and then go online to search for vendors in your area. Many firms will also manage your entire trade show program, including the leads you generate.

Be sure to get opinions and quotes from multiple vendors (and ask for credit references and the contact names of some recent clients) before choosing the right company for your job. Also, share your budget constraints upfront to find out whether the company you're talking to is appropriate for you. Some can do very economical, small-scale projects with ease, whereas others are more oriented to large-scale corporate accounts.

Doing trade shows on a dime

A major booth at a big national convention or trade show is costly (somewhere between $15,000 and $50,000, depending on scale), so if that's beyond your current budget, look for more modest ways to participate, such as the following ideas:

>> **Share a booth.** You may want to consider sharing a booth with a similar business if the expenses are too high and you aren't sure you can get a good return on the cost of a booth. If your business has regional affiliates, share space with one or several of them.

>> **Work with a sales rep.** If you can't afford even a shared booth, you may still be able to appear in the exhibit hall of a trade show by working with a sales representative. If your industry has any sales reps, consider contracting with one and letting him include your products in his wider assortment at the next major show.

>> **Make a presentation at the show.** Start early with a proposal to speak at the event. Many trade shows are coupled with conferences, so get in touch with the person in charge of selecting presenters and pitch a workshop during regular conference hours. Speakers are selected as much as a year in advance, so plan ahead. Your presentation can help drive traffic to the booth and make your investment more worthwhile.

Getting people to your booth

Like any form of marketing, your trade show booth competes with others for traffic and staying power. If you just show up and set up your booth, you'll likely be disappointed in your traffic, even if you have the best display or gimmicks to attract visitors. You need to work the crowd before they show up. The best way to do this is to get a pre-show attendee list from the show organizers. You'll most likely have to pay more for this list, but it's often worth the investment.

Here are some direct marketing ideas for using attendee lists to up your trade show ROI:

>> **Offer:** Give people a reason to come by your booth. Are you offering a white paper, a free audit, a chance to win something cool like an iPad or new smartphone?

>> **Experience:** Create an offer or experience at your booth that is worth people's time. Try a free, informational mini-seminar with a proven expert in their field.

>> **Contest:** Offer people a chance to win something they actually want for themselves, such as a free iPad, a trip to Vegas, a gift card.

>> **Free product:** Give a premium "swag" product that's actually useful. Instead of a free pen, come up with something that stands out from what others are giving. (See the next section for more.)

Offering premiums or "swag" that works

Premium items, as the industry calls them but more commonly known as "swag" among business professionals, are gifts you give to your customers, clients, prospects, or employees. Exhibitors at trade shows usually give away premium items as a way to get people to their booths. However, with an overabundance of cheap free pens or candy, it's hard to get the investments in premiums to pay off by driving traffic at the show or achieving recall afterward.

Here are some things August Wittenberg, COO of Say No More Promotions, suggest businesses consider for using premiums best at trade shows:

>> **Demographics:** Who will be coming to the trade show, and what are their interests based on — their age, lifestyle, job level?

>> **Location of use:** Will users be using your premium at home or at work? Which location is most likely to produce thoughts about your brand and value to them? We've seen companies give out hot mitts to marketers. Not sure how oven mitts make you think about your data lists.

Another thing to keep in mind is how well people can travel with your item. If you intend for them to take it home, make sure people can take the items through airport security. One of your kind authors, Jeanette, once went to a trade show where a fairly large brand gave away box cutters that were pretty much mini X-ACTO knives. Umm . . . we're not sure how that idea got approved.

Also don't give away anything big or bulky, like catalogs or big brochures, because those most often end up in trash cans, not business desks back home. Informative, compact brochures stand a better chance of making it home, especially if they contain special offers or introductory discounts.

- >> **Longevity:** If your product lasts longer than it takes to eat a branded candy bar or break or lose a cheap pen, your brand awareness opportunities last longer and could actually generate more mind share than a radio or TV ad.

- >> **Access:** If you have your premiums on a table by the aisle, you're inviting people to take them without talking to you. Make them visible but not something people can get without committing to listening to you. Also make sure you scan name tags for everyone you give a gift to so you at least get something for your investment.

  For example, Twitter takes branded T-shirts to its booths, which are located right in the middle by its sales executives. If you want a T-shirt you can't get elsewhere, you have to spend three minutes at four stations to listen to the product pitches. After you get your card stamped at each station, you get a T-shirt, and Twitter gets your contact information.

When buying premiums, your budget will go further if you purchase products you can use beyond just trade shows. According to a study by Baylor University, using premiums during a sales process can help to increase sales by as much as 20 percent.

TIP

Wittenberg suggests budgeting premium purchases around your normal close rate and average margin per sale. If sending a gift to every prospect you meet will increase your close rate by 20 percent, that could increase your sales by 20 per 100 sales meetings. If your average sales margin is $1,000, that could add $20,000 to your bottom line. Do the math for your business to determine your potential ROI and realistic spending to achieve it.

If you decide to do giveaways at a trade show, harness social marketing to get the word out. Here are some ideas:

- >> Use a hashtag on Twitter to alert customers that they can get your free gift at your booth.

- >> Make people fill out a form with contact information to get a coupon to present at your booth for a nicer premium gift. This way you get their contact information even if they don't show up.

- >> Promote your booth experience and premium on LinkedIn, Facebook, and other social media channels. If appropriate, use Instagram and Snapchat to tease your premium.

REMEMBER

Bringing customers together with your team and each other, whether at your own event or a trade show, sparks relationships that have the potential to pay off for years. Create meaningful experiences that are worth customers' time and will be remembered long after the fact.

5
Building a Brand That Sells Again and Again

Understand how to define your brand's value to consumers and build your brand identity and product line.

Recognize pricing opportunities and obstacles, and become a master at setting prices, dealing with changes, and promoting special offers.

Build your business with strong distribution strategies.

Find the best marketing channel structure for your product or service, discover how to maximize retail sales, and then work the right sales channels that attract and retain customers.

Chapter **13**

Making Your Brand Stand Out

The brand is the heart and soul of any marketing program. If your product is good and has a strong, appealing identity as part of a trusted brand, then your marketing and customer experience programs have a much higher chance of success.

Branding is one of the most powerful tools in the marketer's toolbox, no matter how big or small your brand is or in which industry you operate. Interbrand, which lists the top global brands every year, once stated that the best brands in the world are living entities that reshape reality. So as you read this book, and this chapter, think deep on that concept. How does your brand reshape reality for your industry, your market, your consumers, and your employees?

Beyond the top revenue brands Interbrand listed, the most powerful brands, according to Brand Finance, are those that score high for familiarity, loyalty, promotion, staff satisfaction, and reputation. For 2015, that brand was LEGO, overtaking the top spot from Ferrari in 2014, largely due to the innovative ways it involved customers in generating product and content. This chapter gives you some ideas for how you can increase the power of your own brand. You can find more on LEGO's content strategies in Chapter 6.

Building Sustainable Brand Equity

A brand is not just a symbol, statement, or status. It's a partnership in which consumers invest their personal equity as the relationship grows. The equity consumers have in a brand is not just the money they've spent on products but also their emotional investment.

People become emotionally invested in a brand when they

>> Experience service or quality that surprises them by exceeding all expectations

>> Are recognized and rewarded for their business and loyalty

>> Evangelize about a brand experience or product in the real world or online

>> Refer others to the brand and encourage them to purchase as well

When all the above happens regularly, your emotional equity in a brand goes up and so does the price to switch. In most cases, it will take a really bad experience for you to be willing to pay that price, which often includes losses such as

>> Loss of the thrill that comes with "surprisingly" good customer service

>> Loss of rewards or redeemable points earned

>> Loss of pride when switching from a brand you heavily promoted to others as trustworthy or good

>> Loss of potential discounts and other perks for loyal customers

Smart brands today design customer journeys, reward programs, and service protocols around building lasting brand equity, not just imminent value. Regardless of the size of your company, or whether you're in B2B or B2C, building equity is critical for maintaining loyalty and generating qualified referrals from your best customers. This chapter is all about doing just that.

Brands are defined by the emotional and functional value they provide consumers. Some are defined by their service, overall experience, innovations, status, luxury, and so on.

Brands defined by service

Here are some examples of brands defined by the quality of service that they provide:

>> Nordstrom carries some of the leading brands in fashion, but when you think "Nordstrom," you more often think "service." Its no-questions-asked return policies take fear out of the purchase process, inspire customers to splurge because there is no risk, and invite people back to feel glamorous and appreciated.

>> Hospitality brands are often distinguished by their service because luxury hotels can easily be duplicated. The Waldorf Astoria in Park City, managed by Kerry Hing, is no exception. He has earned top management rewards for the Hilton chain of hotels numerous years for surprising customers with unexpected service, on top of what is already standard at his four-star hotel. Surprises, like sending a six-pack of beer to a guest's room after hearing the guest say how much he needed one after a cold day of skiing, are what make his brand stand out. By observing and then delivering "surprising" service, his guests come back often and bring others with them.

Brands defined by experiences

You don't have to be in hospitality, amusement parks, or other experience-type industries to stand out for extraordinary experiences at the point of sale. Brands that make the shopping experience anything but ordinary are often the most successful because people remember how they felt long after the product novelty has worn off or the product is no longer in use.

Some examples include

>> **Apple:** Everyone talks about Apple, so forgive us for being trite, but few examples are as good. When you walk into an Apple Store, an employee greets you and then assigns you an expert who stays with you as a personal shopper as long as you need. If you buy something, the expert completes the transaction while standing next to you, not behind a clunky obstacle like a sales counter. You feel like a friend just helped you. If you need help, you can meet with Apple's Genius Bar gurus for free, and per experience, you always get a lot more than you went there for in the first place. I (Jeanette) went in for a keyboard fix and walked away with a software update and a new battery I didn't know I needed, all for free. Yes, that experience was memorable beyond the product's life because I no longer have that computer and don't remember the software updated but continue to talk about the experience years later.

>> **Evo.com:** Evo.com is an online outdoor sports equipment store that has so much personality and such fast responsive service that you want to go back to it, even if you don't need anything. Its emails are conversations that make you smile, its prices and return policies are inspiring, and it makes you feel like you have a friend in the business.

Moosejaw.com is another fun online experience with the same type of customer-friendly service and policies.

>> **Neiman Marcus:** Neiman Marcus, known for launching the "customer is always right" philosophy, takes price out of the equation through its personalized shopping experiences. Early in his career, Harlan Bratcher, most recently CEO of Armani Exchange and Reed Krakoff, rose quickly as the brand's lead personal shopper by putting his emphasis on making his customers feel something powerful inside themselves when shopping with him. Instead of just fitting them in a designer gown or jacket, he helped them find a new sense of self and beauty that they hadn't felt before. Feeling accomplished or glamorous brings people back for more no matter what you're selling.

Brands defined by product distinctions and innovation

Before the exploding battery crisis among Samsung's Galaxy Note 7 phones in 2016, Samsung was breaking ground as an innovative technology company that could actually compete with Apple. In fact, *Forbes* did a report that showed the Galaxy S7 substantially outperforming Apple's iPhone 6S on eight of ten features, including the camera quality that's a huge selling feature for phones. These innovations made Samsung one of the few brands that could actually compete with Apple's smartphone business. In fact, in the third quarter of 2015, Samsung had 10 percent more market share than Apple.

How are you best poised to compete? Is your service, quality, or experience a differentiating point that you can build over time into a sustainable advantage? If the answer is no to all three, you need to rethink your business model. Delivering just enough to get by could set you up to struggle in a dynamic world driven by consumers' demands for bigger and better.

TIP

Whether you're starting from scratch or have been in business for some time, take a closer look at how you project your values and advantages in your marketing programs. Your brand needs to offer more than just the products you sell. You need to offer emotional fulfillment that aligns with customers' values and how they see themselves in today's world.

REMEMBER

Your brand identity is not just your logo, colors, or the imagery you use in your ads, on your website, and more. It's not the dialogue you create on your social media pages. It's the emotions you fulfill, consciously and unconsciously, through your experiences, and it's the reputation you have for the good you do in the world and the promises you keep. It's about the story you tell and the stories you inspire others to tell about your products, service, and impact in the world.

Telling Your Brand's Story

Just like every person, every brand has a story. A story reflects your heritage, vision, values, and what you offer to others. It defines your brand persona and aligns people with your cause and purpose. A successful brand story is one in which consumers want to see themselves. Consumers want to see themselves as happy, fulfilled, carefree, self-actualized, purposeful, and respected by the brands they patronize. Brands that have powerful stories about these outcomes are those that are thriving in this new era of consumerism that demands much more than just product quality.

Brands that have powerful stories about movements, not just products, include TOMS, which gives a pair of shoes to a child in need for every pair purchased, Warby Parker, which does the same with eyeglasses, and Patagonia, which spends time and man-hours working to improve the environment over increasing its profits. And you can find stories of personal adventure and joyful living from brands like GoPro, Vail Resorts, and REI. Stories of trusted community and sharing come from Airbnb, Uber, TaskRabbit, and others that bring people with needs together with people with solutions.

Before you can be successful, you need to define your brand story. Here are some tips:

>> **Think of one of your favorite stories.** Does *Pride and Prejudice* keep you enthralled as you anticipate the moment that Mr. Darcy and Elizabeth connect and proclaim their mutual love? Does *Ocean's 12* have you biting your nails, hoping their creative plot goes off unhitched and doesn't get discovered? Or does *Homeward Bound* help you see the human side of your pets and feel even more connected to the unconditional love they give you?

>> **Ask these questions.** What emotional experience is associated with your favorite story — anticipation of a reward, solving a mystery, or increasing the love you have in your world? What is the emotional experience you need associated with your brand per your ESP (see Chapter 2), and how does your brand deliver on that need?

REMEMBER

Your brand story needs to unfold like a compelling novel. You need characters that your consumers can relate to, a cause and a purpose, and a climax and conclusion that make all feel good and excited to come back for more.

Andrea Syverson, a branding strategist and author, suggests that marketers learn to think like publishers by always asking themselves, "What's the sequel?" Don't stop at one story, but keep it going to give your fans more, and more, and then even more. Remember the Twilight series? It was too good to stop at one. Fans wanted more of the Bella and Edward story, and their passion fueled much more than selling books and movies. Just look at all the accessories associated with the Twilight series.

Exercises Syverson suggests for helping define your story include these steps:

1. **List your brand's ideal customers.**

   Think deeply about your brand's ideal customers. What are their values? And how do your products and experiences support them?

2. **Determine what competitive distinctions truly set you apart.**

   List these on a sticky note to help you identify the key phrases or words that are most meaningful and can be used across channels that let you communicate in only short sentences or sound bites.

3. **Outline the fears, uncertainties, and doubts that muddy the decision processes to buy your category and your brand.**

   Do all you can to overcome these pain points for your customers.

4. **Write your manifesto.**

   What is your brand's vision and passion? How do these reshape reality for your customers and employees?

5. **Write a mini brochure.**

   Try to tell your story on a folded panel about 4 x 2.5 inches. What is most critical for you to say to inspire customers to engage and inquire about your services? How can you quickly tell them about your brand and how you can allay their fears, fulfill their needs, and become a trusted partner?

TIP

Outline the elements of your brand story — the characters, plot, climax, and the happy ending. Look for ways to make the plot more interesting and to engage and involve your customers. After all, consumers are a big part of your story, and if you let them help it unfold, it will be their story, too, and one they will tell to others, building your brand even further. See Chapter 6 on user-generated content for some fun examples of how to do this.

The characters

The characters of your story need to reflect the values and persona of those whom you want to attract because, again, people align with others who have similar values and personalities.

Are the characters in your story like Blake Mycoskie who started TOMS after going on a service trip to Asia and deciding to use his business skills to save the world? Or are your characters more like Steve Jobs, who maybe wasn't the nicest person on the planet but had one of the most innovative minds and the personal fierceness to make things happen? Or perhaps your strongest character is make-believe, like the Maytag Man who never had anywhere to go because Maytag appliances never break down. Or, most recently, like Flo who for years has represented Progressive Insurance as a quirky, overly enthusiast sales clerk?

Since using Flo as its persona and telling its story through her character, Progressive has thrived. According to Morningstar, Progressive's net income went from −$70 million in 2008, the year the Flo commercials were launched, to $1,267 billion at the end of 2015, after more than 100 commercials featuring Flo. Her character became so powerful that a Halloween costume was created in her honor, and she was quickly described as an iconic brand character after just one year of representing the brand.

Although you don't need a massive media budget like Progressive's, you do need to project a story that your customers can relate to, or in which they can see themselves. And you need to weave that story into your content, social media, experience, iconology, and marketing programs.

The plot

Like every good story, you need a plot and a climax. A plot is the sequence of main events that take place in your story and lead to the conclusion or moral at the end. Back to the story of TOMS, which is about poverty, the plot builds as TOMS creates more events to raise awareness and funds to provide shoes to children living in slave labor and extremely poor conditions. The climax is when TOMS reports back to its customers that with their help, the movement achieved its mission: thousands of shoes distributed and a better world for those supported through customers' purchases and volunteer efforts.

What's your brand's story line? A product built around a cause, a company known for disruptive innovation, or customer service that redefines your industry? Or a brand that puts customers first every time?

The climax

Every story has a climax and so does every brand. A climax is the point in a story when the conflict is resolved or all the events come together to create the peak of intensity for reading or viewing the story. Like when the villain is revealed or romance finally results in embrace. Apple's climax is the iPhone because it's the product that most distinguishes its innovation in the world and happens to be the bestselling product of all time, selling more than 1 billion units, according to brand analyst Horace Dediu of Asymco. A local pet store's climax may be having the best pet day care experience due to having an obstacle course, scheduled petting hours to avoid loneliness, and so on. Having an iPhone sets you up to enjoy the intensity of Apple's products easily and readily, and a really fun pet day care creates a high level of joy seeing your pet happy at the end of a day without you.

What's your climax? Maintaining a 90 percent customer satisfaction rate or a 70 NPS? Getting the best reviews in your market?

Branding Your Identity

You need to have a standard for your brand that's as hard, clear, and unwavering as the iron brands cattle owners used generations ago. If your brand identity isn't iron-hard and consistent, then you need to review it and settle on a single, strong identity that you can use in all media at all times.

Is your name relevant and meaningful for the emotional fulfillment it offers? Are your colors creating the moods that inspire attachment and sales? Most important, are you presenting a consistent image, persona, and emotion at every touch point and communications episode? Variation in your brand presentation confuses people, reduces recognition, and dilutes the strength of your brand. Set standards for your company to follow and stand tough on making sure they're not broken.

Unifying your brand identity

Business growth is good, but sometimes an organization grows so many branches that achieving branding recognition for all of them is difficult because those multiple branches have evolved into different identities that fail to reinforce and promote each other fully.

A great example of how developing too many branches can backfire is a nonprofit located in the colonial village of Old Deerfield, Massachusetts. The organization was founded so long ago that its name doesn't make all that much sense for what it does today: Pocumtuck Valley Memorial Association. The term *memorial association* used to be more common for civic groups formed to memorialize people or places from history with statues and plaques. That was its first charter, its trunk. Then it branched out by archiving and presenting historical artifacts at the Memorial Hall Museum in Old Deerfield — another brand name, one that appears over the door and on the organization's website and many of its pamphlets, grant applications, and other communications. The website is www.deerfield-ma.org, which reflects the historical interest in the town of Old Deerfield itself, another brand identity. Then there's the Indian House Children's Museum, a popular place for visitors and another brand identity. Plus the fascinating work the organization does to educate teachers on how to better teach history, nested on the brand branch Deerfield Teacher's Center.

To try to unify these many brands, the organization is using PVMA Deerfield as a new umbrella identity, which retains the traditional name as an acronym but adds in the Deerfield identity that pops up in so many of the sub-brands. Still, there's an apparent need to continue to promote the sub-brands, because each has an identity and a function of its own. The question this brand must decide is whether to operate as a consumer brand marketer, where each brand is a separate marketing asset and doesn't dovetail with others, to try to unify by migrating every sub-brand toward a more unified identity. This is the key strategic question, and what it decides to do will affect the amount of resources and money put behind each brand.

How will you avoid distilling the potency of your brand by trying to take on projects that don't directly address your mission and core competencies? Take a look at brands that diversified too much and the failures that cost them, not just substantial revenues but brand respect. Sony is a formidable example. Known as a pioneer in televisions and stereo systems, it branched out in many directions over the years, and few are paying off. Its movie and music branches have failed to turn profits as expected; it just spun off its online entertainment business, and its attempt to prosper in computers ended in selling the Vaio line in 2014. As a top global brand ranked by Interbrand, it continues to fall, ranking 58 in 2016, down from 52 in 2014, and 46 in 2013.

Developing your brand's iconography

As we mention in Chapter 7, every brand has its iconology or iconography that makes a statement about the role it plays in the lives of those it serves. Iconography is the study of visual images. In marketing, iconography is the development of a family of images or imagery that make the brand appealing and build a consistent identity.

EXAMPLE

For example, since 1971, Adidas had the Trefoil brand with its three petal-like shapes radiating upward, bisected by three lines (the three stripes that have appeared on all Adidas shoes since 1949). That Trefoil symbol is an important logotype, but what iconography, or supporting images, should be associated with it? For some years, Adidas used simple action figures neatly silhouetted in black, performing athletic movements.

Over time, the Adidas action images began to feel a little too static, so Adidas retained EIGA Design (of Hamburg, Germany) to update them. The new versions are also action figures in black and white, but the originals are hand-drawn in felt tip pen, with exciting lines adding to the sense of dynamic movement and grace of each action figure. You can see the updated iconography in animated sequences in some Adidas commercials or by doing an Internet search for "Adidas brand iconography."

In developing your brand's iconography, you may want to create a family of artistic images to illustrate it, as Adidas did. Or you may want to take a more general approach, collecting a handful of the sorts of images you think work well to guide designers of marketing materials. For instance, a natural, old-fashioned cookie brand may have a set of images of traditional farms and farm kitchens, drawn from Flickr or stock photography houses. The exact images need not be used in marketing, but they help advertisers, packagers, point-of-purchase display designers, blog and web designers, and other marketers zoom in on a general look and style, perhaps even a setting, for displaying the cookies.

Identifying your brand's personality traits

Research psychologists rarely agree on anything, but they do agree that human beings have five broad dimensions to their outward personalities. Every person can be defined by where he or she falls on these five dimensions. To define your brand more clearly, and achieve psychological relevance, find ways to align your communications with these five factors of human personality: extroversion, agreeableness, conscientiousness, emotional stability, and openness to experience.

TIP

Table 13-1 shows the range of these outward personalities. You can discover how these traits apply to your customers through the research you do, as discussed in Chapter 4, and by studying consumer trends and studies about the age, lifestyle, attitudes, and values of consumers within your age and geographical parameters. Circle the answer on each row that best defines the personality traits of your high-value customers, rating them on a scale of 1 to 5, with 5 being high. Then develop your brand's iconology, messaging, content, and, most important for branding purposes, your persona and personality. If your customers tend to be more open-minded to new ideas and experiences, use colors, fonts, and images that reflect creativity, innovation, and fun in your brand iconology. Reference this table often to make sure your marketing communications are consistent with the brand personality you've chosen.

TABLE 13-1

Defining Personality Traits That Describe Your Customers

Do Your Customers Tend to Be . . .	Rating
Extroverted: Outgoing. Make friend easily. Sociable. Take charge.	1 2 3 4 5
Agreeable: Make people feel at ease. Are on good terms with nearly everyone. Trust people. Think of others first.	1 2 3 4 5
Conscientious: Do a thorough job. Well prepared. Get chores done right away. Do things according to a plan.	1 2 3 4 5
Emotionally stable: Relaxed. Calm. Handle stress well. Not easily bothered.	1 2 3 4 5
Open to experiences: Imaginative. Creative. Intelligent. Have many interests. Quick to understand things.	1 2 3 4 5

Source: Alex Hiam, The Big Five Personality Test, Trainer's Spectrum, 2009

Now go back and rank your brand's characteristics and persona on the same attributes by using Table 13-2. How closely do you match up?

TABLE 13-2

Defining Your Brand's Unique Personality

Does Your Brand Seem to Be . . .	Your Answer
Extroverted: Outgoing. Makes friends easily. Sociable. Takes charge.	Yes / No
Agreeable: Makes people feel at ease. Is on good terms with nearly everyone. Trusts people. Thinks of others first.	Yes / No
Conscientious: Does a thorough job. Well prepared. Gets chores done right away. Does things according to a plan.	Yes / No
Emotionally stable: Relaxed. Calm. Handles stress well. Not easily bothered.	Yes / No
Open to experiences: Imaginative. Creative. Intelligent. Has many interests. Quick to understand things.	Yes / No

Source: Alex Hiam, The Big Five Personality Test, Trainer's Spectrum, 2009

Does the number of yes answers line up with the personality traits of your consumers? If not, your branding efforts need to include changing this situation.

Perhaps you discover that your brand and consumers tend to be conscientious. This trait aligns well for a line of business products designed to keep important files organized and readily available. It would also work well for a legal firm that wants to be seen as conscientious to people's losses and what's fair for all involved.

REMEMBER

You can't change your own personality or that of your best customers very easily, but you do get to pick the traits you consider most helpful for marketing your brand. For instance, a new line of cosmetics may be portrayed as extroverted and open to experiences. Dynamic, exciting colors and sounds will help convey this sociable, creative, enthusiastic personality to consumers who'll buy the brand to add those traits to their own lives when they feel the need for them.

Developing brands within brands

How you name your product lines, offerings, and experiences can often make them more intriguing and help distinguish your products for your different consumer segments. Sub-branding your product lines can help you offer a little bit of something to everyone, thus widening your reach, relevancy, and profits. Just like you wouldn't name your used-car business Lemon Used Cars or your party-planning services Grimm and Gray Events, you need to give your products and programs inviting names. Take a look at the Toyota car company. The Toyota brand stands for durability, quality, performance, and trust to many people. Under the Toyota brand are many products that reflect very different lifestyles for different consumer segments within the driving population. Consider the following Toyota models:

>> Avalon: A sedan that appeals to middle-aged adults and professionals wanting a nice ride and image without the high luxury price

>> Highlander: A sleek, high-performance SUV for rugged terrain and adventurous lifestyles that comes with luxury options if you want a nicer ride

>> Corolla: An economical small car for entry-level car owners that provides strong performance and trusted reliability

The maintenance and 24-hour road service package Toyota offers is named ToyotaCare, playing off the double meaning of "care" to communicate the free services offered that provide care for your car and a program with the kind of service, coverage, and prices that lets customers know that Toyota really cares for them. Fun innuendos are often the most memorable.

Here are some tips to consider:

>> Create intrigue for your products by giving your product lines names that reflect the values, aspirations, and lifestyles of your customers. Make them interesting or fun enough to be remembered.

If you're a retail shop and sell others' products, have some fun naming your product categories. For example, instead of listing product lines on your site as Dog Food, Dog Toys, and Dog Accessories, why not come up with names at your point of sale and on your website like Nibbles and Staples, Playtime, and Just Because Items. Creativity sparks attention and interest and creates connections that make customers feel like friends rather than just a number.

>> Can't think of any names out of the ordinary that reflect a new product or product line you're launching? Make one up. When you use meaningful components for your made-up names, they're called *morphemes,* which NameLab, Inc. (a San Francisco–based leading developer of such names) defines as the semantic kernels of words. For example, NameLab started with the word *accurate* (from the Latin word *accuratus*) and extracted a morpheme from it to name a new car brand: Acura. The company also developed Compaq, Autozone, Lumina, and Zapmail in the same manner. Each one is a new word to the language, but each word communicates something about the product because of the meanings consumers associate with that word's components.

>> Many names are formed by semi-scientific recombinations of root syllables, which make them sound semi-scientific. Melodious words are more memorable than technical or awkward ones. People recall poems and songs and even marketing text that rhymes better than those that don't. For example, more people are willing to try a Singapore sling than a gin sling as indicated by a jump in sales when the cocktail drink changed its name.

Updating your brand

Just because you may be bored with your brand image and even your products, it doesn't mean your customers are. Don't change something just because you can. Remember the epic and costly failure of New Coke? Product changes and brand updates rarely work. Logo changes, which nearly every new ad agency hired wants to do first off to make its mark, usually don't pay off. Some do, as referenced in Chapter 7, but in most cases, it's risky and can waste a lot of money, unless you need to project a new value or attribute. Changing just because with no strategic reason to do so can backfire.

Consider what happened with The Gap, which switched from a distinctive GAP logo, white on a deep blue square, to a generic-looking Gap logo on black with only a small remnant of the old blue square. Instant loss of brand equity. Nobody liked it. Now the old logo has quietly reasserted itself, and the new one has been retired. *USA Today*'s distinctive white caps logo on a blue box was scrapped in favor of dull black letters next to a strange light–blue circle that seems to symbolize nothing.

If you want to make changes, make change matter. Make change only because your consumers have changed and you need to be in line with their new interests and values. If your products are out of date functionally, make a change. If your iconology reflects the past and your product needs to reflect cutting-edge technology, update it to make your brand look current. If you look out of touch or out of date, people will unconsciously feel like your technology must be, too.

Designing a Product Line

A *product line* is any logical grouping of products offered to customers. You usually identify product lines by an umbrella brand name with individual brand identities falling under that umbrella. After you establish a strong brand, you can extend it to a line of products. Strong brands often have long lines of products, but as pointed out earlier with the example of Sony's failed product lines, you still have to be careful to keep product lines within your core competency and within your consumers' realm of logic for what you do best. Some of the greatest brands extended in ways that just didn't make sense, such as BenGay moving into headache medications. BenGay Aspirin is one of the top product failures of all time. Not hard to quickly figure out why.

The sections that follow provide valuable insight about what to consider when developing your product line, how to manage the product line after you develop it, and what to do to protect its identity.

Eyeing depth and breadth

You have two key issues to consider when designing your product line: depth and breadth.

Depth

How many alternatives should you give customers within any single category? For example, should you make a single T-shirt design in a range of sizes? How about offering the design in a variety of colors? Both of these options increase depth because they give customers more options. Depth gives you an advantage because it improves the likelihood of a good fit between an interested customer and your product.

Increase depth when you're losing customers because you don't have a product for them. Increasing your depth of choice also reduces the chance of disappointing a prospective customer.

Breadth

Breadth comes from offering more types or categories of products. For example, if you sell one popular T-shirt design, you can increase your product line's breadth by offering more T-shirt designs, adding sweatshirts, baseball caps, and other related items. When you add anything that the customer views as a separate choice, not a variant of the same choice, you're adding breadth to your product line. A broad line of T-shirts includes dozens and dozens of different designs. A broad and deep product line offers each of those designs in many sizes, colors, and forms.

Increase breadth whenever you can think of a new product that seems to fit in the product line and that you believe will increase your sales without sacrificing profits. By *fit*, we mean that customers can see the new product's obvious relationship to the line. Don't mix unrelated products because you'll end up with a product line that doesn't have a clear, logical identity to customers. But do keep stretching a successful line as long as sales continue to grow. Doing so makes sense for one simple reason: You sell new products to old customers. Of course, the line may also reach new customers, which is great. But you can sell to your old customers more easily and affordably in a way that offers them new products and becomes a true win-win.

Managing your product line effectively

The secret to good product management is reflected in the motto "Don't leave well enough alone." Yet if you keep growing your product lines, you can obviously bump into some practical limits after a while. Instead of just adding new products because you can and you're looking for new revenue streams, build a plan and stick to it. More new product launches fail than succeed because in many cases brand managers move too far off their core competencies.

Here are some questions to guide you in product development:

>> **Does it make sense to your customers?** Customers compartmentalize expectations for brands, just like most people compartmentalize expectations in virtually all aspects of their lives. Customers expect the newest latte flavor at Starbucks to be as good as the ones it's produced for years. Customers wouldn't have that same expectation if going to Subway for a latte because that isn't the expertise or quality associated with that brand.

>> **Does it support your current product line?** Product expansions, especially for smaller businesses, shouldn't be about adding new brands and branches as much as it should be about adding products that support your current product line. Look at Apple. When it decided to go into the smartphone business, it quickly went into the business of building products, or purchasing products, to use with its smartphones. It now owns Beats, a market leader, and makes several phone accessories and apps that support its core and are must-have products for a fuller product experience. And because finding aftermarket products that support Apple products is difficult, it has your loyalty whether or not you intended to give it. A great example of this is the iPhone 7, which initially launched without a headphone jack, along with the launch of Apple's wireless Bluetooth earbuds, which of course work with the iPhone 7.

>> **Do you have enough capitalization to make it work?** Never start on a journey you can't finish. If you branch out and fail, that failure transfers to the perceived value of other products and sends a signal to your customers that maybe you're not so good, or you've lost your edge, or you could be in trouble. People don't want to keep purchasing from a brand that may fail and leave them with no service options or a bunch of incompatible accessories.

Protecting your product line and brand

You can gain legal protection for your product, a specific line of products, or even your entire company by using and getting legal recognition for a unique identifier. This protection can apply to names, short verbal descriptions, and visual symbols. All these forms of identification are marks that can represent the identity of whatever you apply them to. A tangible product's name and/or visual symbol is a *trademark*. A service name is termed a *service mark* (U.S. law treats a service mark similarly to a trademark). A business name is a *trade name* (again, with similar protection under U.S. law).

REMEMBER

In the United States, you establish and protect your rights to exclusive use of any unique trademark by using it. Yes, you should register it (with the U.S. Patent and Trademark Office — contact any law firm that handles intellectual property to find out how). But registering the trademark isn't nearly as important as *using* the trademark. In other countries, usage and registration also matter, but sometimes governments reverse the emphasis, meaning that without registration usage gives you no protection. So check with local authorities in each country where you plan to use a trademark.

For more information on establishing and strengthening trademarks, contact your lawyer, any experienced ad agency that does brand marketing, or a name lab. You can find more detailed coverage of the topic in *Patents, Copyrights & Trademarks For Dummies,* by Henri Charmasson and John Buchaca (Wiley). Additionally, free information is available at the U.S. Patent and Trademark Office's trademark-specific website (www.uspto.gov/trademarks/index.jsp). There, you can download a free book, search the database, and discover info about U.S. trademark law. You can also file a trademark application online by using the Trademark Electronic Application System (TEAS), although we don't really recommend doing it yourself unless you have working knowledge of trademark law.

To register your trademark in other countries, you must contact a lawyer who specializes in intellectual property. Most of the countries in which you may want to do business (including the United States) subscribe to the Berne Convention, which means your legal protection for a published work (even a label or ad) in one participating country is also honored in other participating countries.

Strengthening an Existing Product

Your existing products have some degree of brand identity and a certain amount of customer loyalty already. Often, your best investment is to boost the strength of your brand image or improve your design or packaging. Doing so takes advantage of any existing brand equity, which is easier than starting from scratch.

Here's a list of simple and quick actions you can take to build customer loyalty and grow sales by working on your product:

>> **Update the appearance.** Many companies present good products to the world in poorly designed exteriors that don't dress those products for success. Look at the product itself. Do the colors, aesthetics, and shapes appeal to your top consumers? Is your brand name visible in an appropriate manner? In a world where minimalism is big, can you streamline your product to be smaller, to take up less space, and to be more efficient?

>> **Rethink the packaging.** Most often, refreshing the look of your packaging is easier than updating the look of your product. If you want to increase your prices, change your packaging to make it look like it's worth the new price tag. Adding "Improved Formula" seems to work for many consumer goods. Always make sure your new packaging adheres to the ESP you've developed and uses the colors you've selected to project your brand's best and most relevant attributes. Highlight your best features and achievements, such as "98% of our customers refer friends," on your packaging, too. Using recycled packaging materials makes customers of all generations feel better about purchasing from you, so consider this as often as you can.

>> **Make sure the product is attractive and easy to use.** Your product should also feel nice — smooth, polished, soft, or whatever texture is appropriate to the product's use. Tactile experiences add value to the product even in today's digital world. Even minor changes in your product's look, feel, and function can improve its appeal and customer satisfaction.

>> **Refresh any printed materials that come with the product.** Can you improve their appearance? Dress them up? Make them clearer or more useful? Whatever you do, make sure these printed materials instill pride of ownership in the product. A professional, attractive web page should also support the product.

>> **Choose your product's best quality.** Coin a short phrase to communicate your ESP and put that phrase in prominent places on the product, its packaging, and its literature. If you don't want to throw out a large inventory of boxes in your warehouse, you can communicate your new features or advantages with stickers.

>> **Eliminate confusion about which product does what for whom.** If you have more than one product, or variations for different segments you serve, clarify the differences and uses of your products by pricing and naming them distinctly (to make them obviously different). You'd be amazed how confusing most product lines look to the average buyer.

Simply put, you're only as good as your products. Always be looking to update, upgrade, or perhaps even replace your current line of products. It's a long-term but vital marketing strategy. Consumers' wants, needs, styles, likes, and trends change quickly, and when you don't provide what they're looking for, they can quickly find someone else who does.

Introducing New and Successful Products

Being innovative can give you a strong competitive advantage. A competitor's major new product introduction probably changes the face of your market — and upsets your sales projections and profit margins — at least once every few years. So you can't afford to ignore new product development. You should introduce new products as often as you can afford to.

For most, coming up with a new idea is the first hurdle. In addition to the ideas listed in Chapter 7 on coming up with creative new ideas for campaigns and products, survey your customers, ask your salespeople what they come up against the most, and so on. There's no single formula for inventing new products.

Give customers a chance to be involved in product development. Daybreak Game Company, LLC, formerly Sony Online Entertainment, invites users to help develop its new online game adventures and has achieved amazing loyalty and brand equity as a result. You just need to engage in a new and different thinking process. *Remember:* Do something new to produce something new.

Partnering with experts to build new products

One of the most effective and powerful ways to develop and launch new products is to partner with experts in a given field. They provide the insights and technology for a product for which you are the exclusive commercial business partner and co-owner of the product patent. Most such relationships involve licensing and royalty agreements that benefit and protect both parties.

More often than not, these experts can be found in the academic and research science fields as PhD research scientists and/or professors. If you're in the sports industry and want to make a product to help improve the game and personal joy for weekend warriors who tend to be hitting middle age and the issues that go with it, it may make sense to work with sports scientists to develop a product that's functional for sports activities and valuable for injury prevention, too.

That is what Kim Gustafson did when he launched Opedix, LLC, which produces compression tights to help ligaments avoid taking the wear and tear of prolonged motion. His goal was to create a product that would enable professional and recreational athletes to stay active longer, enhance their performance, and prevent injuries, too. Gustafson determined that no existing companies making similar products for injury prevention and performance support had scientific evidence to back up their product claims, so he teamed up with the world's leading sports medicine laboratories, The Steadman Philippon Research Institute and the Human Dynamics Laboratory.

The team hypothesized that if a non-stretch banding material were strategically integrated into the design of traditional compression tights, the banding should provide anatomical benefits. Using state-of-the-art motion analysis systems/equipment, the hypothesis proved to be correct. This new product provided "directional compression," and they applied for a patent for the Opedix Knee-Tec Tights (check it out at www.opedix.com), which offer valid results for runners, skiers, and other athletes.

They identified both the sports and medical markets as opportunities. The sports market offered the path of least resistance (easier market entry).

Doing this alone would have been difficult and costly. Partnering with experts not only helped Gustafson develop a strong product, but it also added scientifically valid credibility for performance claims that would have been hard for him to get on his own.

Teaming up with experts in a field of science or technology to let them develop products for you offers many advantages, and you can do so in many different ways, including the following:

>> Pay developers upfront to create apps or technological products for you and assign ownership of the patent to you.

>> Split the costs of research and development and assign royalties on sales accordingly.

>> Secure an arrangement where you provide marketing and distribution and your partner all the R&D and production and then share the profits according to what makes sense given each party's expenditure upfront.

REMEMBER

Whatever you do, make sure you think of the short-term and the long-term impact of your contract. Partnering with experts can enable you to develop products your competitors don't have and can't get without developing them on their own, which is cost-prohibitive. As a result, you can emerge as the leading innovator in your industry and the one to watch for consumers, investors, and more.

You have to be only one step ahead of your competition to win the game, not several, but you must stay ahead. Continuing to add products that are exclusive to your brand is a pretty sure way to do just that.

Getting insights from customers

As discussed in Chapter 4 on research methodology, one of the best sources for new product ideas that fit your brand's competencies and customers' perceptions of you is to ask them. When you do a customer satisfaction survey, add a simple question that gives you powerful insights. Try asking the following:

>> Is there anything missing from our current product line that you would like to see us add?

>> Are there any services we can provide that would help you get greater efficiencies or functionality out of the products you currently purchase from us?

>> Of the following products or services, what are you most likely to trust us to deliver to you with the same quality we currently provide? (List new product or service ideas.)

Using the significant difference strategy

Remember, nearly all new products fail. Even big brands that once dominated their markets fail. Just do an Internet search for brands that have failed in 10 or 20 years and check out the long lists that pop up. Read how these brands fail and take notes not to follow their path.

REMEMBER

To achieve real success, you have to introduce something that really looks new and different to the market. The product needs a clear point of difference. Innovations that consumers recognize quickly and easily provide the marketer with a greater return. Researchers who study new product success use the term *intensity* to describe this phenomenon. The more intense the difference between your new product and old products, the more likely the new product can succeed.

TIP

The Product Development and Management Association (PDMA) publishes reviews of good new books on product development via its website, www.pdma. org. PDMA also offers conferences, training, and other services to its members.

Upgrading or Expanding an Existing Product

Some products are so perfect that they fit naturally with their customers, and you should just leave them alone — for example, the original formula for Coca-Cola or another food that has a taste and effect that transcends generations. Instead of changing your winning formula, if you're not losing sales or discovering flaws with what you're selling, find ways to expand it. After learning from its failed new formula launch, Coca-Cola updated its original formula by adding Vanilla Coke, Black Cherry Coke, Lime Coke, and Orange Coke and of course the greatest success, Diet Coke. All but Diet Coke fizzled out and now lay in the Coca-Cola product failure graveyard, but they did generate revenue for a time.

How expensive is your upgrade or expansion, and how long will it take to pay off? If a change represents a strong potential profit for even a short period of time, it may be worthwhile. Just weigh the costs and payoff ratio, and make sure your new product is relevant to consumers' needs and attitudes to avoid creating a graveyard of your own. When an update is no longer cool or selling, cut your losses and move on. Don't make the mistake of hanging on to a product for nostalgia or hopes it will come back. You stand to lose more than you gain if you do.

REMEMBER

You're competing on a changing playing field. Your competitors are trying hard to make their products better, and you have to do the same. Always seek insights into how to improve your product. Always look for early indicators of improvements your competitors plan to make, and be prepared to go one step further in your response. And always go to your marketing oracle — the customer — for insights into how you can improve your product.

Following are two tests that a product must pass to remain viable. If your product doesn't pass, you need to improve or alter it somehow.

Passing the differentiation test

Your product must pass a differentiation test by being better than its competition on certain criteria due to inherent design features or added service components. Or it needs to be equally as good but offer a great overall value that you can sustain over time. Don't change prices as your point of differentiation, higher or lower, unless you'll be able to keep it up indefinitely. Restaurants that raise prices without changing the menu or adding something new to really add a difference worth paying for don't usually fare well. On the flip side, if you lower your prices to gain more sales, you need to be able to keep it up or suffer bigger losses if you have to raise them back.

Passing the champion test

Champions are those customers who really love your product, who insist on buying it over others, and who tell their friends or associates to do the same. Champions are great to have, but they're also rather rare.

The championship test is tougher to pass than the differentiation test. Many products lack champions. But when a product does secure them, that product is more likely to live a long and profitable life. Generating champions who are so passionate about your product that they evangelize about it without being asked and pass their passion on to the next generations in their families should be your constant goal as you manage the life cycle of your product.

Products with champions get great word of mouth, and their sales and market shares grow with little cost and efforts on the brand's part as a result. Even better, champions faithfully repurchase the products they rave about. And this repeat business provides your company with high-profit sales, compared with the higher costs associated with finding new customers. Always stay in touch with your champions, invite them to provide feedback, reward them, and listen to them. If they like something, chances are others will, too.

Branding across channels

Make sure your have consistent branding across all channels you use. Whether you're marketing through your blog, a YouTube video or channel, outdoor advertising, brochures, events, or other means, you need to present the same values and persona for your brand. Evaluate your brand identity to make sure it's presented consistently and that it appears everywhere possible. Stick with your color palette, fonts, and so on to avoid confusion and weaken the instant brand recognition you're trying to build.

REMEMBER

Your brand name and logo don't have to be the most beautiful, sophisticated, or clever to be successful. In fact, many top brands are strikingly simple. What sets them apart from other brands is that they're recognizable and known, which in turn gives them value and helps them sell products. Rolling your brand out consistently and strongly is even more important than perfecting your logo design. Choose something that's clear and simple, reflects your values and persona, and then stick to it no matter what.

Chapter **14**

Finding the Right Pricing Approach

As simple as it may seem, pricing is actually one of the most complicated parts of marketing. You need to establish what customers are willing to pay for your category and your brand and develop sound pricing strategies. Is your best strategy to set a low price so you can grow revenue faster? Or raise prices for higher profits? How do you best apply discounts and promotions without minimizing your overall pricing and brand value? This chapter gives some insights about the role of pricing for long-term growth and profitability.

Pricing Opportunities and Obstacles

It's easy to think that price is the primary driver for sales and that the lowest priced product wins over customers' sales and loyalty. Yet, as we mention in earlier chapters about the emotional drivers of choice, being the low-price leader can actually be detrimental to your long-term success. Pricing opportunities and obstacles include many elements depending on your market, competition, required profit margins, consumer demand, and perception for your product and brand. Check out Table 14-1 for some examples.

TABLE 14-1 **Examples of Pricing Opportunities and Obstacles**

Opportunities	Obstacles
Setting your initial price to be attractive for trial	Pricing to be competitive with established brands
Increasing price as perceived value grows and so does demand	Under-pricing to attract new customers
Providing special offers to spark sales and loyalty	Deep discounting and its impact on existing customers and long-term sales
Pricing for profitability	Pricing's impact on profit margins

Raising your price and selling more

Your pricing goal should be to see how much you can sell your product for, not how little. Keep in mind that if you start out as the low-price leader in your market, you'll have a hard time moving away from that position. To counteract that, you may have to engage in aggressive branding campaigns to justify a new price, which can be expensive and lower your profit margin.

If you want to raise your price *and* sell more, consider the following:

>> **Building brand awareness:** Better-known brands command a premium price. You can use some of the growth hacking, social media, and publicity methods discussed in earlier chapters such as Chapters 7 and 8.

>> **Increasing quality:** Create new and improved versions of your product that give consumers a perceived reason to spend more on it.

>> **Upping your social dialogue:** Inspire word of mouth by encouraging happy customers to post about their experience with your products on social channels. Word-of-mouth marketing can earn a 5 to 10 percent higher price than competing products.

>> **Using prestige pricing:** Adding a more sophisticated look to your packaging and advertising can help you successfully boost your price 20 to 100 percent. Take a look at your packaging. Does it look like it belongs on the clearance shelf or one for bestsellers?

All these activities take time, resources, and money, so it's important to weigh the potential consequences and returns.

WARNING Sometimes competitor pricing can force you to lower prices to a point that you barely make any profits. If you find yourself in this situation, you may need to consider changing your distribution model or getting out of that line of business if some of these tactics don't work.

Avoiding the dangers of deep discounting

Using deep discounting to attract prospects to try your product is often tempting, but beware. Often more perils than pay-offs occur from using programs like Groupon and other big discount platforms. Here are some facts from a Business Insider survey to consider:

>> Nearly 80 percent of Groupon users surveyed discounted their prices between 50 and 75 percent.

>> Many businesses earned revenues as low as 25 percent of normal.

>> Restaurants that typically earn 6 to 8 percent profit margins earned 3 percent margins, which doesn't help long-term sustainability.

>> More than 50 percent of companies retained only a handful of Groupon customers. Some retained about 25 percent, and none retained 50 percent or higher.

>> The majority say they won't use Groupon again, and 50 percent would not refer it to a friend.

In addition to the disappointing income figures, deep discounting for customer acquisition presents some other dangers. For one, loyal customers that aren't offered the same deal as new customers can feel unappreciated and lose interest in buying from you. Additionally, you've just disvalued your brand. After you offer really low prices, customers will start to see you as less prestigious than before, and that hurts business.

Because of the high frequency of sales many consumer brands offer, customers are being conditioned to wait for the next sale. This strategy has helped usher out the era of department stores ruling retail and has resulted in many store closings and mergers.

REMEMBER

Lowering prices is easier than raising them. When you lower it, you may lower people's interest in buying it again at a higher price and be stuck with a price that hurts your profits despite maintaining or increasing volume.

Exploring the impact of pricing on customers' purchases

Price sensitivity is the degree to which purchases are affected by price. You need to estimate how price sensitive your customers are and how much you stand to gain or lose from a specific price increase or decrease.

The best way to find out is to do a small test. Asking customers won't help because people don't raise their hand for price increases just because, and asking about their willingness to pay more could just be a red flag that something isn't right with your brand or that you're just getting greedy. Neither inspires sales or loyalty.

To get a valid result from testing price, try the following:

>> Select a market where sales reflect normal trends for your business, month over month and year over year.

>> Raise your price at the point of sale without any prior marketing messages.

>> Keep all other variables constant so you can truly determine whether price influenced sales.

>> Use the same packaging and marketing messages as you have in other markets so you have one difference to analyze rather than several, which makes it hard to determine what really drove a change in sales.

If sales were the same or went up with a higher price, you're likely safe to increase your price to the level tested. If your results were the opposite, raising your price would be very risky.

Another indicator of price sensitivity is if you're losing sales to competitors' lower priced products. If this is the case, look for opportunities to change price and cost controls so you can maintain your market share and profit margins.

REMEMBER

Price sensitivity can change as markets change despite your product's constancy. Stay on top of market and economic trends so you can plan ahead rather than scramble to keep up.

Increasing profits without increasing prices

Many factors drive cash flows and profits, not just price. Here are some ways to boost profits without raising prices:

>> **Monitor frequency of discounting.** Are customers shopping only your discounts? Are they stocking up when your price is low? If so, change your sales promotions, not your list prices.

>> **Examine how you assess fees.** Perhaps your company is failing to collect appropriate fees from customers. This is particularly important if you offer a

service at a base price, or a product that requires maintenance, and charge additional fees for extra options or service. Review your fees models and make sure they're priced appropriately to cover your costs, generate a profit, and be within market value.

» **Make sure your fee structure is current.** As customers shifted to online checking, they expected unlimited transactions for free. Many banks had to change their fee structure to compensate. Instead of charging a per-check fee that customers won't pay anymore, many now charge a monthly fee if the balance goes below a certain level. Make sure you have processes in place to compensate for services you have to reduce or give for free due to changing market demands.

Setting or Changing Your List Price

In the following sections, we provide some guidelines for setting or changing your pricing. Figure 14-1 illustrates the process that we describe.

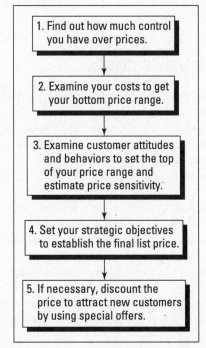

1. Find out how much control you have over prices.

2. Examine your costs to get your bottom price range.

3. Examine customer attitudes and behaviors to set the top of your price range and estimate price sensitivity.

4. Set your strategic objectives to establish the final list price.

5. If necessary, discount the price to attract new customers by using special offers.

FIGURE 14-1: A helpful pricing process.

© *John Wiley & Sons, Inc.*

Step 1: Consider all the influencers

You can set your price however you want, but customers set the threshold that they won't go over. At the end of the day, the retailer has the final word determining price and profit margins that meet business goals. Remember, when you set your price, you have to figure in distributors or wholesalers and the impact of their costs on your profits, and be sure not to lower their share to the point that they won't carry your products in their channels.

TIP

As you determine your pricing, consider asking distributors and wholesalers for input on your pricing goals and what obstacles they may see in your way. They can help you determine the price discount retailers expect so you can price according to the profit you need to reach your capitalization and business goals.

Marketers who operate in or through a *multilevel distribution channel*, meaning that they have distributors, wholesalers, *rack jobbers* (companies that keep retail racks stocked), retailers, agents, or other sorts of intermediaries, need to establish a trade discount structure. *Trade discounts* (also called *functional discounts*) are what you give these intermediaries. They add a cost to you, so make sure you know the discount structure for your product before you move on. Usually, marketers state the discount structure as a series of numbers, representing what each of the intermediaries gets as a discount. But you take each discount off the price left over from the discount before it, not off the list price.

Step 2: Examine your costs

Having a good, accurate view of the true costs of a specific product or service is not always easy. As a result, you need to carefully examine all your expenses so you can identify the actual costs, which include opportunity costs and dormant costs, such as those incurred from inventory sitting in warehouses or not moving off your shelves. Did you add your utility bills to your overhead and all your transportation and inventory storage costs? Every detail adds up.

Examining costs carefully should give you a fairly accurate idea of the minimum amount you can charge to go ahead and avoid going under. At times, you may want to give away a product for less than your costs to introduce it to new consumers, but be careful with this ploy because you can be sued for dumping. See the later section "Staying on Top of U.S. Regulations" for the dirt on dumping.)

In general, your price should cover your costs and a profit margin of maybe 20 or 30 percent, which puts your costs at 70 or 80 percent of the price. Determine where you need to be and test it.

Your cost-plus-profit number is the bottom of your price range (see Figure 14-2). Your charge is to make your product perceived to be so valuable that you can raise your prices to meet your goals, not just market demands.

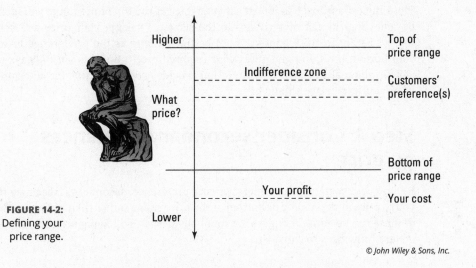

FIGURE 14-2: Defining your price range.

Step 3: Evaluate customers' price preferences

Simply put, you need to figure out what price customers are willing to pay for your product category and your products in general. It's not always or usually one and the same. A consumer is willing to pay more for a Porsche Cayenne than a Volkswagen Touareg, although they are built on the same platform and have many of the same parts. It's all about branding and the perceived value and, as we discuss in Chapter 2, the emotional fulfillment attached to the brand.

With this said, the price customers are willing to pay now may not be their limit. The difference between the customer's desired price and a noticeably higher price is the *indifference zone*. Within the indifference zone, customers are indifferent to both price increases and price decreases. However, the zone gets smaller (on a percent basis) as the price of a product increases. How big or small is the zone of indifference in your product's case? The zone is small if your customers are highly price sensitive; the zone is large if they aren't.

You can identify customer preference by looking at pricing for comparable products with similar sales records. Are these prices going up or down? Are prices stable?

Be sure to analyze prices online and at physical retail locations because pricing and discounts often differ online. Doing so also helps make sure you know what options are available to your customers.

The simplest approach is to just set your price at the top of the range you identify by following the list of activities in the section "Raising your price and selling more," earlier in this chapter. You'll be fine as long as the price range is above your bottom limit and generates your required profit. But this isn't always possible in the real world. The next section provides additional tips for determining what your final price should be.

Step 4: Consider secondary influences on price

Beyond your costs and customers' pricing preference, secondary issues may force you to price in the middle or bottom of the price range rather than at the top. Some of these can be game changers for small businesses. Following are some key secondary influences to consider:

>> **Competitive issues:** Do you need to gain market share from a close competitor? If so, do you need to adjust your price to be slightly but noticeably below its price? If so, how will you avoid a price war, which could substantially hurt your margins if the competitor counterattacks?

>> **Likely future price trends:** Are prices trending downward in this market? Is your category at risk of being a commodity or being dominated by a low-price leader? How do you need to prepare your costs and other factors if this happens to your market?

>> **Currency fluctuations:** Any fluctuation in currency may affect your costs and, consequently, your pricing options. If you're concerned that you may take a hit from the exchange rate, better to be safe than sorry and price at the high end of the range.

>> **Product line management:** This factor may dictate a slightly lower or higher price. For example, you may need to price a top-of-the-line product significantly higher than others in its line just to make it clear to the customer that this product is a step above its competition.

Step 5: Set your strategic objectives

Before you set your pricing, you need to have a clear short-term and long-term business strategy in place. Some questions to ask yourself include

>> Do you need more market share to attract investors and new customers?

>> Do you want to be the luxury leader so you can charge higher prices and fill a specific niche?

>> Is your goal capitalization so you can fund new product development, market expansion, and so on?

>> Do you need to add ancillary services or accessories to your core products like Apple does to build new revenue streams?

The answers to these questions will have pricing influence as your enter a market, expand your base, and plan for future growth.

Sometimes marketers price high to minimize unit volume, like when introducing a new product. Instead of initially producing enough to sell to the mass market, they *skim the market* by selling at a high price that only wealthy or the least price-sensitive customers can afford. Then they lower prices upon achieving profitability goals and expand production capacity. You see this in the luxury market. What once used to be a luxury product sold at exclusive stores can now be found at mid-range retailers like JCPenney and Sears at mid-market prices.

TIP

Doing this takes you out of the luxury market, so be sure this is where you want to go. Don't use a skimming strategy unless you're sure that you're safe from aggressive competition in the short term.

Step 6: Master the psychology of pricing

As we discuss throughout this book, psychology plays a big role in pricing. How you set your price influences customers' perception of value and ultimately their willingness to buy. Following are some insights about different psychology-based pricing methods.

Odd-even pricing

Odd pricing substantially outweighs even pricing when consumers have a choice. Many studies back this up. Some show that 70 percent of customers prefer a price of $9.99 over $10.00 for the very same thing. Even though the difference is just one penny, the price is perceived as significantly lower. That's how our rational and irrational minds work. Using this strategy of lowering your price by one penny isn't going to hurt you, so there's not a lot of reason not to do it. Walmart goes a step further and prices many of its goods ending with 98 or 88 cents rather than 99 to help create the perception that a product it sells is priced substantially lower than those of competitors.

Rounding down to 99, 98, or even 95 works for dollars, not just cents — consider $1.99 or $199 over $2 or $200.

Price lining, a.k.a. price anchoring

The *price lining* method fits your product into a range of alternatives, giving the product a logical spot in customers' minds. Dr. Dan Ariely, a psychologist and professor of psychology and behavioral economics at Duke University, has studied this phenomenon in various settings and finds that most often people choose the price in the middle when given a choice of similar products at a range of different prices. Instead of splurging on the most expensive item available, people often opt for something in the middle because it feels more responsible, and they avoid the lowest price item because they feel they deserve more.

The psychological term for this reaction, or cognitive bias, is *mental anchoring*, which refers to how people often frame their choices around the first piece of information they see. This is a common tendency in investing and can be further explored by reading behavioral economic studies.

Price anchoring is common in the restaurant business. You'll often find a very high priced item on the specials list, which few people are willing to buy, but somehow, when they see the lower priced menu items, even if those are still over-priced, they seem reasonable. This is an easy and effective strategy because it appeals to "rational" thinking by tapping into the irrational drivers that help people justify doing things they may not have done otherwise.

Framing

How you present or frame an offer impacts its perceived value. Studies show that "Buy one, get one free" offers drive more sales than "Two for the price of one." Additionally, stating, "You can have this car for just $600 a month," influences behavior more than stating, "Buy it for $40,000." It's all about framing offers and pricing to be acceptable to consumers' state of mind. When you make purchases seem more reasonable than overwhelming, you help create a sense of comfort and take fear out of the purchase process.

Descriptives

In addition to framing, little things, like adjectives, can help a great deal. For example, adding the word *small* before your actual price can actually increase sales by around 20 percent, according to a study by Carnegie Mellon University.

Competitive pricing

Competitive pricing involves setting your price relative to that of your competitors. Price above if you offer more benefits and overall value; price below if the opposite applies. If you're not as well known as a competitor, lower your price to inspire people to try your product.

EXAMPLE

Price creates prestige, which is what fuels the luxury industry. If you drop the price, you drop the sense of status that results and much of the emotional fulfillment of a product beyond its functional value. This actually happened to Tiffany & Co. when Avon bought it, which then tried to mass-market the Tiffany name by putting it on inexpensive jewelry. Millions of dollars of losses later, Avon sold out, and Tiffany went back to success by charging its usual high prices.

TIP

If you're in a highly competitive market, consider competitive pricing. Decide which competing products customers may view as closest to yours and then make your price sufficiently higher or lower to differentiate your product. How much difference is enough depends on the size of customers' indifference zone as described in the earlier section "Step 3: Evaluate customers' price preferences."

Designing Special Offers

Special offers have a special place in marketing and need special attention so they don't backfire and hurt your brand. Following are some tips to make promotions, coupons, and special offers work most effectively.

Creating coupons and other discounts

Coupons, refunds, *premiums* (gifts), free extra products, free trial-sized samples, and sweepstakes are all special offers that can help you acquire new customers and increase customer satisfaction as customers get excited about getting a good deal from a brand they love. The trick is doing them at the right frequency so that existing customers eagerly anticipate them and prospective customers value them.

Coupons, the printed kind, are one of the most traditional forms of special offers and are often distributed in newspaper inserts, at the point of sale, and on websites where customers can download and print them. Coupon codes are commonly distributed in emails to customers and prospects, promoted on home pages of an e-commerce site, and can often be found on third-party sites, such as www.retailmenot.com, www.coupons.com, and of course www.groupon.com.

You can also use Facebook and other social media sites to distribute coupon codes and hopefully get others to share them for you, enabling you to reach more prospects without having to pay for the extra reach yourself.

QR codes, while fading in popularity and usage, are still used and may be relevant for your consumers. Asking about their use of QR codes may be a good question for your next customer survey.

Perhaps the most exciting way to distribute your coupons is via augmented reality (AR). Valpak, a leader in local print and digital coupons, now offers an AR app. Consumers download the Valpak app on their smartphone, hold their phone up to the horizon, tap the AR icon, and coupons pop up near businesses "on the horizon" that have an active Valpak coupon available. Consumers can tap on the coupons visible to them and interact with the given business in real time. Doesn't get much better than this!

TIP

Distribute your coupons on channels that are relevant to your audience. If you're targeting millennials, you'll be better off using AR, mobile, and social media. If targeting baby boomers and younger silent generation adults, newspaper and highly targeted magazines make sense.

If you use digital coupon codes, adjust your search engine marketing strategy accordingly to make sure your coupon pages come up above the scroll when someone is searching for your product. Purchasing Facebook and Google ads is also a good way to get your coupons to those who stand to use them most.

Direct mail, one of the more traditional methods for coupon distribution, still works, as does advertising in your local newspaper. Mix up your mediums if you want to mix up the demographic response to your offer and to test which channels work best for which special promotions.

REMEMBER

Always remember to put tracking codes in your coupons so you can determine which medium worked best at generating response. Use a different code for each outlet you use — radio, print, newspaper, or email. Your web analytics will be able to tell which websites drove traffic so you're likely covered for your digital distribution channels.

Figuring out how much to offer

Keep in mind that most offers fail to motivate the vast majority of customers, so you need to find ways to make your offer stand out. Apple, at one time, discounted its products only on Black Friday. Because this was the only day that you could get $100 off a MacBook Pro, it got attention and a lot of response. Maybe $100 off isn't a big deal given the full price of the product, but because it happened only once a year, people eagerly waited to jump online the minute it was valid.

Here are some tips for figuring out what and how much to offer:

>> When offers rise above the 50-cent level, coupons are a lot more attractive, appealing to up to 80 percent of customers. Within this larger percentage of interested consumers, you can incentivize your loyal customers to purchase more and your competitors' customers to switch.

>> Unless you want to be seen as the budget or economy brand and give customers a reason to never pay full price for your products, err on the side of infrequent coupon offers and sales.

>> Make your offers reciprocal. If you offer 20 percent off your prices, it's not unreasonable to expect takers to give you something in return, like their contact information or opt in for more emails from you so you can add them to your database. Consumers appreciate and seek reciprocity, and it works both ways.

Forecasting redemption rates

The trickiest part of giving a special offer is guessing the *redemption rate* (or percentage of people who use the coupon). You raise the stakes when you use big offers, which makes them riskier to forecast. Test an offer on a small scale first and gather some real data about how it works. Then use the info in this section to help make your guesstimate a bit more accurate.

REMEMBER

On average in North America, customers redeem a little more than 3 percent of coupons (and the average coupon offers around 50 cents off the list price). These numbers can be used as a good starting point for your estimate, but the range can be wider or lower depending on how appealing your offer is to your customers. As with all things marketing, relevance matters.

TIP

A point-of-purchase and very easy-to-redeem offer will have far higher redemption rates than an offer that's remote from the point of purchase. For example, an offer placed in a web banner ad or newspaper insert may redeem at a rate of 2 percent, but when the same offer is made available electronically at the register, it may redeem at 12 percent. This is where the value of GPS shopping and mobile marketing (as discussed in Chapter 8) plays a big role.

To forecast whether your coupon will have a high or low redemption rate, compare your offer to others. Are you offering something more generous or easier to redeem than you have in the past? Than your competitors do? If so, you can expect significantly higher-than-average redemption rates. Test on a small scale, especially if the offer is generous. Try posting your offer on the web for one hour to see what happens. Take a look at the redemption rate, evaluate your costs at scale, and determine how to execute further without spending too much.

REMEMBER

Mathematical formulas for estimating the effect of a discount or coupon offer exist, but they can be complex, difficult to use, and more theoretical than practical. The best way to estimate the effect of an offer is to test it on a small scale. If you get the bump-up in sales you want, then keep using it. If not, change the value of the offer or the communications channel you used to determine whether it's worth trying again.

If you find an offer that boosts sales, make sure it's profitable. If sales go up only a little but lots of existing customers make their regular purchases at a discount, then you won't make a profit from the offer. What you want is lots of new customers who buy because of the offer and then become regular users.

Predicting the cost of special offers

Always factor in the cost of the promotion. You may find that the cost was too high to enable increased unit sales to really make a difference in profit. You need to determine your total costs involved and subtract these from your projected revenue gain. Total costs include advertising costs, fulfillment, even payroll increases if you have to add staff hours to handle the demand. You need to assess the impact these and other costs will have on future sales with this offer in place.

Assess your opportunity cost. For example, if you discount to have a great revenue stream in November, what will that do for your sales in December?

Try this formula: Analyze your ROI if 4 percent of customers redeem a coupon offering a 10 percent discount on your product. To estimate the cost of your coupon program, you must first decide whether this 4 percent of customers accounts for just 4 percent of your product's sales over the period in which the coupon applies. Probably not. Customers may stock up to take advantage of the special offer, so you must estimate how much more than usual they'll buy.

If you think customers will buy twice as much as usual (that's a pretty high figure, but it makes for a simple illustration), just double the average purchase size. Four percent of customers, buying twice what they usually do in a month (if that's the term of the offer), can produce how much in sales? Now apply the discount rate to that sales figure to find out how much the special offer may cost you. Can you afford it? Is the promotion worth the money? That's for you to decide, and it's a true judgment call — the math can't tell you what to do.

Keeping special offers special

Price cuts are easy to do but hard to undo, which makes special offers a better option because they allow you to temporarily discount your price while still maintaining your list price. When the offer ends, the list price is the same and you haven't permanently discounted your revenue and brand image.

If you keep your price list steady and use discounts infrequently, you'll have more flexibility for changing price when you have a special need, such as wanting to

>> Counter a competitor's special offer or respond to a new product introduction.

>> Experiment with the price (to find out about customer price sensitivity) without committing to a permanent price cut until you see the data.

>> Stimulate consumers to try your product or service, and you believe that after they try it, they'll buy it again at full price.

>> Keep your list price high to signal quality (*prestige pricing*) or be consistent with other prices in your product line (*price lining strategy*).

>> Match a competitor's special lower prices or meet other market expectations.

If you have competitors that frequently deploy special offers so that consumers wait for an offer before they buy, they have effectively lowered their prices because consumers are no longer willing to buy at list price. You need to consider then their discount price is their normal price with which you're competing.

WARNING

When competitors get too focused on making and matching each other's special offers, they flood their customers with price-based promotions. Discounts and other freebies begin to outweigh brand-building marketing messages, focusing consumer attention on price rather than brand and benefit considerations. Special promotions can and do increase customer sensitivity to price. They attract *price switchers*, people who aren't loyal to any brand but just shop on the basis of price. Frequent special offers encourage people to become price switchers, thus reducing the size of the core customer base and increasing the number of fringe customers.

As a result, special offers have the potential to erode brand equity, reduce customer loyalty, and cut your profits. Be careful not to lose your footing on this slippery slope!

Staying on Top of U.S. Regulations

Although it's always wise to check with your attorney before making any final decision concerning special offers, you should be familiar with the following list of the more common and serious illegal pricing practices, as indicated by the federal laws of the United States. Make sure you *never get fooled into* engaging in any of the following:

>> **Price fixing:** Simply put, price fixing is where businesses that compete with each other discuss and agree on prices to take fair options away from consumers. No form of this is legal or ethical on any level.

>> **Price fixing by purchasers:** If retailers you sell to are joining together to dictate the wholesale prices they want you to give them, that may also be price fixing. Have a lawyer review any such plans.

>> **Exchanging price information:** You can't talk to your competitors about prices. Ever. If you or anyone in your company gives out information about pricing and receives some in return, you could be in trouble. Announcing a planned price increase is called price signaling and is often seen as an unfair exchange of price information to signal to others that everyone should make a price increase.

>> **Bid rigging:** If you're bidding for a contract, the preceding point applies. Don't share any information with anyone. Don't compare notes with another bidder. Don't agree to make an identical bid. Don't *split* by agreeing not to bid on one job if the competitor doesn't bid on another. Messing with the bidding process in any manner is *bid rigging* and can get you in trouble.

>> **Parallel pricing:** In some cases, the U.S. government can charge you with price fixing, even if you didn't talk to competitors, just because you have similar price structures. After all, the result may be the same — to boost prices unfairly. In other cases, the law considers similar prices as natural. To be safe, avoid mirroring competitors' prices exactly.

>> **Price squeezes, predatory pricing, limit pricing, and dumping:** To the average marketer, these four illegal acts are effectively the same (although they're tested under different U.S. regulations). They all involve using prices to push a competitor out of business or to push or keep a competitor out of a particular market.

REMEMBER

Pricing is only part of the equation. How you position your product's ability to help consumers reach their tangible and intangible goals helps establish your perceived value and the highest price they will pay for that value. Offering discounts and special pricing should be seen as a reward for customer loyalty or first-time trial, not pricing as usual.

Chapter **15**

Distribution and Merchandising in an Augmented World

Y ou can build the greatest product ever invented, but it won't matter if you don't have an equally great distribution channel and strategy in place.

Quality and quantity of retailers and distributors are important considerations for B2C and B2B businesses and impact not only access to your product but also the prestige and perceived value that drives your pricing limits. If you produce luxury goods, where you sell them is critically important. People expect to pay more at finer retail stores like Saks Fifth Avenue and Neiman Marcus. But the minute you start selling your luxury item at discount department stores like JCPenney, the perceived value of your brand will drop drastically, and that can forever change your pricing as well.

Distribution strategies need to consider the impact of access on overall branding and pricing. Again, if you're a luxury brand, you maintain your status and price point through exclusivity. If too many people have access to your products due to a high number of channels and low pricing, you cease to be a luxury or even high-point brand. Case in point: Yves St. Laurent, Halston, Liz Clairborne, Juicy Couture, and so on.

Outlet stores, a growing trend even in our digital world, can do more damage to an aspirational or luxury brand in the long term and quickly offset any short-term gains. This is due to greater access to a greater number of people, which diminishes the exclusive appeal for those who are willing to pay more to be different. And it gives consumers access to your products at a lot lower price than other channels, which can impact relationships with distributors as well as your profitability.

This chapter outlines many of the considerations all brands in all industries must address to grow sales, profits, and brand equity through sustainable distribution strategies.

Considering Distribution Strategies

Often, the first thing marketers do to increase sales is to expand their distribution systems, adding retailers or distributors to get more product out and sold. However, this is not always the best solution, especially for building a strong brand for the long term. Distribution strategies need to be built on your overall business and marketing goals.

Today, there are many distribution channels to consider for any given product, including

>> Online, e-commerce channels

>> Multi-level marketing channels

>> Mainstream retail outlets

>> Wholesale retail outlets

>> Discount stores

>> Catalog sales

Your channel strategy also needs to address how you present and project your products at a given point of distribution. In the retail world, that involves purchasing prime display space, such as end-aisle displays at a grocery store and kiosks near the main entrance to a department store; and online, that means purchasing search terms for browsers, pop-up ads via programmatic marketing, and mentions on shopping cart pages, such as "Other customers also bought," and so on.

For business-to-business marketers, distribution strategies include a concerted focus on getting in front of purchasing managers at conventions, industry and trade showrooms or events, as well as in online directories. As with all the other elements of marketing, innovations are changing distribution, and this chapter helps you find out more about new options along with more conventional ones.

Distribution strategies are key to launching and growing any business in any industry. Consider the following factors before putting your products out to the world:

» **Selective distribution strategy:** Employed by the luxury industry, selective distribution is just that — selective. You select a few outlets that represent the image and values of your product and charge a high price to compensate for the lower volume of goods sold and to establish a luxury image and thus price point for your overall brand.

» **Exclusive distribution strategy:** This strategy is the extreme version of a selective strategy, in which you sell through one or a few specialized distributors only. Doing this can work well for unique products for which you want to create a sense of exclusivity, justify a high price, and secure low distribution costs.

» **Intensive distribution strategy:** If you're marketing a retail product with mass appeal and want to achieve mass access, this is likely your best approach because it involves making your product widely available in as many outlets as possible. It involves getting onto the roster of accepted vendors for the giant retail chains, like Target and Walmart. You can also expect to give up some pricing and inventory control to big retail outlets such as these and to put a lot of money into your production to assure that you can meet their demands. Before you negotiate terms with the big boxes, make sure you can scale appropriately with little risk.

» **80/20 strategy:** Because most marketers get 80 percent or more of sales from just 20 percent of distributors, this strategy is important. Simply put, it's all about providing top attention, service, and trade deals to your best distributors so that they will stay loyal to you in terms of shelf presence and quantity. Your goal should be to also increase the volume sold through weaker distributors because getting even a small increase in these channels can boost your bottom line significantly.

You also have to decide whether you want to develop *parallel distribution channels*, also known as *competitive channels.* This involves selling directly to consumers, not just through distributors or retail outlets, which puts you in direct competition with those you depend on to get your products out en masse. While this used to be considered taboo, it's increasingly more common and accepted. For example, Apple sells through retail distributors, through its own Apple Stores, through retail computer web stores, and through its own website. Dell does the same thing. So does Patagonia. Determine how this can work in your industry and how you can make it work with the least amount of risk or disruption to your loyal distributors and retailers.

Here are a couple of more ways to get the most out of your distribution program:

>> **Expand your distribution network.** Never quit looking for new outlets for selling your products. Look to the web, community events, e-commerce, and even trade shows where you can actually set up sales transactions.

>> **Increase your visibility.** One way you can use distribution strategies to boost sales is to increase the visibility of your product or service within its current distribution channel by making sure it's better displayed or better communicated.

Many retail chain stores provide better shelving (such as end-cap displays or eye-level shelving with a sign) if you offer them special promotional discounts or cooperative advertising fees. Look into these options and take advantage of them when you can afford to do so.

Shelf strategies to avoid getting benched

Getting your products on shelves, physical and digital ones, of high-traffic retail sites is the first big step to distribution success. Getting your products noticed on those shelves is the second. As private labels increase and new products emerge, along with other factors, getting your products shelved at eye level rather than just inches above the floor is getting more competitive. For digital sales, the challenge is being one of the options for products searched that pops in the main pane of your screen instead of one of the last.

This is where data meets distribution. Data analytics are not just for your direct marketing campaigns, personalized communications, and such. You need information about what drives your best customers to the store, which stores, and what other products they may be shopping for. You then need to work with your retailers to negotiate shelf space that's on your shoppers' traffic patterns and maximize visibility on a shelf with other products in your category. You get to negotiate similar placement on digital stores in which you may post your products. The products that pop up on screen don't do so randomly but more often by what price the marketer was willing to pay for them to show up early in the search and above the scroll.

You can leverage your sales data to get better visibility at a better price as well. If you can show retailers that your product gets maybe 30 percent of the sales for their store in your category and you're getting only 15 percent of the shelf space, or your products are displayed inches above the knee rather than at eye level, you now have negotiating power to get better visibility for your product and likely more space so you can sell more.

End caps, or end-aisle displays, are the most coveted space in a retail setting. These displays are getting better all the time at capturing attention and luring shoppers closer in hopes of getting a new sale. Walmart's videos at end-cap displays are a great example of this. You can watch a product demo or a short video on current promotions. Paying more for end-cap displays may pay off if you're launching a new product that you want to stimulate trial and awareness for or if you have demo stations for end caps whereby shoppers can test out your product easily — for example, feeling the texture of a new cleaning cloth, smelling a candle, or testing a cosmetic product's color.

Add beacons like those we mention in Chapter 10 and you'll be able to make that investment in end-cap displays pay off sooner than later.

Whatever your outlet for sales is for your products, you need to make sure you have top visibility during the sales process, can be easily found by those who come looking for you, and pop up near related items to spark impromptu purchases. For example, if you're selling cherry jam, maybe purchase some space on refrigerator shelves that house goat cheese. You may spark a favorite idea for an appetizer.

E-commerce channels pros and cons

The two biggest e-commerce outlets are of course Amazon and eBay, and both are great for getting your products out to the masses. But they're different. Amazon offers you a retail structure and will often fulfill your sales as well as offer your products on its site for a fee. eBay is mostly a marketplace provider and offers you the tools to help you better promote your products to its site visitors. With both sites, you have access to a lot of shoppers, while of course having to overcome a lot of competition. For example,

	Amazon	eBay
Active users	244 million	157 million
Annual income 2014	$88.9 billion	$17.94 billion
Number of independent sellers	2 million	25 million
Number of products available	480 million	1 billion

As you can see, a lot of selling takes place on these sites, and your product will be one of dozens, or rather nearly 1 billion if you choose eBay. However, it often pays off. For Amazon, some merchants report that their sales went up when selling on Amazon and that the volume of sales outweighed the costs of selling fees.

So the question: to eBay or to Amazon? The main differences eBay offers are really quite simple:

>> The atmosphere is different. It's more of a market for individuals to list and sell personal goods at discount.

>> eBay doesn't offer to take inventory of your goods and sell them for you as Amazon will. eBay provides you with guidelines and tools for selling your items successfully, but you do the rest. With Amazon, you can sell your products with Amazon.com as the payment processing system for your shopping cart or Amazon's; or you can become an Amazon seller, paying a monthly fee for Amazon to list and fulfill your product.

>> The selling fees are lower with eBay; so, too, is the volume.

>> Consumer perception is that eBay is like a big garage sale with a few new items mixed in, and Amazon is a trusted brand with everything new and trendy and easily returnable.

Regardless of where you sell your products, the key is to get your product to pop up on the first page or two of the search results. Here are some tips that can help you get noticed.

>> **List your product in two categories.** Some customers may not know which category to search in, so list your products in the categories that make sense. For example, if you're selling a winter coat, list it as a jacket and a winter sports coat and see what happens. You should be able to track which listing made it to the shopping cart as well. It may cost more to do this, but if you don't get noticed, you don't get sales.

- >> **Offer free shipping.** eBay prefers listings with free shipping and gives them preference in its rank ordering of search results. Amazon offers free shipping to Prime customers, so it's becoming more and more expected. If you offer free shipping, make sure you cover at least the cost of standard shipping in the overall price you list.

- >> **Avoid keyword spamming.** *Keyword spamming* is when you slip a popular keyword into your item description that doesn't really belong there. For example, saying, "If you love Ralph Lauren's designs, you'll love these bath towels," is against eBay policy and may get your listing — and you — kicked off if the towels aren't actually Ralph Lauren towels.

- >> **Become the top seller.** Both sites rate independent sellers and list reviews. Be sure to offer fast, responsive, and honest transactions at all times to maintain a high seller rating. Just one bad review can send shoppers to the next item listed, and because it takes only seconds to move on in a digital store environment, they most assuredly will.

Also consider advertising on both eBay and Amazon. Because both sites attract millions of shoppers per day, if you place relevant ads with strong incentives and offers, you'll likely get a positive return. With Amazon, a product search produces both catalog items and sponsored links advertising off-site web stores (which can be enabled to sell to Amazon customers), so you can troll for those millions of Amazon customers in multiple ways by listing in the Amazon catalog plus advertising products and special offers from your own web store.

Tracking Down Ideal Distributors

Distributors want items that customers want to buy. It's that simple. Your job is to determine which distributors can best reach your customers and are aligned with outlets that your customers want to buy from. Following are some questions to ask:

- >> Which retail outlets (for example, Walmart or Nordstrom) best fit the emotional and social values associated with your product?

- >> What outlets are most trusted in terms of customer service, return policies, and so forth?

- >> Who's willing and able to distribute for you? Are wholesalers or other intermediaries going to be helpful? If so, who are they, and how many of them can you locate?

Here are some sources for helping you identify distributors:

» **Reach out to a trade association or trade show specializing in distributors in your industry.** For example, the International Foodservice Distributors Association (www.ifdaonline.org) puts on an annual conference for food distributors.

» **Attend major conventions in your industry.** Browse the expo hall around the convention center until you find the right distributors.

Understanding Channel Structure

Efficiency should be the driving goal behind your distribution channel strategy. Channel efficiency is based on having a small number of transactions involved to get the product to the end user.

As Figure 15-1 shows, a channel in which 4 producers and 4 customers do business directly has 16 (4×4) possible transactions because each producer has to make 4 separate transactions to get its product to all 4 consumers. In reality, the numbers get much higher when you have markets with dozens or hundreds of producers and thousands or millions of customers.

You lower the number of transactions greatly when you use an intermediary (someone who handles the business transactions for you) because now you have to do only simple addition rather than multiplication, as shown in $16 - 1$. As you can see, you need only 8 ($4 + 4$) transactions to connect all 4 customers with all 4 producers through the intermediary. Each producer or customer has to deal with only the intermediary who makes all the necessary connections. Even with markups or commission fees, intermediaries can lower your overall distribution costs due to lower transactions in your channel.

This example is simplistic, but you can see how the logic applies to more complex and larger distribution channels. Introduce a lot of customers and producers, link them through multiple intermediaries, and you have a typical *indirect marketing channel*.

If you choose to use a direct channel whereby you deal with customers directly for sales, services, returns, and so on, be prepared for a lot more work on your end, which may not be worth your time and the opportunity cost of dealing with customers' needs over executing more marketing programs to gain new customers and sales.

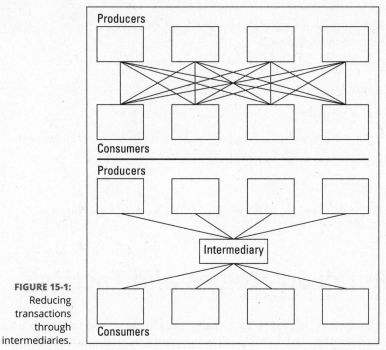

FIGURE 15-1:
Reducing
transactions
through
intermediaries.

REMEMBER

The trend is toward simpler, more direct channels, and you need to be prepared to handle a large number of customer transactions to be in step with this trend. A good general rule for you as a marketer is to use only as many intermediaries and layers of intermediaries as seems absolutely necessary to reach your customers. Try to keep it simple and add more parties only if you can't do it well yourself.

TIP

When reviewing distributors and intermediaries to help you get your products to market, think about the most valuable role they can play for you besides getting your product on shelves or online. Here's a starting list of functions you may want to look for in your intermediaries:

>> Finding more customers for your product than you can on your own

>> Researching customer attitudes and desires

>> Buying and selling

>> Breaking down bulk shipments for resale

>> Setting prices

>> Managing point-of-purchase promotions

- >> Advertising at the local level (*pull advertising,* which is designed to bring people to a store or other business)

- >> Transporting products

- >> Inventorying products

- >> Financing purchases

- >> *Qualifying* sales leads (separating poor-quality leads from serious customers)

- >> Providing customer service and support

- >> Sharing the risks of doing business

- >> Combining your products with others to offer appropriate assortments

Reviewing Retail Strategies and Tactics

If you own your own store, you have many considerations and tactics for a successful retail strategy. These include drawing planograms (diagrams showing you how to flow and display your merchandise), counting SKUs (stock-keeping units), planning your end-aisle displays, and plotting product placement on shelves. Although these are important and impact sales, the most important achievement is traffic flow.

Attracting traffic

Beyond choosing a location that has built-in traffic flow to bring customers to your products, you need to have curb appeal. If you're in an indoor shopping mall or a strip mall, you need to project your persona and convey your emotional fulfillment with your signage, displays, and atmosphere. Although your products and branding insignia create a big part of your storefront appeal and may draw people in, your atmosphere is what will keep them there, which is key to closing a sale.

Think about the stores that draw you in past the front door. Do they appeal to your senses with soft lights, large brilliant colors, smells of candles or cinnamon buns, or pleasant music?

Harlan Bratcher elevated sales for Armani Exchange when he was the brand's CEO by creating an atmosphere that was emotionally engaging beyond the products he sold. His target audience was young, single adults, who enjoyed the metropolitan social scene. So he turned his stores into a night club. His team researched the music his customers loved to listen to while dancing, created spot-on playlists, which they played loudly, and added lighting that reflected a dance atmosphere. Sales took off immensely. This strategy not only made people feel fun, attractive, and glamorous, which in turn made them buy more, but it also drew people off the streets as the music and lights were audible and visible outside the door.

Creating atmosphere

A store's *atmosphere* is the image that it projects based on how you decorate and design it and the experience you create by appealing to the senses. To create the right atmosphere, pay attention to your customers' lifestyle, persona, and why they shop. It's often for more than just the products.

In consumer societies, shopping is an important activity in its own right. Surveys suggest that less than a quarter of shoppers in malls went there in search of a specific item. Consumers often use shopping to alleviate boredom and loneliness, to avoid dealing with chores or problems in their lives, or simply to entertain themselves. Determine what motivates your customers and build your store atmosphere accordingly.

Sophisticated retailers hire architects and designers to create the right atmosphere and then spend enormous amounts on ambient lighting, artwork, trendy decor and finishes, and racks. Your biggest risk is having a store that looks like all the other ones designed at the same time because trends seep across branding boundaries and can put you in the "me too" category, which hurts your chances to secure a distinct advantage.

TIP

Trust your instincts and imagination. Experiment with your ideas and dare to be different. REI did a great job with atmosphere by adding climbing walls to its store floors. What can you do to create an experience beyond the sales transaction and make shopping memorable and something people want to do again?

The American Girl doll company is one of the first brands to really change the retail experience. Its Fifth Avenue location in New York City is a tourist destination for many mothers and daughters because it offers experiences beyond purchasing its inspirational and aspirational dolls. It has a cafe and a charming tea parlor where mothers, daughters, and dolls can all sit at the table together, and at one time it even had a theatre presenting performances about the lives of the dolls you could buy in the store. It also has a photo studio for daughters and doll portraits and a beauty salon. It offers special performances for customers at Radio City Hall with the Rockettes, a design studio for girls to create fashions for their dolls, and more. The experience has become so popular that it offers vacation packages with discounts at partner hotels.

What can you do to make your store an experience destination, not just a place to buy something? This strategy is critical if you want to compete with online stores that don't require getting in the car, driving in traffic, and then standing in line to buy something.

Developing merchandising strategies

Merchandising strategy, the selection and assortment of products offered, creates the foundation of competitive advantage or disadvantage for retailers. The more creative the product offerings, the greater advantage you have over other retailers.

Following are some general strategies and ideas that may get you thinking in new ways about your business.

General merchandise retailing

The *general merchandise retailing strategy* allows you to appeal to more people due to having a wide and deep assortment of products, but it also puts you in a very competitive category, which requires a lot of resources to survive. Competitors include department stores, like Macy's and Lord & Taylor, and big-box retailers, like Target and Walmart. These businesses have been in place for years and have shrewd negotiators who can get costs down below reason in many cases, making it hard for you to match their prices. Now with the huge sizes of Super Targets and Walmart Supercenters, it can be even harder to match the selection they offer in any category.

Limited-line retailing

The *limited-line retailing strategy* is another term for specialty or boutique store. A specialty bakery offers more depth and variety of baked items than a grocery store because that's all it does. Starbucks is a great example of a limited-line strategy. It sells coffee — coffee-based specialty products, coffee cups, coffee mugs, cookies that go with coffee, and so on.

TIP

If you're competing with an established brand like Starbucks, find a new or local twist that makes your experience a bit different. Where I (Jeanette) live, the only coffee shop that really competed with Starbucks and won is one that catered to the healthy sports activist. It sponsors a bike team, sells bike paraphernalia, and offers a sports-bar type atmosphere, which draws local sports enthusiasts after a great workout or bike ride. Its prices are similar to Starbucks, but it caters to the locals' lifestyle and offers healthy alternative snacks instead of just rich pastries, something Starbucks has not done well. It's been successful for many years and even added a new location.

Scrambled merchandising

Consumers have preconceived notions about what product lines and categories belong together, but retailers have been redefining those notions and succeeding. People used to go to one store for one thing and another store for another thing. But now, you can pretty much find a bit of everything almost anywhere — fast-food restaurants in big-box stores, coffee shops adjacent to gas stations, and bookstores and ski shops with coffee shops interweaved. This combination of non-related product lines is called *scrambled merchandising* and works well in many locations because it adds interest to the shopping experience and offers consumers convenience at the same time. Think on what you can do to combine two product lines of interest to your consumer base in a way that makes sense, is interesting, and is something people want to buy at the same time.

Stimulating sales at point of purchase

The *point of purchase* (POP), where customer meets product, represents a critical opportunity to increase your sales. Although customers may have a planned purchase in mind when heading to your store, research shows that the majority of their purchases are actually unplanned ones. It's like going to the grocery store for just one thing you need and ending up with $100 worth of groceries you didn't have in mind at the time. This is the phenomenon of POP advertising, those signs on the shelves or end-cap aisles that "remind" consumers they need these items, too. Table 15-1 shows you just how important POP is given the percentage of unplanned purchases at grocery stores and mass merchandise stores. (The statistics are from Point of Purchase Advertising International.)

TABLE 15-1 ## Nature of Consumers' Purchase Decisions

	Supermarkets Percent of Purchases	Mass Merchandise Stores Percent of Purchases
Unplanned	60%	53%
Substitute	4%	3%
Generally planned	6%	18%
Specifically planned	30%	26%

REMEMBER

Your direct, mass, and display advertising and social media drives people to your store. Your merchandise selection, POP advertising and messaging, pricing and display strategies, atmosphere, and interactive experiences get them to purchase more. And when it all comes together in ways that are inspirational and aspirational, they come back for more and bring others with them. This should be your ultimate goal.

TIP

Here are some tools you can use to improve engagement and enthusiasm for shopping at your store:

>> Place signage on shelves to draw attention to products that you want to boost sales.

>> Set up free-standing floor displays that grab attention for products and promotional prices.

>> Add QR codes to displays, signage, and other POP communications if you want to give customers ways to link directly to a promo or an informational web landing page.

>> Display signage with a scannable app code (supplied by a 3D app maker) that in turn produces an augmented reality display on the shopper's phone or tablet. Let your shoppers see in augmented reality how that hat, bracelet, or other product will look on them. When you make the experience "real" through engaging technologies, consumers internalize the value of your products and become emotionally charged, and that is when you up your chances to close the sale. See the nearby sidebar on augmented reality for more.

Exciting displays increase atmosphere and the entertainment value of the shopping experience. If you're a retailer, create displays to promote your specials. If you're the manufacturer, create displays to help retailers sell more of your product. A good display should

>> **Attract attention.** Make your displays novel, entertaining, or puzzling to draw people to them.

>> **Build involvement.** Give people something to think about or do to involve them in the display. Again, end-cap demonstration stations or product demo videos work well.

>> **Sell the product.** Make sure the display communicates the *positioning* of your brand and the emotional and functional values of your product. Make it as inspirational and aspirational as possible.

Before spending a lot of money on displays to ship out to retailers to help sell your products at their places of business, survey them first to assess the likelihood of use. Between 50 and 60 percent of marketers' POPs never reach the sales floor. If you're a product marketer who's trying to get a POP display into retail stores, you face an uphill battle. The stats say that your display or sign needs to be twice as good as the average, or the retailer simply tosses it into the nearest dumpster.

TIP

For purely e-commerce sales that don't involve POP advertising, you can create similar attention for your product and spark unplanned purchases during the online shopping process. Consider using more aspirational photographs, streaming video demonstration of the product, testimonials, and special offers with time limits to create a powerful sense of urgency. Video blogs showing your product's function and features can help drive traffic to your online store as well.

REMEMBER

Technology changes and changes quickly for all businesses. You must stay on top of marketing technology changes that impact how you distribute, sell, and market your products and the type of experiences you can create. If you don't, others will, and you may not survive. Best advice for anyone in marketing today? Don't blink!

A CLOSER LOOK AT AUGMENTED REALITY

Augmented reality is the overlay of digital imagery, often 3D, on some underlying context, usually what you see in front of you. So, for example, customers encounter a sign that says What Does This Watch Look Like on You? Then they hold out their arm, and suddenly they see themselves wearing the very watch. In a B2B setting, a sales rep uses a tablet to photograph a factory floor and then shows a 3D simulation in which new equipment is placed in context.

Firms such as Layar (www.layar.com) and Augment (www.augmentedev.com) are potential sources of 3D pop-up images and information that marketers can use to enrich the shopping experience. Generally, what you do is set up an account with an augmented reality supplier, upload 3D images, exploded views, within-the-package sequential 3Ds, videos, or other content associated with specific scannable symbols for your products, and then let shoppers know that they can download a free app that will give them an interactive and interesting experience at point of purchase (or elsewhere — for example, why not a 3D model or video leaping off a page of your brochure, catalog, or subway poster?). Introducing this experience could be the subject of a fun, interactive email campaign.

» **Working sales channels that attract and retain customers**

» **Using your ESP in the selling process**

» **Organizing and compensating sales staff**

» **Practicing great service and recovering unhappy customers**

Chapter **16**

Succeeding in Sales and Service

Sales is no longer about offering a product, taking an order, and delivering it on time and on budget. In fact, it never really was. Sales efforts that work are about nurturing relationships, having dialogues not sales monologues, and caring for customers' product, functional, and emotional needs.

Successful organizations in all industries, and both B2B and B2C, don't just create a sales plan and materials to support it; they create a sales cultural. A successful culture is one in which all team members see their top role as serving the customers' needs, taking care of every detail, and delivering the kind of attention and care that make customers feel like your only customers, or at least your most valued. Although this may seem a bit idealistic, it's not, because if you don't do it, a competitor will, and more realistically, a few competitors already are.

In addition to a strong selling and service culture, the key to sustainable profitability for any business is to have robust strategies in place for nurturing sales from existing customers to obtain lifetime loyalty, securing new sales from new customers, and generating referrals among highly qualified leads. In other words, you need to have strong retention and acquisition programs in place that focus on capturing the lifetime value of each customer.

This chapter outlines some selling strategies for customer retention and acquisition and tips for building strong sales channels.

Selling for a Lifetime

Lifetime value is the foundation of sustainable brands. Technically, it's the projected net value customers represent to a brand over their entire life cycle.

Capturing lifetime value is critical to any business, in any industry, B2B or B2C. It is far cheaper to retain current customers than it is to acquire new ones. And when you keep customers and keep them happy, they often become ambassadors who bring more business to you at no additional cost to you.

As you develop plans to capture lifetime value, keep in mind that it is more than customer loyalty. The calculated lifetime value for your business reflects customers' total value throughout their life cycle for your category. For your marketing plan, it should also reflect the value of the customers they refer to you. And your marketing and selling strategies need to thus include incentives for capturing valuable referrals.

Calculating lifetime value

You can calculate lifetime value in three ways. Whichever method you use, you must build your selling strategies around lifetime value because you need to retain customers to be profitable. Continuing to sell to the customers you already have is far less costly than to always be striving to acquire new customers.

TIP

When you increase customer satisfaction, you increase their lifetime value to your business. A report by Harvard Business School showed that even a 5 percent increase in customer retention could generate an increase in profits from 25 to 95 percent. That pretty much sums up what your top selling priorities should be.

To be profitable, your cost of acquisition, or COA, must be below that amount and within your target profit margin.

Simple

This simplistic formula just calculates the average value per week to show what your customers can generate each year and over their lifetime.

52 weeks (average customer value/week)(years in life cycle)

For example, if you're a sandwich shop and your average customer visits three times a week, spends a total of $25 a week, and the average life span in terms of being your customer is 20 years, your calculation would look like this:

52(25)(20) = $26,000 per customer for 20 years

Complex

This formula takes into consideration individual variables per customer and your average profit margin.

(lifespan in years)(weeks per year)(average purchase/visit)(visits/week)
(profit margin/customer)

Using the sandwich shop example, with a profit margin per customer of 20 percent, the customer's lifetime value would look like this:

20(52)(8.3)(3)(0.20) = $5,179

Scientific

Another formula, which is the most complex because it takes into account your discount rates, is as follows:

$M(r/1 + i - r)$

In this formula, M represents a customer's gross margin over his life cycle, r equals the retention rate, and i equals the discount rate, used to project the present value of future cash flows. Typically this rate is between 8 and 15 percent.

For a business with gross margins of $1,000 for a customer's lifetime, a discount rate of 10 percent, and a retention rate of 75 percent, this formula might look like this:

1,000(0.75/1 + 0.10 − 0.75) = $2,142

Understanding the importance of customer loyalty

A customer's lifetime value is often greater than the numbers calculated with the formulas in the previous section. If you can retain customers for their life span or life cycle, you're likely satisfying them to the point that they're referring others. Consider that if each customer who's worth $26,000 to the sandwich shop referred just three customers who lasted the customer's life span of 20 years, each customer is now worth $104,000. This alone illustrates the importance of customer loyalty and referrals, especially because you didn't incur any expenses bringing in the $78,000 each customer referred.

REMEMBER

Even with all the marketing technology available to nurture relationships, loyalty is difficult to attain. Many studies, including those from the Consumer Council on Loyalty, show that in one year's time, many consumer goods companies lose up to 40 percent of their customer base, and that even low-priced products, such as Cheerios, lost substantial sales from more than 50 percent of their highest loyal customers. Gaining that back every year requires a lot of resources and expense that could be better spent on building year-over-year (YOY) growth.

Selling for Sustainability

Successful selling strategies today are focused on retaining customers through pricing and subscription models that build equity that's hard to walk away from because switching brands costs a significant price — whether loss of money, time, or convenience.

Following are some guidelines about developing selling strategies to attract and retain customers.

Subscription and retainer-based selling

One of the best examples of a customer retention strategy is your cellphone service carrier. You don't just buy a cellphone service and then switch brands on a whim like you might toothpaste, pasta sauce, or ice cream at your grocery store. It has you "retained" from the minute you sign your first contract, whether you want to be or not. If you get a free smartphone that would otherwise cost you $1,000 or more, you agree to be "retained" for at least two years or pay back the cost of the phone or a big fee to get out of your contract. Not a lot of people do that. Even if they don't like their phone service carrier, they stick it out to avoid the losses they'll incur.

On the B2B side, many agencies sell their services on retainers rather than one-time projects so that the investment they make in managing an account or project has a better chance of paying off; therefore, they can secure revenue streams they can count on instead of having to find new clients every month to make payroll. Software companies are now doing this through Software as a Service (SaaS), Infrastructure as a Service (IaaS), and other selling structures. Instead of selling you a product outright and then looking to find more customers just like you, they sell monthly usage rights to use their applications, servers, platforms, and infrastructures. They retain a committed income, and customers avoid the hassle of maintaining the systems themselves.

How can you sell your products through a monthly subscription? Can you add competitive service contracts that make it hard for customers to switch brands?

The plus side for this sales model is that every customer represents a committed revenue stream that you, the seller, can count on. If you're selling sandwiches, customers can come and go freely, and you can't rely on them to come back ever again. If you're not in a business where your product or service can be sold via subscriptions or retainers, find ways to build equity through reward points, punch cards, or something else customers won't want to walk away from.

EXAMPLE

Dollar Shave Club is a good B2C example of "retained" customers who subscribe to refills of a product on a monthly basis, giving Dollar Shave Club a solid consistent income without the pressure of having to acquire new customers constantly to maintain revenue. Chances for capturing lifetime value also go up with this sales approach because canceling subscriptions is often burdensome, so many consumers tend to stay longer, even if they're not completely happy.

Some considerations for customer retention include

>> Contracts that secure customers to your brand and make it costly to switch.

>> Service contracts for products sold that only you can fulfill. Manufacturers of medical device equipment, such as ultrasound machines, install locks on their machines so that less expensive third-party repair and maintenance experts can't repair or service machines, forcing customers to contract with the original equipment manufacturer (OEM) for all extended care. This approach can backfire as an unfair business practice, so be careful if considering this option.

>> Loyalty programs such as frequent flyer and guest points that are lost if the customer switches brands.

>> Customer service that surpasses expectations for your category and consistently makes customers feel valued and recognized.

Selling channels

Selling in today's fragmented market can make you a little crazy. It's not like it used to be: Get your goods on a shelf, let them sell, and then restock. You now have to develop prime channels for each of your segments. Some like mobile channels; others don't know how to use them. Some like online shopping; others prefer going to the store or business to shop and see the product in person.

To achieve lifetime value and ongoing sales goals, you need to optimize the various selling channels that cater to the needs, lifestyle, and expectations of your customer segments.

Sales channels for consumer-oriented businesses include the following.

Direct to consumer

This route is risky, but it can be very profitable, too. Top methods include

>> **Retail stores you own:** Microsoft, Dell, and Gateway computers all had stores of their own at one time. With this method, you end up competing with your distribution channel, and that can compromise overall sales while adding more work for you to manage and run your own outlets. But you get the chance to build relationships directly with consumers at all touch points.

>> **Multi-level marketing (MLM):** MLM companies depend on independent distributors to recruit more independent distributors and pay them a percentage of their recruits' sales. In many cases, businesses make money off entry fees for distributors who don't always make that money back. As a result, this model may carry some negative connotations among some consumers. Additionally, most home-based distributors don't succeed for the long term, which can require you to spend a lot of time and resources in continual recruiting efforts. However, many companies like NuSkin, Mary Kay, and Amway have beaten this challenge and earn upwards of $1 billion a year. If you know what you're doing, you can ramp up quickly.

>> **E-commerce:** Many companies that still have third-party distribution channels use this method and increase their profit margins as a result. Patagonia sells direct to consumer via its website and sells via stores like REI.

The key to successful e-commerce is to create a community, not just a website that takes orders. Amazon.com is clear evidence of this. Amazon is a community where you can get customer reviews, connect with other customers, buy just about anything (often with free shipping), and sell just about anything as well. You can also listen to music, choosing from numerous radio stations and artists, and watch videos and TV shows.

Additionally, you need to treat your online customers much the same as you would customers visiting a physical store. After you get people to your website, you need to provide meaningful interaction that makes them want to linger and browse. The experience needs to be smooth — from browsing to shopping cart fulfillment to order confirmation. And you need to make it efficient and affordable. Think about dropping shipping fees as an incentive for trial, and make sure you can deliver goods in a timely manner. See Chapter 10 on direct marketing for tips on preventing shopping cart abandonment.

REMEMBER

When customers walk into a physical store, someone is there to greet them, offer to help, and answer any questions they may have. You need to do this online and can easily and affordably do so with the technology available for online chat. In fact, if you don't offer online chat, you'll struggle to keep up with competitors and to sustain your business in general.

Here are some very telling statistics from ATG Global Consumer Research about what customers expect from e-commerce stores:

>> 90 percent of consumers shopping online say that live chat is helpful to the shopping process.

>> 63 percent say that they're more likely to return to a site that offers live chat and are more likely to purchase again.

>> 40 percent made a purchase because of a helpful online chat experience.

To add online chat to your selling strategies, you can purchase a SaaS system, where you pay per user per month to execute, and assign your staff to "chat" online with your own scripts and protocols. Or you can hire a company that provides the software, trained staff to chat, and analytical tools and reports to help you improve conversion rates and build data models for future selling efforts.

Convertant is a system that offers what it calls online engagement. It provides the staff, trains them to be experts in your field, and develops emotionally engaging protocols for discussions. It claims to have increased conversion rates by as much as 300 percent.

Either way, you need a system that lets you chat, collect data, generate reports on who's coming to your site, what their interests are, conversion rates, and more. Robust systems are set up to analyze all browsing and chat activity to recommend data models and create sales projections.

TIP

You can review the many types of online chat software available at www.capterra.com, where you can get reviews and compare systems like Salesforce that targets companies that could have thousands of users to DontGo, which targets smaller companies with up to 99 users. Price ranges are as robust as services available, so do your research, determine how much you'll use it, who at your company will use it, and what makes sense for your business.

M-commerce, or mobile

This channel may be easy to ignore, but don't. In 2015, m-commerce, or mobile sales, represented 24 percent of all e-commerce sales, and in 2016, that number grew to 29 percent. Mobile sales are projected to keep growing through 2020, when they're expected to represent 49 percent of all e-commerce sales.

Other research shows that 98 percent of consumers switch between their mobile and computer screens daily. On average, people check their phone 40 to 76 times a day, and more than 185 million people in the United States have a smartphone. Adding that together shows that Americans check their phones 8 billion times a day.

With numbers like this, you can't afford to leave m-commerce or at least mobile communications out of your marketing mix. Mobile selling tactics take on several forms, including

>> **Ads that appear on free mobile apps:** Many ads appear before users can use those free running, fitness, and game apps. Even if you just get a few seconds of their attention, you still get your name out and a direct link to your mobile site.

>> **SMS or text messaging to customers who have given you permission to text them coupons, discounts, and so on:** Bed Bath & Beyond lets you get its 20 percent off coupons via text so you can review them on your smartphone while you're shopping at its physical or online stores. You can download coupons from your cloud-based account and manage your offers in real shopping time. As you shop with your phones in physical outlets and while shopping online, mobile access and text messaging are critical to influencing sales in real time — or real shopping time versus just thinking or browsing time.

>> **GPS shopper apps:** These apps turn smartphones into an interactive sales assistant. Shoppers can enter your bricks-and-mortar location and use a GPS shopping app to scan product barcodes, check your inventory, access location-based promotions to spark impulsive or unplanned spending, reserve products while they continue shopping, and much more.

>> **Beacons:** These are a relatively inexpensive way to increase sales during the shopping process. Essentially, they are Bluetooth Low Energy (BLE) signals that reach up to 300 feet. When shoppers walk in and have the app on their

phone and have location services turned on, they can get your messages on their phone while shopping. You can tell them about a free gift at the end of Aisle 14, a special product demo by the home appliances department, or how to get 20 percent off anything they buy before leaving your store, or you can simply say, "Welcome, Susan. Thanks for stopping by."

Apple and Google and other companies have mastered the use of this technology, which is quite affordable to implement. The cost can range from $5 to $30 per Beacon depending on signal range, battery life, and manufacturer.

Although beacons may seem like a cool technology for now but not really necessary to capture a sale over the use of other in-store displays, they may very soon be the difference you need to succeed. Beyond triggering impulsive sales or directing a decision process in store, beacons enable you to collect cellphone numbers and permission to communicate directly with customers on their smartphone, which is usually within a few feet of every owner 24 hours a day.

Retail outlets

Retail is and will always be a valid selling channel no matter how much of our purchasing behavior goes online. We like going to shopping destinations such as large retail malls, specialty boutiques, and fun places such as Aspen, Colorado, and New York's 5th Avenue where shopping is more an experience than a necessity.

Humans are tactile beings. We still like to touch, and we still like the human touch. We want to feel the fabric, touch the glossy surfaces, see the sparkle and craftsmanship, and smell the aroma. And we want to be served and meet the people making the promises we want to believe. In other words, we want "experiences" that engage our senses. Digital may capture our convenience needs, but shopping in real stores fills our social and human needs.

Ironically, Amazon, which pioneered and continuously leads the e-commerce genre, is now building physical bookstores where you can experience hardcover books again in a setting that makes you want to linger, relax, and buy. Small bookstores with coffee shops have been resurging from 2012 as people are going back to tangible versus digital books and like places to hang with other people over coffee or a good read.

The key to being successful in retail today is to offer a creative experience, an inviting environment that encourages lingering and mingling, and comfort drinks and food. When you do this, you don't just attract people and give them a gathering place, you can create new revenue streams. For examples, bookstores that also sell coffee now report non-book sales are about 30 percent of their proceeds.

TIP

Look for ways to create an environment worth going back to, an experience that is enlightening, memorable, and efficient.

Adding the Beacon and GPS shopping features provides an experience based on your consumers' direct needs, makes it stand out, and is fun and engaging at the same time. And it can save you money because you don't have to staff as much if people can get their questions answered immediately on their phones, which are usually in hand.

Getting to Yes via ESP Selling

To manage sales effectively, divide sales into multiple steps and focus on one step at a time as you prepare a sales plan or look for ways to improve your sales. As with any complex process, a weak link always exists. Try to find the step in your sales process that you perform most poorly right now and work to improve it.

Figure 16-1 displays the sales and service process as a flowchart. Note that the chart doesn't flow automatically from beginning to end. You may be forced to cycle back to an earlier stage if things go wrong. But ideally, you never lose prospects or customers forever — they just recycle into sales leads, and you can mount a new effort to win them over.

Adapt this flowchart for the variable emotions and emotional selling propositions (ESPs) associated with your customer segments. For example, if you're a creative designer selling your services to a 30-year-old manager at a high-tech company, you may want to build your initial steps around building trust in you as a person then credibility for your competency by sharing examples of your work and the associated results. If you're selling to baby boomers, your focus may be on the heritage and history of your brand and then your reputation as a supplier.

Figure 16-1 integrates the sales and service processes because they go hand in hand. Customers choose the partners that provide the best support, not just the best overall value regarding price, functionality, and quality. This happens in B2B and B2C. You can't stop nurturing a sale when you close a sale and write the order. You need to sell and nurture with the goal of capturing lifetime value at all times. Your competitors certainly don't stop trying to win that client or account. So you need to think of a completed sale as the beginning of a relationship-building process. More sales calls, further presentations, and efforts to find new ways to serve the customer can help you retain and grow the account. The next sections delve into facets of this flowchart in more depth and help you seal the deal.

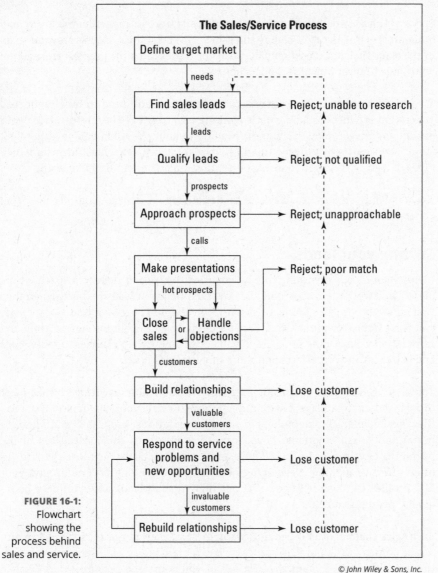

The Sales/Service Process

Define target market

↓ needs

Find sales leads → Reject; unable to research

↓ leads

Qualify leads → Reject; not qualified

↓ prospects

Approach prospects → Reject; unapproachable

↓ calls

Make presentations → Reject; poor match

↓ hot prospects

Close sales — or — Handle objections

↓ customers

Build relationships → Lose customer

↓ valuable customers

Respond to service problems and new opportunities → Lose customer

↓ invaluable customers

Rebuild relationships → Lose customer

© John Wiley & Sons, Inc.

FIGURE 16-1:
Flowchart showing the process behind sales and service.

Generating sales leads

It goes without saying that lead generation is perhaps the most critical foundation you can lay for any business. And it can be the most challenging. No matter how many good customers you have today, you have to continuously gain more to sustain your current level of profitability, compensate for attrition or defection, and grow your business to a new level.

Successful lead generation programs track leads from introduction to closure and build prospecting databases upon the same attributes, life cycle factors, and so on of the leads that were most quickly closed or represented the greatest transaction value, most repeat business, and so on.

This is where good CRM programs come into play. You need to build your lead generation activities around what's working best to get the best return from your efforts and investments. Having information about the leads you've generated, closed, and nurtured for growth will help you qualify new leads, identify which types of leads should get your most attention, and where to find like leads.

The following sections provide some tactics and tips to help you improve your lead generation efforts.

Sorting your leads

Identify your leads according to how qualified they are to close in a specific time period, and work them accordingly. If you qualified your leads properly when they first entered your sales funnel or system, you should know each lead's propensity and time frame for purchasing. Sort them on a value scale for closing time and transaction value. Doing so will help you better identify your highest quality leads and better direct your efforts and those of your sales team.

You also need to sort your leads according to the emotional triggers that most influence them to engage, trust, and purchase. Review your customers' ESP profiles (see Chapter 2), and build your sales presentations, proposals, and messaging around those emotions. If you can allay any fears and insecurities in the beginning of your process, you'll have a much greater chance to move them to yes in an effective manner. Developing questions or screening criteria around your ESP profiles can also help you sort out high-quality leads and eliminate poor-quality prospects quickly.

Each sales channel offers specific advantages and ways to reach customers in different phases of the purchase process. The more you use and the more you test, the more you can pinpoint the best use of your time and resources and what to expect from your various channels. For example:

>> Your website may produce leads with the highest level or readiness to buy.

>> Joining a professional group or association may help you network and mingle with leads that are high quality but have a long closure timeline.

>> A direct-mail campaign may produce leads from your current customers.

>> Direct-response advertising may help you find and close impulsive leads.

>> Online chat, telemarketing, trade shows, and events can help generate leads as well.

Enhancing lead generation on your website

Although websites are clearly good mechanisms for generating leads and starting relationships, don't make the mistake of relying too heavily on yours. Many websites are still relatively passive. They showcase content but don't actively recruit qualified leads.

You need to use other channels to drive leads to your website, and when you get them there, you need to make your site more interactive, give them reasons to share their contact information, and inspire them to inquire and engage.

TIP

Do the following to turn visitors on your website into leads:

>> Require visitors to register on your site to get access to white papers, industry insights, and your blog for current updates on actionable topics.

>> Create and post videos that provide thought leadership interviews, how-to tips, and demonstrations of new technology and products. Require visitors to register with their email address for access.

>> Post a one-question survey and change it weekly. Ask meaningful questions that spark dialogue and reasons to go deeper on your site. Require email registration to participate in your survey and see the results so people can compare their response to others.

>> Draw visitors to your website by reaching to social media groups whose interests align with your products and encourage them to register on your website for white papers, informative emails, webinars you may host, and so on.

Purchasing lists for B2B lead generation

Buying lists of households and consumers is easier than buying a list of actual decision makers at a given company. However, you can find good B2B lists.

Hoover's, a Dun & Bradstreet company, is one of the leading sources for building a list of decision makers at companies you may be interested in targeting. This database groups U.S. companies by *SIC code* — which stands for *standard industrial classification*, a U.S.-government designation based on product type — location, and size (as indicated by annual sales) so you can target companies by industry and city and eliminate any that seem too small. You pay a monthly subscription fee to access leads, which you can download into an Excel file or other format and use as many times as you want without having to repurchase. The leads you purchase are based on the criteria you set so you can create highly customized lists for all your products and segments.

Purchasing these leads and calling them or reaching out to qualify them further can help increase your close ratio by as much as 70 percent because the leads you deliver to your sales team are based on the decision maker and readiness to purchase.

REMEMBER

As you identify characteristics of your most qualified leads through your ESP profile, database analytics, and so on, create marketing content and content marketing that support associated values and behavior. Positioning your brand as a subject matter expert in your field paves the way for brand recognition and higher open and response rates.

For example, if you're selling ERP systems and find that the decision makers you're targeting struggle most with onboarding, you may want to start populating your social channels with articles about training and getting teams up and running as quickly as possible to start saving and realizing top ROIs. Position your executives as experts, and send emails offering free consultations with them.

Tapping your own business networks online can be another huge source for qualified leads. Many of your connections on LinkedIn are likely strong candidates for your services or products and are connected to even more prospects with whom you may have not yet connected. By accepting each other's invitation to connect, you have permission to reach out.

Consultative selling

Consultative selling is just what is says it is: consulting versus selling. Consumers, clients — everyone — prefer to be informed and involved rather than sold anything. Consultative selling involves providing information and insights that help your customers achieve their goals for budget, performance, and so much more.

Beyond providing information that helps with the decision process in an objective manner, consultative selling includes the following actions:

1. **Consult first, build trust second, and sell third.**

2. **Start a relationship by listening to your customers' needs, identifying their personal values associated with your category, and building rapport as someone who's like them and understands them.**

3. **Offer suggestions and solutions that meet their goals, not your sales quota.**

4. **Address their fears.**

   Find ways to identify their greatest fears so you can present your promise, messages, and offers as a solution to overcome these challenges. (See Chapter 2 for more on unconscious drivers for survival.)

5. **Ask thought-provoking questions that inspire your prospects to think about their problems and solutions from new angles.**

When you follow these steps, you take price out of the equation and build value that your competitors can't match.

Here are additional tips for consultative selling.

>> Gather information about your customers and prospects to identify the following:

- Specific issues and needs per the level they're at in their jobs and the influences of the current market environment

- What competitors are likely calling on them so you can address their messaging and promises and build your case

>> Anticipate the questions your customers and prospects are likely to ask of you, and be prepared to answer with confidence, validation, and facts.

>> Ask what criterion drives your customers' decision for products and partners they choose. Don't assume that you already know this answer.

Consultative selling also goes far beyond the first closing. It's about nurturing the account for an entire lifetime and adding new levels of value along the way. Always do the following to keep accounts and lower attrition and defection rates:

>> Follow through after the sale to ensure that all expectations were met.

>> Do periodic reviews to help identify issues that can be improved and new opportunities.

>> Continue to share insights to help them with all aspects of the job.

TIP

If you lose a sale to a competitor, call that lead after a few months to see how happy he is with his choice. If he isn't happy, you just opened the door for a second chance with fewer competitors to beat this time around.

Creating sales presentations with ESP power

What makes a sales presentation great? Pretty much any presentation that gets customers to say yes quickly and creates the kind of enthusiasm that makes them internal ambassadors for getting approval up the ladder if needed. Achieving these outcomes has a greater chance of success when your sales presentations are built on emotional values, your ESP, functional promises, and industry stats and facts that build upon the psychological triggers associated with authority, social proof, and trust.

Inform, involve, inspire

The goal of any sales presentation is clearly to convince the prospect to become a customer. Presentations that build upon psychological triggers and follow the three-*Is* process can help get you an *in* with decision makers:

>> **Inform.** When you provide information that enables purchasers to make wise informed decisions, you become a partner, not just a supplier or vendor. People typically trust partners more than salespeople and tend to listen to and heed their advice. This is where white papers and industry reports are valuable for nurturing relationships that can turn into high-value customers and clients.

>> **Involve.** We've all heard the age-old wisdom of presenting your ideas in a way that makes others think they're actually *their* ideas. Well, this works exceptionally well in selling. You accomplish this by involving the clients in the discussion about solutions rather than just presenting solutions. Build on what the client is doing right, acknowledge and praise his successes, and show how you can build on his current foundation to help achieve even greater outcomes.

>> **Inspire.** Along the lines of involving prospects in the discussion, your goal needs to be to inspire them to trust you to try your products or services. Inspiration comes from being validated for what you've already done and being encouraged to take your successes to a new level. It doesn't come from being given a contract with a pen. It comes from many directions, including

- Never being told what you're doing is wrong

- Being given new tools and insights for building on current successes

- Knowing others have succeeded by making similar choices or working with the given supplier or vendor

- Knowing that the risk is low for trial and that you can change your mind if you so choose

A proven method for inspiring trial is to give a free trial. You see it all the time — 30-day free trial for a movie or music channel, news subscription, even Amazon Prime. To start the free trial, you have to use your credit card, which will be charged as soon as the free trial period ends. Most people like those free trials and don't cancel them when they expire. So that "free" trial often results in revenue. Most important, it takes the fear out of purchasing a commitment that's hard to cancel and makes the initial purchase more comfortable.

A sales presentation that's smart and thoughtful should cover basic facts, emotional drivers, and anticipated needs and wants. Your presentation needs to inform while also making the prospect comfortable and excited. Present yourself with confidence and do your homework about your prospect just like you would in a job interview.

Tell your brand story

A sales presentation needs to be built much like your brand story. As we discuss in Chapter 13, a compelling brand story is one in which others can positively and enthusiastically see themselves. Sales presentations need to accomplish this mission-critical goal.

A key difference in a brand story and a sales presentation is that you're not just engaging in an emotionally fulfilling story; you're trying to persuade listeners to trust you and invest in you and most often choose you over others who may be courting them, too.

Some tips for creating "stories" that close sales include

>> **Building your main points:** Like any persuasive communications effort, you need to clearly define your main points and present them in a way that's critical and engaging. Make a bullet list of three to five main selling points that support your ESP, validate the function or performance goals you promise to deliver, confirm your position in the market, and differentiate you from the rest of the field.

>> **Backing it up:** Don't expect people to believe your product claims, promises, successes, and all the other things you say about your brand because they hear similar chatter from every salesperson who walks in their door. Back up every claim with stats, facts, or testimonials from third parties to make your claims real. Better yet, back it up with a discounted trial offer to let them see for themselves what your product or services can really do for them.

TIP

If your successes can be seen as "too good to be true," find a way to validate them. I (Jeanette) once was asked to respond to a request for proposal (RFP) through a business broker who told me to not include achieving a 3,100 percent ROI for a client because no one would really believe that. As it was true, I found a way to include it and make sure it was believable.

>> **Showing and telling:** Showing is usually better than telling, which is validated by the growing use of videos to promote products and close sales. Videos engage more of the senses, which adds to message recall, and they're relatively easy and inexpensive to produce and deploy on multiple channels — YouTube, Facebook, LinkedIn, websites, trade show displays, and more.

Even if you have a good slide show or video, don't use it as a substitute for a face-to-face conversation. Make your strategic points in person, and base them on what you learned while listening to your prospect. Use a video if you need to back up your claims with third-party statements or demonstrate how a product works.

Responding to problems

To avoid problems with onboarding new customers, treat them like prospects no matter how long you've been managing that account. Pay attention to every detail of their account to ensure that nothing is set up to fail and that they're being serviced properly throughout your entire organization.

Ironically, the most faithful customers are the ones who've had a problem that you managed to solve in a fair and generous manner. Many research studies back this up. Inevitably, something will go wrong that will upset, disappoint, or even anger your customer. That's why the sales process has to include a *service recovery* step. Make sure the customer knows who to contact when a problem occurs and that your entire team is trained to correct the problem immediately.

TIP

Set up protocols and processes that empower your sales team to do whatever it takes to make frustrated clients happy ones. When you do, their loyalty will be stronger because they know they can trust you to fix problems and take care of their needs. This works only when you're willing to make sacrifices to make them happy, so define how you will do this and what costs you're willing to incur to keep customers based on their value to you now and in the future.

Service recovery starts by answering key questions before issues occur and training your staff of response protocols. For example, what potentially could go wrong, what has made customers unhappy in the past, and what are the points of frustration for customers?

Organizing Your Sales Force

Who does what, when, and where? Such organizational questions plague many sales or marketing managers, and those questions can make a big difference to sales force productivity. Should your salespeople work out of local, regional, or national offices? Should you base them in offices where staff members provide daily support and their boss can supervise their activities closely? Or should you set them free to operate on the road or out of their homes? Or, if you have a small business, should you do all the selling, or does bringing in a salesperson on commission make sense?

The following sections provide some conventional wisdom to help you answer these questions and act in a way that best meets your individual needs.

Determining how many salespeople you need

If you have an existing sales force, you can examine the performance of each territory to decide whether more salespeople can help or whether you can do with less and where basic sales service may be falling through the cracks. Ask yourself the following questions to help you optimize your sales organization:

>> Are some territories rich in prospects that salespeople just don't have time to get to? Then consider splitting those territories or adding salespeople.

>> Are you experiencing high customer turnover in a territory as a result of poor service or other factors that can be controlled?

>> Are you operating in some territories with little sales potential that could be detracting your efforts from those with higher potential?

Hiring your own or using reps

You have to decide whether to hire salespeople yourself or subcontract. Most industries have good sales companies that take on the job of hiring and managing salespeople for you. Called *sales representatives* (or just *reps*), they usually work for a straight commission of between 10 and 20 percent, depending on the industry and how much room you have in your pricing structure for their commission. Reps that perform consultative selling and customized service often expect, and deserve, a higher commission.

TIP

If you have a small company or a short product line, using sales reps makes the most sense. They're the best option whenever you have *scale problems* that make justifying the cost of hiring your own dedicated salespeople somewhat difficult. Scale problems arise when you have a too-short product line, which means that salespeople don't have very much to sell to customers, and/or sales calls produce small orders that don't cover the cost of the call. Reps usually handle many companies' product lines so that they have more products to show prospects when they call making the potential of a return much higher.

If you have a long enough product line to justify hiring and managing your own dedicated salespeople, doing so will give you more control and better feedback from the market. A dedicated sales force generally outsells a sales rep by two and ten times as much because their sales focus is your product line.

Finding good sales reps

How do you find sales reps? Word-of-mouth referrals or meeting at a trade show or industry conference are great ways to find out who is reputable, presents well, and is available. Or, even simpler, ask the buyers of products such as the one you sell for names of reps who currently call on them.

TIP

A growing number of hub websites offer access to sales reps and manufacturers reps as well as freelance salespeople who work under short-term contracts. These sites provide leads, not final answers, so make sure you do your screening carefully, and if you do hire someone, do it on a trial basis to start. Here are some of the options on the web today:

>> Goodcall (www.goodcall.io), which claims to have "everything you need to run an outsourced sales team"

>> Time to Hire (www.timetohire.com), which helps you locate sales reps

>> Guru (www.guru.com), which cues up sales reps' ads or posts your project description for them to respond to

>> RepHunter (www.rephunter.net), which specializes in manufacturers reps and independent reps

>> SalesAgentHUB (www.salesagenthub.com), where you can register as a company in need of reps

>> GreatRep (www.greatrep.com), where you can search the rep database, view postings of Lines Wanted, or post under Reps Wanted

Managing reps effectively

After you have reps lined up for each territory, you must monitor their sales efforts on a regular basis. Which rep firms sell the best (and worst)? Usually, 10 or 15 percent of the reps make almost all your sales. Monitor your reps to find the best and make changes quickly to cut your losses and maximize your sales potential. And train each rep in how to tell your brand story so your message and ESP are consistent across all reps and marketing channels.

Compensating your sales force

If you want to recruit top-tier salespeople, you need to offer them a top-tier compensation plan. Find a way to make your compensation model different from the norm in your industry to make your job openings really stand out. For example, if you want to make sure your salespeople take a highly consultative, service-oriented approach with long-term support and relationship building, make your compensation salary-based. If you give them sales incentives, consider bonuses linked to long-term customer retention or to increased value among existing customers. Your compensation plan will then stand out from competitors and send a clear signal about the kind of sales behavior you expect. Similarly, if you want the most self-motivated salespeople, offer more commission than the competition.

TIP

The details of what you must offer in base salary and in commissions vary so much from industry to industry and region to region that you need to research comparable positions to establish a base before you design your compensation plan.

Whatever you pay them, salespeople and reps do best when they have high *task clarity*, defined as clear links from their sales efforts to positive results. Make sure they have the products, leads, knowledge, and support to be successful. You'll find that success is the greatest motivator, and your sales force enjoys the process of selling for you.

Retaining Customers with Great Service

Sales and service go hand in hand. When your business relies on personal selling — like in many business-to-business markets and a variety of consumer markets — you won't succeed without great service.

Do you know your *customer turnover rate* (the percent of customers who leave each year, also called a *churn rate*)? If your turnover goes over 5 percent in most industries, you probably have a customer service problem, and you need to build retention to lower that percentage. Find out by comparing customer lists from two consecutive years — or by asking your salespeople (if you have any) to gather the data if you can't do so easily from your central customer data base or billing records.

As we mention in Chapter 4, customer surveys regarding product satisfaction, service satisfaction, NPSs, and so on can help you identify customer engagement protocols that are and aren't working.

Sometimes companies define a lost customer as one whose business has fallen by more than half, which gives you a more conservative measure than one based only on customers who've stopped ordering entirely.

To figure your rate of customer turnover, follow these steps:

1. **Compare last year's and this year's customer lists to find out how many customers you lost during the year.**

   Ignore new customers for this calculation.

2. **Count the total number of customers on the list from the previous year.**

   That gives you your *base,* or where you started.

3. **Divide the number of lost customers (from Step 1) by the total number of customers (from Step 2) to get your turnover rate.**

For example, if you started the year with 1,500 customers and lost 250, your turn-over rate is 250, or nearly 17 percent. If you find yourself in that situation, it's time to focus on improving customer service.

REMEMBER

Successful selling depends not only on good systems and service protocols but also on having good products that people actually want. If your product or service isn't relevant, your sales efforts can't compensate.

Always stay on top of your consumers' needs, market trends, and technological innovations to make sure you're relevant in terms of your offerings, not just your selling channels.

6

The Part of Tens

Discover ten common marketing mistakes, such as trying to marketing to everyone and relying on discounts, and find out how to avoid them.

Understand what you need to measure to get the real results of your marketing campaigns.

Chapter **17**

Ten Common Marketing Mistakes (And How to Avoid Them)

Learning from others' mistakes is always better than making your own. This chapter presents ten all-too-common marketing mistakes businesses of all sizes make and how to avoid them so you can keep your sales and marketing efforts on track.

Making Assumptions

Assuming that you know your customers, their preferences, their loyalty to you, and the competitive environment in which you operate is one of the most costly mistakes you can make. In most cases, you're likely wrong.

With all the research and feedback tools available today to help you monitor the voice of your customers and their real needs and attitudes, there's no reason to ever assume anything. Regularly survey your customers to see what they like and don't like about your brand, your products, and your service. Do surveys to update your Net Promoter Score (NPS) as well. During transactions, ask for individual feedback and engage in social listening. Analyze results to identify trends and things you can do to maintain and increase satisfaction.

Ignoring Customer Complaints

With all the social media channels available, unhappy customers can share a bad brand experience with literally thousands of people in a matter of minutes. In addition to their Facebook, Twitter, and other social accounts, they can quickly post negative reviews about you and/or your products on Yelp, Google, Amazon, and other sites that masses of consumers browse daily. Whenever this happens, and it will, respond immediately on the site the customer used for the complaint, and let the unhappy customer and others know that you care about each customer and ask what you can do to make it right.

Faking Popularity

Just like all the "fake news" on social media channels, there's often also a lot of "fake likes." Just look at your Twitter messages; chances are you have an offer from someone trying to sell you "followers." Like fake news, this isn't acceptable by any business standards because you're portraying your brand as more popular and successful than you are and misleading consumers about your market position.

Using Dirty Data

Nothing's quite like getting a great offer from a brand you've been loyal to for years only to find out that the great offer applies only to new customers! When this happens, it's often the result of a brand not cleaning up its data to sort out prospects and customers. With all the customer relationship management (CRM) and data management systems available today at many price points, there's no excuse for this anymore. Customers expect personalized communications about their relationships with you and rewards for their loyalty, and when, after years of giving you their business, non-customers get a better offer than you've given them, you can damage that relationship beyond repair.

Competing on Price

Discounts and price cuts have their place but only temporarily, such as when you're trying to stimulate first-time trial and build a base of customers for future email or social media campaigns. Keeping prices low for an extended period of time or offering low prices frequently just puts customers on notice to hold off and never pay full price. You quickly position your brand as the budget option, which limits your appeal, and once you lower a price, you'll have a hard time ever raising it again. Although reducing prices to meet sales goals may be tempting, keep in mind that repeated price promotions can erode brand value and create fickle customers who abandon you for the competitors' promotions.

Ignoring the Emotional Drivers of Choice

As mentioned in Chapter 2, 90 percent of people's thoughts and behavior are driven by their unconscious minds. People respond more to dopamine rushes that make them feel euphoric and unbeatable and oxytocin that makes them feel connected, accepted, and loved than they respond to clever ads or blow-out pricing specials. When you tap the emotional drivers that influence how people feel about themselves and the world around them, you influence behavior. All you do should be based on creating positive feelings and on building trust. Without trust, you can't tap into much of anything else.

Forgetting to Edit

If your letter, email, website, print ad, sign, or billboard has a typo in it, people remember that goof and forget the rest. Not only can sloppy mistakes make a bad first impression among prospects, but they can also make people question the amount of attention you pay to detail when producing your products, managing your invoices, and executing on customer service. Edit carefully and get someone else to look over your shoulder to make sure nothing slips by. Your brand is only as good as your reputation.

Offering What You Can't Deliver

When you make promises you're not sure you can deliver on, you put yourself in the category of bad salespeople who can't be trusted. In addition, if you try to roll out a product that doesn't work yet or before you've worked out all the details for execution, service, and troubleshooting, you set customers up to have a bad experience with you. Either way, you lose trust and potential sales. In most, if not all cases, those disappointed customers can find another supplier from whom to purchase and to whom to assign their loyalty.

Treating Customers Impersonally

Every customer is a person who likes to be treated as such. No one likes to be a number. Today, with all the CRM technology, you can usually identify who is on the other end of a phone call. When you can, you should address that person by name, thank her for her business, and ask if you can do anything else to make her happy.

Put yourself in the customer's shoes and take a hard look at all your customer interactions. Are they as personal as they should be? If not, invest in better list-checking, a central database of customers, training in how to pronounce customer names, and whatever else it takes to allow your business to treat all customers like important individuals.

Blaming the Customer

It's easy to think that an irate customer is out of line and overreacting. But regardless, you need to take the high road and let the customer be right — within reason, of course. As Neiman Marcus is famous for stating, "The customer is always right" when it to comes to how she feels she should have been treated or the quality of product she thought she was buying. This doesn't mean you have to let people take advantage of you. But when someone has to vent, listen. Try to offer a solution that you both can live with. Whether you work it out or not, you need to remain professional, reasonable, calm, and courteous. If you don't and even if you were justified, the customer can easily smear your reputation online, and that's a risk you can't take.

campaigns

» **Measuring the true impact on your bottom line and discovering key insights for future endeavors**

Chapter **18**

Ten Ways to Measure Results (Beyond ROI)

Marketing and measurement are a science and an art, and it takes a commitment to learning how to do both aspects right to grow sustainable results and profits. This chapter presents ten methods to help you measure the real impact of your marketing campaigns and programs and gain insights on how to best execute future campaigns for boosting results and efficiencies.

Chuck McLeester, a pioneer in marketing metrics and popular contributor to *Target Marketing* magazine, shares the following steps to measuring what matters most for long-term success. You can find out more about Chuck's insights and measurement approaches at www.measuredmarketingllc.com.

Establish Clear Objectives

Like any investment or initiative, you need to define what you want to accomplish and what you want to measure. Too often, marketers don't end up with the correct data points at the end of a campaign to effectively measure the outcomes. And this is most often the result of not defining upfront what you want or need to measure.

What are the most important results to measure at each stage of your business to help you determine if you are growing at the desired rate, slowing down, or not growing at all? Some key objectives to measure include your cost to generate each lead and your costs to nurture each lead into a profitable customer.

Tie Your Metrics to Your Objectives

Keep things simple so you can identify measurements without confusion. One way to do this is to track only metrics that are directly related to your objectives. It's easy to think that you need to measure "everything but the kitchen sink" just in case you need more insights later, or so you don't have to do another campaign to learn something, or, better yet, because senior management will want all the data.

Set Learning Priorities

Building on the previous step, be selective about the data points you need to gather and how often you need them, especially with online metrics. You don't need to track every possible navigation path and page view. Doing this will just cause confusion and chaos, which is hard to decipher and sort into meaningful actions. Try to sort your priorities by (1) the things you need to know right away, (2) the information that's good to know but can wait for later, and (3) the data that you don't need anytime soon, if ever.

Establish a Target ROI

Two primary ways for marketers to measure ROI are

>> Calculating simple ROI, which is simply dividing revenue that you can measure and link directly to marketing programs by your marketing costs

>> Determining your incremental ROI, which you find by deducting your marketing costs from your revenue

Either of these definitions and calculations is consistent with the classic marketing principles of customer lifetime value (the "R") and allowable acquisition cost (the "I"), which we cover in the following two sections. (We describe customer lifetime value calculations in detail in Chapter 16.)

Know Your Customer Lifetime Value

Every marketer needs to answer the question, "What is a customer worth to you over time?" Some companies limit customer lifetime value to the first-year revenue, which defeats the whole concept if their purchasing behavior lasts more than one year of their life. Others base lifetime value on the possibility that a customer will stay with them and continue to purchase for three, five, or even ten years. Delve into your customer history (if you have the data) and see how long your customers, on average, tend to remain loyal to you, how much they spend per transaction and over time, and how much they refer to you. To do this, you need to be able to track referrals to customers, which should be part of your learning and measurement plan.

Know Your Allowable Customer Acquisition Cost

Knowing how much it costs for you to acquire a customer is important for any marketer of any size business to determine because it directly impacts your target ROI and your customer lifetime value. For example, if your customer value is $100 for the time period you're measuring or the customer's lifetime of purchases and your target ROI is 2:1, then you can afford to spend $50 to get a customer. That's your allowable customer acquisition cost.

Establish Benchmarks

Chances are you're familiar with the concept of a marketing funnel that illustrates how an impression progresses to a sale and how you can use this progression to forecast marketing results. For example, you estimate a number of impressions your campaign will generate and how many of those impressions will funnel down to responses, qualified leads, sales conversions, and revenue. You can use the final number of impressions that make it to revenue status to calculate your cost per sale by dividing that number into your marketing costs for a given campaign or annual budget.

Turn the Funnel Upside Down

Most often, marketers start at the top of the funnel, or the mouth, with the number of prospects and work their way down by applying historic or projected response rates at different points in the sales cycle. Another way to determine how much you can afford to spend for a qualified lead is to work backward by starting at the bottom of the funnel with your actual or estimated cost to acquire a customer. Then use your conversion to sales percentage (actual or estimated) to determine how much you can afford to spend for a qualified lead, response, and impression. These benchmarks will become goals for your campaign. As with anything, test and test again to determine what your actuals are.

Adjust Your Funnel Benchmark Assumptions When You Have Real Data

After you get real data from actual campaign results rather than just your projections based on estimates, rerun your scenarios from the earlier exercises. Make the appropriate adjustments to your funnel assumptions so you can launch new campaigns with realistic goals in place. To reach the ROI goals you define as a result of actual campaign data, you may need to adjust your media purchasing costs to lower your promotion costs, or you may have to accept higher customer acquisition cost and adjust your target ROI downward.

Avoid the Dashboard Trap

Just because your dashboard, or central location for reviewing all your data points simultaneously, *can* measure everything doesn't mean it *should*. Don't become obsessed with *what* you can count. Focus on what you need to count to identify profits, losses, and opportunities. A carefully thought-out measurement plan that's tied directly to your sales and profitability goals should provide only actionable information to drive decisions. Otherwise, it's just busywork that keeps you going but leads to nowhere.

Index

Numerics

80/20 distribution strategy, 331
99designs, 201

A

A/B tests, 242
Accenture, 9
Accounting For Dummies (Tracy), 114
action steps (in marketing plans), 104–108
Adbeat, 84
Adbusters, 14
AdClarity, 84
Addictomatic, 82
AdGooroo, 84
Adidas, 299–300
Adobe Cloud, 201–202
Adobe Marketing Cloud, 201, 227
Adobe Typekit, 202
advertising
  mobile, 352
  print, 210–216
  sex-oriented ads, 135
  web, 189–192, 335
advertising research, 84
Advertising Standards Authority, 160
Airbnb, 96, 295
Alchemist Distilleries, 201
Alexa, 86
Allegra, 234
AlphaGraphics, 234
Amazon, 263, 333–335, 350, 353
ambush marketing. *See* guerilla marketing
American Express, 41, 97, 280
American Girl doll company, 339
analogies, 159–160
animus archetype, 35
Anson Calder, 51
Apple, 19–20, 49, 75, 150, 154, 293–294, 297–298, 305, 332, 353

Apple iTunes, 180
AR (augmented reality), 22, 324, 343
archetypal theories, 34–35
Ariely, Dan, 322
Armani Exchange, 338–339
assignment of loyalty (component of decision process), 17–18
Asymco, 298
ATG Global Consumer Research, 351
Augment, 343
augmented reality (AR), 22, 324, 343
authority, as social influencer, 36
automated customization, 192–194
average session duration, 253–254
Avon, 323

B

B2B. *See* business to business
B2C. *See* business to consumer
Baby Boomers, 10, 12, 195
Bagchi, Rajesh, 144
banner ads, 191–192
Beanie Babies, 53
belief
  schemas and, 26–27
  tenets of, 19–20
Belkin, 126
benchmarks, 56–58, 104–105, 375
BenGay, 304
bestsellers, 51–52
beta testing, 49–50
bid rigging, 328
Bing, 189
Birren, Faber, 145
Bissonnette, Zac, 53
blogs, 68, 124, 257, 268–269
BlogTalkRadio, 180
Bluetooth beacons, 352–354
body copy (copy), 197

Boost post feature (Facebook), 173

"born this way" theory, 32–33

Boston Aquarium, 83

bounce rate, 252–253

brainstorming, 158–159

brand anchors, 207

Brand Finance, 291

brand iconology and iconography, 144–146, 299–300

brand identity

   brand iconography, 299–300

   brands within brands, 302–303

   general discussion, 298

   personality traits, 300–302

   unifying, 298–299

   updating, 303

brand recall, 133, 195

brand story

   characters of, 296–297

   climax of, 297–298

   overview, 295–296

   plot of, 297

   sales presentations, 361–362

Brand24, 82

BrandColors, 146

branding

   brand identity, 298–303

   brand story, 295–298

   creativity and, 154–156

   defined by experiences, 293–294

   defined by product distinctions and innovation, 294

   defined by service, 292–293

   emotional equity in, 292

   overview, 291

   product lines, 304–312

   updating versus changing logos, 154–155

Brandwatch Analytics, 87

Bratcher, Harlan, 294, 338–339

brevity, 172–173, 180, 184

brochures, 208–210

budgeting, 111–113

Building Websites All-in-One For Dummies (Karlins and Sahlin), 262

buildup forecasts, 114–115

bullet points, 207

Burberry, 125

Business Insider magazine, 155

business to business (B2B)

   direct marketing, 222

   distribution strategies, 331

   influencers, 100–101

   psychological drivers, 28

   retainer-based selling, 349

   thought leaders in, 69

   videos, 185–186

business to consumer (B2C)

   direct marketing, 221–222

   distribution strategies, 332

   influencers, 100–101

   psychological drivers, 28

   retainer-based selling, 349

   thought leaders in, 69

   videos, 185–186

But You Are Free concept, 148, 161

BuySellAds, 270

BzzAgent, 80

C

C2C (consumer to consumer), 272

Cahners Publishing Co., 214

call and chat centers, 244–246, 351–352

calls to action (CTAs), 127, 185, 197, 232–233

Canada Post, 196

Capterra, 352

captions, 198

Carnegie Mellon University, 322

Carolla, Adam, 181

cash position, 95

cash-based accounting, 114

CataBoom, 187

CCI Color Institute for Color Research, 144

celebrity endorsements, 133, 156

chambers of commerce, 281

champion test, 311

charitable activities and giving. *See* corporate social responsibility

Cheema, Amar, 144

Cheerios, 348

Chick-fil-A, 14

chief experience officers (CXOs), 16

Christie's, 41

churn rate (customer turnover rate), 365–366

Cialdini, Robert, 37

clarity, 123, 129, 155, 262–263

Clemson University, 171

click bait, 129–130, 147–149, 232

client advisory boards, 275

client-appreciation events, 274

climate change, 78–79

Clinton, Hillary, 117–118

cloud-based systems, 194

CMI (Content Marketing Institute), 118

Coca-Cola, 39, 125, 171–172, 185, 205, 311

collaboration
  corporate social responsibility, 97–98
  cross-promotion, 163
  funding events, 277–278
  kinship strategies, 98–99
  overview, 96–97
  partnering to build new products, 308–310
  sponsoring cause-related events, 279–281
  trade shows, 283, 286

color
  brand iconology, 144–146
  color wheel meanings, 145
  creative briefs and, 151
  print media, 200
  psychology of, 144
  values and, 144–146

Color Association of the United States, 144

Color Psychology and Color Therapy (Birren), 145

comment cards, 83

community (tenet of belief), 19–20

community building, 15–16, 23–24, 250

community events, 275

community theaters, 213

competitive channels (parallel distribution channels), 332

competitive pricing, 323

Competitor Monitor, 86

competitors, research into, 83–84, 86

Competitrack, 84

Cone Communications, 13–14, 40, 130, 278

Conference Board, 111

confirmation and reassurance (component of decision process), 17–18

Conquest Imaging, 132

consistency of message, 123, 132–133

Constant Contact, 74, 80

consultative selling, 358–359

consumer choice
  appealing to consumers' happiness and purpose, 39–42
  ESP grids, 42–44
  overview, 25
  psychological drivers, 29–33
  psychology theories, 33–35
  social influencers, 35–38
  unconscious mind, 26–28

Consumer Council on Loyalty, 348

consumer to consumer (C2C), 272

content analytics, 194

content marketing
  channels for, 121–122
  content library, 120
  creating content marketing plans, 122–124
  defined, 118
  drawing attention to brand, 120
  goals of, 119
  overview, 117–119
  user-generated content, 125–126
  writing for, 128–135

Content Marketing Institute (CMI), 118

conversion rate, 267–268

Convertant, 351

copy (body copy), 197

copyrighted fonts, 205

Corbett, Julie, 97

Corbis, 261

corporate social responsibility (CSR)
  building customer relationships through, 16
  building trust through, 13–16
  effect on consumer trust, 13–15
  guerilla marketing and, 23–24
  marketing that focuses on happiness and purpose, 40–42
  marketing content, 127
  marketing plans involving, 97–98
  reciprocity, 37–38
  sponsoring cause-related events, 279–281
  website creation and, 249

cortisol, 30

Co-Society, 97

cost per acquisition (CPA), 221

Costco, 51

coupons and coupon codes, 233, 323–324

Coupons.com, 323

CPA (cost per acquisition), 221

creative
  color, 144–146
  creative briefs, 149–153
  creativity audits, 140–141
  fonts, 146–147
  overview, 139–140
  questioning everything, 141–142
  strategy for, 143
  word choice for click bait, 147–149

Creative Bloq, 147

creative briefs
  color palette, 151
  constraints, 151–152
  defined, 149
  emotional drivers, 150–151
  execution, 152–153
  goals of, 149
  golden triangle pattern, 151
  promises and offers, 149
  support statement, 150
  tone or persona statement, 150
  wannabe profiles, 151

creative envelopes, 232

creativity
  activities to engage imagination, 156–157
  branding and, 154–156
  as group activity, 157–161
  identifying sources and constraints, 142–143
  managing creative process, 161–163
  product development and, 153–154
  tips for creative thinking, 163

Crimson Hexagon, 82

CRM. *See* customer relationship management systems

crowdfunding, 49

Crowdsite, 201

CSR. *See* corporate social responsibility

CTAs (calls to action), 127, 185, 197, 232–233

"culture jamming," 14

currency fluctuations, 320

Customedialabs.com, 254

customer events, 273–274

customer experience (CX)

beyond sales process, 18–20

customer experience planning, 17–18

defining, 17

direct marketing, 230–231

as go-to-market strategy, 50

improving for sustainability, 16–20

marketing plans, 101–102

overview, 16

customer experience department, 16

customer journey, 19, 102

customer loyalty
  importance of, 348
  special offers and discounts, 327–328
  strengthening existing products, 307–308

customer relationship management (CRM) systems, 75, 226–228, 356, 370

customer segments, 55

customer turnover rate (churn rate), 365–366

customers and consumers
  blaming, 372
  creating trust equity among, 12–16
  distractedness of, 9
  generations of, 9–12
  guerilla marketing, 20–24
  ignoring complaints, 370
  multitasking when consuming media, 9
  personal contact with, 67
  personality traits and branding, 301
  research into, 66–68, 71–73, 82–83, 86–87
  social media, 67–68
  state of mind of, 9
  technology and, 7–8
  treating impersonally, 372

Cvent, 278

CX. *See* customer experience

CXOs (chief experience officers), 16

Cyrus, Miley, 133

D

Darwin's Data, 80

Data and Marketing Association (DMA), 69, 195, 220, 222, 225, 239

data management platforms (DMPs), 226, 228–229

Daybreak Game Company, LLC, 308

decision grids, 70–71

decision process
    guiding with customer experience planning, 17–18
    identifying customer feelings, 72–73
    interactions during, 17
Dediu, Horace, 298
Dell, 332
Deloitte, 9, 130
Demand Metric, 220
demand side platforms (DSPs), 226, 229
demographics
    changes in, 88
    surveys, 74
descriptives, 322
DesignContest, 201
DesignCrowd, 201
dictionary.com, 146
differentiation test, 312
Digimind, 86
digital marketing
    automated customization, 192–194
    challenges of, 166
    Facebook, 167–174
    forgetting to edit, 371
    games, 187–188
    Instagram, 175
    LinkedIn, 175–177
    online review sites, 186
    overview, 165–166
    overview of channels and tools for, 167
    Pinterest, 177–178
    podcasts, 179–181
    Twitter, 174
    videos, 183–186
    web advertising, 189–192
    webinars, 181–183
direct marketing
    call and chat centers, 244–246
    calls to action, 233
    channels for, 336–337
    customer relationships management systems, 226–228
    data, 224–225
    data management platforms, 226, 228–229
    demand side platforms, 226, 229
    email, 237–244
    emotional appeal, 223
    foundation of, 222
    messaging, 231–232
    metrics of, 220–222
    overview, 219–220
    print, 232–235, 243
    purchasing lists, 235–237
Data and Marketing Association (DMA), 195, 239
direct response. See direct marketing
direct to consumer sales, 350–352
discovery (component of decision process)
    defined, 17
    guiding with customer experience planning, 18
distribution
    channel structure, 336–338
    overview, 329–330
    selecting distributors, 335–336
    strategies for, 330–335
    tactics for, 338–343
DMA (Data and Marketing Association), 69, 195, 220, 222, 225, 239
DMPs (data management platforms), 226, 228–229
doing good in the world. See corporate social responsibility
Dollar Shave Club, 349
domain names, 250–251
dopamine, 29–31
DSPs (demand side platforms), 226, 229
Duhigg, Charles, 272
Duke University, 322
dumping, 328
DuPont, 160
dynamic content, 258

E

E2MA (Exhibit & Event Marketers Association), 285
eBay, 333–335
Ecologic Brands, Inc., 97–98
e-commerce. See also website creation
    coupon codes, 323
    efficiency, 250
    merchandising strategies, 343
    overview, 350–351
    pros and cons of, 333–335
    triggered email campaigns, 239–240
The Economist, 41
Edelman, 12, 14, 40, 130

education-based marketing, 17–18

ego, 34

eHost, 261

EIGA Design, 300

80/20 distribution strategy, 331

Elateral, 152, 193

email

    direct marketing, 237–244

    for feedback and surveys, 83, 86

    fishing, 61

    one-question surveys, 85

    testing ads before printing, 216

eMarketer, 9, 69

emotional selling propositions (ESPs)

    brochures, 208–209

    collaboration, 97

    direct marketing, 223

    emotional drivers, 150–151

    example of, 39

    grids, 42–44

    ignoring the emotional drivers of choice, 371

    overview, 31

    positioning strategy, 58–60

    print media, 197

    researching to identify, 71

    sales strategies, 354–362

    scarcity, 38

    surveys, 78–79

end caps (end-aisle displays), 332–333, 341

Enloop, 103

Entrepreneur, 104

Entrepreneur on Fire podcast, 180

envelopes, 232–233

environmental responsibility. *See* corporate social
    responsibility

EPA (Event Planners Association), 278

Epsilon, 239

ERDM Corp, 230–231

Ernan's Insights on Marketing Best Practices blog, 230

ESPs. *See* emotional selling propositions

evaluation (component of decision process), 17–18

Event Manager Blog, 278

Event Planners Association (EPA), 278

Event Planning blog, 278

EventCrazy, 282

events

entertaining, 276

    hosting, 276–278

    sponsoring, 279–282

    trade shows, 283–288

    types of, 273–275

Evo.com, 293

exchanging price information, 328

exclusive distribution strategy, 331

Exhibit & Event Marketers Association (E2MA), 285

Expanded Ramblings, 174

F

Facebook

    advertising, 173–174

    content creation, 172–173

    facts regarding, 168

    general discussion, 167–168

    marketing plan for, 169–172

    monitoring to better understand customers, 67

    testing ads, 229

    testing ads before printing, 215

Facebook Insights, 170

The Fashion Spot (blog), 121

fees, 316–317

Ferrari, 291

First Bank, 37

fishing, 61

Flaming Text, 201

flash mobs, 22

Flickr, 67, 262

fliers, 207–208

flow, in print media, 206

fonts

    brand iconology, 146–147

    copyrighted, 205

    creative briefs, 200

    overview, 202

    sizes, 204, 206

    styles, 202–204

    typeface versus, 205

Forbes, 294

Forrester and Gartner, 47

four Ps (price, product, promotion, place), 92–93

Foursquare, 97

framing, 322

free product trials, 23
free shipping, 240, 335
Freelancer, 201
"freemiums," 23
frequency (quantity) of communication, 123
Freud, Sigmund, 34
"From Promotion to Emotion" (Google/Motista), 28
Fun Theory, 21–22
functional discounts (trade discounts), 318
fundraising dinners, 275

G

G Suite, 104
gamification, 163, 187–188
Gap, 303
Gartner's Magic Quadrant, 96
GDELT Project, 118
GDP (gross domestic product), 115
GE Capital Retail Bank, 148
general merchandise retailing strategy, 340
Generation X, 10–11
genetically modified organisms (GMOs), 26
Getty, 261–262
GoDaddy, 261
golden triangle pattern, 151, 259–260
Goodcall, 364
Google, 28, 83, 155, 186, 189, 353
Google AdSense, 270
Google AdWords, 190–191
Google Alerts, 86
Google Analytics, 253–254
Google Hangouts, 181
Google Trends, 190
GoPro, 295
go-to-market (GTM) strategy
    beta testing, 49–50
    building presence, 49
    crowdfunding, 49
    customer experience, 50
    overview, 49
GoToWebinar, 181
GPS shopping apps, 352, 354
Graves, Charles, 17
The Great Beanie Baby Bubble (Bissonnette), 53
GreatRep, 364

gross domestic product (GDP), 115
Groupon, 315, 323
growth hacking
    fishing, 61
    hiring growth hackers, 62
    networking, 61
    overview, 60
    search, 60
    tripwires, 61–62
growth rate
    measuring, 46–47
    responding to flat or shrinking market, 47–48
growth strategies
    bestsellers, 51–53
    go-to-market strategy, 49–50
    growth hacking, 60–62
    hot sellers, 53–54
    increasing product line, 50–51
    market segmentation strategy, 54–56
    market share strategy, 56–58
    overview, 45
    positioning strategy, 58–60
growth waves, 45
GTM. *See* go-to-market strategy
Gueguen, Nicolas, 148
guerilla marketing (ambush marketing)
    augmented reality, 22
    captivating displays, 22
    community building and, 23–24
    defined, 20
    flash mobs, 22
    free product trials, 23
    "freemiums," 23
    Fun Theory, 21–22
    goals of, 20–21
    return policies, 22
Guru, 364
Gustafson, Kim, 309
GutCheck, 80

H

Haidt, Jon, 39–40
happiness, 39–40
The Happiness Hypothesis (Haidt), 39
Harley Owners Group (H.O.G.), 274

hashtags, 173, 288

Hatchwise, 201

headlines, 197

Health magazine, 215

Hing, Kerry, 293

H.O.G. (Harley Owners Group), 274

Hootsuite, 82

Hoover's, 357

Hostess Brands, 38

how-to guides, 256

HubSpot, 69, 86, 125, 183, 238–240, 256, 268

Human Dynamics Laboratory, 309

I

IaaS (infrastructure as a service), 349

IBM, 8, 267

iconology, 146

id, 34

IEG (International Events Group), 281

IHOP, 155

indicator forecasts, 115

indifference zone, 319

indirect marketing channels, 336–337

influencers

  B2B and B2C, 100–101

  blogs, 68

  customer experience planning, 18

  economic, 110–111

  growth initiatives, 60

  list price guidelines, 318, 320

  as marketing plan target, 100–101, 121

  social, 35–38

  unconscious mind, 26–28

infrastructure as a service (IaaS), 349

Instagram, 67, 175

intensive distribution strategy, 331

interactive ads, 192

Interbrand, 299

Intermountain Healthcare, 251

International Events Group (IEG), 281

International Foodservice Distributors Association, 336

Internet Archive Television News Archive, 118

Internet service providers (ISPs), 262

inverted pyramid format, 128

iStock, 262

J

Jaguar, 160

JCPenney, 321

Jennings, Jeanne, 240

JIAN Marketing Plan Builder, 103

Jobs, Steve, 297

Jung, Carl, 34–35

K

Kahnemann, Daniel, 31

Kamel, Perry, 121, 152, 193

Kantar Futures, 99

key performance indicators (KPIs), 116

keyword spamming, 335

Kickstarter, 49

KidzEyes, 80

kinship strategies, 98–99

KPIs (key performance indicators), 116

L

landing pages, 266–267

Larson, Ken, 206

Layar, 343

lead capture pages (transactional landing pages), 267

lead generation programs, 355–357

learning plans, 107–108

LEGO, 125–126, 291

lifetime value (LTV)

  calculating, 346–347

  customer loyalty, 348

  direct marketing, 220, 226

  overview, 346

  target audience, 100

limit pricing, 328

limited-line retailing strategy, 340

LinkedIn

  driving engagement through, 177

  elements of, 175–176

  groups, 176–177

  lead generation, 61

  monitoring to better understand customers, 67

  overview, 175

  testing ads before printing, 215

links, 264–265
list purchasing, 235–237, 357–358
list suppliers, 235–237
LivePlan, 103
local supply chains, 275
Logo Design Guru, 201
Logo Garden, 201
Logo Maker, 201
LogoArena, 201
logos, 154–155, 198, 201
long-tail keywords, 189–190
Lord & Taylor, 340
LTV. *See* lifetime value
LXR Marketplace, 86

M

Macy's, 340
market segmentation strategy
  advantage of, 54
  customer segments, 55
  niche marketing, 56
  overview, 54
market share strategy
  defining metrics, 56
  establishing benchmarks, 56–58
  overview, 56
  projections and goals, 58
marketing communications audits, 122
marketing content, 118, 126–127
Marketing Metaphoria (Zaltman), 159
marketing mistakes
  blaming customers, 372
  competing on price, 371
  dirty data, 370
  faking popularity, 370
  forgetting to edit, 371
  ignoring customer complaints, 370
  ignoring the emotional drivers of choice, 371
  making assumptions, 369–370
  offering the undeliverable, 371–372
  treating customers impersonally, 372
marketing plans
  action steps, 104–108
  budgeting, 111–113
  collaboration, 96–99

components of, 90–92
controls, 116
economic influences, 110–111
expanding target audience, 100–102
expense and revenue projection, 113–116
four Ps, 92–93
functional alternatives, 95–96
justification for time spent on, 103
management, 113
overview, 89–90
SWOT analyses, 93–95
tips for, 108–110
tools for, 103–104
Maytag, 297
McGee, Todd, 187–188
MCI, 277
McLeester, Chuck, 373
McMurtry, Jeanette, 17
m-commerce (mobile commerce), 352–353
Measured Marketing, LLC, 373
mental anchoring, 322
Mercedes-Benz, 160
merchandising strategies
  defined, 340
  general merchandise retailing strategy, 340
  limited-line retailing strategy, 340
  point of purchase, 341–343
  scrambled merchandising, 341
metaphors, 159–160
metrics
  adjusting assumptions to real data, 376
  allowable customer acquisition cost, 375
  benchmarks, 375
  dashboard trap, 376
  direct marketing, 220–222
  Facebook, 170
  growth rate, 46–47
  learning priorities, 374
  lifetime value, 375
  market share strategy, 56
  objectives for, 373–374
  print advertising, 215–216
  reversing the funnel, 376
  target ROI, 374
  websites, 252–255

Microsoft, 97, 274

Microsoft Dynamics 365, 227

Microsoft Dynamics For Dummies CRM 4 (Scott, Lee, and Weiss), 227

Milgram, Stanley, 36

Milken Institute, 111

Millennials, 10–11

The Minimalists (blog), 68

MIT, 206

MLM (multi-level marketing), 350

mobile commerce (m-commerce), 352–353

Modern Man in Search of a Soul (Jung), 35

MonetizePros, 270

Moosejaw.com, 294

Morningstar, 297

morphemes, 303

Motista, 28, 83

Mplans, 104

multilevel distribution channels, 318

multi-level marketing (MLM), 350

multiple-scenario forecasts, 115

Mycoskie, Blake, 297

MyView, 80

N

NameLab, Inc., 303

Neilsen, 14

Neiman Marcus, 294

Neistat, Casey, 268

Net Promoter Score (NPS), 37, 75

networking
  events, 273–288
  growth hacking, 61
  social hives, 271–273

networking groups, 213–214

neurotransmitters, 29–31

newspapers, 213–214

niche marketing, 56, 265

Nielsen, 9, 100, 130

Nike, 154

Nimblwit, 78

99designs, 201

nonprofit clubs and charities, 213

Nordstrom, 75, 293

Norins, Hanley, 159

NPS (Net Promoter Score), 37, 75

NPS Calculator, 75

O

Occupy Wall Street, 14

odd-even pricing, 321–322

Offer ads (Facebook), 174

offset printing, 210

one-to-one marketing. *See* direct marketing

on-hold messages, 245

online review sites, 186

Opedix, LLC, 309

Opinion Outpost, 80

Opinion-Place, 80

opportunities (component of SWOT analysis), 94

opportunity cost, 318, 326, 336

Oracle CRM on Demand Marketing, 226–227

Oracle Data Cloud, 227

Oreo, 34, 119

outlet stores, 330

oxytocin, 30

P

Page like ads (Facebook), 173

pages per session, 255

PaidViewpoint, 80

pain, avoidance of, 29

Panelpolls, 80

parallel distribution channels (competitive channels), 332

parallel pricing, 328

Parks, Rosa, 272–273

Pascual, Alexandre, 148

pass-along game, 160–161

Patagonia, 15, 295, 332

Patel, Neil, 62

Patents, Copyrights & Trademarks For Dummies (Charmasson and Buchaca), 306

pay per click (PPC), 120, 270

pay per impression, 270

PC Magazine, 82

PDMA (Product Development and Management Association), 310

perceived minutes, 245

persona archetype, 35

persona statements, 150

personality theory, 34

personalization. *See* direct marketing

personalized email campaigns, 240–241

persuasiveness of communication, 123, 133–134

Pew Research, 26

Pinterest, 67, 156, 177–178

Pinterest For Dummies (Carr), 178

Pinterest Marketing For Dummies (Carr), 178

pleasure, pursuit of, 29

podcasts, 179–181

point of purchase (POP), 341–343

Pokémon, 24

Polldaddy, 80

pop-up ads, 243

positioning strategy, 58–60, 126

The Power of Habit (Duhigg), 272

power words, 133

PPC (pay per click), 120, 270

PR Newswire, 85

predatory pricing, 328

premium items ("swag"), 287–288, 323

presence, as go-to-market strategy, 49

press releases, 124

prestige pricing, 314, 323

price fixing, 328

price lining (price anchoring), 322

price sensitivity, 315–316

price squeezes, 328

price switchers, 327

pricing
  list price guidelines, 317–323
  opportunities and obstacles, 313–317
  regulation, 328
  special offers, 323–327

print advertising
  coding for metrics, 216
  considerations for, 211–212
  keys to successful, 210–211
  measuring impact of, 215–216
  outlets for, 212–214
  sizes, 214–215

print collateral
  brochures, 208–210
  fliers, 207–208
  self-mailers, 208–209

print media
  advertising, 210–216
  designing, 198–206
  direct marketing, 232–235, 243
  elements of, 197–198
  forgetting to edit, 371
  importance of, 195–196
  print collateral, 207–210
  purpose of, 196
  refreshing, 307

problem or need identification (component
    of decision process), 17–18

Proctor and Gamble, 150–151, 186

product category, 57

product comparisons, 256

Product Development and Management Association
    (PDMA), 310

product life cycle, 62

product lines
  breadth, 304–305
  creativity and, 153–154
  defined, 304
  depth, 304
  effective management, 305–306
  increasing as growth strategy, 50–51
  introducing new and successful, 308–310
  protecting, 306
  strengthening existing, 307–308
  upgrading or expanding existing, 311–312

professional associations, 213–214

professionalism, 134–135, 182

Progressive Insurance, 297

promises (tenet of belief), 19–20

Psych2go.net, 144

psychological drivers
  in B2B, 28
  neurotransmitters, 29–31
  overview, 29
  rewards versus loss, 32
  survival instincts, 32–33
  from USPs to ESPs, 31

psychology
  of color, 144
  Freud's personality theory, 34
  Jung's archetypal theories, 34–35
  overview, 33–34
  pricing and, 321–323
pull power, 135
purchasing guides, 256
PURLs, 267
purpose
  defined, 41
  marketing that focuses on, 40–42
  sincerity and, 42
The Purpose Driven Life (Warren), 40, 272
PVMA Deerfield, 298

Q

QR codes, 124, 324, 342
quality of communication, 123
question brainstorming, 158–159
QuickList service, 257

R

rack jobbers, 318
rack rates, 211
ReadyTalk, 181
reciprocity, as social influencer, 37–38
Red Hat, 205
redemption rates, 325–326
reference landing pages, 267
REI, 295, 339
relationship marketing. *See* direct marketing
religious tenets, 19–20
RepHunter, 364
research plans and programs
  avoiding assumptions, 65
  competitor research, 83–84
  customer observation tools, 82–83
  customer records, 86
  demographics, 88
  guidelines for, 66–75
  information needs of decisions, 70–71
  interviewing defecting customers, 87
  Net Promoter Scores, 75

overview, 65–66
  paid market research tools, 80–81
  process for, 72
  surveys, 74–79, 84–85
  testing marketing materials, 86–87
  trend reports, 85–86
  web analytics, 87
RetailMeNot, 323
retainer-based selling, 348–349
return on investment (ROI)
  automated customization, 193
  comparison of marketing channels, 222
  target, 374
  unthinkable, 31
return policies, 22, 249, 293
reviews, 83
RFM (recency, frequency, monetary value) of
  customers, 55
risk
  affective system driving thrill seekers, 33
  new products, 51
  rewards versus, 32
rituals (tenet of belief), 19–20
Ritz-Carlton, 75
ROI. *See* return on investment
Roman, Ernan, 230–231

S

SaaS (software as a service), 48, 82, 187, 194, 263,
  349, 351
Saddleback Church, 272
sales channels
  direct to consumer, 350–352
  m-commerce, 352–353
  retail outlets, 353–354
sales force organization
  compensation, 365
  hiring salespeople, 363–364
  number of salespeople, 363
  sales representatives, 363–365
sales presentations, 286, 360–362
sales representatives (sales reps), 363–365
sales strategies
  customer turnover and service, 365
  emotional selling propositions, 354–362

lifetime value, 346–348
overview, 345–346
sales force organization, 363–365
sustainability, 348–354
SalesAgentHUB, 364
Salesforce, 113
Salesforce Marketing Cloud, 227
Salesforce.com For Dummies (Wong, Kao, and Kaufman), 227
Samsung, 254, 294
sans serif typeface, 202–203
Satmetrix, 75
Say No More Promotions, 287
SBA (Small Business Administration), 104
scale problems, 364
scarcity, as social influencer, 38
schemas, 26–27
SCORE, 104
scrambled merchandising, 341
search engine marketing (SEM), 60, 243, 263–265
search engine optimization (SEO), 60, 120, 257, 263–265
Sears, 321
"Secrets and Lies" (Young & Rubicam), 27
SecurePlan, 103
selective distribution strategy, 331
self archetype, 35
self-mailers, 208–209
SEM (search engine marketing), 60, 243, 263–265
sensory appeal (tenet of belief), 19–20
SEO (search engine optimization), 60, 120, 257, 263–265
serifs, 202–203
serotonin, 30
service marks, 306
service recovery, 362
Seventh Generation, Inc., 97
sex-oriented ads, 135
shelf archetype, 35
shortcode, 67
Shutterstock, 262
SIC (standard industrial classification) codes, 357
simplicity, 134, 155–156, 262–263
site maps, 264
situational analyses/summaries, 104
skimming the market, 321
Skype, 181
Sleeman, Raewyn, 78

slogans, 198
Small Business Administration (SBA), 104
smartphones, distraction of, 9
Smartsheet, 104
Smith, J. Walker, 98–99
SMS messaging, 352
Social CRM For Dummies (Lacy, Diamond, and Ferrara), 227
social influencers
authority, 36
general discussion, 35
reciprocity, 37–38
scarcity, 38
social proof, 36–37
social media
content marketing, 120, 124
engaging followers, 67
honesty, 68
identifying trends, 67
listening tools, 68, 82
monitoring to better understand customers, 66–68
one-question surveys, 85
photo sites, 67
Social Media Marketing All-in-One For Dummies (Zimmerman and Ng), 166
Social Mention, 82
social proof, as social influencer, 36–37
Social Studies Group, 87
software as a service (SaaS), 48, 82, 187, 194, 263, 349, 351
Sony, 299, 304, 308
source citations, 133
special offer envelopes, 232
special offers
coupons and other discounts, 323–324
determining amount to offer, 324–325
frequency of, 327
predicting cost of, 326
redemption rates, 325–326
Sprout Social, 82
Squarespace, 261
standard industrial classification (SIC) codes, 357
Starbucks, 340
static content, 258
Statista, 46, 58, 69, 240
Steadman Philippon Research Institute, 309

stealth approach envelopes, 232

Stitcher, 180

stock photography, 261

stopping and sticking power of communication, 123, 131–132

strengths (component of SWOT analysis), 94

subheads, 197

subscription-based selling, 348–349

superego, 34

superiority, feeling of, 31

support statements, 150

SurePayroll, 239

SurveyMonkey, 74–75, 77, 80

SurveyPolice, 80

surveys
  asking good questions on, 76–77
  communicating brand through, 75
  demographics, 74
  emotional selling propositions, 78–79
  for guidance in product line development, 75
  levels of statistical significance, 76–77
  oversurveying, 79
  paid tools for, 80–81
  scales of 1 to 5, 74
  website, 257

survival
  affective system driving, 33
  sense of, 31
  tapping into instinct for, 32–33

sustainability
  improving customer experience for, 16–20
  retainer-based selling, 348–349
  sales channels, 350–354
  subscription-based selling, 348–349

"swag" (premium items), 287–288, 323

SWOT (strengths, weaknesses, opportunities, threats) analyses
  of competitors, 93–95
  example of, 94
  growth rate, 46
  overview, 93
  starting points for, 94

symbolism (tenet of belief), 19

Synthesio, 82

System Pavers, 52–53, 234, 236

Syverson, Andrea, 295–296

T

Tarantik, Sven, 227–229

Target, 14, 47, 144, 340

Target Marketing magazine, 373

task clarity, 365

TaskRabbit, 96, 295

tear sheets, 197

TEAS (Trademark Electronic Application System), 306

teaser envelopes, 232

technology. *See also* e-commerce; email; social media; website creation
  distraction of, 9
  knowledge and power for customers through, 8
  learning about customers through, 7–8
  multitasking when consuming media, 9

telemarketing, 245–246

television stations, 282

tellwut, 80

templates, 194, 199

testimonials, 130, 186, 249

text messaging, 352

theme calendars, 123

thought leaders, 69

threats (component of SWOT analysis), 94

Tiffany & Co., 323

Time to Hire, 364

time-period forecasts, 116

TOMS, 15, 24, 41, 295, 297

Toyota, 97, 302

trade associations, 336

trade discounts (functional discounts), 318

trade names, 306

Trade Show News Network (TSNN), 285

trade shows
  booths, 284
  driving traffic, 286–287
  locating, 285
  minimizing expenses, 286
  overview, 274
  plan for, 283
  premium items, 287–288
  selecting distributors, 336
  selecting floor space, 285–286
  tips for, 283

Trademark Electronic Application System (TEAS), 306

trademarks, 251, 306

transactional landing pages (lead capture pages), 267

Traveling Creative Workshop, 159

Trefoil brand, 299

trends
demographic, 57, 88
economic, 57
in growth, 47, 55
identifying through customer records, 86
identifying through social media, 67
identifying through surveys, 74
monitoring and reacting to, 101
in prices, 320
trend reports, 85–86

trial or purchase (component of decision process), 17–18

triggered email campaigns, 239–240

tripwires, 61–62

True Impact, 196

Trump, Donald, 117–118

trust equity
creating, 12–16
creative strategy and, 143

TSNN (Trade Show News Network), 285

TuneIn, 180

TweetReach, 82

Twinkies, 38

Twitter, 67, 174

typefaces, 205

U

Uber, 96, 295

unconscious mind, 25–28

UNICEF, 23

unique selling propositions (USPs), 31

University of Virginia, 144

University of Winnipeg, 144

URLs, 250–251

U.S. Census, 57, 85

U.S. Patent and Trademark Office, 251, 306

USA Today, 303

USAA, 75

Usnik, Toby, 41

USPS, 209

USPs (unique selling propositions), 31

V

Vail Resorts, 295

Vaio, 299

Valpak, 324

values
conscious versus unconscious, 27–28
creative strategy and, 143
marketing plans that define, 13–15
print advertising, 212
religious and political, 19

Verizon, 155

videos
B2C and B2B considerations, 185–186
creating effective, 184–185
reasons for using, 183–184
vlogs, 268–269
on websites, 254, 258, 262

Viewpoint Forum, 80

viewthrough, 244

Virginia Tech, 144

Virtual Press Office, 285

vlogs, 268–269

Volkswagen, 21–22

W

wait times, 245

Waldorf Astoria, 293

Walmart, 47, 53, 144, 321, 333, 340

wannabe profiles, 151

Warby Parker, 295

Warner, Ty, 53

Warren, Rick, 40, 272

Watch My Competitor, 86

Watson supercomputer, 8

weaknesses (component of SWOT analysis), 94

web advertising
banner ads, 191–192
general discussion, 189
Google AdWords, 190–191
interactive ads, 192
search-term marketing, 189–190
widgets, 192

web identity
  customer expectations, 249–250
  defined, 248
  standardizing, 250–251
web persona development, 260–261
webcams, 254
WebEx, 181
webinars, 181–183
website creation
  blogs, 268–269
  content, 255–258
  deployment, 261–263
  design elements, 259–261
  first impression, 252
  general discussion, 247–248
  landing pages, 266–268
  metrics, 252–255
  monetization, 269–270
  search engine marketing, 263–265
  search engine optimization, 263–265
  web identity, 248–251
Welch, Jack, 41
WhatRunsWhere, 84
white papers, 123, 256
white space, 206
widgets, 192
Wildfang, 15, 261

Winterberry, 69
wishful thinking, 159
Wittenberg, August, 287–288
Wix.com, 261
WordPress, 261
words
  But You Are Free concept, 148, 161
  for click bait, 147–149
  power words, 133
WordStream, 190
workshops, 275
Wpromote, 257
Wunderman, Lester, 223

Y

Yahoo!, 189
year-over-year (YOY) objectives, 92
Yelp, 83, 186
Young & Rubicam, 27, 159
YouTube, 126, 134, 184–185, 269
YOY (year-over-year) objectives, 92

Z

Zaltman, Gerald, 159

About the Author

Jeanette McMurtry first became obsessed with marketing when she stumbled upon a marketing textbook just before graduating with her college degree in journalism. Having realized her passion lie in creativity and analytics, she pursued jobs in marketing upon graduation and eventually landed at DDB Worldwide and Ketchum, where she learned the science and art of advertising and public relations. After career positions at American Express, Intermountain Health Care, and a few high-tech start-ups, she became a CMO for a direct marketing agency in Denver, Colorado, where she became entrenched in database marketing and personalization. She then started her own consulting firm and emerged as a leading authority on psychology-based marketing, helping brands trigger the unconscious mind in order to achieve "unthinkable" ROI.

Jeanette is a frequent speaker at global marketing events, a columnist for marketing magazines, and has been featured as a subject matter expert by CNBC, Forbes. com, and others. She is the author of *Big Business Marketing for Small Business Budgets* (McGraw-Hill) and *The Cat Diaries,* an ebook on the adventurous tale of when cat meets dogs, which she uses to raise funds for another passion: animal rescue.

When not focusing on the next big marketing idea, Jeanette enjoys spending time with her husband, three daughters, dog, poodle, and cat in the Colorado mountains she's called home for years.

Author's Acknowledgments

Just like it takes a village to raise a child, it can take a family to write a book. Writing this book would never have happened without mine. I am forever grateful to the most supportive, loving, and spunky family ever. Thank you John, Jessica, Jenevieve, and Jordan. Your lights inspire me beyond words. A huge big thank you to Tracy Boggier, editor extraordinaire, for inviting me to share my voice and experiences by writing this book, and Tim Gallan for keeping me on course. And finally, thank you to everyone reading this book, trusting me to provide powerful insights for your journey to marketing excellence. Learning is the first step to achieving greatness. Shine on!

Publisher's Acknowledgments

Acquisitions Editor: Tracy Boggier

Project Editor: Tim Gallan

Copy Editor: Jennette ElNaggar

Production Editor: Siddique Shaik

Cover Image: © Buena Vista Images/ Getty Images